IN THE REALM OF ORGANIZATION

The study of organization in recent years has been dominated by administrative, economic and performative concerns. The contributors to this book acknowledge the impact of Robert Cooper on their own work and develop further his insistence that organizational analysis must be understood in terms of the rationalization of society as a whole.

Among the contributors are many of the leading experts in organizational theory. Chapters cover a wide area of interest, including organizational science and postmodernism, the logics of organizing and instrumental experience. In doing so, the book breaks new ground, departing from an emphasis on 'organizations' as social objects and moving towards a position of analysis which situates itself in the wider context of late modernity. It is therefore essential reading for students across a range of disciplines, including sociology, management and organizational behaviour as well as political studies. It will also be of interest to all professionals who desire to have a better understanding of organizational society and of the future direction of organization studies.

Contributors: Kenneth J. Gergen, Tojo Joseph Thatchenkery, Haridimos Tsoukas, Paul Jeffcutt, Muffy Thomas, John Law, José Malavé, Rolland Munro, Jannis Kallinikos, Pippa Carter, Norman Jackson, Hugh Willmott.

Robert C. H. Chia is senior lecturer in organizational studies at the University of Essex. His previous publications include *Organizational Analysis as Deconstructive Practice* (Berlin, 1996).

IN THE REALM OF ORGANIZATION

Essays for Robert Cooper

Robert C. H. Chia

London and New York

First published 1998 by Routledge
2 Park Square, Milton Park, Abingdon, Oxfordshire OX14 4RN

Simultaneously published in the USA and Canada
by Routledge
711 Third Avenue, New York, NY 10017

First issued in paperback 2014

Routledge is an imprint of the Taylor and Francis Group, an informa company

Editorial matter © 1998 Robert C. H. Chia
Individual contributions © 1998 individual contributors

Typeset in Baskerville by Routledge

All rights reserved. No part of this book may be reprinted or reproduced or utilised in any form or by any electronic, mechanical, or other means, now known or hereafter invented, including photocopying and recording, or in any information storage or retrieval system, without permission in writing from the publishers.

British Library Cataloguing in Publication Data
A catalogue record for this book is available from the British Library

Library of Congress Cataloging in Publication Data
A catalogue record for this book has been requested

ISBN 13: 978-0-415-12699-1 (hbk)
ISBN 13: 978-0-415-75654-9 (pbk)

CONTENTS

Notes on contributors vii
Acknowledgements viii

Introduction 1
ROBERT C. H. CHIA

PART I
Postmodern knowing 13

1 **Organizational science in a postmodern context** 15
   KENNETH J. GERGEN AND TOJO JOSEPH THATCHENKERY

2 **Forms of knowledge and forms of life in organized contexts** 43
   HARIDIMOS TSOUKAS

3 **Order, disorder and the unmanageability of boundaries in organized life** 67
   PAUL JEFFCUTT AND MUFFY THOMAS

4 **After meta-narrative: on knowing in tension** 88
   JOHN LAW

CONTENTS

PART II
Logics of organizing   **109**

5 **From bounded systems to interlocking practices: logics of organizing**   **111**
JOSÉ MALAVÉ

6 **On the rim of reason**   **142**
ROLLAND MUNRO

7 **Utilities, toys and make-believe: remarks on the instrumental experience**   **163**
JANNIS KALLINIKOS

8 **Negation and impotence**   **188**
PIPPA CARTER AND NORMAN JACKSON

9 **Re-cognizing the other: reflections on a 'new sensibility' in social and organization studies**   **213**
HUGH WILLMOTT

Index   242

CONTRIBUTORS

Pippa Carter is Senior Lecturer in Organization Studies at the University of Hull, UK.

Robert C. H. Chia is senior lecturer in Organizational Studies at the University of Essex, UK.

Kenneth J. Gergen is the Mustin Professor of Psychology at Swarthmore College, Pennsylvania, USA.

Norman Jackson is Senior Lecturer in Organizational Studies at the University of Newcastle Upon Tyne, UK.

Paul Jeffcutt is Director of the Institute for Organizational Analysis at the University of Hull, UK.

Jannis Kallinikos was formerly Associate Professor and head of the Department of Organization Studies at Stockholm University, Sweden.

John Law is Professor of Sociology at Keele University, UK.

José Malavé is Professor at the Instituto de Estudios Superiores de Administración, Caracas, Venezuela.

Rolland Munro is a Reader in Accountability at Keele University, UK.

Tojo Joseph Thatchenkery is Assistant Professor of Organizational Learning, George Mason University, Fairfax, Virginia, USA.

Muffy Thomas is Senior Lecturer in Computing Science at the University of Glasgow, UK.

Haridimos Tsoukas is Associate Professor in Organization Studies at the University of Cyprus, Cyprus.

Hugh Willmott is Professor of Organizational Analysis at the University of Manchester Institute of Science and Technology, Manchester, UK.

ACKNOWLEDGEMENTS

This volume, the first of a two-part series exploring the connections made in the work of Robert Cooper between technology, modernity and organization, has been three years in the making. I owe a special debt to Pippa Carter and Norman Jackson for their initial enthusiasm when the idea for this collection was conceived during a workshop in Utrecht in January 1991. However, the idea remained dormant for several years until a chance encounter with Rosemary Nixon, then a commissioning editor at Routledge, revived it as a definite possibility through her assurance of Routledge's keen support. Many other people have contributed to the realization of this volume through their enthusiastic support, even though their names do not appear here. I am of course most grateful for their continuing support as well as their ideas and suggestions which have helped shape this final version of what has been a truly collective enterprise. Finally, I would like to thank Stuart Morgan, Mark Dibben and Uwe Haiss for their invaluable assistance in the preparation of this manuscript.

Robert C. H. Chia
Boxted, Essex
September 1997

INTRODUCTION

Robert C. H. Chia

The work of Robert Cooper on systemness, information, representation and the logic of organization has substantially influenced and animated debates on the implications of modernism and postmodernism for the analysis and understanding of organizational society, and for the future direction of organization studies. This collection of essays has been brought together as a tribute to the potency and fertility of his ideas and their continuing influence on contemporary organization and institutional studies. It, therefore, represents significant acknowledgement and confirmation of the impact that Cooper's thinking has had on the field of organizational analysis and which is reflected more specifically in the work of the various contributors to this volume who are themselves established figures in the field. The essays have been written in response to the scholarly attempts of a social thinker who persistently reminds us that the contemporary obsession with the study of organizations must be understood in broader terms as part of the inexorable rationalization and organization of society.

Cooper is essentially a social theorist with wide interests in social science and philosophy, all of which he brings to the study of organizational and institutional developments in the contemporary social world. His work is distinctive for the range of intellectual resources he draws on as well as for its analytical complexity and imagination. He is, therefore, better seen as a social theorist of modern organizing and institutionalization rather than as an academic specialist who focuses on the study of organizations. This is a deliberate strategy on his part since he recognizes that academic specialisms are themselves institutional (and institutionalized) forms that create and preserve their own professionalized objects of knowledge. The field of organizational studies is no exception to this general rule inasmuch as it defines itself precisely through the definition of *organizations* as its object of study. For Cooper, this means that the academic field of organization theory assumes the institutionalized form of the objects it studies. To overcome this, it is necessary to question and problematize the established discursive strategies and conventions, which Cooper has attempted to do more generally by de-objectifying *organization* into a diffused and generic process as opposed to a specific structure. This is more evident in his various recent essays, especially those which deal with representation and 'cyborganization'.

INTRODUCTION

The essays contained in this collection, therefore, seek to develop a social scientific analysis of modern organizing/organization and to demonstrate the potential richness and insights that can be derived from adopting this intellectual stance. In their various ways, they exemplify Cooper's rigorous concern with showing how micropractices of punctuating, informing, representing, abbreviating, assembling and ordering, collectively constitute the macro-organizational world that especially characterizes late modernity.

Cooper's concerns

Organizing is fundamentally an advantage-gaining socioeconomic activity involving the 'transformation, use and exchange of matter and energy' (Cooper, 1987: 406), whereby the remote, the obdurate and the intractable are rendered more accessible and hence more amenable to control and manipulation. It is this generalized understanding of organization as a social process of ordering which offers a promising alternative to the more economic-administrative preoccupations of contemporary organization studies. The revival of this more comprehensive approach to organizational analysis owes much to the influence of Cooper's recent writings which have served to question the dominant performative mode of thinking in organization studies (see, for instance, Cooper, 1986, 1987, 1992; Cooper and Law, 1995). They testify to the significant influence Cooper's work has had in resisting the prevailing tendency to subsume organizational theorizing within the conceptual rubric of a 'theory of organizations', and in redirecting attention to the wider implications of organization theory for the analysis of contemporary institutional and social life. In this way, the more fundamental issues relating to the assumptions we make about the nature of social reality (ontology) and its construction, and the knowledge (epistemology) thus created, are raised into focus and questioned in a manner which throws fresh light on the nature of modernity.

As Bergson (1911) reminds us, a theory of life and a theory of knowledge are inseparable. A theory of social life that is not accompanied by a critique of knowledge necessarily relies on pre-formed conceptual frames which it can only regard as ultimate. As a result, it 'obtains a symbolism which is convenient', but it cannot obtain a 'direct vision of its object' (1911: xiii). On the other hand, 'a theory of knowledge which does not replace the intellect in the general evolution of life will teach us neither how the frame of knowledge has been constructed nor how we can enlarge or go beyond them' (ibid.: xiii). It is therefore crucial that these two inquiries, the theory of knowledge and the theory of life, should 'by a circular process, push each other on unceasingly' (ibid.: xiv). Knowledge of organizing and the organizing of knowledge implicate and explicate each other and are thereby inextricably intertwined. Awareness of this mutuality is what has characterized Robert Cooper's work over the past two decades.

Cooper's theoretical preoccupations have been arrived at after a long and careful distillation of the rich intellectual traditions which have formed the scholarly priorities of the human sciences in general and organization studies in particular. In the course of his intellectual journey, Cooper has also developed a particular *style of thinking* which is traceable to the influences of 'process' thinkers such as Alfred North Whitehead on the logic and primacy of process, the anthropologist Gregory Bateson on the cybernetics of difference, the historian of science Michel Serres on the equivalence of literature, science and philosophy, the philosopher of science Gaston Bachelard on science and representation, and the philosopher Martin Heidegger on language and technology. For Cooper, such writers remain the key sources of intellectual inspiration and sustenance in his attempts to think of organization as a general process and as a sociotechnical accomplishment. Their trenchant critiques against scientism and the technologizing of the world as well as the overwhelming dominance of a representationalist epistemology is echoed in Cooper's own emphasis on the primacy of action, movement, transformation, becoming and the inevitable mixing or 'mediation' of events in the actual practice of social life. Cooper's own unique style of thinking can, therefore, be best understood against the background of the intellectual concerns shared by these critical thinkers.

The term 'style' as conventionally understood can carry with it negative connotations of superficiality and lack of substance. However, in its finest sense, a *style of thinking*, as Whitehead (1932) puts it so eloquently, is a cultivated 'aesthetic sense, based on admiration for the direct attainment of a foreseen end, simply and without waste' (1932: 19). It is the ultimate morality of mind and one characteristic of what Whitehead deemed to be an *educated* person. This personal intellectual style, evident in Cooper's scrupulously theoretical expositions, means that it has not always been easy for those unfamiliar with his theoretical aspirations, to appreciate fully his approach to the analysis of organization and hence to recognize the exemplary intellectual rigour and insightfulness of his contribution to our understanding of modernity. Thus, this approach seeks to be 'precise about the imprecise, it's singularly multiple, it thrills to the hybrid, it loves the animus of motion, and reveres the unfinished and infinite' (Cooper, 1995: xxv).

Despite the clarity and rigour of his work, Cooper has been too often misconstrued as a 'postmodern' organization theorist. The recent rise into prominence of the debates between modernism and postmodernism in organizational analysis and the unfortunate but conceptually convenient location of Cooper's work within the restricted and restrictive orbit of populist postmodern discourse have only served to distract attention from the more general significance of his analyses of the fundamental nature of human organizing. It would be greatly regrettable, as Kallinikos in Chapter 7 of this volume points out, to confuse such academic parroting of postmodern clichés with Cooper's serious and considered attempts (since the early 1970s) to deal with the complex issues underlying the processes of modern social transformation. Cooper's concerns are more to do with a social science of modern organizing and far less to do with so-called 'postmodern' organization theory. A brief historical survey of his writings over the past twenty-five years can help orient the interested reader to the enduring themes that inform his work.

INTRODUCTION

Intellectual themes

Four enduring themes are traceable in Cooper's writings. They are variously accentuated in each of the pieces of work he has produced. First, there is an unmistakable commitment to thinking *movement*, *process* and the *becoming* of organization as a social phenomenon. This commitment to an *epistemology of process* is emphasized in his earlier works and revisited in the writings of more recent years. Perhaps the most explicit articulation of this concern is in an early essay, 'The Open Field', *Human Relations* (1976), in which he drew substantially from the philosopher A. N. Whitehead and the geneticist C. H. Waddington to articulate the nature of a processual and emergent form of knowing and its consequences for strategies of intellectual inquiry.

Second, a *logic of otherness*, whereby the shadow of the Other is always implicated in the articulation of the One, is consistently emphasized to 'loosen' apparently unproblematic oppositional categories and to direct attention to the organizing function of conceptual 'boundaries' which simultaneously both separate and join oppositional terms (e.g. organization and environment, self and other, subject and object, inside and outside). The necessary self-interference and 'contamination' of a term by its 'other', and the inevitable undecidability of the meanings of each individual term that this involves, with its radical questioning of such taken-for-granted concepts as identity and location, are repeatedly emphasized in many of his works. In his essay on 'Information, Communication and Organization: a Post-Structural Revision', for example, he notes that 'language itself is structured around the sense of a primal lost unity or originary void' (Cooper, 1987: 403). It is this intuition of an intrinsic link between 'language' and 'loss' which prompts Cooper to conclude that language is not rooted in an external world, but 'in the act and process of division' through which object identities are created at the expense of a necessary 'suppressing' of their ontological Otherness. The insistence on the validity of a *logic of otherness* in the analysis of social organization is, therefore, an attempt to reverse this tendency and to redress the current asymmetry in theoretical accounts of organizational processes.

Third, a recurrent feature of Cooper's work has been the close examination of the nature of information, writing, organization and communication as highly developed *technologies of representation* intrinsic to the social process of world-making. Through acts of stabilization and location, composition and decomposition, repetition and sequencing, transformation and ordering, deformation and supplementation, technologies of representation help generate the patterned regularities of our increasingly complex and mobile modern world. The manner in which these micro-acts of formation interlock and mediate one another to create possibilities for identity, meaning, simple location, and self-presence provides a key intellectual focus for Robert Cooper's work. Thus, in his discussion of the relevance of Derrida's work for our understanding of organization, Cooper (1989) notes that 'writing' in the Derridean sense, 'is the process by which human agents inscribe organization and order on their environments' (1989: 484). In this generalized conception, writing is not so much concerned with meaning and content of messages but rather with the 'structure and organization' of representation. Like organization, writing is a technology of representation that involves the active arresting and fixing of the continuous flux and flow of the world in order to facilitate the construction of our life world; an activity that McArthur (1986) describes as the 'taxonomic urge'. Cooper notes that Derridean 'writing' can be understood as a form of organization involving a 'labour of division' where effort is applied to arrest and punctuate the flow of human experience. In this way, writing as a form of organization works to stabilize, objectify and bring 'to hand' the remote, obdurate and intractable aspects of the world for the purpose of manipulation and control. Through his imaginative connections Cooper shows us how writers such as Derrida are fundamentally concerned with similar issues of organizational and institutional process.

Finally, a lasting preoccupation in Cooper's work has been the task of making clearer the ways in which the modes of modern organizing are deeply embedded in our attitudes towards ourselves and towards the everyday objects that make up our social world. Organizing is an all-pervading feature of modernity, which is why Cooper views it as integral to our sociocultural lifeworlds rather than just as an economic-administrative structure. To understand this wider conception of organization, we have to rethink the conventional meaning of *scale*. Scale is not mere size: it is not the idea of the large containing the small. For Cooper, the large and the small *contain each other*. This is why he says that organizing is the *interaction* of human organs and organizations. The telephone exemplifies the organ–organization relationship as the mediation between the human ear–mouth and the telecommunication system; the camera, between the human eye and the photography industry. These examples also underline the increasing interdependence between technology and modern organization, which is why Cooper prefers to think in terms of techno-scientific organization rather than organizations as economic-administrative units. Further, organizational *products* such as the telephone and the camera are not just objects of consumption and functional use. They become objects *to think with* and *live through* and so help constitute our sociocultural lifeworlds. This is why Cooper says that *pro-ducts* are also *pre-dicts*, that is, they are means by which we organize or structure the future or the not-yet-known. (Although Cooper would perhaps prefer to say that pro-ducts pre-dict by structuring the various human organs and senses towards the future.) Organization understood in this expanded realm implies the *immanence* or in-one-anotherness of human organ senses and technical products in a distributed system of continuous space–time construction.

These four themes, each distinctive in itself but also immanent in one another, exemplify Cooper's unique intellectual orientation towards the analysis of institutionalized social trends, including especially the effects of rationality, representation, technology, information and organization.

INTRODUCTION

Exploring the expanded realm of organization

The four themes discussed above as contexts for Cooper's various writings also provide a convenient framework for presenting the various contributions to this volume. The collection is organized into two parts. Each of the two parts contributes to the cumulative, overall thesis that organization must be understood not as economic-administrative units, but as techno-scientific institutionalizing processes. Implicit in the identified themes of process epistemology, logic of otherness and technologies of representation is the fourth concern with the immanence of generic organizational processes in social action and reality. In this way, all the key intellectual strands identified provide the theoretical framework for organizing the diversity of issues considered in this volume and their specific locations in the book reflect their varying theoretical emphases.

Part I is called 'Postmodern knowing'. It comprises four chapters, each of which examines the problems of knowledge and knowing in a postmodern context. Intrinsic to this question of postmodern knowing are issues which reflect our earlier discussion of the epistemology of process. Thus, the essays in this collection set the scene by critically examining the inherent limitations of modernism and rationality and their implications for organization theory. They propose alternative ways of understanding what it means to know 'legitimately' in a world increasingly characterized by fragmentation, discontinuity and the collapse of grand narratives.

Chapter 1 by Kenneth J. Gergen and Tojo Joseph Thatchenkery begins by examining the key underlying presuppositions of modernism and their consequences for the development of organizational science. They trace the modernist impulse to a systematic privileging of an interconnected web of beliefs involving (a) the idea of the individual rational agent, (b) the desirability of systematic empiricism, (c) the idea of language as representation, and (d) the idealizing of the narrative of progress. For Gergen and Thatchenkery, the recent 'postmodern turn' has directed attention to the inadequacies and undesirability of these modernist imperatives in favour of the alternative notions of (a) communal rationality, (b) social constructionism, (c) the view of language as social action, and (d) the celebration of the 'multiculturation' of meaning. Given these alternative 'postmodern' priorities, Gergen and Thatchenkery advocate the development of a 'postmodern organizational science' in which local knowledge, the generation of new social realities, 'modest' theorizing, and critical reflexivity are accentuated. They end by calling for 'catalytic' forms of conversation to continue the development of a new vision for organizational science.

In Chapter 2, Haridimos Tsoukas argues that our forms of knowledge are rooted in our forms of life so much so that the social and knowledge domains are mutually constituted. Organized contexts are both institutions and practices and each of these generate different discourses on knowledge. Organized contexts that are primarily concerned with regularities, rule following and predictability generate propositional forms of knowledge while narrative knowledge serves as a repository of tacit understanding which makes up the spaces left out by propositional knowledge. Tsoukas maintains that while propositional knowledge retrospectively explains how social systems function in terms of rules, it is unable to provide actors with the knowledge for prospective application. This is because propositional knowledge is essentially atemporal in nature. Narrative knowledge, on the other hand, is fundamentally historical in character comprising context-specific accounts of temporarily arranged events that make up the collective memory of a social system. Such narrative knowledge is indispensable to effective action. However, the tacit understanding associated with narrative knowledge must remain 'nonexplicit' in order to keep performance effective, particularly in sociocultural contexts in which science is unquestionably held to be the paradigm for knowlege. In such circumstances organizations have better chances of survival if they are astute enough to adopt propositional knowledge for purposes of expediency.

Chapter 3 by Paul Jeffcutt and Muffy Thomas deals with the complex relationship of information theory and organizational analysis within the context of an *informational society*. Focusing on accidents occurring in safety-critical software applications they reveal the problematical nature of information and the limits of the manageability of boundaries in organized life. Through their unfolding of situation-specific events in several specific accident cases, they reveal the tensions between order and disorder and the inherent instability of informational flows which both pluralize and cross-connect artefacts and subjects in a manner akin to that of the World Wide Web. They conclude by arguing for the 'reorientation of organization studies towards the development of more modest, situated and dynamic forms of theory/practice'. This is because contemporary organized life is essentially uncertain, ambivalent and open-ended and hence characterized by the 'incompleteness of hybridity' and the 'ambiguity of heterogeneity' which are both inherent in information processing and thus unavoidable.

Like Jeffcutt and Thomas, John Law, in Chapter 4, recognizes the inevitability of having to live and know 'in-tension' in a world in which even claims such as 'Meta-narrative is dead' must paradoxically be announced silently. Rather than get caught in an interminable bind of reflexive 'whirls', however, Law suggests that the social studies of science, technology and society offer a productive way out of this reflexivity quagmire. According to this approach, authority, knowledge and the idea of the author, for instance, are effects of material networking processes – constructed in laboratories, in texts, in the lecture hall, and so on. But there an essential tension is generated in the production of these effects. For Law, the tension resides in the fundamental difference between doing and telling. This tension is a form of knowing that must be experienced. Drawing on the work of Frederic Jameson, Law suggests that Jameson's problematization of the materialities of 'knowing in tension' effects a displacement of our attention from knowledge to knowing and from results to process. This knowing in tension is irreducibly complex and it must be lived. Law concludes by inviting us to resist the urge to

INTRODUCTION

simplify and 'centre' our knowing and instead to celebrate complexification and deferral.

Part II comprises five chapters which examine the dominant contemporary logics of organizing and develops a case for overcoming dualisms and for thinking in terms of negativity and otherness. In Chapter 5, José Malavé shows that the conventional postulating of boundaries that separate organizations and environments has imposed an unnecessarily restrictive 'systems' approach on the analysis of social phenomena. Malavé traces the legacy of this systemic thinking in social analysis to the social theorist Thomas Hobbes and in particular to his work, *Leviathan*, in which he advocates a systems view of social order. For Malavé, the systems approach has dominated contemporary social theorizing, especially through the works of influential writers such as Talcott Parsons and Peter Blau. Following the work of Cooper, Law and Callon, and Allport, Malavé argues persuasively for an alternative networking understanding of organization in which the latter is viewed in terms of 'interlocking and extending relations through a widely defined domain' rather than in terms of end states and the properties of clearly delimited systems. For Malavé, the concept of transformation-displacement networks (TDN), whereby organization is seen as the development and strengthening of interlocking chains of relations, enables us to understand better organization in processual terms. This implies that we are able to move from the traditional understanding of organization as a boundary-maintaining system to one where it is viewed as a complex of network-strengthening practices. Malavé concludes by pointing out that one of the wide ranging consequences of this revised understanding of organization is that organization theory must itself now be understood as a form of event-structuring. Theory-building in organization studies, as an organizational effect, results from the strengthening of its network relations through interlocking itself with other established theories in the social scientific domain.

Malavé's concern is to show that the systems view encourages thinking in bounded and dualistic terms (i.e., organization/environment, inside/outside, controllable/uncontrollable, etc.), and that thinking in terms of transformation-displacement networks can obviate this tendency by encouraging a processual orientation to the understanding of organizational phenomena. Rolland Munro, in Chapter 6, proposes that this problem of dualism in organization theory can be overcome by showing how such dichotomies are manufactured in the first place. Munro begins by noting that organization theory is an archaeological site of theorizing in which 'none of the competing dualism making up "organization theory" ever become abandoned'. One such dualism is that concerning the 'separation' and 'joining' simultaneously created by an organization chart. Thus, read one way the organization chart offers an image of connectedness, while read in another, it depicts a series of 'gaps'. Munro argues that this 'double reading' is linked to Cooper's (1989) discussion of 'hierarchy' and 'interaction'. However, he charges Cooper with too readily treating hierarchy and interaction as binary divisions in themselves rather than as always existing in interaction. This means that Cooper's idea of the *labour of division* is actually a continuous and unremitting social process of 'rendering apart' terms in order to enable them to attain their singleness of identity. This leads Munro, like Law and Malavé in this volume, to conclude that binary oppositions such as hierarchy and interaction or formal and informal are actually effects of the labour of division. In the context of several field studies, Munro illustrates how it is that the organization chart, as an effect of the labour of division, serves, not so much as a representation of space, but as a 'device for stabilizing "spaces" of representation'. Hence, not only does the organization chart not represent the world, but by its very construction it leads us to construe the world in static, picture terms. It is this feature which prevents us from seeing organizing as a process that happens *through* the creation of dualisms. Munro therefore urges us to 'stop impaling the study of organizing on our own divisions' and to recognize that our very theories are founded on a circulating currency of dualisms which act as organizing devices.

In Chapter 7, Jannis Kallinikos explores the tendency of the 'instrumental consciousness' to categorize things and actions into functional singularities for the purpose of attaining desired end-states. Like Malavé and Munro in the previous chapters, Kallinikos observes that this is a reflection of the pervasiveness of the rule of rationality, systems thinking and dualism in contemporary systems of production and administration. Such an instrumental orientation expresses itself in the form of anticipatory-consequential models of choice where individuals are portrayed as solid entities with clearly established preferences and an intimate understanding of how such preferences are related to their consequences. Although the rule of rationality has been subjected to a thorough criticism in the last three decades, alternative approaches arguing for a moderation of this extreme rationalism have tended to evolve as counter-reactions rather than as systematic attempts to reframe the relationship between purposeful instrumentality and playfulness. Kallinikos identifies three distinct counter-reactions which he calls the *unconscious*, the *cognitive* and the *antagonistic*. Each of these counter-reactions emphasizes the *constraints* placed upon instrumental action, but does not fundamentally question the hierarchical character of the subject–object relationship implied by the instrumental model. For Kallinikos, instrumental models of choice, rather like Munro's organizational chart, must be reinterpreted, not as statements of truth, but as normative devices which work to produce a version of reality. The convenient bipolar distinction between instrumental and noninstrumental action cannot be attributed to any natural necessity, but to social values and normalized conventions. Drawing on Lévi-Strauss' comparison of the *bricoleur*'s contingent, inductive and playful style of work with the *engineer/scientist*'s more rational, instrumental strategy, Kallinikos shows that instrumental action is also significantly suffused with the logic of 'play', contrary to conventional economic theories of decision-making.

Chapter 8 by Pippa Carter and Norman Jackson, and the final chapter by Hugh Willmott, both draw our attention to the significance of the 'negative' and the 'other' in social theory and practice. For Carter and Jackson, there is the 'known' and the 'not-to-be known' of organization(s). Their essay, therefore, seeks to inquire into the organization of knowledge about organization(s) with a view to articulating 'what is it that cannot be said and why'. They argue that the impotence of dominant forms of organizational knowledge to solve chronic organization problems is a direct outcome of overlooking the potential of this 'negative' knowledge. Negation is often thought of in censorious terms, yet the potential of negative thinking for overcoming the paradoxes created by the obsession for an ordered and predictable world is a real one. However, the totalizing character of the 'affirmative' discourse makes opposition to it extremely difficult. This is exemplified by what the authors call the there-is-no-alternative (TINA) syndrome of the 1980s. Against this view, the authors invoke Keats' concept of 'negative capability' to counterpose the power of the affirmative thesis. For them negative capability 'opens up a world of possibilities' denied by the object-oriented rules imposed by the dominant discourse. For organizations/organization theory, therefore, this means that the redefinition of problems and of admissible solutions can only be pursued *outside* the dominant discourse of organization theory.

Willmott also acknowledges the overpowering dominance of the 'orthodox' discourse in organization theory and, like Carter and Jackson, recognizes that a reflexive understanding of the 'methodical' organization of analysis is crucial to the forging of an alternative, critical organization theory which seeks to 'identify, critique and transform institutional forces of repression or to release proximal practices from their distorting influence'. For Willmott, Cooper's (1983) significant contribution to the methodology debate reminds us that social science is actually the 'study of *method*' for engaging with reality. Our reality is thereby constituted by our method of apprehending it. This implies that the methodical organization of analysis should form a central theoretical focus in reflexive social and organizational studies. Like many who have been influenced by Cooper's thinking, Willmott appreciates that what Cooper has done in his writings, among other things, is to draw attention to the wide ranging implications of a post-Cartesian, deconstructive understanding of science and technology for the social sciences. It is this 'new sensibility' that Willmott finds resonant in the works of the social theorist Melvin Pollner whose 'mundane' and 'constitutive' models of social inquiry Willmott compares with Cooper and Law's (1995) 'distal' and 'proximal' thinking. Adopting a proximal and constitutive understanding of social inquiry helps us to understand that the world appears as it does because of the *structures of methods* we deploy in our engagement with reality. It is this reflexive defamiliarization of our taken-for-granted world that Willmott finds most instructive about Cooper's work. However, Willmott takes issue with Cooper for being more concerned with deconstructing our common sense being-in-the-world than with 'exploring how we might begin to *live*' in a way that is more consistent with the implications of proximal thinking.

Bibliography

Bergson, H. (1911) *Creative Evolution*, trans. A. Mitchell, London: Macmillan.
Cooper, R. (1976) 'The Open Field', *Human Relations*, 29/11, 999–1017.
—— (1983) 'The Other: a Model of Human Structuring', in G. Morgan (ed.) *Beyond Method: Strategies for Social Research*, Newbury Park, CA: Sage, 202–18.
—— (1986) 'Organization/Disorganization', *Social Science Information*, 25/2, 299–335.
—— (1987) 'Information, Communication and Organization: A Post-Structural Revision', *The Journal of Mind and Behavior*, 8/3, 395–416.
—— (1989) 'Modernism, Postmodernism and Organizational Analysis 3: The Contribution of Jacques Derrida', *Organization Studies*, 10/4, 479–502.
—— (1992) 'Formal Organization as Representation: Remote Control, Displacement and Abbreviation', in M. Reed and M. Hughes (eds) *Rethinking Organization: New Directions in Organization Theory and Analysis*, London: Sage, 254–72.
—— (1995) 'Personal Statement', *Research in the Sociology of Organizations, Vol. 13*, Greenwich, CT: JAI Press, xxv–vi.
Cooper, R. and Law, J. (1995) 'Organization: Distal and Proximal Views', *Research in the Sociology of Organizations, Vol. 13*, Greenwich, CT: JAI Press, 237–74.
McArthur, T. (1986) *Worlds of Reference: Lexicography, Learning and Language from the Clay Tablet to the Computer*, Cambridge: Cambridge University Press.
Whitehead, A. N. (1932) *The Aims of Education*, London: Williams & Norgate.

Part I

POSTMODERN KNOWING

1
ORGANIZATIONAL SCIENCE IN A POSTMODERN CONTEXT

Kenneth J. Gergen and Tojo Joseph Thatchenkery

There is a broad agreement that, at least within the Western world, the greater part of the present century has been dominated by an interlocking array of conceptions that – retrospectively – may be termed modernist. These conceptions, in turn, are related to various techno-material conditions, undergirding many forms of institutional life, and informing a broad array of cultural practices – for example, within literature, art, architecture and industry. Analysts focus on differing aspects of this period, often using the term modernity to emphasize a composite of technological, economic, and institutional features (Giddens, 1990; Jameson, 1984), and modernism to speak of intellectual and cultural patternings (Levenson, 1984; Frascina and Harrison, 1982). While unanimity of characterization is far from complete, there is also a general recognition that this interrelated set of modernist beliefs is slowly losing its commanding sense of validity. This consciousness of disjunction is variously indexed by writings on the demise of history (Bernstein, 1989; Fukuyama, 1992), nature (McGibben, 1989), the individual (Ashley, 1990), coherent identity (Gergen, 1991), objective representation (Marcus and Fisher, 1986), modern sociology (Cheal, 1990), empirical psychology (Sampson, 1989; Parker and Shotter, 1990), literary theory (de Man, 1986), expertise (Lerry and Taket, 1994) and philosophy (Rorty, 1979). These and other works examine the pitfalls and potentials of life in a postmodern context (Rosenau, 1992; Callari and Ruccio, 1996; Boje, Gephart and Thatchenkery, 1996; Gottdiener, 1995; W. Simon, 1996; Ellin, 1996; Fox and Miller, 1995; R. H. Brown, 1995; Gergen, 1991, 1994a; Pfohl, 1992).

Drawing sustenance from Robert Cooper's (Cooper, 1987; Cooper and Burrell, 1988) volatile critiques of the systemic orientation of modern organizational theory, one pauses to consider organizational science itself. For the very theoretical suppositions under attack in Cooper's work are wedded to a body of interlocking beliefs concerning organizational science as a knowledge-generating discipline. If the theoretical premises are placed in question, so by implication are the meta-theoretical commitments from which these premises spring. In the present offering, we shall first consider prominent ways in which traditional organizational science is rooted in modernist assumptions, along with several major threats which postmodern thought poses for such assumptions. More importantly, given the waning of the modernist tradition, we must ask what postmodern thought can offer as an alternative conception of organizational science. Are postmodern critiques simply nihilistic, as many believe? As we shall propose, certain arguments within the postmodern dialogues, when properly extended, yield a promising vision of future organizational science. After developing these arguments, we shall explore several significant implications and illustrate their potential in ongoing work.

Modernism and the formation of organizational science

To appreciate the emerging elements of postmodern thought, let us first isolate key presumptions underlying organizational science in the modernist frame. More broadly, this is to articulate a number of the constitutive beliefs which have defined the very character of organizational science – its major forms of research, theoretical commitments, and its practices within the workplace. In effect, the implications of these beliefs have been evidenced in virtually every corner of the discipline – from the classroom, to the research site, forms of publication, theoretical content, and the dispositions carried by specialists into organizations themselves. Although there is much to be said about science in the modernist mould, we shall confine ourselves here to several presumptions of relevance to future developments.

The rational agent

As most scholars agree, modernist thought in the present century has important roots in the Enlightenment (the rise from the 'dark' or 'medieval' ages), a period when the works of philosophers such as Descartes, Locke and Kant were giving sophisticated voice to emerging conceptions of the individual and the cosmos. Although history has furnished many significant detours (for example, nineteenth-century romanticism), Enlightenment assumptions have continued into the present century, fuelled to new heights by various scientific and technological advances (attributed to Enlightenment presumptions), the growth of industry and prevalence of warfare (both of which increased society's dependency on science and technology), and various philosophic and cultural movements (e.g. logical positivism, modern architecture, modern music).[1]

The Enlightenment was a historical watershed primarily owing to the dignity which it granted to individual rationality. Enlightenment thinkers assailed all forms of totalitarianism – royal and religious. As it was argued, within each individual lies a bounded and sacred principality, a domain governed by the individual's own capacities for careful observation and rational deliberation Descartes proposed that it was only his thought itself that provided a certain foundation for all else. It is this eighteenth-century valorization of the individual mind that came to serve as the major rationalizing device for the twentieth century beginnings of organizational science. The effects here are two-fold: first, the individual mind of the worker/employee/manager becomes a preeminent object of study; and second, knowledge of the organization is considered a byproduct of the individual rationality of the scientific investigator. On the one hand, if individual rationality is the major source of human conduct, then to unlock its secrets is to gain provenance over the future well-being of the organization. At the same time it is the individual investigator, trained in systematic rational thought, who is best equipped to carry out such study.

More explicitly, these assumptions have been realized in the conceptions of the individual and the organization emerging from organizational study since virtually its inception.[2] For many scholars (see, for example, Clark and Wilson, 1961; de Grazia, 1960), Taylorism provided the modernist model of organizational life *par excellence*. On the one hand, it views the individual worker as a quasi-rational agent who responds to various inputs (e.g. orders, incentives) in systematic ways. Thus, if the organizational researcher makes a rational assessment of inputs and their effect on time and motions, worker behaviour can be reliably maximized. Although shorn of the dehumanizing qualities of early Taylorism, the general orientation gave rise to contemporary beliefs that management is a process of planning, organizing, coordinating and controlling. Such beliefs continued to pervade organizational science theories and practices. For example, congenial to these beliefs are job enrichment, job rotation, job enlargement, job design (Hackman and Lawler, 1971), and management-by-objectives (MBO) techniques extensively used during the 1960–70s. More recently, Planning-Programming-Budgeting Systems (PPBS) and Total Quality Management (TQM) are often conceptualized as 'input-devices' used to derive the greatest output from employees. Here the manager is typically assisted by consultants and strategic planners trained to make predictions based on the assumption of individual rationality. Managers create short- and long-term predictions of organizational performance based on the assumption that employees are rational beings who, in order to optimize their outcomes, will react to various inputs in reliable ways to produce goods and services.

This applies to the belief in rational agency figures in the conception of the ideal manager. Contingency theories (Lawrence and Lorsch, 1967) reveal steps that the individual manager can take in order to create the optimal balance between the organization and environmental conditions. The field of strategic management similarly rests on the assumption of individual rationality (Thompson and Strickland, 1992). For example, Miles and Snow (1978) have identified four strategic styles of management; Child (1972) similarly proposed a theory of 'strategic choice'. Expectancy theory (Vroom, 1964), the path-goal theory of leadership (House, 1971), and goal-setting theory (E. A. Locke, 1968) are also based on assumptions of individual rationality. The seminal work of Herbert Simon (1957) on 'bounded rationality' – while recognizing limitations in the human capacity to process information – is premised on the assumption of individual 'satisficing', implying that the search for rational alternatives ceases not with an optimal but a satisfying solution. Management education and training programmes are similarly developed to furnish managers with managerial competencies crucial to producing superior performance (Boyatzis, 1982). Similarly, Lobel (1990) has proposed Global Leadership Competencies, individual modes of managerial activity that should have universal efficacy. In short, the prevailing assumption is that individuals are in charge of the organization, and that, through the development of their rational capacities (to think, plan, discern, create, etc.), they can effectively direct or lead the organization.

In addition to informing the view of the individual worker and the function of the manager, the commitment to rational process has also shaped the contours of macro-organizational theories. It is this topic to which Cooper and Burrell have largely addressed themselves. As they point out: 'The significance of the modern corporation lies precisely in its invention of the idea of performance, especially in its economizing mode, and then creating a reality out of the idea by ordering social relations according to the model of functional rationality' (Cooper and Burrell, 1988: 96).

They illustrate this with the work of Bell (1974) and Luhmann (1976). Similarly, cybernetic and general systems conceptions – such as those championed by Boulding, Bertalanffy and Wiener – have directly contributed to the open systems perspectives of organizational theory. As Shafritz and Ott (1987) point out, the systems orientation is philosophically and methodologically tied to Taylorism.

Finally, the belief in rational agency undergirds the self-conception of the organizational scientist and the view of his/her role *vis-à-vis* the organization. At the foundational level, one could argue that organizational theory is the quintessential outcome of rational thought, and this presumption grants to the professional theorist a degree of superiority. In the modernist Zeitgeist, it is the most rational voice that should prevail in the interminable contest of opinions. And it is this implicit claim to reason that has largely provided the justification for organizational consulting: the consultant, by traditional standards, is (or should be) one who – by virtue of scientific training – thinks more clearly, objectively, profoundly or creatively than the layman, and is thus deserving of voice within the organization. This logic is amplified by a second modernist belief.

Systematic empiricism

In addition to the celebration of rationality, a second legacy of Enlightenment discourse is a strong emphasis on the powers of individual observation. It is reason in combination with observation that enables the individual's opinion to count on a par with those of religious and royal lineage. This emphasis has been played out most importantly in empiricist philosophy over the centuries, and surfaces most vigorously in the twentieth century in forms of logical positivist or empiricist philosophy. For logical empiricists (see, for example, Ayer, 1940), only those propositions linked unambiguously to observables are candidates for scientific consideration, and it was only the careful testing of scientific propositions that led to increments in knowledge. Within the behavioural sciences, these views not only became central rationalizing devices – placing the behavioural sciences, as they did, on equal footing with chemistry and physics – they also stimulated enormous interest in research methodology and statistics.

It is within this soil that organizational science initially took root. The presumption was that there is a concrete organizational reality, an objective world, capable of empirical study. To illustrate, in the first issue of the *Journal of the Academy of Management*, William Wolf proclaimed that, 'We can describe an organization as a living thing; it has a concrete social environment, a formal structure, recognized goals and a variety of needs' (1958: 14). Similarly, in his widely cited *Modern Organization Theory*, Mason Haire (1959) discussed the 'shape' and other 'geometric properties' of an organization, arguing that organizations have bodily properties and growth characteristics typical of the biological world. This concrete character of the organization was also evident in Talcott Parsons' contribution to the first issue of *Administrative Science Quarterly*. Here, Parsons defined an organization as a 'social system oriented to the attainment of relatively specific types of goals, which contributes to a major function of a more comprehensive system, usually the society itself' (1956: 63). In the same issue of this journal, James Thompson, writing about the task of building an administrative science, placed the major emphasis on 'deductive and inductive methods . . . operational definitions . . . and measurement and evaluation' (1956: 102).

Within this context, it was the responsibility of the organizational scientist to work towards isolating variables, standardizing measures and assessing causal relations within the organizational sphere. Thus, for example, Pugh *et al.* (1963) proposed to analyse organizational structure in terms of six variables – specialization, standardization, formalization, centralization, configuration and flexibility. These were to be related in causal fashion to such variables as size of the firm, ownership and control, charter and technology. Similarly, in his 'An Axiomatic Theory of Organizations', Hage (1965) defined eight variables (including complexity, stratification, efficiency, production effectiveness, job satisfaction) with corresponding 'indicators' for precise measurement. Warringer, Hall and McKelvey have even urged researchers to formulate 'a standard list of operationalized, observable variables for describing organizations' (1981: 173). And, it is also this emphasis on rigorous observation that leads to the frequent apologies made for organizational theory, its lack of 'strong' methodologies, and thus, its capacities for prediction and control.

At the same time, this celebration of observational process makes its way both into theories of the effective organization, and to the positioning of the organizational scientist in the broader cultural sphere. In the former case, an array of organization theories places a strong emphasis on the necessity for the organization systematically to gather information, facts, or data for purposes of optimizing decision-making.[3] Most early theories of rational decision-making, for example, were closely coupled with an emphasis on empirical fact. For instance, Frederick (1963: 215) pointed to the necessity for linking statistical decision theory and other mathematical decision-making strategies to empirical inputs. Rational decisions – whether in organization or in science itself – are 'primarily a function of available information'. The emphasis placed on rigorous observation within the profession, and its reinstantiation within its theories of optimal organization functioning, also enhances the image of the organizational scientist within the culture. If observational techniques yield information essential to organizational well-being, and the organizational scientist is an expert in rigorous observation, then the scientist's voice is again privileged.[4] By nature of his/her training, the scientist can be an essential *aide-de-camp* for the aspiring organization.

Language as representation

A third modernist text shapes the contours of organizational science. In comparison to the stories of individual rationality and systematic empiricism, it seems of minor significance. Yet, it is one that proves critical as we move to the postmodern context. The emphasis, in this case, is on the function of language in both science and the culture at large. John Locke (1825 [1959: 106]) captures the Enlightenment view of language. According to Locke, our words are, 'signs of internal conceptions'. They stand as 'marks for the ideas within (the individual's) mind whereby they might be made known to others and the thoughts to man's mind might be conveyed from one to another'. It is this view of language, as an outward expression of an inward mentality, that has been passed across the centuries, and now informs organizational science in the modernist mould. At the outset, as scientists, we treat language as the chief means by which we inform our colleagues and our culture of the results of our observations and thought. In effect, we use language to report on the nature of the world insofar as we can ascertain its character through observation. Words, in effect, are carriers of 'truth' or 'knowledge' – whether in journals or books, or in everyday conversation.

This same belief in the capacity of language to represent the real, when coupled with the belief in reason and observation, also sets the stage for modernist understanding of organizational structure and communication. The effective organization should be one in which various speciality groups generate data relevant to their particular functions (e.g. marketing, operations, human resources), the results of these efforts are channelled to the other decision-making domains, and most importantly, higher ranking executives are informed so as to make rational decisions coordinating these various efforts. In effect, the emphasis on rationality, empiricism and language as representation favours strong divisions of labour (specialization) and hierarchy (see, for example, the early works of Rushing, 1967; de Grazia, 1960; V. A. Thompson, 1961 and Rosengren, 1967).

The narrative of progress

Closely related to the preceding assumptions is a final modernist belief, that of systematic progress. If reason and observation work in harmony, the nature of the objective world is made known through language, others can reexamine and give further thought to these propositions, the findings of this assessment are again made available for others' scrutiny, and so on, the inevitable result will be a march towards objective truth. Scientists increasingly will acquire sophisticated knowledge about the nature of the world, be capable of increasingly precise predictions, and ultimately be able to build utopian societies. This presumption of progress is also a constitutive belief within modernist organizational science. In the formative years of the science, Rollin Simonds (1959) gave voice to the progressive narrative in the *Journal of the Academy of Management*:

> As (the science of business administration) develops... there will be more and more stress on stating rather precisely cause and effect relationships and on securing empirical data to substantiate or disprove these statements. Then the results of one investigation may be integrated with another until very substantial evidence is accumulated in support of a set of scientific principles.
>
> (Simonds, 1959: 136)

Thirty years later, Cheal (1990) characterized modernity as a project in which the goal of progress is achieved through the 'managed transformation' of social institutions. The industrial organization is thus a major source of human unity and progress. In Bell's terms, modern (post-industrial) society is 'organized around knowledge of purposes of social control and the directing of innovation and change' (1974: 20). Much the same view of scientific progress is also projected into theories of organizational functioning. It is through continued research that the organization may adapt and prosper. With the consistent application of reason and empirical observation, there should be steady increments in the organization's capacities for control and positive innovation.

The postmodern turn

The vast share of contemporary theory and practice in organizational science is still conducted within a modernist framework. Most remain committed to one or more of the modernist presumptions. However, across many branches of the sciences and humanities – indeed, some would say across the culture more generally – a new sensibility has slowly emerged. Within the academy, this sensibility is predominantly critical, systematically dismantling the corpus of modernist assumptions and practices. Such critiques not only obliterate the modernist logic, but throw into question the moral and political outcomes of modernist commitments. Yet, while critique is pervasive and catalytic, it has not yet been restorative.

While faulting existing traditions, it has left the future in question. How do we now proceed? The question lingers ominously in the wings. In our view, however, there lie embedded within certain forms of critique implicit logics of great potential. Criticism, too, proceeds from an assumptive base, and as its implicature is explored, a vision of alternatives unfolds. In terms of positive potentials, we feel the most promising forms of critique are social constructionist in character. In what follows, we shall outline the nature of the critique and the grounds for a constructionist vision of organizational science.[5]

From individual to communal rationality

While a faith in individual rationality lies somewhere towards the centre of the modernist worldview, postmodern voices turn sceptical. At the extreme, the concept of individual rationality is found both conceptually flawed and oppressive in implication. Its conceptual problems are demonstrated most clearly in the case of literary and rhetorical movements.[6] In major respects, these movements are pitted against the modernist assumption that rational processing lies 'behind' or guides one's 'outward' behaviour. The site of critique in this case is language, which, for the modernist, furnishes the most transparent expression of individual rationality. As semioticians, literary deconstructionists and rhetoricians propose, language is a system unto itself, a system of signifiers that both precedes and outlives the individual. Thus for one to speak as a rational agent is to participate in a system that is already constituted; it is to borrow from the existing idioms, to appropriate forms of talk (and related action) already in place. Or more broadly put, to 'do rationality' is not to exercise an obscure and interior function of 'thought', but to participate in a form of cultural life. As rhetoricians add to the case, rational suasion is thus not the victory of a superior form of logic over an inferior one, but results from the exercise of particular rhetorical skills and devices. In effect, there is little reason to believe that there is a specifically rational process (or *logos*) lurking beneath what we take to be rational argument; to argue rationally is to 'play by the rules' favoured within a particular cultural tradition.

For many scholars, the implications of such arguments suggest the presence of broad and oppressive forces within the culture – appropriating both voice and power by claiming transcendent or culture-free rationality. Critiques of the modernist view of individual rationality are most sharply articulated in feminist and multicultural critiques.[7] As the critics surmise, there are hierarchies of rationality within the culture: by virtue of educational degrees, cultural background and other such markers, some individuals are deemed more rational (intelligent, insightful) than others, and thus, more worthy of leadership, position and wealth. Interestingly, those who occupy these positions are systematically drawn from a very small sector of the population. In effect, while Enlightenment arguments have succeeded in unseating the totalitarian power of crown and cross, it is argued, they now give rise to new structures of power and domination. And, if the exercise of rationality is, after all, an exercise in language, if convincing descriptions and explanations are, after all, rhetorically constituted, then what is there to justify one form of rationality over another? And wouldn't such justifications, if offered, be yet another exercise in rhetorical suasion?

Yet, postmodernist voices also enable us to move beyond critique. For, when these various ideas are linked to emerging arguments in the history of science and the sociology of knowledge, an alternative view of human rationality emerges.[8] Consider again the system of language. Language is inherently a byproduct of human interchange. There can be no 'private language' (following Wittgenstein, 1963). To generate a symbol system of one's very own would essentially be autistic. Viable language, then, depends on communal cooperation – the 'joint-action' (in Shotter's (1984) term) of two or more persons. Making sense is a communal achievement. Now if being rational is fundamentally an achievement in language (or actions consistent with a given language), as previously suggested, then rationality is inherently a form of communal participation. To speak rationally is to speak according to the conventions of a culture. Rational being is not thus individual being, but culturally coordinated action.

From empirical method to social construction

Under modernism, observational methods enjoyed an elevated status. The more sophisticated the mensurational and statistical techniques, it was believed, the more reliable and well nuanced the scientific understanding of the phenomena in question. The road to truth, then, must be paved with rigorous empirical methods. From the postmodern standpoint, methodology does not itself place demands on descriptions or interpretations of data; findings do not inexorably rule between competing theories.[9] This is so because phenomena are themselves theory laden, as are the methods used in their elucidation. It is only when commitments are made to a given theoretical perspective (or form of language) that research can be mounted and methods selected. The *a priori* selection of theories thus determines, in large measure, the outcomes of the research – what may be said at its conclusion.

To illustrate: if the organizational scientist is committed to a view of the individual as a rational decision-maker, then it is intelligible to mount research on information processing heuristics, to distinguish among heuristic strategies and to demonstrate experimentally the conditions under which differing strategies are favoured. If, in contrast, the theorist is committed to a psychoanalytic perspective and views organizational life as guided by unconscious dynamics, then issues of symbolic authority and unconscious desires might become research realities. Projective devices might serve as the favoured research methods. The former research would never reveal a 'repressed wish', and the latter would never discover a 'cognitive heuristic'. Each would find the other's methods similarly specious. To speak, then, of 'the organizational system', 'leadership styles' or 'causal effects' is to draw selectively from the immense repository of sayings (or writings) that constitute a particular cultural tradition.

The present arguments are most fully developed in social constructionist scholarship, that is, writings attempting to vivify the sociocultural processes operating to produce various 'pictures' of reality – both scientific and quotidian. Social constructionist offerings are now emerging across the full spectrum of the academy – including organizational science.[10] Such writings are both emancipatory and expository. In their emancipatory function, they single out various aspects of the taken-for-granted world – the existence of a 'cold war' or a 'space race', the distinction between genders, the existence of mental illness or addiction, for example – and attempt to demonstrate their socially constructed character. They attempt to show, in Bateson's (1972) terms, that 'the map is not the territory', and thereby, free us from the grip of traditional intelligibilities; they invite alternative formulations, the creation of new and different realities. In their expository role, such writings also attempt to elucidate the processes by which various rationalities and realities are created. They sensitize us to our participation in constituting our world, thus emphasizing our potential for communally-organized change in understanding and thus action.

Language as social action

Because language for the postmodernist is the child of cultural process, it follows that one's descriptions of the world are not outward simulacra of an inner mirror – that is, reports on one's private 'observations' or 'perceptions'. On the scientific level, this is to say that what we report in our journals and books is not a mirror or map that in some way corresponds to our observations of what there is. Yet, if the modernist view of language as a representational device is eschewed, in what manner can it be replaced? It is in the later works of Wittgenstein – who, along with Nietzsche, is often viewed as a significant precursor of postmodernism – that the major answer is to be located. As Wittgenstein (1963) proposed, language gains its meaning not from its mental or subjective underpinnings, but from its use in action ('language games'). Or, again emphasizing the significant place of human relatedness in postmodern writings, language gains its meaning within organized forms of interaction. To 'tell the truth', on this account, is not to furnish an accurate picture of 'what actually happened', but to participate in a set of social conventions, a way of putting things sanctioned within a given 'form of life'. To 'be objective' is to play by the rules of a given tradition.

More broadly, this is to say that language for the postmodernist is not a reflection of a world, but is world constituting. Language does not describe action, but is itself a form of action. To do science, then, is to participate actively within a set of sub-cultural relationships. As scientific accounts are made known to the culture – for example, accounts of organizations as information systems, or managers as information processors – they enter the stock of cultural intelligibilities. They shape our modes of understanding and thus our forms of conduct. To treat the organization as an information system and managers as ideally guided by a rational calculus is to favour certain forms of cultural life and to undermine or prevent others. We shall return to the implications of this view shortly.

The multiculturation of meaning

With this relational view of language in place, modernism's grand narrative of progress (Lyotard, 1984) is thrown into question. Because scientific theory is not a map of existing conditions, then research does not function to improve the accuracy of the scientific account. Scientific research may lead to technical accomplishments, but it does not improve our descriptions and explanations of reality. Rather, descriptions and explanations are like markers through which we index our accomplishments. As research operates to displace one scientific theory with another, we are not moving ineluctably 'forward' on the road to truth, we are – as many would say – simply replacing one way of putting things with another. Again, this is not to deny that scientific research enhances our capacities for certain kinds of prediction, and generates new forms of technology, however, it is to question the accompanying descriptions and theoretical explanations as in any way giving an accurate picture of events.

It is again the function of scientific language that primarily concerns the postmodern critic. As a modernist byproduct, scientific endeavours work towards a single language – a monologue. Scientific research operates to narrow the range of descriptions and explanations – to winnow out the false, the imprecise, and the inconsistent forms of language, and to emerge with the single best account – that which best approximates the 'objectively true'. For the postmodernist, the results of this effort towards univocality are disastrous in implication. The culture is made up of a rich array of idioms, accounts, and explanations, and these various forms of talk are constitutive of cultural life. To eradicate our ways of talking about love, family, justice, value and so on, would be to undermine ways of life shared by many people. In its search for the 'single best account', science operates as a powerful discrediting device – revealing the 'ignorance' of the layman in one sector after another. Love is shown to be a myth, families are formed out of the requirements of 'selfish genes', values are merely the result of social influence, and so on. For the culture at large, then, scientific activity does not represent progress but often its reverse. From the postmodern perspective, it is imperative to strive towards pluralism of understanding.

Towards a postmodern organizational science

Postmodern critique encourages a general process of delegitimation. In the scientific sphere, we find a loss of confidence in rational theory, the safeguards of rigorous research methods, the capacity for objective knowledge, and the promise of steady progress in the growth of knowledge. As Burrell and Morgan (1979) maintain, there is a loss in the resumption of an obdurate subject matter – an object of study that is not constituted by the perspectives of investigators themselves.

When translated into the sphere of organizational life, the outcome of such arguments is a threat to longstanding assumptions of effective leadership, the scientifically managed transformation of organizations, the promise of steady growth in organizational efficacy, and the capacity of organizational science to produce increments in knowledge of organizational functioning. These are indeed momentous transformations, and if current discussions continue unabated, we may soon confront a major evolution in the concept of, and practice of, organizational science. Yet, while the vast majority of scientists and practitioners may see these emerging threats as tantamount to nihilism, we have also attempted to locate a reconstructive theme. In particular, we have emphasized the replacement of individual rationality by communal negotiation, the importance of social processes in the observational enterprise, the sociopractical function of language, and the significance of pluralistic cultural investments in the conception of the true and the good. In short, we have derived a rough outline for a social constructionist view of the scientific effort, a view that is congenial to many of the postmodern critiques but enables us to press beyond the critical moment.

In this final section, we turn attention to the possible contours of a positive organizational science within a postmodern context. This task is informed by a range of writings which have already introduced postmodern thought into organizational science – namely the *Organization Studies* series on postmodernism and organizational analysis begun by Cooper and Burrell in 1988. Other writers such as Clegg (1990), Gergen (1992), Boje, Gephart and Thatchenkery (1996), Hassard and Parker (1993) and Schultz and Hatch (1996) have also made attempts to join postmodernist thought to management discourse. And in 1992, the topic of postmodernism figured in the annual meetings of the Academy of Management (Joseph and Pasmore, 1992; Nielsen, 1992; Boland and Tenkasi, 1992; Clegg, 1992; Hetrick and Lozada, 1992; Gephart, 1992; Boje, 1992). These inquiries are also complemented by an impressive array of related work in organizational analysis (Boje, 1995; Bradshaw-Camball and Murray, 1991; Calás and Smircich, 1991; Chia, 1995; Boje and Rosilie, 1994; Martin, 1990; Hassard, 1991, 1994), environment (Gare, 1994), the social construction of leadership and organization (Chen and Meindl, 1991; Srivastva and Barrett, 1988) social inquiry (Dickens and Fontana, 1994) and the language of organization theory (Cooperrider and Srivastva, 1987). In an attempt to integrate various strands of this work, and simultaneously elaborate on the potentials of organizational science in a constructionist mode, we centre on three areas of special significance.

The place of research technologies

Within the modernist frame, the technologies of empirical research (e.g. experimentation, simulation, attitude and opinion assessment, participant observation, trait testing, statistical evaluation) were largely used in the service of evaluating or supporting various theories or hypotheses about behaviour in organizations. Under postmodernism, methodology loses its status as the chief arbiter of truth.

Research technologies may produce data, but both the production and interpretation of the data must inevitably rely on forms of language (metaphysical beliefs, theoretical perspectives, conceptions of methodology) embedded within cultural relationships. Thus, research fails to verify, falsify, or otherwise justify, a theoretical position outside a commitment to a range of empirically arbitrary and culturally embedded conceptualizations.

At the same time, there is nothing about postmodernism that argues against the possibilities of using empirical technologies for certain practical purposes. To be sure, there is widespread scepticism in the grand narrative of progressive science, however, there is no denying that the means by which we now do things called 'transmitting information', 'automating production' and 'quality control' were not available in previous centuries. It is not technological capability (or 'knowing how') that is called into question by postmodern critique, but the truth claims placed upon the accompanying descriptions and explanations (the 'knowing that'). In this sense, organizational scientists should not be dissuaded by postmodernist arguments from forging ahead with methodological and technological developments. First and foremost, within certain limits, the technologies of prediction remain essential adjuncts to the organization. The prediction of team versus individual production on a particular assembly line, management turnover in a specified company, and white collar theft in a particular bureaucracy, for example, may be very useful contributions of research technology within a field of currently accepted realities. In the same way, we may continue to pursue what may be termed technologies of sensitization, that is, means of bringing new and potentially useful ideas or practices into an organization. For example, various forms of skills and competency training, on-the-job education, values clarification and diversity training programmes may have beneficial effects from a particular organization's standpoint. Traditional research methods may very well be used to produce results that sensitize the readership to alternative modes of understanding. So long as one does not objectify terms such as 'team', 'values', 'competencies' and the like, but instead, remains sensitive to the parochial forms of reality which these terms sustain, and to the valuational implications of such work, then such technologies are not inconsistent with most postmodern arguments.

While postmodern critique undermines the function of research in warranting truth, and shifts the empirical emphasis to more local and practical concerns, it also invites a broad expansion in the conceptualization of research. As we have seen, postmodern critique favours a constructionist view of scientific research. From this standpoint, rather than being used to buttress the theoretical forestructures of various scientific enclaves, research technologies serve a variety of social functions. Many organizational researchers have already begun to mine the potential of this alternative. For over a decade, organizational scholars have been exploring the intersection of research and social action (see, for example, Brown and Tandon, 1983). Gareth Morgan has spoken of scientific research as a 'process of interaction... designed for the realization of potentialities' (1983: 12–13). Argyris, Putnam and Smith (1985) and Schön (1983) argued for the inextricability of research and social action. It is within this vein that action research (Reason and Rowan, 1981; Torbert, 1991) and 'appreciative inquiry' (Cooperrider and Srivastva, 1987) have developed forms of research in which the researcher and the researched collapse their traditional roles to collaborate in what may be viewed as the realization of local knowledges.

Yet, the articulation of local knowledges is not the only function of research within a constructionist frame. Various research strategies may also be used to give voice to otherwise marginalized, misunderstood or deprivileged groups. Thus far, the scholars have occupied themselves primarily with exploring the ways in which various voices are silenced. For example, Calás and Smircich (1991, 1993) have used feminist deconstructive strategies to expose rhetorical and cultural means by which the concept of leadership has been maintained as a 'seductive game'. Martin (1990) has looked at the suppression of gender conflicts in organizations, showing how organizational efforts to 'help women' have often suppressed gender conflict and reified false dichotomies between public and private realms of endeavour. Mumby and Putnam (1992) have demonstrated the androcentric assumptions underlying Simon's concept of 'bounded rationality'. And Nkomo (1992) as well as Hamada (1995) have analysed how the organizational concept of race is embedded in a Eurocentric view of the world, and should be re-visioned. While this form of analysis is essential to a postmodern organizational science, innovative practices or methodologies are also required to bring forth the marginalized voices in the organization. Practices must be developed that enable the unspoken positions to be expressed and circulated, and to enter actively into decision-making processes.

Finally, in the broadened conception of research, methods may be sought to generate new realities, to engender perspectives or practices as yet unrealized. Thus far, the most favourable technologies for achieving these ends take the form of dialogic methods (for a range of illustrations, see Reason and Rowan, 1981; Kilmann *et al.*, 1983; Cooperrider and Srivastva, 1987; Senge, 1990; Schein, 1993). Dialogic methods often enable participants to escape the limitations of the realities with which they enter, and working collaboratively, to formulate modes of understanding or action that incorporate multiple inputs. As Covaleski and Dirsmith (1990) suggest, dialogic research often facilitates the generation of unforeseen relationships. If research is understood in its social capacities, these are but a few of its possible functions.

Towards critical reflection

Cultural life largely revolves around the meanings assigned to various actions, events or objects; discourse is perhaps the critical medium through which meanings are fashioned. And, because discourse exists in an open market, marked by broadly diffused transformations (Bakhtin, 1981; Foucault, 1978), patterns of human action will also remain forever in motion – shifting at times imperceptibly and at others disjunctively. This means that the efficacy of our professional technologies of prediction, intervention and enrichment are continuously threatened. Today's effective technology may be tomorrow's history. In this sense, prediction of organizational behaviour is akin to forecasting the stock market; with each fresh current of understanding, the phenomenon is altered.

In this sense, we find organizational science as a generative source of meaning in cultural life. In its descriptions, explanations, technologies and its services to organizations, science is a source of cultural meanings. And, as advanced above, in generating and disseminating these meanings, science also furnishes people with implements for action. Its concepts are used to justify various policies, to separate or join various groups, to judge or evaluate individuals, to define oneself or one's organization, and so on. In effect, organizational science furnishes pragmatic devices through which organizational/cultural life is carried out. From this standpoint, two vistas of professional activity become particularly salient. Here we consider ideological and social critique: we then turn to the challenge of creating new realities.

Within organizational science in the modernist context, there was little justification for moral or political evaluation of science itself. The attempt of the discipline was to furnish value-neutral knowledge and assessments. If this knowledge was used for unethical or untoward purposes, this was not normally the concern of the science *qua* science. Yet, with the postmodern emphasis placed on the pragmatics of language, organizational science can no longer extricate itself from moral and political debate. As a generator and purveyor of meanings, the field inherently operates to the benefit of certain stakeholders, activities and forms of cultural life – and to the detriment of others. Three forms of critical analysis are especially important.

At the outset, organizational science can appropriately develop a literature of self-critique. Required are debates on the cultural implications of its own constructions. With the benefit of the various intellectual movements described above, this form of self-reflection is already under way (see, for example, Cooper, 1989; Kilduff, 1993; C. J. Thompson, 1993). To illustrate, Boyacigiller and Adler (1991) show how US values regarding free will and individualism affect how researchers conceptualize organizational behaviour. Quoting Stewart, they argue that a strong US cultural assumption is that individuals are (or should be) in control of their actions, they can affect their immediate circumstances and can influence future outcomes. By contrast, they explain, 'many other cultures traditionally see causality as determined by factors beyond their control, factors such as God, fate, luck, government, one's social class, or history... the Chinese invoke "Joss", a combination of luck and fate, to explain events' (1972: 273). The US value-orientation explains the unusual preoccupation of researchers in the 1970s and 1980s with the 'locus of control', and their unquestioning assumption that a strong sense of 'internal locus of control' is important if individuals are to control their lives and take responsibility for their actions. The works of feminist scholars, along with those representing various ethnic and political standpoints, also contribute valuably to critical self-reflection. Critical-emancipatory (Alvesson and Willmott,

1992) and radical humanist (Atkouf, 1992) works further extend the horizons. The postmodern transformation not only furnishes a strong warrant for such work, but invites a vigorous expansion of these efforts.

Simultaneous to the valuative appraisal of its own practices, organizational science may also direct its concerns to the dominant and conventional forms of organizational structure and practice. What is to be said in praise of contemporary organizational arrangements and in what ways are they deficient? This is not simply to extend the modernist quest for the most efficient, productive and profitable organizational structure and practices. Rather, it is to inquire into the entity called 'organization' as a form of cultural life. To what extent are the relevant modes of human activity desirable in their present condition, for whom, and in what ways? In certain degrees, comparative studies of organizational life carry with them such valuative standpoints. For example, Allen, Miller and Nath (1988) argue that, in countries where individualism is highly regarded, actors tend to view their relationship with organizations strategically, whereas in collectivist cultures, the individual feels more in harmony with the organization and the environment. There is a strong belief in the US system in the power of the individual to make a difference, which is consistent with the fact that the average US Chief Executive Officer (CEO) earns 160 times more than the average US worker, whereas, in a more collectively oriented culture such as Japan, the corresponding differential is under twenty (Crystal, 1991). While such explorations sensitize the reader to possible biases in the taken-for-granted world of organizational life, in fact they serve as subtle criticisms of Western modes of life. As we find, however, the door is opened to far more pointed and uninhibited forms of critique – directed both to the discipline and to organizational life more generally.[11] This is to say that organizational sciences should be active participants in the more general debates about values and goals within the culture, and most specifically, as these are related to organizational practices. Again, this is a venture effectively launched within organizational science. Pettigrew and Martin (1987) have explored the shape of the organization in terms of its inclusion of black Americans. Srivastva *et al.* (1990) have prompted inquiry into more 'appreciative' management practices; Strati (1992) has inquired into the aesthetics of organizational life; and so on. Again, a postmodern organizational science would extend such discussions in manifold ways. At the present juncture, mainstream positivist scientific training provides very few resources for such explorations. Organizational science has specialized in a language of 'is' rather than 'ought', a language of rational judgment as opposed to an ethics of care (Jacques, 1992; Peck, 1993; Cooperrider and Srivastva, 1990). In this sense, postmodern arguments also favour a revitalization of the organizational science curricula.

The construction of new worlds

One of the most significant and potentially powerful byproducts of organizational science is its forms of language – its images, concepts, metaphors, narratives and the like. When placed in motion within the culture, these discourses may – if skilfully fashioned – be absorbed within ongoing relations. Such relations thereby stand to be transformed. Not only does this place a premium on reflexive critique within the profession, as just discussed, but it also invites the scientist to enter the process of creating realities. Within the modernist era, the organizational scientist was largely a polisher of mirrors. It was essentially his/her task to hold this mirror to nature. For the postmodernist, such a role is pale and passive. Rather than 'telling it like it is', the challenge for the postmodern scientist is to 'tell it as it might become'. Needed are scholars willing to be audacious, to break the barriers of common sense by offering new forms of theory, interpretation, or intelligibility. The concept of generative theory (Gergen, 1994a) is apposite here. Such theory is designed to unseat conventional assumptions and to open new alternatives for action. Through such theorizing, scholars contribute to the forms of cultural intelligibility, to the symbolic resources available to people as they carry out their lives together.

Generative theorizing is already evidenced in the steadily increasing number of contributions drawing from post-structuralist and postmodern analytics to forge new ways of conceptualizing (and challenging) organizations themselves. In these instances, theorists typically view bureaucratic, hierarchical and rationally controlled organizations as constituted and sustained by the particular range of modernist discourses (both in the academy and the market). As it is variously maintained, because of radical changes in the technological ethos, information intensity, economic globalization and the like, the modernist organization is no longer viable. The new wave of postmodern, post-structural, and constructionist discourses are then employed as means of describing and creating what is often called the postmodern organization. Much of this work is foreshadowed in Cooper's (1989, 1990) critiques of systemic organization, and on language as an active force in simultaneous processes of organization/disorganization. Useful extensions of these ideas into re-visioning the organization are compiled in Reed and Hughes (1992) and Boje, Gephart and Thatchenkery (1996) as well as Hosking, Dachler and Gergen (1995). Importantly, this work also carries on a dialogic relationship with the marketplace and, in this way, acquires a constitutive capability (see, for example, Berquist, 1993; Handy, 1989; Morgan, 1993; Peters, 1987).

The challenge of generative theory must also be qualified in two ways. First, organizational science has already produced a vast range of theory. From the postmodern perspective, these myriad formulations are not a deficit – an indication, in modernist terms, of the pre-paradigmatic and noncumulative character of the science. Rather, each of the existing theories represents a metaphoric construction (Morgan, 1986), available for many purposes in a variety of contexts. Such theories should not be abandoned for the sake of the new and 'more relevant'. To abandon these discourses is to foreclose on valuable perspectives and thus alternatives for action. Generative efforts may include reinvigorating the theories of the past, redefining or recontextualizing their meanings so as not to be lost from the repository of potentials.

Second, the move towards generative theory should not be oblivious to issues of use-value, that is, how and whether a given form of language can be absorbed into ongoing relationships. Rather than simply inventing new languages of understanding organizations, there is much to be said for a patient listening. Can the voices of front-line practitioners – struggling to articulate the challenges of the new – be amalgamated into more robust and compelling vehicles of comprehension? There is also much to recommend circumscribed theorizing, that is, descriptions and explanations of more delimited and pointed application. An account of a company's venture into overseas markets, how the basic structure of the organization was changed, how people lost and gained jobs, and the attendant excitements and frustrations, may be vivid and empathically absorbing. The specific details cannot be generalized across time and organizations. However, in these concrete detailings, others can more easily locate relevant analogies. In this sense, the language of the circumscribed theory can have greater use-value than the highly general and abstract offering.

To illustrate, consider the sweeping moves towards globalization currently occupying the business community (see, for example, Hamel and Prahalad, 1996; Bartlett and Ghoshal, 1992; Cooperrider and Pasmore, 1991; Albrow, 1995; Weick and Van Orden, 1990). From the present perspective, organizational science should not strive towards a single best, most rational and empirically grounded theory – a grand or totalizing narrative. Rather, a variety of theoretical perspectives are invited. Views of globalization as a 'post-Fordist model of accumulation' (Albertsen, 1988), or 'flexible accummulation' (in Harvey's terms (1989)), should stand alongside accounts of the global organization as 'post-Copernican' (Peters, 1992) in its existence within a network of collectivities. We may also strive towards new forms of articulation, as in the concept of *systase* (Gebser, 1985). In contrast to the system, the systase is an organization without an absolute centre, around which order – as a 'patchwork of language pragmatics that vibrate at all times' (Lyotard and Thébaud, 1985: 94) – is continuously being established and threatened. At the same time, these overarching conceptualizations need supplementation by accounts at the more concrete level of action. In pursuing this line of argument, Joseph (1994) cites the evolution of a transnational nonprofit organization that went global during the 1970s. By the 1980s, it became clear that their universal model of socioeconomic-cultural development could not be applied across cultures. Needed was a reorganization, whereby each local organization autonomously pursued its own model of development. As a result, the organization developed a remarkable competency to function as an international network of locally disparate organizations.

Yet, in the end, the challenge of constructing new realities is not exhausted through the scholarly and practical actions of the organizational scientist alone. Under welcoming circumstances, organizational actors are fully capable of generating their own theories of 'models' – accounts that can be more organically suited to their practices than the vessels of meaning supplied by the organizational scientist. While such local understandings may lack the elegance and sophistication of official theory, in terms of immediate needs, they can be more valuable. However, integrating new intelligibilities into organizational life is often a difficult challenge, as illustrated by Astley and Zammuto (1992). Required of the organizational scientist is an expanded range of practices, modes of enhancing generative interchange within the organization and between the organization and the academy. This should also include means of enabling self-reflexive critique of the kind discussed above. In effect, the organizational scientist in this case would not be furnishing a theory, a metaphor, or a narrative, but a means of developing and enriching these resources.

Communication in a multinational organization: an illustration

Although we have made reference to a substantial number of inquiries congenial with, or deriving from, a constructionist/postmodern perspective on organizational science, it will finally prove useful to explore a single case in which a number of these ideas have together been put into practice. The case will also help to demonstrate the potentials and limitations of the approach in an organizational setting. The case in point took place in response to a 'cry for help' from a large, multinational pharmaceutical company. As upper-level executives described the problem, the organization had spread over recent decades into some fifty different countries. Considerable difficulty was now experienced both in communicating and coordinating actions effectively. Individuals across the various functions, and across nations, failed either to understand or to appreciate each other's perspectives and decisions. Tensions were especially intense between the parent company and the subsidiaries: each tended to be mistrustful of the other's actions.

From a modernist standpoint, it would be appropriate at this juncture to launch a multifaceted research project attempting to determine precisely the origins of the problem, locating the specific individuals or conditions responsible, and based on the results of such study, to make recommendations for an ameliorative plan of action. From a postmodern/constructionist standpoint, however, there are good reasons for rejecting this option. Not only is 'the problem' continuing to change while the research and intervention are being carried out, but the very idea that there is a single set of propositions that will accurately reflect the nature of the condition (or its 'causal' underpinnings) is grossly misleading. Further, to warrant this interpretation with empirical data ('true' because there are 'findings'), and to present the interpretation as authoritative (as truth beyond perspective), is to perpetrate a bad faith relationship with the organization. Competing realities are suppressed in the name of a 'scientific justification'.

Given these and other problems with the modernist orientation, we first established a series of generative dialogues in which we, the consultants, served in a collaborative role.[12] Interviewing various managers at various levels of the organizations, both in the parent company and subsidiaries, we explored their views on various relationships within the organization. Our attempt was not to locate and define 'the problem' with ever increasing accuracy, but to elicit discursive resources that would enable the managers to remove themselves from the daily discourses of relationship and to consider their situation reflexively. The hope was, on the one hand, to loosen the sedimented realities giving rise to 'the problem', and to multiply the voices they could speak with within their relationships, and thus the range of options for action.

Although these discussions ranged broadly, two forms of questioning were common across all of them: first, we asked the participants to describe instances in which communication and coordination were highly effective. Drawing from Srivastva et al.'s (1990) work on appreciative inquiry, our hope was, first, to deconstruct the common sense of failure ('we have a serious problem'), and, second, to secure a set of positive instances that might serve as model practices (sources of reconstruction). However, we also inquired about areas in which the managers felt there were specific problems in communication and coordination. The point here was to tap common constructions of the problematic within the organization that might be used to generate further dialogues (e.g. a rationale for 'we need to talk').

The second phase of the project served to introduce conceptual resources. Given the reasoning developed above, we see theoretical discourse (when properly translated), as having catalytic potential within the field of practice. By introducing new metaphors, narratives, or images, new options for action are created. To translate the 'sacred' language of the profession into the secular argot, we sent letters to each of the participants summarizing their comments. However, these summaries were set in the context of a set of theoretical departures drawing heavily from postmodern organizational theory. On the one hand, the managers' accounts were used to illustrate shortcomings of the modernist organization – its hierarchies, singular logics, clear separation of boundaries, individualistic views of leadership, and the like. Further, positive cases were often linked to postmodern conceptions of organization, including, for example, participatory performance, interactive decision-making, reality creation, multicultural resources, and coordinating interpretations. In effect, by instantiating a set of concepts and images with ongoing practices from the organization, we hoped that the theoretical resources could be appropriated for conversational use within the organization.

In a third phase, we attempted to broaden the conversational space. That is, after securing permission from the various participants, we shared the contents of their interviews with other managers. These documents were circulated broadly in an attempt to (1) enrich the range of conversational resources available to the participants, (2) furnish a range of positive images for future use, (3) provide a range of problems that might invite further discussion, and (4) inject into the discussions a common language drawing from contemporary theorizing in the profession. We cannot ascertain, at this juncture, the longterm effects of this process, and it would surely be cavalier to suppose that these various moves are sufficient for altering the corporate culture at large. At a minimum, both management training must be instituted and alterations instituted in corporate communication if significant change is to be effected. However, these various interchanges did propel into action a variety of constructionist assumptions, suggested new forms of organizational practice (technology), and fostered an enrichment in organizational theory – all functioning to invite new and transformative conversations.

Towards catalytic conversation

The present offering has first attempted to isolate an interrelated set of assumptions forming an important basis for traditional organizational science. By locating these assumptions within the historical context of modernism, it was also possible to consider a variety of arguments currently sweeping the academic terrain, arguments usefully viewed as postmodernist. These latter views, while placing modernist presumptions in jeopardy, also offer an alternative vision of organizational science, one that places a major emphasis on processes of social construction. From this latter perspective, we outlined a rationale for what we see as a vitally expanded and enriched conception of organizational science.

Yet, these views should scarcely be considered fixed and final. On the contrary, the very conception of a science in the postmodern context is one that emphasizes continuing interchange, continuing reflection and innovation. The present account is thus the beginning of a conversation rather than a termination. Not one of the present arguments is without its problems. For example, Jean-François Lyotard has criticized contemporary science for its abdicating concern with knowledge as an end in itself. As he sees it, 'knowledge is . . . produced in order to be sold, it is . . . consumed in order to be valorized in a new production. Science becomes a force of production, in other words a moment in the circulation of capital' (Lyotard, 1984: 4). Is the present search for the utility of a postmodern organizational science not subject to the same critique? Is there a more promising alternative? There are further questions including, for example, the implicit regime of values contained within this analysis, the possibilities of infinite regress in argumentation, and the intellectual and cultural dangers of relativism. Clearly the conversation must continue.

Notes

1. For a brief but relevant summary of these cultural underpinnings, see Gergen (1991). For more detailed accounts, see Randall (1940), Berman (1982) and Frisby (1985).
2. The present account of modernist organizational science singles out what many feel to be mainstream tendencies. We recognize a variety of competing approaches within the field – for example, psychoanalytic, interpretivist, symbolic – not exclusively wedded to assumptions of individual rationality and objectivity.
3. As with most forms of modernist organizational science, there continues to be a strong commitment to such practices.
4. As only one illustration, a special issue of the *Academy of Management Journal* (1992: 685) focused on 'configurational approaches to organization', committed to the view that 'out of the theoretically infinite set of possible combinations of organizational attributes', the organizational scientist will discover a 'relatively small subset that will characterize organizations empirically'.

5 For an extended discussion of social construction and its application to the human sciences, see Gergen (1994b).
6 See especially Derrida (1976) and Foucault (1979), along with later essays, for example, by Norris (1983) and in Simon (1990).
7 For feminist illustrations, see Joy and Venkatesh, (1994), Holmwood (1995), Mclennan, (1995), Grosz (1988) and Harding (1986). Consider also Cornell West's statement that, 'The scientific racist logic rests upon a modern philosophical discourse guided by Greek ocular metaphors, undergirded by Cartesian notions of the primacy of the subject and preeminence of representation and buttressed by Baconian ideas of observation, evidence and confirmation that promote and encourage the activities of observing, comparing, measuring and ordering physical characteristics of human bodies.... Within this logic, the notions of black ugliness, cultural deficiency and intellectual inferiority are legitimated by the value-laden, yet prestigious, authority of science' (1988: 17).
8 Major contributions to this literature include Kuhn (1970), Feyerabend (1976), Latour and Woolgar (1979), Barnes (1974) and Knorr-Cetina (1981).
9 The best known arguments to this effect are those of Kuhn (1970) and Feyerabend (1976).
10 See, for example, Gergen (1994a) for a discussion of constructionist contributions to human science. In the organizational arena, see also Astley (1985), Morgan (1986), Joseph and Pasmore (1992) and Whitley (1992).
11 See also relevant works of Sinclair (1992), Morgan (1988), and Hoskin and Macve (1986).
12 The consultants in this case were Kenneth and Mary Gergen.

Bibliography

Albertsen, N. (1988) 'Postmodernism, Post-Fordism, and Critical Social Theory', *Environment and Planning*, 6, 339–65.
Albrow, M. (1995) 'Orientalism, Postmodernism, and Globalism', *Sociology: the Journal of the British Sociological Association*, 29/4, 740–1.
Allen, D. B., Miller, E. D. and Nath, R. (1988) 'North America', in R. Nath (ed.) *Comparative Management*, Cambridge: Ballinger, 23–54.
Alvesson, M. and Willmott, H. C. (1992) 'On the Idea of Emancipation in Management and Organization Studies', *Academy of Management Review*, 17/3, 432–64.
Argyris, C. (1964) *Integrating the Individual and the Organization*, New York: Wiley.
Argyris, C., Putnam, R. and Smith, D. (1985) *Action Science*, San Francisco, CA: Jossey-Bass.
Ashley, D. (1990) 'Postmodernism and the "End of the Individual": from Repressive Self-mastery to Ecstatic Communication', *Current Perspectives in Social Theory*, 10, 195–221.
Astley, G. (1985) 'Administrative Science as Socially Constructed Truth', *Administrative Science Quarterly*, 30, 497–513.
Astley, G. and Zammuto, R. (1992) 'Organizational Science, Managers, and Language Games', *Organizational Science*, 3, 443–60.
Atkouf, O. (1992) 'Management and Theories of Organizations in the 1990s: Towards a Critical, Radical Humanism?', *Academy of Management Review*, 17, 407–31.
Ayer, A. J. (1940) *The Foundation of Empirical Knowledge*, New York: Macmillan.
Bakhtin, M. (1981) *The Dialogic Imagination*, Austin, TX: University of Texas Press.
Barnes, B. (1974) *Scientific Knowledge and Sociological Theory*, London: Routledge & Kegan Paul.

Bartlett, C. and Ghoshal, S. (1992) 'Global Strategic Management: Impact on the New Frontiers of Strategy Research', *Strategic Management Journal*, 12, 5–16.
Bateson, G. (1972) *Steps to an Ecology of Mind*, New York: Ballantine.
Bell, D. (1974) *The Coming of Post-industrial Society*, London: Heinemann.
Berman, M. (1982) *All That is Solid Melts into Air: the Experience of Modernity*, New York: Simon & Schuster.
Bernstein, R. J. (1989) 'The End of History, Explained for a Second Time', *New York Times*, (10 December), Section 4, 6.
Berquist, W. (1993) *The Postmodern Organization: Mastering the Art of the Irreversible Change*, San Francisco, CA: Jossey-Bass.
Boje, D. (1992) 'The University is a Panoptic Cage: the Disciplining of the Student and Faculty Body', paper presented at the National Academy of Management Meetings, Las Vegas, Nevada.
—— (1995) 'Stories of the Story-telling Organization: a Postmodern Analysis of Disney As Tamara-Land', *Academy of Management Journal*, 38/4, 997–1035.
Boje, D., Gephart, R. and Thatchenkery, T. J. (1996) *Postmodern Management and Organization Theory*, Newbury Park, CA: Sage.
Boje, D. and Rosile, G.A. (1994) 'Diversities, Differences, and Authors' Voice', *Journal of Organizational Change Management*, 7/6, 8–17.
Boland, R. J. and Tenkasi, R. (1992) 'Postmodernism and its Implications for Information System Design', paper presented at the National Academy of Management Meetings, Las Vegas, Nevada.
Boyatzis, R. (1982) *The Competent Manager: A Model for Effective Performance*, New York: Wiley.
Boyacigiller, N. and Adler, N. (1991) 'The Parochial Dinosaur: Organizational Science in a Global Context', *Academy of Management Review*, 16, 262–90.
Bradshaw-Camball, P. and Murray, V. (1991) 'Illusions and Other Games: a Trifocal View of Organizational Politics', *Organizational Science*, 2, 379–98.
Brown, D. L. and Tandon, R. (1983) 'Ideology and Political Economy in Inquiry: Action Research and Participatory Research', *Journal of Applied Behavioral Science*, 19, 277–94.
Brown, R. H. (ed.) (1995) *Postmodern Representation: Truth, Power and Mimesis in the Human Sciences and Public Culture*, Urbana, IL: University of Illinois Press.
Burrell, G. and Morgan, G. (1979) *Sociological Paradigms and Organisational Analysis*, London: Heinemann.
Calás, M. and Smircich, L. (1991) 'Voicing Seduction to Silence Leadership', *Organization Studies*, 12, 567–602.
—— (1993) 'Dangerous Liaisons: the "Feminine-in-Management" Meets "Globalization"', *Business Horizons*, 36/2, 71–81.
Callari, A. and Ruccio, D. (eds) (1996) *Postmodern Materialism and the Future of Marxist theory*, Middletown, CT: Wesleyan University Press.
Cheal, D. (1990) 'Authority and Incredulity: Sociology between Modernism and Postmodernism', *Canadian Journal of Sociology*, 15, 129–47.
Chen, C. C. and Meindl, J. (1991) 'The Construction of Leadership Images in the Popular Press: the Case of Donald Burr and *People Express*', *Administrative Science Quarterly*, 36, 521–51.
Chia, R. (1995) 'From Modern to Postmodern Organizational Analysis', *Organization Studies*, 16/4, 580–604.
Child, J. (1972) 'Organizational Structure, Environment and Performance: the Role of Strategic Choice', *Sociology*, 6/1, 1–22.

Clark, P. and Wilson, J. (1961) 'Incentive Systems: a Theory of Organizations', *Administrative Science Quarterly*, 6, 129–66.

Clegg, S. (1990) *Modern Organizations: Organization Studies in the Postmodern World*, Newbury Park, CA: Sage.

—— (1992) 'Postmodern Management?', paper presented at the National Academy of Management Meetings, Las Vegas, Nevada.

Cooper, R. (1987) 'Information, Communication and Organization: a Post-structural Revision', *The Journal of Mind and Behavior*, 8/3, 395–416.

—— (1989). 'Modernism, Postmodernism and Organizational Analysis 3: the Contribution of Jacques Derrida, *Organization Studies*, 10/4, 479–502.

—— (1990) 'Organization/Disorganization', in J. Hassard and D. Pym (eds) *The Theory and Philosophy of Organizations: Critical Issues and New Perspectives*, London: Routledge. Previously published in *Social Science Information*, 25/2, 299–335.

Cooper, R. and Burrell, G. (1988) 'Modernism, Postmodernism and Organizational Analysis 1: an Introduction', *Organization Studies*, 9/1, 91–112.

Cooperrider, D. and Pasmore, W. (1991) 'The Organization Dimension of Global Change', *Human Relations*, 44, 763–87.

Cooperrider, D. and Srivastva, S. (1987) 'Appreciative Inquiry in Organizational Life', *Research in Organizational Change and Development*, 1, 129–69.

—— (1990) 'The Constructive Task of Organizational Theory', paper presented at the Conference on Relational Theory of Organizations, Saint Galen, Switzerland.

Covaleski, M. and Dirsmith, M. (1990) 'Dialectical Tension, Double Reflexivity and the Everyday Accounting Researcher: on Using Qualitative Methods', *Accounting, Organizations and Society*, 15, 543–73.

Crystal, G. (1991) *In Search of Excess: the Overcompensation of American Executives*, New York: W. W. Norton.

de Grazia, A. (1960) 'The Science and Values of Administration: I', *Administrative Science Quarterly*, 5, 421–47.

de Man, P. (1986) *The Resistance to Theory*, Minneapolis, MN: University of Minneapolis Press.

Derrida, J. (1976) *Of Grammatology*, trans. G. Spivak, Baltimore, MD: Johns Hopkins University Press.

Dickens, D. and Fontana, A. (eds) (1994) *Postmodernism and Social Theory*, New York: Guilford.

Ellin, N. (1996) *Postmodern Urbanism*, Cambridge, MA: Basil Blackwell.

Elliot, A. (1995) 'Contested Knowledge: Social Theory in the Postmodern Era', *Sociology: The Journal of the British Journal of Sociological Association*, 29/3, 552–4.

Feyerabend, P. K. (1976) *Against Method*, New York: Humanities.

Fox, C. and Miller, H. (1995) *Postmodern Public Administration: Towards Discourse*, Thousand Oaks, CA: Sage.

Foucault, M. (1978) *The History of Sexuality, Vol. 1: An Introduction*, trans. R. Hurley, New York: Pantheon.

—— (1979) 'What is an Author?', in J. V. Harari (ed.) *Textual Strategies: Perspectives in Post-structuralist Criticism*, Ithaca, NY: Cornell University Press.

Frascina, F. and Harrison, C. (eds) (1982) *Modern Art and Modernism*, London: Open University Press.

Frederick, W. (1963) 'The Next Development in Management Science: a General Theory', *Academy of Management Journal*, 6, 212–19.

Frisby, D. (1985) *Fragments of Modernity*, Cambridge: Polity Press.

Fukuyama, F. (1992) *The End of History and the Last Man*, New York: The Free Press.
Gare, A. (1994) *Postmodernism and the Environmental Crisis*, New York: Routledge.
Gebser, J. (1985) *The Ever-present Origin*, Athens, OH: Ohio University Press.
Gephart, R. P. (1992) 'Environmental Disasters in the Postmodern Era: Theory and Methods for Organizational Change', paper presented at the National Academy of Management Meeting, Las Vegas, Nevada.
Gergen, K. J. (1991) *The Saturated Self: Dilemmas of Identity in Contemporary Life*, New York: Basic Books.
—— (1992) 'Organization Theory in the Postmodern Era', in M. Reed and M. Hughes (eds) *Rethinking Organization: New Directions in Organization Theory and Analysis*, 207–26, London: Sage.
—— (1994a) *Towards Transformation in Social Knowledge*, London: Sage, 2nd edn.
—— (1994b) *Realities and Relationships*, Cambridge, MA: Harvard University Press.
Giddens, A. (1990) *Consequences of Modernity*, Stanford, CA: Stanford University Press.
Gottdiener, M. (1995) *Postmodern Semiotics: Material Culture and the Forms of Postmodern Life*, Cambridge, MA: Basil Blackwell.
Grosz, E. A.(1988)'The In(ter)vention of Feminist Knowledges', in B. Caine, E. A. Grosz and M. de Lepervanche (eds) *Crossing Boundaries, Feminism and the Critique of Knowledge*, North Sydney: Allen & Unwin.
Hackman, R. and Lawler, E. (1971) 'Employee Reactions to Job Characteristics', *Journal of Applied Psychology*, 60, 159–70.
Hage, J. (1965) 'An Axiomatic Theory of Organizations', *Administrative Science Quarterly*, 10, 289–320.
Haire, M. (ed.) (1959) *Modern Organization Theory*, New York: Wiley.
Hamada, T. (1995) 'Inventing Cultural Others in Organizations: a Case of Anthropological Reflexivity in a Multinational Firm', *Journal of Applied Behavioral Science*, 31/2, 162–85.
Hamel, G. and Prahalad, C. K. (1996) 'Competing in the New Economy: Managing Out of Bounds', *Strategic Management Journal*, 17/3, 237–42.
Handy, C. (1989) *The Age of Paradox*, Cambridge, MA: Harvard Business School Press.
Harding, S. (1986) *Whose Science, Whose Knowledge?*, Ithaca, NY: Cornell University Press.
Harvey, D. (1989) *The Condition of Postmodernity: an Inquiry into the Origins of Cultural Change*, Oxford: Basil Blackwell.
Hassard, J. (1991) 'Multiple Paradigms and Organizational Analysis: a Case Study', *Organization Studies*, 12, 275–99.
—— (1994) 'Postmodern Organizational Analysis: towards a Conceptual Framework', *Journal of Management Studies*, 31/3, 303–24.
Hassard, J. and Parker, M. (eds) (1993) *Postmodernism and Organizations*, Newbury Park, CA: Sage.
Hetrick, W. and Lozada, H (1992) 'Postmodernism and Anti-theory: the Illusion of Organizational Science', paper presented at the National Academy of Management Meetings, Las Vegas, Nevada.
Holmwood, J. (1995) 'Feminism and Epistemology: What Kind of Successor Science?', *Sociology: The Journal of the British Sociological Association*, 29/3, 411–28.
Hoskin, K. W. and Macve, R. (1986) 'Accounting and the Examination: a Genealogy of Disciplinary Power', *Accounting, Organization and Society*, 11, 105–36.
Hosking, D., Dachler, H. P. and Gergen, K. J. (eds) (1995) *Management and Organization: Relational Alternatives to Individualism*, Aldershot: Avebury.

House, R. (1971) 'A Path Goal Theory of Leadership Effectiveness', *Administrative Science Quarterly*, 16, 321–38.
Jacques, R. (1992) 'Critique and Theory-building: Producing Knowledge "From the Kitchen"', *Academy of Management Review*, 17, 582–606.
Jameson, F. (1984) 'Postmodernism, or the Cultural Logic of Late Capitalism', *New Left Review*, 146, 53–92.
Joseph, T. T. (1994) 'Hermeneutic Processes in Organizations: a Study in Relationships between Observers and Observed', unpublished doctoral dissertation, Case Western Reserve University, Cleveland, Ohio.
Joseph, T. T. and Pasmore, W. A. (1992) 'The Challenge of Postmodernism for the Globalization of Organizations', working paper, Department of Organizational Behaviour, Case Western Reserve University, Cleveland, Ohio.
Joy, A. and Venkatesh, A. (1994) 'Postmodernism, Feminism, and the Body: the Visible and the Invisible in Consumer Research', *International Journal of Research in Marketing*, 11/4, 333–57.
Kelly, S. (1996) 'A Postmodern Feminist Perspective on Organizations in the Natural Environment: Rethinking Ecological Awareness', *Business and Society*, 35, 62–78.
Kilduff, M. (1993) 'Deconstructing *Organizations*', *Academy of Management Review*, 18, 13–31.
Kilmann, R., Thomas, K., Slevin, D., Nath, R. and Jerrell, L. (eds) (1983) *Producing Useful Knowledge for Organizations*, New York: Praeger.
Knorr-Cetina, K. D. (1981) *The Manufacture of Knowledge*, Oxford: Pergamon.
Kuhn, T. S. (1970) *The Structure of Scientific Revolutions*, Chicago, IL: University of Chicago Press, 2nd edn.
Latour, B. and Woolgar, S. (1979) *Laboratory Life: the Social Construction of Scientific Facts*. Beverly Hills, CA and London: Sage.
Lawrence, P. R. and Lorsch, J. (1967) *Organization and Environment*, Cambridge, MA: Harvard Business School Press.
Lerry, W. and Taket, A. (1994) 'The Death of the Expert', *Journal of the Operational Research Society*, 45/7, 733–48.
Levenson, M. (1984) *A Genealogy of Modernism*, Cambridge: Cambridge University Press.
Lobel, S. A. (1990) 'Global Leadership Competencies: Managing to a Different Drumbeat', *Human Resource Management*, 29, 39–47.
Locke, E. A. (1968) 'Towards a Theory of Task Motivation and Incentives', *Organizational Behavior and Human Performance*, 3, 157–89.
Locke, J. (1825/1959) *An Essay Concerning Human Understanding*, New York: Dover.
Luhmann, N. (1976) 'A General Theory of Organized Social Systems', in G. Hofstede and S. Kassem (eds) *European Contributions of Organization Theory*, 96–113. Amsterdam: Van Gocum.
Lyotard, J.-F. (1984) *The Postmodern Condition: A Report on Knowledge*, trans. G. Bennington and B. Massumi, Manchester: Manchester University Press.
Lyotard, J.-F. and Thébaud, J.-L. (1985) *Just Gaming*, trans. W. Godzich, Manchester: Manchester University Press.
Marcus, G. E. and Fisher, M. (1986) *Anthropology as Cultural Critique: An Experimental Moment in the Human Sciences*, Chicago, IL: University of Chicago Press.
Martin, J. (1990) 'Deconstructing Organizational Taboos: the Suppression of Gender Conflicts in Organizations', *Organizational Science*, 1, 339–59.
McGibben, B. (1989) *The End of Nature*, New York: Random House.

Mclennan, G. (1995) 'Feminism, Epistemology, and Postmodernism: Reflections as Current Ambivalence', *Sociology: The Journal of the British Sociological Association*, 29/3, 391–409.
Miles, R. E. and Snow, C. C. (1978) *Organizational Strategy, Structure and Process*, New York: McGraw-Hill.
Morgan, G. (ed.) (1983) *Beyond Method: Strategies for Social Research*, Beverly Hills, CA: Sage.
—— (1986) *Images of Organization*, Beverly Hills, CA: Sage.
—— (1988) *Riding the Waves of Change: Developing Managerial Competencies for a Turbulent World*, San Francisco, CA: Jossey-Bass.
Morgan, G. (1993) *Imaginization: The Art of Creative Management*, Newbury Park, CA: Sage.
Mumby, D. K. and Putnam, L. (1992) 'The Politics of Emotion: a Feminist Reading of Bounded Rationality', *Academy of Management Review*, 17, 465–86.
Nielsen, E. H. (1992) 'Modernism, Postmodernism and Managerial Competencies', paper presented at the National Academy of Management Meetings, Las Vegas, Nevada.
Nkomo, S. (1992) 'The Emperor Has No Clothes: Rewriting "Race in Organizations"', *Academy of Management Review*, 17, 487–513.
Norris, C. (1983) *The Deconstructive Turn*, London: Methuen.
Parker, I. and Shotter, J. (eds) (1990) *Deconstructing Social Psychology*, New York: Routledge.
Parsons, T. (1956) 'Suggestions for a Sociological Approach to the Theory of Organizations-1', *Administrative Science Quarterly*, 1/1, 63–85.
Peck, S. (1993) *A World Waiting to be Born*, New York: Bantam Books.
Peters, T. (1987) *Thriving on Chaos: Handbook for a Management Revolution*, New York: Knopf.
—— (1992) *Liberation Management: Necessary Disorganization for the Nanosecond Nineties*, New York: Knopf.
Pettigrew, T. F. and Martin, J. (1987) 'Shaping the Organizational Context for Black American Inclusion', *Journal of Social Forces*, 43, 41–78.
Pfohl, S. (1992) *Death at the Parasite Cafe*, New York: St Martins.
Pugh, D. S., Hickson, D. J., Hinings, C. R., MacDonald, K. M., Turner, C. and Lupton, T. (1963) 'A Conceptual Schema for Organizational Analysis', *Administrative Science Quarterly*, 8/3, 289–315.
Randall, J. H. (1940) *The Making of the Modern Mind*, Boston, MA: Houghton Mifflin.
Reason, P. and Rowan, J. (eds) (1981) *Human Inquiry: A Sourcebook of a New Paradigm Research*, Chichester: Wiley.
Reed, M. and Hughes, M. (eds) (1992) *Rethinking Organization: New Directions in Organization Theory and Analysis*, London: Sage.
Rorty, R. (1979) *Philosophy and the Mirror of Nature*, Princeton, NJ: Princeton University Press.
Rosenau, P. M. (1992) *Postmodernism and the Social Sciences: Insights, Inroads, and Intrusions*, Princeton, NJ: Princeton University Press.
Rosengren, W. (1967) 'Structure, Policy and Style: Strategies of Organizational Control', *Administrative Science Quarterly*, 12, 140–64.
Rushing, W. (1967) 'The Effect of Industry Size and Division of Labor on Administration', *Administrative Science Quarterly*, 12, 273–95.
Sampson, E. E. (1989) 'The Challenge of Social Change for Psychology: Globalization and Psychology's Theory of the Person', *American Psychologist*, 44, 914–21.
Schein, E. H. (1993) 'On Dialogue, Culture, and Organizational Learning', *Organizational Dynamics*, 22, 40–51.
Schön, D. A. (1983) *The Reflective Practitioner: How Professionals Think in Action*, New York: Basic Books.

Schultz, M. and Hatch, M. T. (1996) 'Living with Multiple Paradigms: the Case of Paradigm Interplay in Organization Culture Studies', *Academy of Management Review*, 21/2, 529–57.
Senge, P. (1990) *The Fifth Discipline: The Art and Practice of the Learning Organization*, New York: Currency Doubleday.
Shafritz, J. M. and Ott, S. (1987) *Classics of Organization Theory*, Chicago, IL: Dorsey Press.
Shotter, J. (1984) *Social Accountability and Selfhood*, New York: Basil Blackwell.
Simon, H. (1957) *Administrative Behavior*, New York: Macmillan, 2nd edn.
—— (ed.) (1990), *Case Studies in the Rhetoric of the Human Sciences*, Chicago, IL: University of Chicago Press.
Simon, W. (1996), *Postmodern Sexualities*, New York: Routledge.
Simonds, R. H. (1959) 'Towards a Science of Business Administration', *Journal of the Academy of Management*, 2, 135–38.
Sinclair, A. (1992) 'The Tyranny of a Team Ideology', *Organization Studies*, 13, 611–26.
Srivastva, S. and Barrett, F. J. (1988) 'The Transforming Nature of Metaphors in Group Development: a Study in Group Theory', *Human Relations*, 41, 31–63.
Srivastva, S., Su, D. L., Cooperrider, D. *et al.* (1990) *Appreciative Management and Leadership: The Power of Positive Thought and Action in Organizations*, San Francisco, CA: Jossey-Bass.
Stewart, E. C. (1972) *American Cultural Patterns: A Cross-Cultural Perspective*, Chicago, IL: Intercultural Press.
Strati, A. (1992) 'Aesthetic Understanding of Organizational Life', *Academy of Management Review*, 17, 568–81.
Thompson, A. A. and Strickland, A. J. (1992) *Strategic Management*, Homewood, IL: Irwin.
Thompson, C. J. (1993) 'Modern Truth and Postmodern Incredulity: a Hermeneutic Deconstruction of the Meta-narrative of "Scientific Truth", in Marketing Research', *International Journal of Research in Marketing*, 10, 332–8.
Thompson, J. D. (1956–7) 'On Building an Administrative Science', *Administrative Science Quarterly*, 1/1, 102–11.
Thompson, V. A. (1961) 'Hierarchy, Specialization and Organization Conflict', *Administrative Science Quarterly*, 5, 485–521.
Torbert, W. R. (1991) *The Power of Balance: Transforming Self, Society and Scientific Inquiry*, Newbury Park, CA: Sage.
Vroom, V. H. (1964) *Work and Motivation*, New York: Wiley.
Warringer, C. K., Hall, R. and McKelvey, B. (1981) 'The Comparative Description of Organizations: a Research Note and Invitation', *Organization Studies*, 2, 173–5.
Weick, K. E. and Van Orden, P. W. (1990) 'Organizing on a Global Scale: a Research and Teaching Agenda', *Human Resource Management*, 29, 49–61.
West, C. (1988) 'Marxist Theory in the Specificity of Afro-American Oppression', in C. Nelson and L. Grossberg (eds) *Marxism and the Interpretation of cultures*, Urbana, IL: University of Illinois Press.
Whitley, R. (1992) 'The Social Construction of Organizations and Markets: the Comparative Analysis of Business Recipes', in M. Reed and M. Hughes (eds) *Rethinking Organization: New Directions in Organization Theory and Analysis*, London: Sage.
Wittgenstein, L. (1963) *Philosophical Investigations*, trans. G. Anscombe, New York: Macmillan.
Wolf, W. (1958) 'Organizational Constructs: an Approach to Understanding Organizations', *Journal of the Academy of Management*, 1/1, 7–15.

2

FORMS OF KNOWLEDGE AND FORMS OF LIFE IN ORGANIZED CONTEXTS

Haridimos Tsoukas

Mainstream Organizational Studies (OS) has historically been antagonistic towards the lay knowledge that organizational members possess. One of OS's foundational assumptions has been that the management of people in organizations will be more effective the more lay knowledge is displaced by social scientific precepts. It has also been assumed that the body of formal knowledge necessary to enable this is increasingly becoming available by OS as the discipline of the social sciences dealing with the human aspects of organizing and managing (see Lupton, 1983; Pinder and Bourgeois, 1982; Simon, 1957 [1976]; Thompson, 1956-7; Donaldson, 1985). 'A unified science of man in organizations', Pugh, Mansfield and Warner characteristically argued, would generate the sort of knowledge that would bring 'increasing benefits if man is to control the social institutions he has established, and hence the nature of the society in which he lives' (1975: 1, 68).

Such an unqualified optimism has been a distinguishing feature of several OS textbooks and of more esoteric mainstream OS research. For example, addressing the readers of his textbook on organizational behaviour (OB), Robbins (1989:) remarked in unequivocal terms: '[O]ne of the objectives of this text is to encourage you to *move away from your intuitive views of behavior* towards a systematic analysis, in the belief that the latter will enhance your effectiveness in *accurately explaining and predicting behavior*' (1989: 4, emphasis added). Similarly, the recent efforts to formalize organization theory through the design of expert systems have been explicitly motivated by the view that intuitive reasoning is inherently 'flawed' and 'prejudiced' (Glorie, Masuch and Marx, 1990: 80; Baligh, Burton and Obel, 1990: 35) and, thus, it ought to be replaced by scientifically derived knowledge.

It is partly my aim here to explore the presuppositions and limitations of such a view of organizational knowledge.[1] More generally, the purpose of this chapter is two-fold: first, to delineate the different types of organizational knowledge and the way they relate to one another; and, second, and more importantly, to ground the different types of organizational knowledge to particular dimensions of organized contexts. My thesis is that the propositional structure of knowledge produced by mainstream (or classical) OS stems from, and is fully realized within, highly institutionalized social contexts (that is to say, in formal organizations or organized contexts – the two terms will be used interchangeably here). However, as will be shown later, even in such contexts, propositional knowledge on its own is of limited utility. It will be further argued that as well as being institutions, organized contexts are practices (or communal traditions – these two terms will also be used interchangeably) in which organizational members live their working lives. Practices are intrinsically related to narrative knowledge, namely to knowledge organized in the form of stories, anecdotes, and examples.

Thus, in the argument put forward here, propositional organizational knowledge is intrinsically related to the institutional dimension of organized contexts, while narrative organizational knowledge is intrinsically related to the latter's practice dimension. The two pairs, however, are in conflict: for practices to endure they need to be sustained by institutions to whose corrosive influence they are inescapably exposed. At the same time, institutions cannot function unless they are supported by communal traditions. The implications of this conflict are explored later in this chapter.

The chapter is organized as follows. In the next section there will be given an outline of the scope of propositional knowledge, underlining its necessary relationship with highly institutionalized forms of social action. Subsequently, the limits of propositional knowledge will be discussed, followed by an outline of the narrative form of organizational knowledge which will be shown to be grounded on communities of tradition.

Organized contexts as institutions: the case for propositional knowledge

The basic characteristic of propositional knowledge is the formulation of conditional 'if, then' statements relating a set of empirical conditions ('If X ... – the factual predicate') to a set of consequences that follow when the conditions specified in the factual predicate obtain (' ... then Y – the consequent') (Johannessen, 1988; Johnson, 1992; Reeves and Clarke, 1990; Payne, 1982; Schauer, 1991; Varela, Thompson and Rosch, 1991; Stillings *et al.*, 1987). With reference to organizations, examples of propositional statements, generated by mainstream OS, are the following: 'If size is large then formalization is high'; 'if technology is routine then complexity is low'; 'if strategy is that of a prospector then centralization is low'; 'if the environment is stable then centralization is high', and so on (see Baligh, Burton and Obel, 1990: 41–4; Glorie, Masuch and Marx, 1990: 87; see also Webster and Starbuck, 1988: 128; Mintzberg, 1979, 1989). The preceding conditional statements serve as explanations of certain recurring organizational phenomena *and* purport to be the basis for formulating rules for guiding human action in the future.

Propositional statements are predicated on the assumption that the phenomenon they refer to is patterned, composed of objectively available elements which can be re-presented via an abbreviated formula (Barrow, 1991; Cooper, 1992; Varela, Thompson and Rosch, 1991). Anything that is assumed to be ordered and nonrandom is thought to be susceptible to propositional formalization and, thus, to abbreviation or, as Barrow termed it, to 'algorithmic compressibility' (1991: 10–11). For example, the sequence of numbers 1 2 3 1 2 3 1 2 3 1 2 3 can easily be seen to be ordered: there is a pattern in it which allows us to replace the sequence with a rule and, thus, be relieved of the burden of having to carry the whole sequence and list all its contents (Barrow, 1995: 46–7). However, in cases where there is no pattern in a sequence of numbers (generated, say, by tossing a coin) there is no abbreviated formula to capture its information content and the whole sequence needs to be listed in full.

Algorithmic compressibility is clearly important insofar as it allows the compression of masses of observational statements into a few clearly stated propositional statements possessing the same informational content but, more importantly, enabling economy of effort, transferability, and remote control (Cooper, 1992; Latour, 1986). A revealing defence of the benefits of algorithmic compressibility that comes about as a result of the accumulation of scientific knowledge was given, some time ago, by Medawar (cited in Feyerabend, 1987):

> As science progresses, particular facts are comprehended within, and therefore in a sense *annihilated* by, general statements of steadily increasing explanatory power and compass – whereupon the facts need no longer be known explicitly, i. e. spelled out and kept in mind. *In all sciences we are progressively relieved of the burden of singular instances, the tyranny of the particular.*
> (Feyerabend, 1987: 122, emphasis added)

Thus an object of scientific study is, in a very crucial sense, thought to be absorbed ('annihilated') by the discipline that studies it, so that its conceptual re-presentation, derived from a selective attention to certain features deemed crucial by the inquiring discipline, is taken to be more important than the object itself. Any other features of an object of study can, therefore, be disregarded (Feyerabend, 1987: 122–3).

As stated earlier, the utility of abbreviated representations stems from their *mobility* (hence their transferability across contexts), their *manipulability*, and from their providing *efficient* ways of achieving results (Cooper, 1992; Latour, 1986).[2] Consider, for example, what one can do with digital representations of material objects. A two-dimensional square can be represented by four pairs of numbers corresponding to each one of its angles. Having this information on a computer one can play with the digital square: it could be made bigger or smaller by respectively increasing or decreasing its coordinate numbers; or it can be 'moved' around by adding to or subtracting from its coordinate numbers (Wooley, 1992: 54). A symbolic world, namely a world consisting of abbreviated representations, is a mobile world (a digitized square can be sent through the network to other computers); it is also a manipulable world (you can experiment with a digitized object and even simulate some of its behaviour); and is, of course, a world in which you can obtain results more efficiently than dealing with the objects themselves (a bigger square can be created instantly on the computer without the need to design physically another one).

What is it that makes abbreviated representations mobile and manipulable, and renders their application efficient? A formal representation is independent of the medium in which it is 'embodied' and, therefore, as Haugeland remarks, 'essentially the same formal system can be materialized in any number of different media, with no formally significant differences whatsoever' (1985: 58). One may play chess, for example, with chessboard and pawns made of all sorts of different materials and sizes without affecting the rules and the syntax of the game. Abbreviated representations are abstract, and are defined exclusively in terms of their syntax (or structure), so that they do not mean anything particular. They are, thus, applicable across a variety of contexts after a particular interpretation (i.e. semantics) has been attached to them in each particular case (Casti, 1989: Chap. 5). Expert systems are a good example of abbreviated representations whose formal syntax needs to be supplemented with the details of a particular case each time they are used.

In extreme cases, once an object of study has been formalized, it can be manipulated without its users having to understand what they are doing, thus increasing economy of effort. Reasoning about the object of study can be carried out by purely manipulating symbols, divorced from meaning or interpretative understanding (Casti, 1989; Reeves and Clarke, 1990). Any time, for example, someone uses a medical expert system, they do not need to understand what it is they are doing as long as they can see the results they expect. Abbreviated representations (and the propositional statements they are associated with) save actors from the burden of interpretative understanding for the sake of efficiently obtaining the desired output.

What must the social world be like for propositional knowledge to be possible? Clearly, it must be, at least to some extent, regularized, patterned, and nonrandom (Castoriadis, 1991) so that it can be described via abbreviated representations in the form of propositional statements. Berger and Luckmann (1966) have, some time ago, provided what still remains the best exposition of how the *ordered* character of reality is socially constructed:

> All human activity is subject to habitualization. Any action that is repeated frequently becomes cast into a pattern, which can then be reproduced with an economy of effort and which, *ipso facto*, is apprehended by its performer *as* that pattern. Habitualization further implies that the action in question may be performed again in the future in the same manner and with the same economical effort.
> (Berger and Luckmann, 1966: 70)

Berger and Luckmann observed that habitualization is the precursor to institutionalization. The latter occurs, they argue, 'whenever there is a reciprocal typification of habitualized action by types of actors' (1966: 72). Notice the link they make between recurring patterns (i.e. habitualization) and quasi-formal cognition (i.e. typification) in the context of institutionalization. Actors attribute motives to each other and seeing actions recur they *typify* the motives as recurrent (hence reciprocal typifications). Individuals begin to cease to be – if they ever were! – unpredictable, randomly acting atoms, and they gradually develop routines (i.e. roles) for dealing with one another. As Berger and Luckmann put it: 'The institution posits that actions of *type x* will be performed by actors of *type x*' (1966: 72, emphasis added). The individual and his/her actions are subsumed under broader categories which may formally be related and described.

Institutionalization renders the social world patterned and routinized so that it is possible to 'freeze' patterns and routines, and formally represent them in an abbreviated explanatory-cum-predictive formula (Tsoukas, 1992). Or to put it more generally: the more institutionalized human interaction is, the more likely it is that the patterns and regularities it gives rise to will be describable in an algorithmically compressed formula. For example, Poole and Van de Ven (1989) have highlighted the possibility of explaining the development of innovations in highly institutionalized contexts in terms of relatively deterministic historical-cum-functional models. By contrast, in the absence of highly institutionalized contexts, innovation patterns are better explained, they argue, in terms of emergent processes. Or to put this in the terminology of this chapter: algorithmically compressible explanations are less likely to be useful in situations in which there are not well developed institutional rules for the regulation of social life.

Hopefully, it should be clear by now that processes of institutionalization imply that actors have delimited modes of interaction and that, therefore, they relate to one another in terms of their roles (see Zucker, 1977; Lee, 1984). Roles consist of sets of rules delineating the scope and direction of individual action. This is most clearly manifested in organized contexts since the latter consist, by design, of sets of processes for reducing equivocality among actors (Weick, 1979), thus generating recurring events by means of rules that are usually explicitly defined and their execution monitored. Rules are prescriptive statements mandating or guiding behaviour in a given type of situation (Haugeland, 1985; Schauer, 1991; Twinnings and Miers, 1991). As Twinnings and Miers remark, a rule 'prescribes that in circumstances X, behavior of type Y ought, or ought not to be, or may be, indulged in by persons of class Z' (1991: 131) (see also Argyris and Schön, 1974: 6).

Notice the similarities between such a definition of rules and the preceding description of the process of institutionalization by Berger and Luckmann (1966). Rules are necessarily generalizations connecting *types* of behaviour by *types* of actors to *types* of situations (see Schauer, 1991: Chap. 2). To assert the existence of a rule is necessarily to generalize and to institutionalize human interaction is, of necessity, to imply the existence of rules. As Weber (1948) insightfully remarked, it is the centrality of impersonal rules that marks out formal organization (bureaucracy) from other forms of administration. 'The "objective" discharge of business', observed Weber, 'means a discharge of business according to *calculable rules* and "without regard for persons"' (1948: 2–15):

> Why are calculable rules so important for bureaucracy? For Weber, it is in the very logic of bureaucracy to demand calculability of results. In his words: '(Bureaucracy) develops the more perfectly the more the bureaucracy is "dehumanized"', the more completely it succeeds in eliminating from official business love, hatred, and all purely personal, irrational, and emotional elements which escape calculation. This is the specific nature of bureaucracy and it is appraised as its special virtue.
>
> (Weber, 1948: 216)

The similarities of formal organization with expert systems are evident. Both rely on explicit rules for their functioning, and it is precisely this property of organized contexts that enables some researchers to pursue enthusiastically the formalization of organization theory (Lee, 1984; Masuch, 1990). However, as we will see below, such formalization is necessarily limited, and insofar as it is considered to be the *raison d'être* of OS, it is definitely problematic. Organized contexts cannot rely on calculable rules alone. Weber's linear logic, implicit in the preceding extract, can be seen at best as a *ceteris paribus* argument for the development of formal organization. We have seen enough in the last hundred years to make us have serious doubts about whether formal organizations can really function effectively as programmable machines.

Imperfect rules, unstable semantics: the limits of propositional knowledge

It has been argued so far that in organized contexts there is an intrinsic relationship between rules and propositional statements. In fact, as we have seen, they are mirror images of one another. For propositional statements to be possible, rules guiding human action must necessarily be in place. Conversely, the existence of rules can be captured via formal methods of investigation relating factual predicates to consequents. Rules, however, are far from perfect: the links between general categories and the particular instances that they seek to relate to is always precarious. In this section it will be explained why this is the case and the implications will be explored.

Particular objects, actions, and events can be subsumed under a number of overlapping categories. A man or a woman, for example, can be described using a potentially infinite number of categories (e.g. nationality, race, occupation, state of health, marital status, hobbies, food preferences, and so on – the list is endless) but, in practice, a very limited set will normally do. Out of a multiplicity of classificatory candidates, all of which are empirically and logically correct generalizations, we normally choose the category 'patient' to describe someone who enters a hospital for treatment. Within this category even more discriminating choices can be made, depending on the kind of treatment a patient is seeking. Such choices are determined not by any of his/her properties – as Schauer remarks, 'no one of the simultaneously applicable categories of which any particular is a member has a logical priority over another' (1991: 19) – but by the *discursive context* in which that person is described (see also Watzlawick, Weakland and Fisch, 1974: Chap. 8).

Through generalizing in one direction and, by default, not in another direction, discursive contexts make organizational action possible (Schauer, 1991: Chap. 2). Saying, for example, that 'Joanna is a thirty-year-old woman' or that 'Joanna is a secretary' is quite different from saying that 'Joanna is a single mother', because the same Joanna is in the company of different particulars depending on the category chosen for attention. Thus, in the discursive context of the Child Support Agency (CSA), launched in 1993 by the British government to track down absent fathers who refuse to contribute towards their children's upbringing, women like Joanna are of interest only by virtue of being single mothers. In every other respect these women are bound to be different (each of them is a particular whose properties extend in different directions and can, therefore, be subsumed under different categories) except for the one single category which constitutes the *raison d'être* of the CSA: single motherhood.

By being generalizations, categories are necessarily selective: as selective inclusions they are also selective exclusions; they suppress as much as they reveal (Schauer, 1991: 21). Furthermore, when categories are joined to make an organizational rule (e.g. 'if a single mother is in danger of being harmed by her ex-partner, then the CSA may not force him to pay maintenance to her') the rule's factual predicate 'consists of a generalization perceived to be causally relevant to some goal sought to be achieved or evil to be avoided. Prescription of that goal, or prescription of that evil, constitutes the justification which then determines which generalization will constitute the rule's factual predicate' (Schauer, 1991: 27). Here the evil sought to be avoided is the ex-partner doing harm to the single mother. Avoiding this evil is judged to be more important than getting the ex-partner to contribute to the maintenance of his children at all costs.

What is noteworthy about organizational rules is that their consequents ('then the CSA may not force him to pay maintenance to her') are meant to be applied to future instances, while their factual predicates ('if a single mother is in danger of being harmed by her ex-partner') are either derived from knowledge of past regularities (which, it is thought, will also be obtained in the future), or are based on current assumptions about behaviour in the future.

However, there is an asymmetry between description-cum-explanation and prescription. While propositional knowledge *retro*spectively explains (or at least describes) the functioning of a social system in terms of rules, it cannot *pro*spectively provide actors with the knowledge of how to apply definitively a set of rules in the future or how to create new rules. This asymmetry can be removed only in closed systems in which internal change and external contingencies have been formally excluded so that the future is a linear extension of the past.[3] Despite their in-built tendencies for closure, however, organizations are inherently open systems in which the above noted asymmetry can, at best, only temporarily be abolished. There are two reasons for this: first, there is the inherently unstable semantics of knowledge representation. All formal systems consisting of explicit rules depend for their functioning on the manipulation of representations (i.e. symbols) (see Casti, 1989; Haugeland, 1985; Varela, Thompson and Rosch, 1991; Winograd and Flores, 1987; Lee, 1984). How do these representations get their meaning? The users of a system decide to interpret the symbols they use in a particular way (that is, the users decide to stabilize the symbol's meaning) so that valid inferences can be drawn. For a formal system to be effective, it requires that its representations have stable meanings for as long as it is possible. In open systems, however, such stability is always precarious and temporary. New definitions inevitably emerge eroding the established ones (Tsoukas, 1994b: 22–7), for example, in the case of the CSA, a 'single mother applying for maintenance to the CSA' is such a symbol and is incorporated into the agency's knowledge representation. In CSA's interpretation, a single mother is eligible for receiving the full maintenance from CSA if she discloses the name of her ex-partner and if, in doing so, her safety is not at risk. For its own internal purposes such definition may suffice, but in an open social system the stability of the definition is precarious. For several single mothers wishing to receive the full maintenance through CSA, and wishing not to get embroiled in arguments with their ex-partners, or even aiming at obtaining some financial assistance from them which would be less than what their ex-partners would have to pay through the CSA, may collude with their ex-partners in claiming that the latter have been threatening them (see the *Independent*, 21 March, 1995). So, the initial interpretation of the Agency must now be supplemented with another whereby the genuineness of claims made by single mothers can be verified.

Although the preceding illustration is an example of how definitions can be eroded from 'within', it is similar in mode to those cases in which definitional control is eroded from 'outside', namely from competitors or outside stakeholders (see Tsoukas, 1994a: 8–12, 1994b: 22–4). The more general point made here is that while an organization is compelled to fix the definition of its representations for its own purposes, insofar as 'it must interact with the larger social world, it no longer has this definitional control' (Lee, 1984: 302). The semantics of knowledge representation in an organized context is intrinsically unstable (although this does not mean permanently unstable) and, therefore, so are the rules underlying its functioning.

Second, several philosophers have pointed out that what ensures that a rule will be followed in the same way, repeatedly in the future, cannot itself be a rule (Taylor, 1993: 57). This is essentially the gist of Wittgenstein's (1958) well-known remark that the application of rules is rooted in customs and public practices, and of Gadamer's (1980: 83) claim that to understand *in concreto* one needs *phronesis* (prudence) for 'the application of rules can never be done by rules'. Anyone, for example, who has attempted to speak a foreign language must have experienced the inadequacy of simply knowing the rules alone in order to practise effectively a language. It is the grounding of language on social practices that makes it necessary for a speaker to learn (not just the rules but also) to discriminate among a large variety of social situations, and this cannot be done effectively except through *participating* in a social practice.

It could be argued, however, that to the extent that contexts, customs, and practices can be studied and classified, it is possible to construct increasingly more refined rules. While this has certainly been happening in medicine (see Hunter, 1991), in artificial intelligence (Schank and Childers, 1984), and in OS (Masuch, 1990), it is churlish to believe that it will eliminate the fundamental imperfection of rules as guides for human action in open social systems (Corbett, 1989; Rosenbrock, 1988; Schauer, 1991). The reason is, as Johannessen (1988), echoing Wittgenstein, puts it:

> Since a definition of a rule cannot itself determine how it is to be applied, there is no point in giving a new rule to lay down how the first should be applied. For then the problem will just transfer itself to the new rule, because this also could be interpreted or followed in several different ways. It will continue thus *ad infinitum* if we try to escape this tangle by formulating more and more new rules to determine the use of the first rule. This is a dead end. We must realize that our application of rules cannot itself be determined through a rule. The application must by necessity be ruleless.
>
> (Johannessen, 1988: 298–9)

Brown and Duguid (1991), Orr (1990) and Spender (1992), have pointed out the problems associated with the propositional structure of knowledge underlying the application of rules in their discussion of the role of directive documentation in helping technicians who service broken photocopiers. The machine manuals that are issued to service technicians contain canonical (i.e. rule full) images of their practice which is only tenuously related to the noncanonical practices technicians frequently employ to deal with a variety of local problems.[4] In a sense, this is inescapable: organizations provide the discursive contexts by means of which certain generalizations are preferred while some others are suppressed (although not negated). For the designers of photocopy manuals, a 'broken machine' is of central importance and manuals are about fixing such an abstract entity. Repairing a machine, however, occurs in a social context the details of which cannot be exhaustively known *ex ante* to designers. Furthermore, although certain generalizations are necessarily selected ('If this error code is displayed then check this, or do that'), it does not mean that the ones that have been suppressed are irrelevant – indeed, in certain conjunctions of circumstances they become central (Schauer, 1991: 22). The technician, for example, needs to fix not only the machine but to attend simultaneously to several other things (usually of a social nature); he/she strives not to lose the customer's trust in him/her, to inquire about the manner in which the customer had been using the machine, to maintain his/her reputation in the community of technicians, and so on (see Brown and Duguid, 1991: 43; Orr, 1990: 173; see also Vickers, 1983: 42–5). In a particular conjunction of circumstances one or more of those concerns may become particularly salient, although there is no way of telling if, when, and what form such conjunction may take. Only the technician faced there and then with a concrete concatenation of events can carry out the diagnosis and undertake effective action.

At any point in time, therefore, what is going on in an organized context is not only unfixed but is inherently indeterminate, so that organizational rules (and the underlying propositional knowledge) are bound to be of limited utility. Several transactions take place at the same time, and no one can describe them all in advance, since to notice what is going on depends on the (ineluctably partial) perspective of the observer (Hayek, 1982: Chap. 2; Tsoukas, 1994a: 16). As MacIntyre has observed, there is no single game that is played but several, and 'if the game metaphor may be stretched further, the problem about real life is that moving one's knight to QB3 may always be replied to with a lob across the net' (1985: 98).

Cannot repair manuals be made more sophisticated by drawing on past experiences and incorporating more and more categories of the social contexts in which broken machines are likely to be found? Should this happen, the technicians would surely be offered better informed, rule-based advice as to how to deal with broken machines. That would certainly be useful but, still, it does not solve the problem. The fact remains that even conditional generalizations are *universal* within their scope of applicability. In Schauer's words: 'Regardless of scope, any rule uses its generalizing factual predicate to make it applicable to *all* of something' (1991: 24). To say, for example, 'if in such and such circumstances this error happens, then do that', is to offer advice that is universal within the scope of 'such and such' regardless of how small that scope is.

Managing an organized context exclusively by rules leads inescapably to paradoxes. The reason is that time is not included in the propositional logic underlying the use of rules. As Bateson (1979: 63) observed, the 'if, then' of causality contains time, but the 'if, then' of propositional statements is timeless (see also Capra, 1988: 83). Take, for example, the case of the CSA again. One of the CSA rules is that if a single mother does not disclose the name of the father to the CSA, her benefit will be reduced. What is the justification for this? Obviously, the legitimate need for the CSA is to identify irresponsible fathers who have not contributed towards the upbringing of their children, and to force them to do so. Putting pressure on the mother (the only person the CSA is likely to have, initially, any contact with) seems a sensible thing to do. But, if a mother refuses to tell the CSA the father's name, then her benefit must be reduced. Notice the paradox. On the one hand there is an agency whose primary goal is to provide single mothers with money considered minimally necessary for the upbringing of their children. On the other hand, if a single mother does not conform to the agency's rules, her maintenance will be reduced. And if the state benefit is reduced, those who will most likely suffer will be the children, whose welfare is supposed to be the sole reason for the existence of the CSA. A classic Catch-22. The paradox is created because of a confusion of logical levels induced by timeless propositional logic. One logical level is that of single mothers' *real* demands, namely maintenance sufficient for the welfare of their children. A logically higher level is that of single mothers' demands as they are *represented* by the CSA's rules, namely state benefits with strings attached. Conflating meeting single mother's demands with 'meeting' their demands as the CSA's rules prescribe, creates the paradox. Hence, if the single mothers' demands are met, then they are not 'met'. If they are 'met', then they are not met! The system oscillates, it cannot get things right.[5]

Organized contexts as practices: the case for narrative knowledge

The impossibility of guiding practical action in organized contexts by rules alone underlines the gnosiological[6] indispensability of examples, anecdotes, and stories – in short: narratives – for stating what rules cannot state. As Wittgenstein famously remarked: 'Not only rules, but also *examples* are needed for establishing a *practice*. Our rules leave loopholes open, and *the practice has to speak for itself* (1969: 145, emphasis added). We have earlier seen why rules leave loopholes open, but in what sense are 'examples' needed for establishing a practice? What does 'practice' mean, and how can it 'speak for itself'?

In the preceding excerpt Wittgenstein uses the word 'example' in this double meaning: I hold someone up as an example, as embodying the standards of excellence I myself aspire to, *and* also, I use examples, illustrations, and stories to convey to someone else the knowledge that is necessary for engaging in a set of practical activities. In the former sense, I learn a practice through actively participating in it through engaging with and learning from all those who have been there before me. In the latter sense, a community shares a set of narratives through which it articulates its self-understanding, its historicity and its identity, and preserves its collective memory. Thus, it follows that a practice speaks for itself *actively*, namely through letting others see what its members are up to. Also, a practice speaks for itself *gnosiologically*, namely through the narratives articulating the knowledge employed in (the) practice. On this account, therefore, narratives are intimately linked to practices. As will be shown below, unless organized contexts are also seen as *practices* (and not merely as institutions) it is difficult to be adequately understood.

What are practices, and why do we need to distinguish them from institutions? MacIntyre's attempt to ground sociologically his theory of morality makes use of the concept of 'practice', and in what follows I will draw extensively on his analysis. 'By a "practice" I am going to mean' writes MacIntyre:

> any *coherent and complex form of socially established cooperative human activity* through which *goods internal* to that form of activity are realized in the course of trying to achieve those *standards of excellence* which are appropriate to, and partially definitive of, that form of activity, with the result

that human powers to achieve excellence, and *human conceptions of ends and goods involved are systematically extended*.

(1985: 187, emphasis added)

So what might be examples of practices? MacIntyre again:

> Tic-tac-toe is not an example of a practice in this sense, nor is throwing a football with skill; but the game of football is, and so is chess. Bricklaying is not a practice; architecture is. Planting turnips is not a practice; farming is. So are the enquiries of physics, chemistry and biology, and so is the work of the historian, and so are painting and music.
>
> (1985: 187)

There are four crucial features of a practice borne out by MacIntyre's definition. First, a practice is a complex form of social activity that involves the cooperative effort of human beings; it is coherent and, therefore, bound by rules and it is extended in time. For practices to survive for any length of time they need to be carried out within institutions for, as we saw earlier, it is the latter that gives social life its duration and coherence. Obviously, this is a matter of degree: practices are more or less institutionalized as, for example, when one is doing solitary research in, say, physics, as opposed to carrying it out within a university laboratory. However, one thing is clear: although practices alone are articulate forms of social action, if they are to be sustained, they will inevitably become institutionalized.

Second, every practice establishes a set of what MacIntyre calls 'internal goods', meaning goods that cannot be achieved in any other way but by *participating* in the practice itself. For example, the particular analytical skills and strategic imagination that are associated with playing chess, the kind of satisfaction derived from caring for patients, or the thrill that comes from exploring new avenues of scientific research, cannot be achieved in any other way but by respectively *playing* chess, *nursing* patients, and *researching* in a particular field. Naturally, 'those who lack the relevant experience are incompetent thereby as judges of internal goods' (MacIntyre, 1985: 189). By contrast, 'external goods' such as status, money, career, fame, etc., are only contingently attached to a practice and they can, therefore, be achieved by alternative ways without having to participate in a particular practice.

Whereas the achievement of internal goods benefits potentially the whole community who engage into a particular practice (e.g. major conceptual shifts in physics), the achievement of external goods benefits only individuals, and this accounts for the competition that is often associated with acquiring external goods. Practices are intrinsically linked with internal goods, whereas institutions are linked with external goods. The result is conflict: 'the ideals and the creativity of the practices are always vulnerable to the acquisitiveness of the institution' (MacIntyre, 1985: 194).

Third, participating in a practice necessarily involves attempting to achieve the standards of excellence operative in the practice at the time. Unless one accepts the standards of the practice into which one has entered, and the inadequacy of his/her performance *vis-à-vis* those standards, he/she will never learn to excel in that practice.

Fourth, every practice has its own history which is not only the history of the changes of technical skills relevant to a practice, but also a history of changes of the relevant ends to which the technical skills are put. It is the *historicity* of a practice that impels MacIntyre to argue that:

> to enter into a practice is to enter into a relationship not only with its contemporary practitioners, but also with those who have preceded us in the practice, particularly those whose achievements extended the reach of the practice to its present point. It is thus the achievement, and *a fortiori* the authority, of a *tradition* which I then confront and from which I have to learn.
>
> (MacIntyre, 1985: 194, emphasis added)

If what has been argued so far in this chapter is accepted, it follows that organizational rules are intimately connected with the institutional dimension of organized contexts, and are necessarily couched in the language of selective generalizations, while at the same time remaining inherently open-ended in their future applications. Thus, the task of, say, service technicians is located at the interface between the generic rules mandated by a particular manual *and* the local context of application. It is the ability to mediate between these two levels that marks out an effective technician, and such an ability is largely acquired and enhanced through participating in a practice (i.e. in a community of other technicians) (Brown and Duguid, 1991; Orr, 1990; Schön, 1987: 35–40).

From a gnosiological point of view, what does it mean to participate in a practice? The answer has already been alluded to: it is to share in the narratives a community of practitioners employ. Why is this sharing important, and why sharing in *narratives*? It is because the *history* of the practice into which I have entered, and from which I have to learn if I am to become an effective member of the community of practitioners, is conveyed to me through the *stories* my fellow practitioners tell me. Stories about the good old days, about achievements and failures, about awkward people and memorable episodes; stories, in short, about everything that matters to those participating in the practice (Hunter, 1991: Chap. 4). Narratives, therefore, are context-specific accounts, replete with the actions (or omissions) of concrete individuals, containing events that are temporally arranged and, in an organized context, they usually imply suggestions for desirable ways of acting.

Rules cannot have the role that narratives have: rules are impersonal, generic, and atemporal formulae bearing only an apparent relation to what I am exactly experiencing 'on the ground' (Bourdieu, 1990: 80–97; Taylor, 1993: 56–7). I am a concrete individual with my own aspirations, skills, and vulnerabilities – in short, having my particular context-dependent experiences obtained in the course of my life. As such, I am an inescapably historical human being and I have entered into an ineluctable historical setting (or context). If I want to find out about why certain patterns of behaviour are dominant in my practice, I have to inquire about intentions, desires, and goals of those already engaging in them. But in order to do so I need to relate those intentions to the settings in which the behaviours occur. Now, to understand the setting(s) of a behaviour I need to find out about its history, for the setting itself consists of individuals and their relationships extended in time (MacIntyre, 1985: 204–17). As Mulhall and Swift, echoing MacIntyre, remarked:

> Rendering an action intelligible is a matter of grasping it as an episode in the history of the agent's life and of the settings in which it occurs. . . . In other words, narrative history of a certain kind is the basic genre for the characterization of human action. . . . Because action has a basically historical character, our lives are enacted narratives in which we are both characters and authors; a person is a character abstracted from history.
> (1992: 87)

The suggestions for action implied by narratives do not follow the 'if, then' structure of rules.[7] To understand the practical utility of narratives, it is helpful to see them as analogous to the inputs into an individual considered as a black box, the output of which is individual action. Why is the individual thought of as analogous to a *black box*? In a black box there is nothing known about how inputs are connected to outputs (Beer, 1966: 293–8). What is so interesting about a black box? Look at it this way: in a transparent box its internal connections are known, hence its variety (namely, the number of possible states the box can take up) is constrained. Individuals following rules are enjoined to act as if they were transparent boxes: the consequents (i.e. the outputs of action or behaviour) are linked to the factual predicates (i.e. the inputs) in specific ways – as rules mandate. A particular set of inputs is supposed to lead to a pregiven set of outputs. No interference from (to quote Weber again) 'love, hatred, and all purely personal, irrational, and emotional elements which escape calculation' is allowed.

The reverse happens with a black box. Because it is 'assumed to be able to take on any internal arrangement of input-output connectivity at all' (Beer, 1966: 293), a black box can have maximal variety, and thus it is better suited to cope with unforeseen circumstances. Narratives conceived as inputs leading to individuals-considered-as-black-boxes can be linked to the specific experiences individuals have already acquired in the course of their lives, in numerous, unforeseeable ways. How is this possible? Three reasons. First, nobody fully knows what an individual's specific experiences are; or, to put it differently, it cannot be fully known by an observer what an actor's stock of past experiential knowledge consists of (Tsoukas, 1994b). Second, no observer can ever possess all the local information each actor *happens* to possess by virtue of his/her particular location in the organization (Hayek, 1945, 1982; Tsoukas, 1994a). And third, no one is in a position to tell which parts of, and how, an individual's stock of experiential knowledge and of local information will be connected with the in-coming narratives. Hence, the link between narratives and individual actions is bound to be contingent and, therefore, ambiguous.

From the above it follows that the utility of narratives lies not so much in the particular suggestions for action they may imply as in their mode of use: their contingent connections to individual actions help bridge the gap between generic rules and local circumstances in a flexible and inconclusive manner. Commenting on the extensive narration used by service technicians in their work, Brown and Duguid aptly remark: 'The stories have a flexible generality that make them both adaptable and particular. They function, rather like the common law, as a usefully underconstrained means to interpret each new situation in the light of accumulated wisdom and constantly changing circumstances' (1991: 44). To the extent that this happens, narratives help provide unexpected clues which may trigger new ways of thinking and thus initiate fresh courses of action (McKelvey and Aldrich, 1983; Spender, 1992; Weick, 1987). Contrary to the linear structure of propositional knowledge, the dynamic structure of narratives is such that it allows events to be flexibly connected along time, social interactions to be preserved, and local contexts to be taken into account. Narratives have also a mnemonic value since they are registered in, and recalled from, human memory more easily than complex sets of propositional statements (Brown and Duguid, 1991; Daft and Wiginton, 1979; Weick, 1987; Weick and Browning, 1986).

Narration, therefore, facilitates social interaction, preserves a community's collective memory, and enhances a group's sense of shared identity as participants in a practice (Brown and Duguid, 1991; Orr, 1990). Starbuck (1985) has given a vivid account of the intimate links between organized-contexts-as-practices and narration. In a research project he investigated how a worker, Charlie Strothman, drafted production schedules, including in particular how he estimated machine run times. No one had taught him an explicit procedure and he could not quite put it in words how exactly he was able to estimate run times: 'He had just learned from experience, and he doubted that he always used the same procedure' (Starbuck, 1985: 354). After an in-depth study, the researchers concluded that Charlie's complex thought processes could be reduced to a linear equation which produced his speed estimates fairly accurately. Having shown him the linear equation and demonstrated the benefits from using it in his daily work, the researchers expected Charlie to start using it. Alas, this did not happen! 'Six years of habit and the frame of reference that went with it were too strong. The familiar program worked and he trusted it. Who knows what errors lurked in an unfamiliar program?' (Starbuck, 1985: 355). What is more important, however, is the link between narration and organized-context-*qua*-practice that Starbuck alludes to:

> [T]he familiar program meshed with other programs used by other people: the whole organization talked and reported data in terms of speeds, not times. . . . *If Charlie were to shift to a time frame of reference, he would*

isolate himself from other people in his organization, and their talk about speeds would lack meaning for him. It was no accident that he had earlier told us: 'When I first came to work here, I was told what the average speeds were'.

(Starbuck 1985: 355, emphasis added)

Starbuck dismisses the possible explanation that Charlie's resistance might be due to apathy, ignorance or conservatism. Charlie is described as intelligent, extremely cooperative in the research project, having had some engineering training, and being renowned for his willingness to introduce innovations at work. Such apparent resistance cannot be understood unless one sees an organized context also as a communal tradition: namely as a practice whose main mode of understanding and communication is narration. The particular set of social relationships existing at Charlie's work place were underwritten by a particular form of organizational knowledge; changing one would inevitably have implications for the other.[8]

An attempt to represent organizational knowledge via an abbreviated propositional formula may be necessary for institutional purposes (e.g. individual or group target-setting, efficiency, accountability, etc.), but it highlights the external goods to be achieved in an organized context. A particular abstraction, such as, for example, the productive capacity of individuals (or of *individual* groups, departments, etc.) becomes the prime focus of attention, individual calculation, and potential dispute. The more this happens, the more the institutionalized character of organized contexts is underscored at the expense of their communal dimension and the internal goods the latter is associated with.

An organized context deprived of the experience of a communal form of life manifested in a shared tradition, in stories and memorable episodes, has a truncated collective memory which undermines its ability to cope with novel problems (Weick, 1987; see also Engestrom *et al.*, 1990). Insofar as organized contexts are inherently open systems, and to the extent that organizational rules are intrinsically open-ended in their application, every problem has some degree of novelty or, as Piaget remarked, 'in each act of understanding some degree of invention is involved' (1970: 77). Individuals, therefore, faced with problems will have to transcend their reliance on rules and draw also on narratives shared in their practice if they are to tackle their problems effectively.

Furthermore, Charlie Strothman's resistance to apply the researcher's mathematical formula at work, stemmed not only from the important fact that doing so might have distanced him from the community of his fellow workers, but also from an intuitive appreciation that unless practical knowledge is known *tacitly* it is ineffectual. Polanyi (1966) and Polanyi and Prosch (1975) cogently argue that all practical knowing is tacit, in the sense that the focal target of our attention (e.g. a pair of stereoscopic pictures) always relies on particulars of which we are only subsidiarily aware (e.g. the individual pictures), and which need to be integrated tacitly by the knower with the focal target. In Polanyi and Prosch's words:

> (T)he structure of tacit knowing . . . includes a joint pair of constituents. Subsidiaries exist as such by bearing on the focus *to* which we are attending *from* them. In other words, the functional structure of from–to knowing includes jointly a subsidiary 'from' and a focal 'to' (or 'at'). But this pair is not linked together of its own accord. The relation of a subsidiary to a focus is formed by the *act of a person* who integrates one to another.
>
> (Polanyi and Prosch, 1975: 37–8)

Although Polanyi and Prosch's argument refers to the structure of individual knowing, it is equally relevant to the structure of collective knowing. As an individual is unable to learn to balance on a bicycle by trying to follow a mathematical formula relating the velocity of the bicycle to its angle of imbalance, so a collectivity of individuals cannot undertake effective action unless its knowledge is known nonexplicitly, that is to say, nonpropositionally. Narratives provide the subsidiaries which individuals integrate tacitly with the focus of attention.

Thus, what Starbuck's workers practically do with respect to run times is based on a host of subsidiaries such as machine speeds and specific features of the production schedule, which they as individuals have tacitly learned to integrate. Collectively, they share a number of stories about machine breakdowns, time miscalculations, successful estimates, etc., which, although they may have little to do directly with the estimates of run time for a particular schedule at a particular point in time, do bear tacitly on it (see also Brown and Duguid, 1991). How? Stories make workers (and practitioners in general) aware of the knowledge that has been historically accumulated in a practice, and this subsidiary awareness is merged into the focal awareness of trying to tackle a particular problem. Practitioners watch (namely, they are focally aware of) the effects of their problem-solving efforts by keeping subsidiarily aware of the hitherto known episodes concerning similar problems in the past. Narratively organized experiences (both personal and vicarious) provide actors with the subsidiary particulars which bear on the focal activity *to* which actors are attending *from* (Polanyi and Prosch, 1975: 37–8).

Summary and conclusion

Organizing consists of a set of processes aimed at institutionalizing human interaction and, as such, it is intimately related to quasi-formal cognition. Actors attribute motives to each other and, seeing actions recur, they typify the motives as recurrent. Institutionalized human interaction gives rise to patterns and regularities which are, in principle, amenable to algorithmic compressibility. Knowledge of regularities is cast in a propositional mould so that the right type of action can be initiated in the right type of circumstance. Thus, propositional knowledge is closely linked with the institutional dimension of organizing: organized contexts tend to be, by design, institutionalized systems, replete with regularities which can be represented via propositional knowledge.

However, knowledge of regularities alone cannot be an effective guide for (prospective) action. For organized contexts are also open systems in constant flux. Particular organizational practices continue to exist only to the extent that actors' interpretations of them continue to be stable. Also, actors' capacity for learning and self-reflection has the effect that actors have the potential for self-transformation, and thus the social reality they help constitute is also transformable.

The intrinsic openness of organized contexts implies that the future may always be different from the past, and that there is no guarantee that the rules guiding individuals' behaviour now will also be applied in the future as intended. Rules on their own are imperfect coordinating devices: how they will be interpreted and applied in particular situations will always be uncertain. Therefore, rules need to be supplemented by narratives containing the collective memory of a social system and enabling it to cope with novel problems.

Narrative knowledge is an indispensable input to effective action because organized contexts, in addition to being institutions, are also practices. As practices, organized contexts are communal traditions having their own standards of excellence as well as their own internal goods which only participants can judge and achieve. To participate in a practice is to share in the narratives that a community of practitioners employ. Narratives are indeed an important unit of organizational knowledge and discourse, and are constructed around memorable episodes derived from participating in a practice. Unlike propositional statements, narratives are contingently linked to individual action thus facilitating individual adaptation to a large number of unforeseeable circumstances. Furthermore, narration facilitates social interaction, preserves a community's collective memory, enhances a group's sense of shared identity as participants in a practice, and serves as a repository of tacit organizational knowledge.

From the above it follows that the knowledge and social domains are interdependent: forms of organizational knowledge are rooted in forms of organizational life, and vice versa. In order for actors to be able to realize their plans, their immediate (human and nonhuman) environment needs to be rendered predictable (i.e. to be institutionalized), and the acquisition (as well as the generation) of propositional knowledge is necessary (as well as feasible). At the same time, however, through participating in a practice, actors need to preserve their free will, their autonomy and creativity which, valuable although these are in themselves, are also necessary for *en*acting (as opposed to merely *re*acting to) a predictable environment. As MacIntyre has remarked:

> It is necessary, if life is to be meaningful, for us to be able to engage in long- term projects, and this requires predictability; it is necessary, if life is to be meaningful, for us to be in possession of ourselves and not merely to be the creations of other people's projects, intentions and desires, and this requires unpredictability. We are thus involved in a world in which we are

simultaneously trying to render the rest of society predictable and ourselves unpredictable, to devise generalizations which will capture the behaviour of others and to cast our own behaviour into forms which will elude the generalizations which others frame.

(MacIntyre, 1985: 104)

Propositional knowledge and narrative knowledge are the two ends of the spectrum of organizational knowledge.[9] Insofar as organized contexts are institutions they necessarily generate and use propositional knowledge; to the extent that organized contexts are practices they also generate and draw upon narrative knowledge. Furthermore, other things being equal, the more institutionalized a social system is, the more the propositional type of knowledge will tend to be used (e.g. total asylums). Conversely, the more organizational knowledge is understood in terms of propositional knowledge, the more institutionalized a social system will tend to become, and narrative knowledge will tend to be underestimated. In those sociocultural contexts in which classic scientific argumentation is held to be the paradigm of reliable knowledge, propositional knowledge will tend to dominate over narrative knowledge. In such rationalized sociocultural contexts, organizations have more chances of surviving by adopting a rationalistic discourse manifested in explicit rules. Thus, as well as being gnosiologically indispensable, rules are also politically expedient for they enhance organizations' chances of survival in rationalized contexts. Although exploring the influences that shape the forms of organizational knowledge is important, such exploration is beyond the scope of this chapter.

Acknowledgements

I have greatly benefited from several discussions with Alan B. Thomas whose ideas, criticism, and suggestions were invaluable in improving an earlier draft. I would also like to thank Gibson Burrell, Robert Cooper, Kenneth Gergen, Jannis Kallinikos, Steen Sorensen, Richard Whitley and Arndt Sorge for their very useful comments. The responsibility for any mistakes or omissions is obviously mine.

Notes

1. By 'organizational knowledge' I primarily mean knowledge used by actors *in* organizations, not knowledge *about* organizations. There is, obviously, a clear relationship between the two. For example, the propositional knowledge used in organizations in the form of rules is certainly related to the formal knowledge about organizational phenomena generated by organizational researchers – the former is supposed to be aided, refined and, ideally, replaced by the latter. For the sake of conceptual clarity, however, it makes sense to keep these two logical levels of organizational knowledge separate.
2. Transferability is an important property of social scientific knowledge which was well appreciated by Thompson (1956–7), and was part of his justification for the desirability and possibility of an administrative science. In his words:

If every administrative action, and every outcome of such action, is entirely unique, then there can be no transferable knowledge or understanding of administration. If, on the other hand, knowledge of at least some aspects of administrative processes is transferable, then those methods which have proved most useful in gaining reliable knowledge in other areas would also seem to be appropriate for adding to our knowledge of administration.

(Thompson, 1956–7: 103)

Similarly, the efficiency (or economy of effort) that comes with the application of social scientific knowledge has been praised by Huczynski and Buchanan. They write: 'If (for example) we know what motivates you, we then know what buttons to press to make you work harder, we know what levers to pull to make you change your attitudes, we know what rewards and sanctions will get your support for a particular package of changes – so we can influence your behaviour in directions we think desirable' (1991: 54).

3   A social system is intrinsically open in the sense that it is impossible to obtain stable regularities across space and time (see Bhaskar, 1979; Sayer, 1984). Why? Regularities are generated by repeated individual actions (namely, acting similarly in similar circumstances) and are possible only when the following two conditions obtain: first, the mechanisms (that is, individual action) producing regularities must not undergo qualitative change (the intrinsic condition of closure); second, the relationship between mechanisms and the external conditions that matter for their operation must remain constant (the extrinsic condition of closure). To the extent that individuals' meanings and interpretations differ across contexts, and change over time, social systems violate both conditions of closure (Tsoukas, 1994a: 8–9).

4   Parenthetically, it may be noted that although Brown and Duguid, and Orr rightly underline the imperfection of rules in guiding practical action, they fail to see the intrinsic relationship between rules and organized contexts. The mismatch between canonical (propositional) knowledge and noncanonical, context dependent practical action is not so much the result of organizations 'misunderstanding' the work of technicians as Brown and Duguid (1991: 53) suggest, as an intrinsic property of the generalizations employed in organized contexts.

5   The paradoxes, and the oscillating management of social systems that ensues, have been also explored in the context of the recent UK reforms in local government, focusing in particular on the introduction of league tables (see Tsoukas, 1994a: 6–8).

6   *Gnosis* is the Greek word for knowledge. 'Gnosiological', therefore, is the adjectival form of 'knowledge'. I use this neologism here for I want to avoid using the term 'cognitive' which has been related to a particular type of representational thinking in cognitive science (see Stillings *et al.*, 1987); and I also want to avoid using the term 'epistemological' which has been traditionally used in connection with formally assessing knowledge claims. 'Gnosiology' means 'discourse on knowledge' – knowledge in general, not cognition nor formal knowledge.

7   On the one hand, it could be argued that insofar as knowledge in general implies or suggests propositions for action, all knowledge (including narrative knowledge) is propositional. However, such an assertion would miss the most salient features of propositional knowledge proper – namely, the *abbreviated representation* of social phenomena via abstract thinking for the purpose of instrumental intervention at a distance (Cooper, 1992). Thus, while 'industry recipes' are knowledge bases that structure senior managers' ways of looking at particular industries as well as offering strategists sets of background ideas and elemental judgments concerning their business domains (see Spender, 1989: 185–98; Sackmann, 1992), the guidance they offer is partial, ambiguous, and inconsistent (Spender, 1989: 190). Industry recipes, albeit

consisting of actionable knowledge, lack the degree of abstraction, and do not include the systematic co-variation of a few salient features of their objects of reference, which are the key characteristic of propositional knowledge as defined above. Later in the chapter it will be argued that individuals applying propositional statements in the form of organizational rules are analogous to 'transparent boxes', while when acting under the influence of narratives they are analogous to 'black boxes'. Both types of knowledge entail or imply action, but in different ways.

On the other hand, it could be argued that all knowledge is narrative in a generic sense – even propositional knowledge is a particular form of narrative. That is true, but please note that the term 'narrative' has been used in this chapter in a restricted sense to mean story-like accounts (see Hunter, 1991).

8 Of course, it could be that in time the same workers might end up using times instead of speeds as the basis for drafting production schedules. However, it would still be the case that, for the new metric's daily use to be effective, it would have to rely on knowledge cast in a narrative form, albeit one with a different content. New narratives would be expected to be invented, a different set of memorable episodes would become the focus of attention, and the new members would be initiated into the new method of working out production speeds. In short, a more or less different pattern of social interaction would be expected to emerge, and new stories would inevitably be told. But stories there would be!

9 The classification of organizational knowledge suggested here (propositional versus narrative) is not the only one available, although as I hope has become clear, it is the most suitable for the purpose of showing the links between organized contexts and types of organizational knowledge. Other researchers have suggested different classifications. For example, as is well known, Weber (1947: 184–6) distinguished between 'formal' and 'substantive rationality', Ryle (1947) between 'knowing that' and 'knowing how', and Habermas between 'strategic' versus 'contextual rationality' (see White, 1988: 10–21). Similarly, Nonaka (1994), drawing on Polanyi (1966), has made the distinction between 'explicit' versus 'tacit' organizational knowledge, which is also one dimension in Spender's (1995) typology of organizational knowledge (the other one being the individual versus social dimension). All the above classifications parallel to some extent the distinction between propositional versus narrative knowledge, although it needs to be said that they were developed for different purposes and in different contexts, which makes them irreducible to the classification employed here.

Bibliography

Argyris, C. and Schön, D. (1974) *Theory in Practice*, San Francisco, CA: Jossey-Bass.
Baligh, H. H., Burton, R. M. and Obel, B. (1990) 'Devising Expert Systems in Organization Theory: the Organizational Consultant', in M. Masuch (ed.) *Organization, Management, and Expert Systems*, Berlin: de Gruyter, 35–57.
Barrow, J. (1991) *Theories of Everything*, London: Vintage.
—— (1995) 'Theories of Everything', in J. Cornwell (ed.) *Nature's Imagination*, Oxford: Oxford University Press, 45–63.
Bateson, G. (1979) *Mind and Nature*, Toronto: Bantam Books.
Beer, S. (1966) *Decision and Control*, Chichester: Wiley.
Berger, P. and Luckmann, T. (1966) *The Social Construction of Reality*, London: Penguin.
Bhaskar, R. (1979) *The Possibility of Naturalism*, Brighton: Harvester Wheatsheaf.
Bourdieu, P. (1990) *The Logic of Practice*, trans. R. Nice, Cambridge: Polity Press.

Brown, J. S. and Duguid, P. (1991) 'Organizational Learning and Communities of Practice: towards a Unified View of Working, Learning, and Innovation', *Organization Science*, 2: 40–57.

Capra, F. (1988) 'The Pattern which Connects: Gregory Bateson', in F. Capra (ed.) *Uncommon Wisdom*, London: Flamingo, 73–92.

Casti, J. (1989) *Paradigms Lost*, London: Cardinal.

Castoriadis, C. (1991) *Philosophy, Politics, Autonomy*, (edited by D. A. Curtis) New York: Oxford University Press.

Cooper, R. (1992) 'Formal Organization as Representation: Remote Control, Displacement and Abbreviation', in M. Reed and M. Hughes (eds) *Rethinking Organization: New Directions in Organization Theory and Analysis*, London: Sage, 254–72.

Corbett, M. (1989) 'Automate or Innervate? The Role of Knowledge in Advanced Manufacturing Systems', *AI & Society*, 3, 198–208.

Daft, R. and Wiginton, J. (1979) 'Language and Organization', *Academy of Management Review*, 4, 179–91.

Derrida, J. (1976) *Of Grammatology*, trans. G. Spivak, Baltimore, MD: John Hopkins University Press.

Donaldson, L. (1985) *In Defence of Organization Theory*, Cambridge: Cambridge University Press.

Engestrom, Y., Brown, K., Engestrom, R. and Koistinen, K. (1990) 'Organizational Forgetting: an Activity-theoretical Perspective', in D. Middleton and D. Edwards (eds) *Collective Remembering*, London: Sage, 139–68.

Feyerabend, P. K. (1987) *Farewell to Reason*, London: Verso.

Gadamer, H. G. (1980) 'Practical Philosophy as a Model of the Human Sciences', *Research in Phenomenology*, 9, 74–85.

Glorie, J. C., Masuch, M. and Marx, M. (1990) 'Formalizing Organizational Theory: a Knowledge-Based Approach', in M. Masuch (ed.) *Organization, Management, and Expert Systems*, Berlin: de Gruyter, 79–104.

Haugeland, J. (1985) *Artificial Intelligence*, Cambridge, MA: MIT Press.

Hayek, F. A. (1945) 'The Use of Knowledge in Society', *The American Economic Review*, 35, 519–30.

—— (1982) *Law, Legislation and Liberty*, London: Routledge & Kegan Paul.

Huczynski, A. and Buchanan, D. (1991) *Organizational Behaviour*, Hemel Hempstead: Prentice Hall.

Hunter, M. K. (1991) *Doctor's Stories: The Narrative Structure of Medical Knowledge*, Princeton, NJ: Princeton University Press.

Independent (1995) 'Mothers in Fear of Ex-partners Lose Out to CSA Defrauders' (21 March).

Johannessen, K. (1988) 'Rule Following and Tacit Knowledge', *AI & Society*, 2, 287–302.

Johnson, P. (1992) *Human-computer Interaction*, London: McGraw-Hill.

Latour, B. (1986) 'Visualization and Cognition: Thinking with Eyes and Hands', *Knowledge and Society: Studies in the Sociology of Culture Past and Present*, 6, 1–40.

Lee, R. M. (1984) 'Bureaucracies, Bureaucrats and Information Technology', *European Journal of Operational Research*, 18, 293–303.

Lupton, T. (1983) *Management and the Social Sciences*, London: Penguin, 3rd edn.

MacIntyre, A. (1985) *After Virtue*, London: Duckworth, 2nd edn.

Masuch, M. (ed.) (1990) *Organization, Management, and Expert Systems*, Berlin: de Gruyter.

McKelvey, B. and Aldrich, H. (1983) 'Populations, Natural Selection and Applied Organizational Science', *Administrative Science Quarterly*, 28, 101–28.
Mintzberg, H. (1979) *The Structuring of Organizations*, Englewood Cliffs, NJ: Prentice Hall.
—— (1989) *Mintzberg on Management*, New York: The Free Press.
Mulhall, S. and Swift, A. (1992) *Liberals and Communitarians*, Oxford: Basil Blackwell.
Nonaka, I. (1994) 'A Dynamic Theory of Organizational Knowledge Creation', *Organizational Science*, 5, 14–37.
Orr, J. E. (1990) 'Sharing Knowledge, Celebrating Identity: Community Memory in a Service Culture', in D. Middleton and D. Edwards (eds) *Collective Remembering*, London: Sage, 168–89.
Payne, R. (1982) 'The Nature of Knowledge and Organizational Psychology', in N. Nicholson and T. Wall (eds) *Theory and Method in Organizational Psychology*, New York: Academic Press, 37–67.
Piaget, J. (1970) *Genetic Epistemology*, New York: W. W. Norton.
Pinder, C. C. and Bourgeois, W. V. (1982) 'Controlling Tropes in Administrative Science', *Administrative Science Quarterly*, 27, 641–52.
Polanyi, M. (1966) *The Tacit Dimension*, London: Routledge & Kegan Paul.
Polanyi, M. and Prosch, H. (1975) *Meaning*, Chicago, IL: University of Chicago Press.
Poole, M. S. and Van de Ven, A. H. (1989) 'Towards a General Theory of Innovation Processes', in A. Van de Ven, H. L. Angle and M. S. Poole (eds) *Research on the Management of Innovation: The Minnesota Studies*, New York: Harper & Row, 637–62.
Pugh, D. S., Mansfield, R. and Warner, M. (1975) *Research in Organizational Behaviour: A British Survey*, London: Heinemann.
Reeves, S. and Clarke, M. (1990) *Logic for Computer Science*, Wokingham: Addison-Wesley.
Robbins, S. (1989) *Organizational Behavior*, Englewood Cliffs, NJ: Prentice Hall, 4th edn.
Rosenbrock, H. (1988) 'Engineering as an Art', *AI & Society*, 2, 315–20.
Ryle, G. (1947) *The Concept of Mind*, London: Hutchinson.
Sackmann, S. A. (1992) 'Culture and Subcultures: an Analysis of Organizational Knowledge', *Administrative Science Quarterly*, 37/1, 140–61.
Sayer, A. (1984) *Method in Social Science*, London: Hutchinson.
Schank, R. and Childers, P. (1984) *The Cognitive Computer*, Reading, MA: Addison-Wesley.
Schauer, F. (1991) *Playing by the Rules*, Oxford: Clarendon Press.
Schön, D. A. (1983) *The Reflective Practitioner: How Professionals Think in Action*, New York: Basic Books.
—— (1987) *Educating the Reflective Practitioner*, San Francisco, CA: Jossey-Bass.
Simon, H. (1957) *Administrative Behavior*, New York: The Free Press, 3rd edn, 1976.
Spender, J.-C. (1989) *Industry Recipes*, Oxford: Basil Blackwell.
—— (1992) 'Knowledge Management: Putting Your Technology Strategy on Track', in T. Khalil and B. Bayraktar (eds) *Management of Technology III*, Norcross, GA: Industrial Engineering and Management Press, Institute of Industrial Engineers, 404–13. (Proceedings of the third international Conference on Management of Technology, 17–21 February, Miami, Florida.)
—— (1995) 'Organizational Knowledge, Collective Practice and Penrose Rents', *International Business Review*, 3, 353–67.
Starbuck, W. H. (1985) 'Acting First and Thinking Later: Theory versus Reality in Strategic Change', in J. M. Pennings *et al.* (eds) *Organizational Strategy and Change*, San Francisco, CA: Jossey-Bass, 336–72.

Stillings, N., Feinstein, M., Garfield, J., Rissland, E., Rosenbaum, D., Weisler, S. and Baker-Ward, L. (1987) *Cognitive Science*, Cambridge, MA: MIT Press.

Taylor, C. (1993) 'To Follow a Rule', in C. Calhoun, E. LiPuma and M. Postone (eds) *Bourdieu: Critical Perspectives*, Cambridge: Polity Press, 45–60.

Thompson, J. D. (1956–7) 'On Building an Administrative Science', *Administrative Science Quarterly*, 1/1, 102–11.

Tsoukas, H. (1992) 'Ways of Seeing: Topographic and Network Representations in Organization Theory', *Systems Practice*, 5, 441–56.

—— (1994a) 'Introduction: from Social Engineering to Reflective Action in Organizational Behaviour', in H. Tsoukas (ed.) *New Thinking in Organizational Behaviour*, Oxford: Butterworth-Heinemann, 1–22.

—— (1994b) 'The Ubiquity of Organizational Diversity: a Social Constructivist Perspective', Warwick Business School Research paper no. 120.

Twinnings, W. and Miers, D. (1991) *How to Do Things with Rules*, London: Weidenfield & Nicholson, 3rd edn.

Varela, F., Thompson, E. and Rosch, E. (1991) *The Embodied Mind*, Cambridge, MA: MIT Press.

Vickers, G. (1983) *The Art of Judgment*, London: Harper & Row.

Watzlawick, P., Weakland, J. and Fisch, R. (1974) *Change*, New York: W. W. Norton.

Weber, M. (1947) *The Theory of Social and Economic Organization*, trans. A. M. Henderson and T. Parsons, New York: The Free Press.

—— (1948) *From Max Weber: Essays in Sociology*, in H. H. Gerth and C. W. Mills (eds), London: Routledge.

Webster, J. and Starbuck, W. (1988) 'Theory Building in Industrial and Organizational Psychology', in C. Cooper and I. Robertson (eds) *International Review of Industrial and Organizational Psychology*, London: Wiley, 93–138.

Weick, K. E. (1979) *The Social Psychology of Organizing*, Reading, MA: Addison-Wesley, 2nd edn.

—— (1987) 'Organizational Culture as a Source of High Reliability', *California Management Review*, 29, 112–27.

Weick, K. E. and Browning, L. (1986) 'Argument and Narration in Organizational Communication', *Journal of Management*, 12, 243–59.

White, S. (1988) *The Recent Work of Jurgen Habermas*, Cambridge: Cambridge University Press.

Winograd, T. and Flores, F. (1987) *Understanding Computers and Cognition*, Reading, MA: Addison-Wesley.

Wittgenstein, L. (1958) *Philosophical Investigations*, Oxford: Basil Blackwell.

—— (1969) *On Certainty*, Oxford: Basil Blackwell.

Wooley, B. (1992) *Virtual Worlds*, London: Penguin.

Zucker, L. G. (1977) 'The Role of Institutionalization in Cultural Persistence', *American Sociological Review*, 42, 726–43.

3

ORDER, DISORDER AND THE UNMANAGEABILITY OF BOUNDARIES IN ORGANIZED LIFE

Paul Jeffcutt and Muffy Thomas

Introduction

In a paper exploring the relationship between information theory and organizational analysis, Cooper (1993a) connected cybernetics with post-structuralism: relating the understanding of systems as patterns of difference with the understanding of language as the ordering of difference. In the light of these interconnections, he suggested that the 'time had come' for the theory of information to take a more explicit and significant role in the understanding of organization. We shall argue that while in some respects such a development of organization studies has undoubtedly come to pass, its concern has been to emphasize the controllability rather than the undecidability of these interconnections. In this chapter we contribute to the redressing of this imbalance through an examination of the interconnections between information and organization in the context of computer software.

Organization and information in an information society

In organization studies, particularly over the past five years, there has been an increasing examination of the relationship between information systems and the nature of transition in complex organizations. While information systems have become understood as both the catalyst for and the medium of contemporary organizational transition (see, for example, Zuboff, 1988), this transitional process has tended to be represented as a process of change with a character which is either utopian (e.g. innovation, devolution, synergy or empowerment) or dystopian (e.g. exploitation, divestment, surveillance, or management through blame). But, we shall argue that such either/or analyses both oversimplify and understate the nature and complexity of transition in contemporary organized life.

Following Cooper (1993a), several distinctive avenues of development characterize the relationship of information theory and organizational analysis. On the one hand, as argued by Cooper, the continuing convergence of systems/complexity theory and post-structuralist thinking is concentrated around the problems of structure and order (see also Cooper, 1992, 1993b). On the other hand, as acknowledged but not developed by Cooper, the continuing convergence of information technologies and socioeconomic transition is concentrated around the problems of electronic media and organized life (see Poster, 1990; Lash and Urry, 1994).

These distinctive avenues of development are interconnected most explicitly through theorizations of the nature and form of organized life in an *information society* (Lyon, 1988). This is a condition in which time and space compression (i.e. the rapid, simultaneous intensity of flows of information across all contexts) is interconnected with both disembodiedness and disembeddedness (i.e. the implosion of boundaries within and between subjects and objects). Through these dynamic and unpredictable flows and relativities, an information society is characterized by the explosive pluralization of subjectivity, interconnection and artefaction, forming a hyperreal marketplace of semiotic exchange where information becomes the transient medium and message.

For the field of organization studies, the conjunction of such developments in the understanding of information articulates a series of significant problems with which this chapter is concerned. First, seeking to understand the organization of information in an information society emphasizes the inevitable range of the field of knowledge and practice of organization studies. This range not only spans and interconnects a spectrum from the humanities to natural and engineering sciences, but also confirms the field's essential hybridity (see, for instance, Hayles, 1991a). However, as the field debates crucial questions surrounding the nature and form of what is coming to be called its *neo-discipline* (Burrell *et al.*, 1994), the determination of an integrated core of theory and practice has become recognized as an impossible quest (Jeffcutt, 1994). Second, although the nature and form of contemporary information society has become imbued with very different potentials by different interpreters (for example, Lyotard, 1984; Baudrillard, 1988; Bauman, 1993), complex organization has become comprehensively problematic. For in an unstable and contingent world of rapid, multiple transactions effected through a panoply of communications media (e.g. information highways and byways), between a multiplicity of transactors (e.g. producers and consumers), the characteristic features of complex organization (e.g. control, unity, consistency and stable bounding) become both problematic and ephemeral. As Castells (1989: 142) observes, 'flows rather than organizations become the units of work, decision, and output accounting' across shifting networks of information. With both the coherence of organizations as structural entities and the stability of exchanges between transactors becoming problematic, our attention is directed towards organizing as a constituent of, and a contribution to, the implosions of boundary and form effected by the complex flows and relativizations of an information society. In other words, organization becomes an unfolding process of tension between order and disorder in unstable flows which both pluralize and cross-connect artefacts and subjects, in, so to speak, a worldwide web.

The implications of this intensive and expansive process of transition for the theory and practice of organized life are considerable. Yet, in contemporary organization studies, the frames in which these matters have been addressed have been primarily in terms of the manipulability of information systems and the extension of organized activity (e.g. Galliers, 1995) rather than in terms of the problems of information and the limits of manageability (e.g. Lyotard, 1991). Under these circumstances, information systems become understood as being able to extend the boundaries of the manageable in the turbulent complexities of an information society, either through facilitating more interactive and egalitarian forms of organizing (Mulgan, 1991) or facilitating the refinement and spread of exploitation and organizational surveillance (Lyon, 1988). Whether empowering or exploitative, both of these understandings of the interrelationship of information and organization concentrate on issues of organizational form and behaviour (e.g. types of network) and overlook the form and behaviour of the media (e.g. computer software) which makes such networking possible. But, as the Pentium processor 'bug' (Pratt, 1995) and the Therac-25 accidents (Leveson and Turner, 1993) illustrate, computer software (and hardware) does not always behave in reliable or predicted ways. As software becomes more pervasive, providing new forms of organizational control and extension, enabling new behaviours (e.g. in medical techniques such as neurosurgery) and encouraging more tightly-coupled complex systems, an examination of the organizational limits of software becomes more urgent. However, these have been largely overlooked, leading Leveson to observe that 'with the introduction of computers into the control of complex systems, a new form of complacency appears to be spreading – a belief that software cannot "fail" and that all errors will be removed by testing' (1995 : 63).

This chapter thus considers the interrelationship of information and organization through a focus on the form, behaviour and usage of computer software. We explore the problematical nature of information and the limits of manageability within this context through issues of safety, risk and the software development process. We propose that there are fruitful relationships to be explored between software and organization, with respect to both behaviour and form, with consequences for a deeper understanding of questions of manageability. Our aim is to address both software engineers and organizational analysts through the development of these significant connections in the hope that further insight into one another's areas of concern and better appreciation of mutualities can be achieved.

Software engineering

The construction of large software systems has long been recognized as an *engineering* problem – the discipline of software engineering (Sommerville, 1992; Pressman, 1992) emerged in response to the so-called 'software crisis' of the late 1960s. Over the past decade there have been numerous calls for software engineering to venture beyond a purely engineering approach based on the natural sciences, and subsequent developments include, for example, the interdisciplinary 'art and science' design approach of Ehn (1991). However, only recently has the concept of *uncertainty* of software behaviour and software development processes been acknowledged (e.g. in Littlewood and Thomas, 1991; Littlewood, 1994). As we shall consider, acknowledgment of these uncertainties strikes hard at the very core of the engineering mainstream, raising significant concerns about the nature of the gap between theory and practice. While this opens up a variety of management and organizational aspects to be explored and developed, we focus here on the linking idea that computer software ought not to be understood as just a technological artefact with an assumedly pre-determined existence but rather as *text* open to a multiplicity of meanings. The novelty of our association is our focus on the media, i.e. consideration of software *itself* as text, rather than on the network, i.e. on the *role* of software in the creation of text (as considered, for example, in Poster, 1990), or on the nature of information held within an electronic information system (as considered, for example, in Mouritsen and Bjorn-Anderson, 1991).

Before developing this association, we give a very brief overview of the discipline of software engineering. The issues of software reliability and design became prominent in the late 1960s with the advent of third generation computers requiring the implementation of large software systems; there was increasing recognition that software must be managed, or *engineered*. Software engineering is now a mature subject with design principles, methods, methodologies, strategies, policies and tools which aim to aid the production of software that is reliable, maintainable, efficient, and usable. The discipline includes both consideration of the human and sociological factors of software development and use, as well as mathematical methods and tools which are used to reason about behaviour.

The engineering approach has produced numerous generic and domain-specific process models of developing software. While still the subject of research, the most widely used models are variants of the so-called 'waterfall model' (Sommerville, 1992). In as much as the stages, and progression between stages, depend on the particular model, the important aspects can be summarized as: requirements (description of the behavioural requirements of the software and any constraints or relevant context), specification and design (rigorous description, usually semi-formal, of how the software will behave and the constraints or context), implementation and unit testing (representation and implementation of components of the solution in a programming language and testing of the components), and integration (of all components) and testing.

While the stages are conceptualized as distinct, in practice, stages overlap and feed back into each other. In any nontrivial software development, the process returns to various stages several times. The process is therefore not a linear one and the movement between the stages can take various forms: from transformation and iteration to refinement and rupture. Furthermore, the textuality is rich and complex: the languages used at each stage range from natural language to mathematics and formal programming languages and machine languages. Ideally, at each stage the result is *verified* (with respect to the upper layers), and *validated* (as to whether it is the kind of result intended). By progressing through the development stages of any process model in this way, it is hoped that the complexity of the software system can be managed. In all this, it is assumed that the success of this depends, at least, on the extent to which relationships between the results of the various stages in the process model, and between the model and the operational world, can be (formally or otherwise) subjected to logical reasoning.

Tools which may be used in the reasoning process within the model may involve the application of discrete mathematics (e.g. formal grammars, automata, algebra, logic) and may be used at all stages of the development process, as languages for unambiguous, rigorous expression, and for proof. Moreover, by their very nature, they also lend themselves to automatic verification and validation by software tools such as computer-aided theorem provers and simulators (themselves, complex pieces of software). But, to what extent can we rely on these organizational and analytic methods, formal or otherwise, to develop and argue that software has the behaviour we predict and that it can and should be trusted?

Software as text

What are the consequences of thinking of the formal and informal notations for computer software as a form of writing? Post-structural theories of language/discourse, as discussed by authors such as Derrida (1984), Knoespel (1991) and Poster (1990), are concerned with the handling of written texts: how they are read and understood; how a text 'works'. Since any software process provides us with a rich set of texts to consider, such as natural language texts, programming language texts, machine language texts, and mathematical texts, we may also ask how these texts 'work'. In a post-structural approach, with a variety of *readers* and *writers*, these texts are thus open to a multiplicity of interpretations. Following Turner (1994) we may try to understand the potential multiplicity of a computer program as a system of Derridean 'marks'. However, Turner considered program texts only while here we extend our consideration to all texts in the development process.

According to Derrida, a mark is an element of language which conveys meaning but which has an existence that cannot be directly tied only to the intentions of the writers and the understandings of the readers. Three essential properties of a mark are identified: there is no natural bond between a mark and the thing it denotes, its identity lies in its difference from other marks, and it is re-markable; we can recognize it when it occurs; it is single, atomic, indivisible. To appreciate the meanings of marks, one must both consider the *present* relationships with other marks, and the *future* relationships with other marks, as the context of the marks changes. Because of these properties, marks are used in ordering activities. But to be useful, a mark must be repeatable, in different contexts. A mark can be 'released' from any one of its contexts, enabling it to emigrate or move to another role elsewhere. Thus, the author may lose control of the mark and one is left with a tension between the properties of marks which make them amenable to ordering activities on the one hand, and their ability to have multiple meanings and to migrate from one context to another. Because there is no assured destination or single role for a mark there is an element of indetermination or *chance*. Together, these properties contribute to a tension between ordering, codification and randomness.

There is a compelling argument to support this proposal for software systems because the concept of codification is central to both the development of software and to *computability* – the theory of what is computable by (abstractions of) computers. One can easily argue that Gödel numbering (the way of encoding symbols and sequences of symbols in numbers used in computability theory) is a system of marks, as is the ASCII encoding (the encoding used for characters as bit patterns). Moreover, the concept of the stored program depends upon the difference between a program instruction and data being distinguished *only* by the context in which it is 'read'. For example, the byte 00010001 might mean the instruction 'load from register A', or the number 17, depending on whether an instruction or data is expected.

However, while computer programs are developed in a rich social context, from requirements derived from texts developed in 'natural' languages and notations, they are still *formally* defined objects; the analogy between the Derridean theory of writing and the formal languages of computer programs is somewhat tenuous. On the other hand, the view it offers of increasing complexity as disorder is a very important and appealing one, and an example of Prigogine's (1989) argument that the concept of instability has, in some way replaced determinism in the way that it changes our relationship with and understanding of science. This is also the view prescribed by the theory of *chaos* – a re-evaluation of the relationship between order and disorder, which recently has been the subject of widespread attention in both the natural and the social sciences, from mathematics and science (Peitgen and Richter, 1986) to literary criticism (Hayles, 1991a). In an unstable world, 'although we may know the initial conditions to an infinite number of decimal points, the future remains impossible to forecast' (Prigogine, 1989: 399). With disorderly behaviour in complex systems being seen as rich in information, rather than lacking in order, unpredictability may be characterized as deriving from microscopic changes. So, microscopic changes can have macroscopic effects; a phenomenon commonly observed in complex systems, including software systems.

To summarize, the conventional engineering approach to software implicitly adopts a deterministic orientation by attributing to it discrete, mathematical characteristics which thereby render it (potentially) completely understandable through the process of systematic analysis. We can regard such 'grand' explanatory narratives (Norris, 1982) as approaching the text as a 'bearer of stable (if complicated) meanings', positioning the interlocuter (e.g. the software engineer) as seeking to render the text predictable and controllable. Thus, conventional software engineering is seen as a project of managing risk which seeks to unify and explain a complex system (i.e. making order) through the process of totalization (i.e. eradicating disorder). On the other hand, approaching software as text leads us to consider how behaviour (e.g. 'normal' and 'abnormal') affects the mode and content of data, and hence the information it carries within a complex system (i.e. organization) of which it is a constituent. The *difference* between meanings attached to software is vitally important when software is used in safety-critical or high-risk situations. In the remainder of this chapter, we focus on software within these systems, and examine particular cases which articulate the organizational significance of failure and breakdown in such complex systems.

Accidents in safety-critical systems

The systemic interconnection between the production of 'goods' and 'bads' has been recognized in recent studies of accidents and breakdowns in complex systems across a broad range of organizational and cultural contexts (e.g. Turner, 1978; Shrivastava, 1987; Perrow, 1984). These studies have exposed how large-scale system breakdowns (e.g. 'disasters' such as the Bhopal incident in India) result from the interrelationship and development of small-scale problems in unanticipated ways. Two significant and interlinked issues are raised by these analyses.

First, all complex systems are to some extent 'safety-critical', where the consequences of failure are more or less catastrophic (e.g. from the loss of an airliner due to the breakdown of an air traffic control system to the loss of student grades due to the breakdown of a data-processing system). Second, in complex systems, the management of risk (i.e. the achievement of appropriate levels of safety) should be understood as both an important need and a problematic objective.

These issues are central to the examination of the organizational significance of software, since it is a primary means by which complex systems are both connected and extended, as well as a primary means by which increasing complexity is sought to be managed (e.g. safety-critical process control). While all complex systems can be regarded as 'safety-critical' in the sense described above, our attention here is directed towards the use of software in systems in which a failure poses a serious threat to human life, both directly or indirectly. In such systems, an *accident* is an unplanned, or abnormal, event, or sequence of events, leading to human injury or death (we extend this to serious environmental damage); a *hazard* is a condition with potential for causing or contributing to an accident; and *risk* is a combination of the likelihood of an accident and the potential severity of its consequences (Leveson, 1986). Software is used increasingly in the management of these systems and the software therein is referred to as *safety-critical* software. Examples of such systems include aircraft control, air traffic monitoring, medical process monitoring (e.g. continuous drug delivery), medical treatment equipment (e.g. radiotherapy), and control systems for chemical and nuclear power processes.

As noted above, software is a means whereby such systems are extended and managed. There are numerous advantages to using software: software can be flexible and easily adapted; a wider range than purely electro-mechanical conditions can be monitored; physically small and reliable computers are involved. Moreover, software can allow the introduction of strategies which reduce the amount of time humans need to spend in particularly hazardous situations.

While software may increase the safety of a system, for example, in the ways described above, we must conclude that it may also increase the complexity of the system and hence increase the associated risk. Of course, software alone cannot pose a threat to human life or the environment; it is the embedding system breakdown (resulting in a hazardous hardware operation) which ultimately poses the threat. Thus, we must always consider the interactions between heterogeneous elements such as software, hardware, and human and mechanical users in complex hybrid systems. In this chapter, we focus on what is called primary safety-critical software (Sommerville, 1992): software which is embedded in a hardware process used to manage another process where a failure leads directly to an accident. But we must also be aware of secondary safety-critical software which can indirectly lead to an accident, for example, a computer-aided design (CAD) tool which may be used to design a component in a (primary) safety-critical system.

There have been various fatal accidents involving safety-critical software (see Leveson, 1986; MacKenzie, 1994); some of the more recently publicized ones under investigation are the Airbus A320 aircraft crashes, the Saab Griffen aircraft crashes, and the 1993 London Ambulance Service breakdown. During the finalization of this chapter (in June 1996) a spectacular (although not fatal) accident involving safety-critical software occured – the explosion of the Ariane 5 rocket launcher (European Space Agency 1996).[1] However, the most serious *civilian* deaths to date attributable to malfunctions of safety-critical software are the Therac-25 computer-controlled linear accelerator accidents (Leveson and Turner, 1993; Jacky, 1991). Linear accelerators are used for medical radiation therapy (e.g. in cancer treatment); the accidents referred to involved the delivery of sometimes fatal overdoses to patients in medical clinics in the USA and Canada during the late 1980s.

The danger of radiation overdose in a linear accelerator has long been acknowledged (at least since 1966 when the control on a traditional electromechanical machine failed at Hammersmith Hospital – see *British Medical Journal*, 1966) and since then most machines have contained a safety system of hardware interlocks. While the Therac-25 was not the first computer-controlled linear accelerator (its predecessor Therac-20 was also computer controlled), it was unique in that it was *entirely* software controlled; there were no hardware interlocks. Thus, abnormal software behaviour in the Therac-20 which might blow a fuse could have an entirely different effect in the Therac-25. In their analysis of the Therac-25 accidents, Leveson and Turner explain that the accidents are not attributable to just one software error, but that they are *system* accidents stemming from complex interactions between the various software and hardware components. An example of one particular software error involved the software controlling the way in which the operator entered and edited the treatment parameters, e.g. mode of treatment (electron or X-ray therapy), intensity of electron beam, positioning of beam, etc., at the computer terminal. If the operator made a mistake when entering the treatment data, the operator could edit parts of the data on the screen instead of re-entering all of the data from the beginning. As a consequence of a software design error, it was possible, under rare and unforeseen circumstances, for the operator to *appear* to edit the data, i.e. the corrected values for the treatment parameters appeared on the screen, but the control process ignored these values and continued with the values which were originally entered. As a result of this hazard, patients could be and indeed were delivered incorrect and sometimes fatal radiation doses.

It is relevant to relate at this point some findings from the analysis of two aspects of the Therac-25 software (Thomas, 1994a, 1994b). In the former, a mathematical model of the overall system design of a linear accelerator was constructed and the results of the specification and design stages were analysed. The formal aspect of the analysis, using discrete mathematics and carried out by hand and by using a simulation program, revealed the system's ability to deliver a radiation overdose under certain circumstances. In the latter, details of the implementation were considered: some assembler (a low-level programming language) routines from the editing software were shown to be faulty. Specifically, the assembler routines are first represented as a formal (algebraic) system. A computer-aided theorem prover based on first order logic is then used to prove some 'bad', or unintended, properties of the formal system. In these studies, both mathematics and software embodying mathematics were used to reason about the software in the software development process. That is, they were used for verification and validation of the relationships between various stages in the process model (See also Thomas, 1996 on the role of mathematics in developing safe systems). In both cases, the primary goal of the analysis was to investigate expressibility and the power of analytical methods in a real case study; the analysis took place *after* the accidents, with the aid of hindsight.

While the fact that the analysis was *post hoc* does not mean that it could not have been carried out before the fact (a good example of such an investigation revealing undetected faults is the analysis of the AAMP5 microprocessor microcode by Miller and Srivas, 1995), it is arguable whether such an analysis could, and would, have been envisioned before these accidents.[2] First, the analysis was enormously time consuming and involved a high degree of expertise. Second, this kind of analysis is not feasible, in general, for an entire large-scale system, except when targeted at 'high-risk' components. Thus, the identification of such components is crucial. Indeed, one can only formally (or otherwise) analyse the properties that one has had the one *foresight* to identify. While there are numerous generic properties which are recognized in software engineering,[3] inevitably some crucial properties which impact on the safety or reliability of a system are unique to that system.

It is also arguable whether the results of analysis would have been interpreted in such a way as to prevent the accidents; such an interpretation might require what has recently been called the 'extra-logical' factors involved in complex software engineering. For example, MacKenzie (1993) argues for a sociological treatment of mathematical proofs of correctness of software (or hardware) systems; namely, proofs that may be negotiated, depending on context. He refers to one of the first analyses of a microprocessor, the VIPER microprocessor chip, and subsequent litigation concerning the claim by the UK Ministry of Defence that VIPER was 'the first commercially available microprocessor with a proven correct design' (MacKenzie, 1993: 53). Interestingly, critics of the claim of proof include members of the verification team, one of which (in Cohn, 1989) stressed that only a formal, abstract description had been verified. As discussed earlier, the relationship between the formal model and the operational model is crucial; from the intended to the operational behaviour of a complex system one needs to consider a series of exchanges between designers, verifiers, manufacturers, and user groups, as well as the performance of physical components.

Another crucial aspect of these examples is the relationship between error and system accident. Whereas a single software error or bug is an incident, as we have seen, errors interacting in an *unpredicted* way may result in an accident. It follows from this that the concepts of order, disorder, chance, and coincidence are fundamental to the understanding of such accidents. But, these are just the concepts which hitherto have been absent from software engineering. While we can observe that there are accepted limitations and uncertainties concerning the use of analysis methods (such as human ability, applicability of abstract system models, consistency of theories, tool quality and availability, notation quality, process maturity, evidence of success and management pressure – to cite a few), we ask whether these offer an adequate framework for understanding organizational issues, particularly given the complexity of exchanges between such heterogeneous elements (see Law, 1994, for an extended discussion of heterogeneity in sociotechnical networks).

In a pioneering study of 'man-made' disasters, Turner (1978) argued that accidents have an 'incubation period' in which a series of events running counter to established beliefs about the way in which the system operates remain unnoticed. The period of order ends when some event(s) draw(s) attention to the discrepancy between the system as it is believed, and as it is operating, resulting in a sudden shift in information levels. Both the Therac-25 and Ariane 5 accidents illustrate these translation or migration issues well. For example, the (errant) software behaviour in the Therac-20 went unnoticed (although its effects were potentially observable, e.g. as blown fuses) until the code was reused in the Therac-25 when it directly affected patients in an adverse way. Moreover, as we explained earlier, safety-critical analysis involves only the properties which have been identified as such; the key properties here might have been overlooked because in the Therac-20 the errant behaviour had an apparently innocuous form. Höpfl and Jennings (1994) further develop Turner's argument, maintaining that it is the 'pursuit of coherence that imposes the appearance of order on a wide range of behaviours and experiences *including* the discrepant and irrational. Thus, multiple meanings are likely to be glossed over by a privileged interpretation of events' (1994: 8). They conclude that a safety culture is not just a set of assumptions, shared values, and behavioural routines, but at the same time it must create an environment which is receptive to multiple sources of information, and which protects itself from its own delusion and which problematizes learning.

While conventional software engineering recognizes 'flaws' in its safety cultures, articulated largely in Leveson's (1995) pioneering work, the perceived 'flaws' relate to issues such as complacency and overconfidence, disregard or low prioritization, and faulty procedures. The consequences of interpreting software as text – Cooper's (1993a) and Turner's (1994) concepts of information shift, based on information as difference/transformation – appear to be largely absent.

However, some recent re-orientation within the software engineering community towards these goals can be detected. For example, in Littlewood, Neil and Ostrolenk (1996), the authors contend that software problems can only be managed through acknowledging their *inherent uncertainty* both with respect to design and operational behaviour. They propose that future research should be directed towards developing a framework for managing uncertainty in dependability arguments (i.e. claims that a software system is dependable/safe). While they do not go on to develop such a framework in detail, they have given an outline which acknowledges that evidence is based on a variety of quite disparate models and development methods (e.g. formal models of functional behaviour, life-cycle models, models of human–computer interaction). We believe this to be just one example of how our organizational approach offers new avenues of development in the understanding of software management, and also presents another new domain for exploring the tensions between text and organization.

There are two general conclusions for software engineering which we draw from in considering the textuality of software and its relationship with contemporary organized life. First, since accidents in safety-critical systems have appeared to be 'normal accidents' (Perrow, 1984), resulting from the complex interaction of different components and activities in a complex system, we may deduce that while software contributes as a cause, such accidents must be beyond the discrete control of such software. Second, from the above flows the understanding that the inadequacy of software is not a problem which could be solved by additional resourcing (i.e. scale, time, etc.) or enhanced sophistication (e.g. ever more grand and inclusive parameters of engineering), since it is the engineering approach and not the particularities of each case which requires attention. In a post-structural perception of science, where order and disorder are created simultaneously (as suggested in Prigogine, 1989), codification must be associated with unpredictability: we cannot seek to design absolutely error-free software, or even the zero-fault designs sought by Gaudel (1995). Thus, there is no single 'grand narrative' role for engineering methods: we have, in essence, an *incompleteness* result.

These conclusions do not discourage us from doing mathematics or writing computer programs; rather they make us aware of the need for different approaches to different problems in complex systems. For example, we may scale down rather than scale up, thus limiting applicability to that which is dependably achievable. Analogously, we do not propose to reject engineering methods, or to give up on safer software, because there is no complete solution to the problem of risk in complex systems. Rather, we must develop an approach which will guide us on how to deal with approximations and relatively safe or *safe-enough* systems in practice.

Whereas software may be introduced to reduce risk in safety-critical systems, we must recognize that it also introduces its own multiplicity of meanings and risks. Software engineering analysis methods and risk and reliability measures are neither the panacea hoped for by the UK Ministry of Defence (and prescribed in their DefStan-0055), nor are they to be rejected out of hand as in the European Joint Airplanes Requirements standards for onboard aircraft systems.[4]

The current incapacity of software engineering to develop in this important middle ground is understood, in our framework, to be a consequence of there being too great a concentration on computer programs, or software components, as indivisible, atomic objects in the present, with insufficient emphasis on the future relationships which result from changes of context. Prigogine (1989) urges us to think of 'time as the essential variable', that trajectories of many systems are unstable because we have only a limited window on the universe, and from our window we must extrapolate and guess what the mechanisms could be. While future relationships, in the context of software reuse, have been acknowledged within software engineering, we would suggest that this has been undertaken in a strictly linear way, looking to the past in a determinate mode in a search to eradicate future disorder. Yet, as we observed in the cases of the Therac-25 and the Ariane 5, software reuse is becoming increasingly important. Very few systems are built from 'scratch', with the majority being built upon existing systems (the so-called 'legacy' systems). Thus we argue for a post-structural approach to software development that places more emphasis on textuality, migration of meaning, and trajectories of ordering: a practice of learning to work with the increasing complexity, and hence risk, associated with the reuse of code in such software and systems.

The organization of information: engineering the manageable

Our examination of the form and behaviour of computer software has raised significant issues for the understanding of the form and behaviour of information systems in contemporary organized life. As we have seen, the conventions of software engineering can be closely related to the conventions of organization studies.

Indeed, since both of these territories are interconnected through organization and information, this interrelationship thus articulates crucial tensions between management, the theory and practice of ordering, and manageability and the limits of that theory and practice.

As we have suggested, understandings of the form and behaviour of information systems in organization studies (whether empowering or exploitative) rely on conventional readings of relationships between information and organization, hence, the contemporary 'knowledge work' of network organization becomes strangely familiar, since it re-presents mainstream theory and practice as novel (e.g. Beaumont and Sutherland, 1992). First, a hierarchical model of organizational communication which emphasizes a master system for the coding and decoding of information has become translated into the extended capacities for information processing of the networked organization. This seeks to revitalize the authority of a central managerial authority for the coordinating and controlling of organizational complexity. Second, the understanding of technology as an intrinsically neutral medium for the extension of human capacities has become translated into information systems as the facilitators of sophisticated but controllable organizational change. This seeks to revitalize the authority of complex organizations as vehicles of progress in a turbulent and uncertain risk society. Third, the structuring principle of core and periphery has become translated into both the reconfiguration (i.e. disassembly and reconnection) and extension (i.e. globalization) of complex organizations through information systems. This seeks to revitalize the centrality of the core and the power of the centre in the policing and adjustment of the network's boundaries and margins.

Together, these revitalizations may be understood as attempting the resuscitation of an 'old' order (i.e. organizational unity, coherence, clarity) through yet another novel persuasive form – information systems – in a search to regain mastery in face of the disturbances and dislocations of contemporary transition. However, for giants to be able to learn this flexible dance of networking (see Kanter, 1992) presumes that not only are they currently stabilized on relatively solid ground, but also that their diverse and disaggregated elements are manipulably interconnected through a central nervous system. However, as we have already suggested in our brief analysis of the nature of an information society, and as the shaky, stumbling and safety-critical nature of contemporary organized life emphasizes, such presumptions of coherence and groundedness are clearly unrealistic. The antecedents of this new orthodoxy are significant. For, as Boland (1987) argues, underpinning the contemporary development of information systems in the extension of complex organization is the work of Herbert Simon, a crucial figure in the establishment of the 'new paradigm' of organization studies (R. Locke, 1989), which paralleled the development of software engineering. Simon's characterization of complex organization as technologies of decision-making that articulated 'rules for moving through a problem space' (Boland 1987: 368) has informed significant oversimplifications of the nature of information which Boland describes as 'fantasies'.

First, the assumption of a master system for the organization of communication requires both the transparency of meaning and a central, determining authority. However, as we considered in the design of safety-critical software, a totalizing master-narrative is unreachable with information as a translation process of mutually constituting exchange and representation. Second, information systems cannot be assumed to be solely predisposed towards the extension of progressive human control over a threatening periphery. Indeed, electronic media, like other technologies, are not intrinsically neutral extensions, but complex systems of mediation and representation which interact in the hybrid constitution of an information society, where, as in the cases of the Therac-25 and the Ariane 5, meaning migrates. Third, under these interconnected strains and in spite of policing and surveillance, the organizational centre will not be able to hold on to its conventional pre-eminence and mastery. Hence, through a process of radical pluralization, multiple, simultaneous centres of ordering inevitably emerge, articulating both local and worldly contingencies. The contemporary transition of organized life through information systems cannot then be simply characterized as either empowering or exploitative, since these are conventional analyses which rest on either prioritizing a 'managerial' orthodoxy or overturning it with a 'critical' alternative. Instead, contemporary organizational transition needs to be approached as both empowering and exploitative rather than either/or. As such, contemporary 'knowledge work' has both rewritten the labour process by shifting access, patterns and places of work (e.g. remote tele-working) as well as translating established sexual divides (e.g. the gendering of new technologies; see Cockburn, 1985). Furthermore, while the information society has developed through an infrastructure which has pluralized and dispersed access (both local and global), organized life at the same time has become further socioculturally and spatially divided as its flows have translated risk society into 'wild' and 'tame' zones (see Lash and Urry, 1994).

These complex interconnections are inherent to the contemporary transition of organized life and articulate the virtual limits of organization and management. Indeed, contemporary information systems are paradoxical, for their very scale, speed and complexity leads to the organizational processes they seek to inscribe and order becoming effectively unaccountable and unmanageable. For example, the patterning of international financial markets (i.e. interconnected through the Internet) can only be approached as chaotic: characterized by an unruly order that is discontinuous, incomplete, unpredictable and unregulatable, articulating sustained growth as well as spectacular falls. Furthermore, the very complexity of these heterogeneous and hybrid computer-mediated networks enables new subversions, such as hacking and viruses, as well as new deficiencies, such as software 'bugs' and 'crashes'.

In relation to these expanding problematics in the computer-mediated forms of contemporary organized life, we have examined the development of safety-critical software engineering. However, despite the considerable focus on techniques of proof and the normalization of methods and standards, we have questioned the ability of this arena to achieve its previously held error-free objectives. As Leveson (1995) has shown, these software controlled systems can fail due to errors that are both generated by unspecified implementations of, and unspecified interactions within, the specified system. In other words, these complex systems can generate errors as part of their normal activities which are both beyond their operational parameters and beyond any human or nonhuman intervention. The implications of these cases are significant, because they concern complex computer-mediated and controlled systems that have been carefully engineered (i.e. designed and tested) to be closed and complete, which, through their complex heterogeneity, interactively generate incompleteness and develop unspecified aspects of their process. This would seem to exemplify the two defining characteristics of the process of organizing described by Cooper and Law:

> First ... it is an indeterminacy which ... uses the distal (i.e. structure) to exceed and transgress it. But second, it is also a diversity – *not* a fragmentation – of possibilities and processes, a set of processes in which partial alternatives which exceed any particular alternative, partial codes which exceed any particular code, are endlessly played out.
> (Cooper and Law, 1995: 271)

Approaching the un-modern

The broad significance of our investigation of the nature and form of computer software is that it opens up aspects of the interrelationship between organization and information that have been both under-recognized and under-explored. On the one hand, as we considered in the previous section, where the interrelationship between organization and information is articulated in terms of a dialectic of transcendence, the form and behaviour of computer software is largely overlooked. As we suggested, this has been the case because of a concentration on information systems as a master code where a progressive narrative of becoming has no theoretical limit to manageability. Consequently, the privileged medium of extension, computer software, has to be theorized as homogenous and neutral, since the role of the medium is to manage order from incoherence through the consumption, conversion and coordination of difference. Hence, the inherent hybridity of computer software, such as the multilingual and reversible process of exchange by which the medium evolves and then works, cannot be recognized. On the other hand, where the interrelationship between organization and information is articulated in terms of a dialogic of transgression, the form and behaviour of computer software is largely underexplored. As has been considered, our analysis of the hybridity of software as text is analogous to Cooper and Law's (1995) reading of contemporary organized life as composed of heterogeneous networks of humans and nonhumans shaped by the dynamic transactions of randomness and code. Here the concentration is again on systems of information, but with a very different understanding which emphasizes difference, hybridity, under-determination and instability in a process of 'cyborganization'.[5] Media of translation and exchange between heterogeneous elements are of course crucial to complex cyborganized systems, such as the software mediated systems we have been considering in this chapter. However, as we have observed, through the inherent incompleteness and undecidability of such media, the cyborganization process must be beyond both human (e.g. regulatory structures) and nonhuman (e.g. safety-critical software) forms of control. In these circumstances, the limits to manageability are ambiguous, shifting and reversible, making ordering become patterned but not predictable (i.e. chaotic in the mathematical sense) and plural but not compatible (i.e. unmanageable in the conventional sense). Indeed, such a transition in the understanding of the interrelationship of information and organization from the dialectics of transcendence to the dialogics of transgression has enormous implications for both contemporary organized life and contemporary organization studies.

This chapter has examined some of the characteristics of this transition and, following Cooper (1989, 1992) and Bauman (1992, 1993), we also find the engineering of modern organized life to have become theoretically and practically unreachable. In the light of the eventual exhaustion, failure and emptying out of the principles and practices by which a modern order had been sought to be achieved, we conclude by arguing for the reorientation of organization studies towards the development of more modest, situated and dynamic forms of theory/practice.

From this basis, the unbounding and pluralization of contemporary organized life is not symptomatic of an information society which exceeds modern order (i.e. a newly disordered and untamed condition), but, rather, of an instability that is implicit and hence definitively unmasterable, where order and disorder are mutual processes (see Prigogine, 1989). Contemporary organized life thus needs to be understood as ordered by a deconstructive and metaphorizing reflexivity in which the incompleteness of hybridity and the ambiguity of heterogeneity are both inherent and unavoidable. These conditions do not mean that organization is unable to take place, only that there cannot be a single, dominant centre – but rather a series of multiple, simultaneous and partial nodes; likewise, there cannot be a complete, controlling code unfolding through a unified narrative – but rather a series of discontinuous, incomplete and incompatible patterns. Hence, what occurs at the relational interstices of nodes and patterns is *organizing*, however, this is as much being managed by, as the managing of, particular interconnections. This dynamically hybrid process of transition is also paradoxical, being multilayered and multifaceted as well as partial and incomplete: accordingly, the ordering that is made (i.e. the bounding, forming and shaping of interrelationships) is necessarily temporary and transitory, since through heterogeneity and incompleteness these arrangements will always become unbound and reshaped, and so on. In short, we are irretrievably part of an un-modern process of organizing that is intertextual, fuzzy and in a perpetually subversive state of motion, in which media (particularly computer software) have both constitutive and transgressive effects.

Contemporary organized life is thus a process of becoming that is uncertain, ambivalent and open-ended. Under these circumstances, contemporary transition is neither benign nor authorially controllable, but imbued with both unwritten opportunity and the limits of contestation. Hence, we can only go on with resourceful fortitude in everyday struggles for 'safe-enough' and 'managed-enough' forms of ordering, a critical form of involvement in complexity that is neither nostalgic nor nihilistic. Ultimately, like Cooper and Law (1995), we would argue that such an (un-modern) engagement with contemporary organized life is both more modest and more urgent:

> processes of organization are fluid and flexible; that everything is mobile and malleable; that everything could be otherwise; that everything is incomplete; that everything is in a state of both tension and motion; and that if matters are more or less stable for a moment, then this is, indeed, an achievement; an outcome achieved in a series of reversible translations.
>
> (1995: 264)

Postscript

As we have suggested, the ideas which have interconnected to inform these un-modern understandings of organization and information have travelled from different directions; on the one hand, from the humanities, language as comprising contingent interrelationships that are both constitutive and subversive (following Derrida); on the other hand, from the natural sciences, mathematical and physical relationships as being incomplete, undecidable but patterned (following Gödel). Hence, where intertextuality, chaos theory, information and undecidability cross-connect, can be found the conditions for an un-modern understanding of the process of organizing. As has already been noted, a crucial contribution to the interrelationship of these ideas around the understanding of organization has been made through the work of Robert Cooper (particularly Cooper, 1986, 1989, 1992, 1993b; Cooper and Law, 1995), and this chapter has sought to both build on and develop aspects of this interdisciplinary approach.

However, it also needs to be acknowledged that the unbounding and pluralization of organization studies into an un-modern 'field' of knowledge and practice is not an inherently liberating process. Indeed, this process has to be understood as bringing the field into touch with major problematics, since the hybridity and heterogeneity of the un-modern is constituted by a landscape of multiple simultaneous nodes, but without the possibility of a unified authoritative centre. This landscape is thus unfolding and enfolded between the push of the canonical, with its repressive excesses, and the pull of the carnivalesque, with its opportunistic excesses. This means that the interdisciplinarity and cross-functionality of un-modern organization studies is necessarily articulated through subtle and fragile exchanges between knowledge and practice that cannot be conveniently reduced and separated into discrete theoretical or practical arenas. But, in the absence of any feasible centre, we need to be very concerned with the nature and form of the exchanges which both cross and reform boundaries of knowledge and practice. For un-modern organization studies, this means the building of a syncretic dialogue which recognizes both mutuality and difference, maintaining a heteroglossic in-between that is both diverse and hybrid as well as creative and critical. However, such a process of reflexive reconstruction needs to recognize the colonial practices by which modern organization studies has consistently sought transcendence and renewal. Accordingly, as the canon of modern organization studies becomes increasingly exhausted and bereft, so does the character of transition in the mainstream become more turbulent, fragmentary and reactionary. In this context, the rich landscape of interconnections developed throughout this volume offers particularly timely avenues of exploration.

Acknowledgements

When the two authors of this chapter first met, we thought that, given our respective subjects, we would have little academically in common. How wrong we discovered we were, for we have progressively found that organization studies and computer science are both fields of ordering, with parallel concepts of form, flow and undecidability. In this work we are particularly indebted to Robert Cooper, Ursula Martin, and the late Barry Turner, all of whom have offered astute advice.

Notes

1. This accident is relevant because it illustrates very starkly the textuality of computer software. Briefly, the flight control system for the Ariane 5 included much of the software developed for the Ariane 4 (its predecessor). Shortly after taking off, the horizontal velocity of the Ariane 5 exceeded the upper limits of an internal variable; these limits had been defined according to the requirements of the Ariane 4 (and were never exceeded during the operation of the Ariane 4). The result was an 'overflow' error in one of the inertia reference systems. This error was then transmitted to the flight control system where it was interpreted, not as an error message, but as *flight data*. Consequently, the engines and boosters were set according to this (bogus) data, resulting, shortly thereafter, in an explosion due to impossible aerodynamic forces.
2. After the Therac accidents, the software was not initially investigated as it was not considered possible for it to behave hazardously.
3. Some of these were overlooked in the software development.
4. This standard defines requirements for hardware only and ignores software reliability entirely because of the difficulties involved (Mellor, 1993).
5. The concept of 'cyborganization' is introduced by Cooper and Law (1995: 269–72).

Bibliography

Baudrillard, J. (1988) *Selected Writings*, in M. Poster (ed.) Cambridge: Polity Press.
Bauman, Z. (1992) *Intimations of Postmodernity*, London: Routledge.
—— (1993) *Postmodern Ethics*, Oxford: Basil Blackwell.
Beaumont, J. and Sutherland, E. (1992) *Information Resources Management*, London: Butterworth-Heinemann.
Boland, R. (1987) 'The In-formation of Information Systems', in R. Boland and R. Hirschheim (eds) *Critical Issues in Information Systems Research*, New York: Wiley, 363–79.
British Medical Journal, (1966) 'Radiation Accident at Hammersmith', *British Medical Journal* (23 July), 233.
Burrell, G., Reed, M., Calás, M., Smircich, L. and Alvesson, M. (1994) 'Why *Organization*? Why Now?', *Organization*, 1/1, 5–17.
Castells, M. (1989) *The Informational City*, Oxford: Basil Blackwell.
Cockburn, C. (1985) *Machinery of Dominance*, London: Pluto Press.
Cohn, A. (1989) 'The Notion of Proof in Hardware Verification', *Journal of Automated Reasoning*, 5, 127–39.
Cooper, R. (1986) 'Organization/Disorganization', *Social Science Information*, 25/2, 299–335.
—— (1989). 'Modernism, Postmodernism and Organizational Analysis 3: the Contribution of Jacques Derrida', *Organization Studies*, 10/4, 479–502.
—— (1992) 'Formal Organization as Representation: Remote Control, Displacement and Abbreviation', in M. Reed and M. Hughes (eds) *Rethinking Organization: New Directions in Organization Theory and Analysis*, London: Sage, 254–72.
—— (1993a) *Información e Institutión: Dos Ensayos sobre Estética y Comunicación en el Análysis Organizacional*, Caracas, Venezuela: Ediciones IESA.
—— (1993b) 'Technologies of Representation', in P. Ahonen (ed.) *Tracing the Semiotic Boundaries of Politics*, Berlin: Mouton de Gruyter, 279–312.
Cooper, R. and Burrell, G. (1988) 'Modernism, Postmodernism and Organizational Analysis 1: an Introduction', *Organization Studies*, 9/1, 91–112.
Cooper, R. and Law, J. (1995) 'Organization: Distal and Proximal Views', *Research in the Sociology of Organizations, Vol. 13*, Greenwich, CT: JAI Press, 237–74.
Derrida, J. (1984) 'My Chances/Mes Chances: a Rendezvous With Some Epicurean Stereophonies', in *Taking Chances: Derrida, Psychoanalysis and Literature*, Baltimore, MD: Johns Hopkins University Press.
Dunlop, C. and King, R. (1991) *Computerization and Controversy: Value Conflicts and Social Choices*, London: Academic Press.
Ehn, P. (1991) 'The Art and Science of Designing Computer Artifacts', in C. Dunlop and R. King (eds) *Computerization and Controversy: Value Conflicts and Social Choices*, London: Academic Press.
Galliers, R. (1995) 'A Manifesto for Information Management Research', *British Journal of Management*, 6, special issue, 45–52.
Gaudel, M.-C. (1995) 'Advantages and Limits of Formal Approaches for Ultra-High Dependability', in *Predictably Dependable Computing Systems*, 241–51, Berlin: Springer Verlag.
Hayles, N. K. (1991a) *Chaos and Order: Complex Dynamics in Literature and Science*, Chicago, IL: University of Chicago Press.

—— (1991b) 'Introduction: Complex Dynamics in Literature and Science', in N. K. Hayles (ed.) *Chaos and Order: Complex Dynamics in Literature and Science*, Chicago, IL: University of Chicago Press.

Höpfl, H. and Jennings, M. (1994) 'Safety Culture, Corporate Culture: Organizational Transformation and the Commitment to Safety', unpublished manuscript, Bolton Institute of Higher Education, Bolton, UK.

Jacky, J. (1991) 'Safety-Critical Computing: Hazards, Practices, Standards and Regulation', in C. Dunlop and R. King (eds) *Computerization and Controversy: Value Conflicts and Social Choices*, London: Academic Press.

Jeffcutt, P. (1994) 'The Interpretation of Organization: a Contemporary Analysis and Critique', *Journal of Management Studies*, 31/2, 225–50.

Kanter, R. (1992) *When Giants Learn to Dance*, London: Routledge.

Knoespel, K. J. (1991) 'The Emplotment of Chaos: Instability and Narrative Order', in N. K. Hayles (ed.) *Chaos and Order, Complex Dynamics in Literature and Science*, Chicago, IL: University of Chicago Press.

Lash, S. and Urry, J. (1994) *Economies of Signs and Space*, London: Sage.

Law, J. (1994) *Organizing Modernity*, Oxford: Basil Blackwell.

Leveson, N. (1986) 'Software Safety: Why, What and How', *ACM Computing Surveys*, 18/2, 25–69.

—— (1995) *Software: System Safety and Computers*, Reading, MA: Addison-Wesley.

Leveson, N. and Turner, C. (1993) 'An Investigation of the Therac-25 Accidents', *IEEE COMPUTER* (July), 26/7, 18–41.

Littlewood, B. (1994) 'Why We Should Learn Not to Depend too Much on Software', in *Transcript of IFIP Congress 94, 13th World Computer Congress*, Hamburg, 254–61, North Holland.

Littlewood, B. and Thomas, M. (1991) 'Reasons Why Safety-critical Avionics Software Cannot be Adequately Validated', in *Proceedings Safety and Reliability Society Spring Conference on 'Air Transport Safety'*, Manchester: Safety and Reliability Society, 77–87.

Littlewood, B., Neil, M. and Ostrolenk, G. (1996) 'Uncertainty in Software-Intensive Systems', *High Integrity Systems*, 1/5, 402–15.

Locke, R. (1989) *Management and Higher Education Since 1940*, Cambridge: Cambridge University Press.

Lyon, D. (1988) *The Information Society: Issues and Illusions*, Cambridge: Polity Press.

Lyotard, J.-F. (1984) *The Postmodern Condition: A Report on Knowledge*, trans. G. Bennington and B. Massumi, Manchester: Manchester University Press.

—— (1991) *The Inhuman: Reflections on Time*, trans. G. Bennington and R. Bowlby, Cambridge: Polity Press.

MacKenzie, D. (1993) 'Negotiating Arithmetic, Constructing Proof: the Sociology of Mathematics and Information Technology', *Social Studies of Science*, 23, 37–65.

—— (1994) 'Computer-related Accidental Death: an Empirical Exploration', *Science and Public Policy*, 21, 223–48.

Mellor, P. (1993) 'The Noncertification of Flight-critical Software', *Safety-Critical Systems Club Newsletter*, 3/1, 4–5.

Miller, S. and Srivas, M. (1995) 'Formal Verification of the AAMP5 Microprocessor', in *Proceedings of Workshop on Industrial-Strength Formal Specification Techniques*, Boca-Raton, FA: IEEE Press, 2–16.

Mouritsen, J. and Bjorn-Anderson, N. (1991) 'Understanding Third Wave Information Systems', in C. Dunlop and R. King (eds) *Computerization and Controversy: Value Conflicts and Social Choices*, London: Academic Press.

Mulgan, G. (1991) *Communication and Control*, Cambridge: Polity Press.

Norris, C. (1982) *Deconstruction, Theory and Practice*, London: Methuen.

Peitgen, H. and Richter, P. (1986) *The Beauty of Fractals*, Berlin: Springer Verlag.

Perrow, C. (1984) *Normal Accidents*, New York: Basic Books.

Poster, M. (1990) *The Mode of Information: Post-structuralism and Social Context*, Chicago, IL: University of Chicago Press.

Pratt, V. (1995) 'The Anatomy of the Pentium Bug', *Lecture Notes on Computer Science*, 915, 97–107.

Pressman, R. S. (1992) *Software Engineering: A Practitioner's Approach*, New York: McGraw-Hill, 3rd edn.

Prigogine, I. (1989) 'The Philosophy of Instability', *Futures* (August), 396–400.

Reed, M. and Hughes, M. (1992) *Rethinking Organization: New Directions in Organization Theory and Analysis*, London: Sage.

Shrivastava, P. (1987) *Bhopal: Anatomy of a Crisis*, New York: Ballinger.

Sommerville, I. (1992) *Software Engineering*, Reading, MA: Addison-Wesley, 4th edn.

Thomas, M. (1994a) 'The Story of the Therac-25 in LOTOS', *High Integrity Systems Journal*, 1/1, 3–15.

—— (1994b) 'A Proof of *Incorrectness* Using the LP Theorem Prover: the Editing Problem in the Therac-25', *High Integrity Systems Journal*, 1/1, 35–48.

—— (1996) 'Formal Methods and Their Role in Developing Safe Systems', *High Integrity Systems Journal*, 1/5, 447–51.

Turner, B. (1978) *Man-Made Disasters*, London: Wykeham Press,

—— (1994) 'Software and Contingency: the Text and Vocabulary of System Failure?', *Journal of Contingencies and Crisis Management*, 2/1, 31–8.

Zuboff, S. (1988) *In the Age of the Smart Machine: The Future of Work and Power*, New York: Basic Books.

4

AFTER META-NARRATIVE: ON KNOWING IN TENSION

John Law

Foreword

This is a chapter. An article. Or a paper. Let us take note of that. But the business of writing – and talking – raises serious problems. Difficult questions. Questions to do with materiality. To do with method. To do with knowing, representing, signifying. To do with authorship, authority. To do with the nature of our field. To do with the character of what it is to be an expert in 'our' field. Whatever that field may be. Science, technology and society. Organizational studies. With any field. With the very notion of a 'field'.

So there are plenty of questions. And these are the topics to which I want to attend. But how should I do so, author, speaker, 'authority' that I am? There is no right answer. But here I will tell some stories. Stories that raise questions about what it is to be an author, what it is to be an authority. Stories that I hope reflect on some methodological and theoretical choices that confront practitioners in organizational studies. In science, technology and society. That confront practitioners who sense the restrictions performed in disciplinary knowledges.

Story 1

A lecture hall. A square of tables. An overhead projector. Thirty-five graduate students. Two organizers. And me. It is the beginning of a summer school. One of the organizers is speaking. He is welcoming us all. But he is offering a special welcome to me: I am to be the guest lecturer and the resource person for the first three days of the summer school. The summer school is on postmodernism and science, technology and society (STS). And today, in this first lecture, I am going to talk. I am going to give a lecture on 'Did the Modern Fail?'.

He stops talking. There is a silence. It is time for me to start. This is the moment for which I have been preparing for weeks. I thank him. I say I am looking forward to the week, to talking with people. I put my first overhead on the projector. Everyone looks at the screen. And they see some quotations. Here are two of them:

AFTER META-NARRATIVE

> Savoir pour prévoir, prévoir pour pouvoir.
> (Auguste Comte, nineteenth-century social philosopher, 'positivist')

> Simplifying to the extreme, I define *postmodern* as incredulity towards metanarratives.
> (Jean-François Lyotard, late twentieth-century social philosopher)

Two authorities.

I explain that these quotations are going to define the intellectual space occupied by the summer school; that, on the one hand, there is a view, an attitude, which is sometimes called 'modernism'. Modernism suggests that one can *know*; one can know (at any rate) reasonably well if one uses method, perhaps the methods of science; and that one can use the knowledge obtained by using the methods of science to make improvements to the world; to make a better society; to build a beautiful world, one that is just. So modernism is about knowledge, method and improvement. It is an attitude of optimism. It believes that things can be made better; that there is the possibility of progress; that justice is an attainable ideal. The authorities here are Auguste Comte (or for that matter, Karl Marx who is apparently quite different, but 'really' very similar).

But if this is modernism, then what about postmodernism? Well, Jean-François Lyotard is the chosen authority on 'postmodernism'. He talks about incredulity to meta-narratives.[1] That is, beliefs, forms of story-telling, that act as foundations: firm foundations upon which other more specific forms of belief and action can be built. Lyotard, I tell the students, talks of two great meta-narratives: 'science' and 'philosophy'. One way or another, belief in philosophy and scientific method have underpinned specific stories. They have guaranteed them. Have offered some form of warranty. Reasonable. True. Workable. They have told us that a specific finding, for instance out of chemistry, or sociology, is likely to be reliable, so long as the scientific method has been properly followed.

This, then, is a redescription of modernism. But, there is the twist. For Lyotard does not believe in meta-narratives any more. Or, better, he does not think that the great meta-narratives of modernity work any more. And this is postmodernism: 'incredulity towards meta-narratives'. Doubt. Pessimism about the possibility of truth. And, at any rate in Lyotard's version, a commitment to lots of little narratives: a plurality of stories. Many methods. The blooming of a thousand flowers.[2]

Now I shift. For the argument is that something has happened. Something has happened in the period between Comte (or Marx) on the one hand, and Jean-François Lyotard on the other. I find myself saying that 'we' are different from Comte and Marx. Some of us, at any rate are more sceptical than we were. We have lost certainty and find that matters look complex. We have become ambivalent about science, about its benefits. Perhaps we no longer have faith in progress. Perhaps we no longer think that science has the power to bring about the good life. And, I say, that this is what the summer school will be about. It will be about the space between modernism and postmodernism. About the space between the nineteenth century and the end of the twentieth century. It will be about the implications of abandoning master-narratives.

Which is, at any rate in one version, what we are also about here. The implications of abandoning master-narratives. The study of organization and STS are, or so I take it, practical studies, two of many, that come after master-narrative.

Commentary 1

I apologise. I think that you know all this. You know about the difference between modernism and postmodernism. You have followed and contributed to the debates about the death (or otherwise) of meta-narrative. The death (or otherwise) of method. The political impotence, real or supposed, of postmodernism and post-structuralism and, like me, you have watched the refraction of these debates in organization studies or science, technology and society; you have read and written studies which show that knowledges and orderings are relatively local matters, constructed in language communities or in heterogeneous networks. These are debates which explore the ways in which subjects and objects are constituted together and work such as Donna Haraway's (1992) on primates and the men and women who studied them, or Karin Knorr-Cetina's on epistemic fields in high energy physics and molecular biology,[3] or Sharon Traweek's on the gendering tropes in high energy physics,[4] or Robert Cooper's on the mutual constitution of order and disorder in the process of ordering.[5] They are debates which show the heterogeneous organizational work that is concealed when the voice of truth speaks: debates about the forms of silencing involved in organizational work; about hidden technicians, women, people of colour, Jews, androids, and nonhumans. These are debates about the way in which entities are constructed and given voice, debates about the way in which voices are made and distributed.[6]

These, then, are the moves: the issues that we open up when we imagine that sciences, technologies and organizations are socially constructed and when we link that imagination to the effervescence that comes after methodology, an effervescence sometimes called postmodernism or post-structuralism. But if we know the moves, then we must know that there are also lots of questions to be asked. Questions, for instance, about:

> what it means to *narrate* – that is to write or give a lecture;
> what it is to be an *authority*;
> what it is to be an *author*;
> what it means to treat someone as an *expert*;
> what it means to *imagine* such a thing as expertise.

Lots of questions and by now, perhaps, classic questions. Questions opened up by Michel Foucault (1969) over twenty-five years ago and widely explored since then. But we must be specific and narrow down the focus of inquiry. We must think about one, and only one question. Let us think about what has happened, what follows afterwards, if someone, an authority, someone like Lyotard, announces the end of meta-narrative. Let us imagine some responses. First, we could insist on principles, on, as it were, drawing things together:[7] connecting them, assembling them into a whole, trying to take an overview. Indeed, this is what I have done, very briefly, in the first story. There are other things going on there too. More on those in a moment. But the lecture that I gave to those students – which is also, in this respect, the same as this chapter – was a summing up, an overview, a description, an account offered by someone performed as an authority, someone who knows, who can see, who can tell about it. This is all very well for it is the modernist pattern. There are knowers and known; subjects and objects; those who do not yet know and those who already know. All very well, that is, unless the authority, the knowing subject, also announces the end of meta-narrative, the end of the modern project, with its concern to sum up: to see things in the round, to bring them together.

So what is the difficulty? Well, it is clear enough. To make this claim is to be self-refuting. She/he who announces the end of meta-narrative precisely prevents her/himself from making that announcement. She/he silences her/himself.[8] Principles. This is an argument that insists on principles. On the importance, indeed perhaps the necessity, of drawing things together. In principle. As I did when I spoke to the students. As I am doing now. With claims about the structure of the intellectual field. About how different bits and pieces cohere and relate together. As a whole. About change, about history, about the move from modernity to postmodernity. About the links, or the contrasts, between this author and that author. About moves from structuralism to post-structuralism. Claims that distribute subjectivity and objectivity and perform a distribution of objects, an *overall* distribution of objects. An order. An order that derives from an overview, the overview of the authority, the author. An order that derives from system, the system of method, a system embodied in authority.

When a monarch died in the middle ages they cried from the walls: 'The king is dead! Long live the king!'. So it was that continuity was celebrated within supposed discontinuity. So this is the question. When we announce that meta-narrative is dead, do we also, and necessarily, at the same time declaim, 'long live meta-narrative!'? Are reports of the death of meta-narrative greatly exaggerated? Is it that we could only ever make the announcement silently? Or are there other possibilities? Possibilities which we might explore if we wanted to try to renounce the seduction of its delights? Pondering this, I think that work in science, technology and society is useful. For STS is informed by post-structuralism and also by parts of sociology – for instance the work of Elias and Goffman.[9] And the argument which we can draw from these sources – an argument which is perhaps by now familiar – is that *authority is an effect*; that knowledge too is an effect, something generated for instance in a centre of calculation;[10] that it is a consequence of a network of bits and pieces; that it is a product of the performance of certain kinds of materialities,[11] which sometimes produce knowledge effects, authority effects, epistemic fields, ontological distributions, narrative outcomes, positioned speakers such as lecturers, local universalities. Sometimes. If the conditions are right; if the local conditions are right. If the narrow networks are in place,[12] and kept in place for long enough to generate the circulation of immutable mobiles.

So, we know how knowledge effects, author effects, authority effects are *made*. We know how it is that in practice local authorities can sometimes announce the end of meta-narrative and get away with it. But the question is: what happens afterwards to the authorities who announce the end of meta-narrative? Or, a more interesting twist to the question is, *what might we imagine would go in their places?* What might replace these men and women who assembled their bits and pieces to stand before us and tell us? Or these authoritative books that we read? What are the materialities of knowing if the authorities, the centres of translation, are scaled down? That is the next question: what are the *materialities of decentred knowing?* Let me tell another story about the summer school.

Story 2

The organizers of the summer school have gone away: the authorities, the experts, the bodies of power/knowledge. They are too powerful to make it easy for the students to do the exercises. For there are exercises in the summer school, exercises for the students. Exercises about knowing. One of these has to do with 'textures', the textures of knowledge/power, with how it is that knowledge and power are all rolled up together and how it is that they are *performed*.

Although they were not told this, the students were asked to enact plays, games, or mimes: for instance, of 'ethnographies of the summer school so far'. I watch these – for, incongruously, I am still there. In the mime there is no sound. Nothing is said. Nothing at all. It is all done in silence. With bodies. For instance, there is someone playing 'John Law', the lecturer. He sits at the table, the place where I, the 'real' lecturer have sat throughout. Elsewhere, facing him, there are people who are going to play the students, the audience, those who will listen to the lecture. The lecture starts. The lecturer's mouth opens. Nothing comes out. He talks. And he talks some more. There is silence. Complete silence. (Apart, that is, from the laughter of the onlookers.) He stops for a moment to scratch his head. And then he starts again. He continues to talk. More silence. Suddenly he turns and puts up an invisible overhead transparency. The students direct their gaze upwards to the screen. There is nothing to be seen, no writing, but nonetheless we watch them reading. The lecturer gestures. They turn their attention back to him. We laugh again as he plays with an apple, as he continues in silence to talk. Suddenly a student raises her hand. She looks diffident, worried, uncertain. The lecturer stops. Indicates that she should speak. She poses a silent question. Very tentatively. He reflects for a moment. Then he nods to himself. He has worked something out. He rises from his chair, takes a marker pen and begins to draw a diagram on the whiteboard. First a vertical line and then the 'detail' – boxes, arrows and concentric circles. Those of us who are watching are amused. We have sat in that room for three days and we all know that the 'real' lecturer has made diagrams like this too. Especially when he is in trouble and cannot think what to say next.

The lecturer turns round. He looks at the student who asked the question. Has his explanation solved her problem? Does she understand now? Quickly we see that it has not. She looks puzzled, she hesitates, and then she gestures. Silently elaborates her question. Again the lecturer pauses for a second. And, again, quite suddenly, he sees what he might say. The marker is picked up and again he starts to draw. More boxes. More arrows. More subheads. More interconnections. He talks. He talks more. He talks silently. By now everything is connected with everything else in the diagram. Or so it seems. Arrows pointing in every direction. The audience is laughing again. It seems that they have been there. But the lecturer does not react to the onlookers. Straight-faced, he looks back questioningly at the student, but she is still looking puzzled. She shrugs her shoulders. It is not obvious that this new elaboration has made any difference to her. The end of the mime. There is a moment. A moment for questions and discussion. We have all laughed. But, more important, there is also puzzlement. Puzzlement about what this exercise is *really* about. We have watched, but what have we learned? What, asks one of the other students, was the group really trying to say in its mime? There are murmurs of agreement around the room. This is something that exercises people. Something that they want to know. One of the actors volunteers that what we wanted to show was how power is exercised – power and knowledge – how these are carried out by material means, with materials such as the overhead projector, the layout of the room, with a prominent desk for the lecturer, with the students sitting below the lecturer. A representation or performance of submissiveness. Assisted by other performances. The ability of the lecturer – unlike the students – to get up and walk about. And again, the performance of the whiteboard and the diagrams. We wanted to show how power (and with it knowledge) is locally performed. To do that the simplest thing was to cut out the talk, to do it without any words at all. The students are nodding. We are all nodding. Now we know. We know what the mime was about. The uncertainty, the tension which we have experienced, begins to subside.

Commentary 2

You know this argument. We can extract it from the figurational sociology of Norbert Elias. Or the symbolic interactionism of Erving Goffman. But in this particular version it is post-structuralist. The performance of knowledge/power, its syntax, what we might call its 'texture': this is a concern that we learned from Michel Foucault.[13] Although analogous concerns inform large parts of feminism and cultural studies, in its particular STS version as enacted here, we watch out for the artful performance of scientific authority, for instance, in laboratories, texts, the lecture hall, in the management practices of science-administrators:[14] the textures of knowledge/power. We watch methods for creating and distributing the voices and silences of nature, and with this, the methods for making scientific authority, authorized knowledge, and its materiality when these are projected through an array of persons and objects. We watch, then, the materialities of scientific knowing, of natural knowledge, of creative heroism, of the performance of method.

I apologize since you know this story: this story that tells us how it is, in practice, that grand narrative narrates – if only in appearance. But, my reason for insisting on the materialities and textures of knowing is not primarily to make this point. Rather, it is because I want to ask a supplementary question. I want to ask more precisely *where* those materialities are located, the materialities of knowing. To do this I would like us to attend to the question of *tension*. For the story about the mime is also a story about tension.

What then, of this tension? First, it seems that there is some kind of strain between *doing or performing*, on the one hand, and *telling*, on the other. The two are different, to do and to tell, and they do not necessarily fit together. But I think there is also a second form of tension: one that is generated in the onlookers as a result of the performance of the mime. So there are two forms of tension, but I also think that they are linked together. This is because the tension generated in the onlookers by the mime is a concern, an anxiety, which asks, in the first case speechlessly: what is it all about? Which poses the question: *what precisely is being said?* Ponder this, for a moment. There is an initial problem in this particular context at least in that it is not possible to imagine, or treat with anxiety, or tension without turning it into words: words that match and provide for those that will follow, those that will tell what precisely is being said. So, at least in this context (I repeat the proviso), the words are, so to speak, a trap. Or, as Derrida (1981) reminds us, at any rate, a circumstance out of which we cannot emerge. But, let us put that on one side. For the in-mime tension is important in its own right. For it is, I think, an expression of indecision and uncertainty; an expression of openness; it is, in some sense, a refusal of the option of bringing things to a point. Perhaps it is, then, an expression of, a confrontation with, undecidability.[15] The experience that matters are – necessarily – deferred.

But, what might we make of this expression of deferral? In the summer school what we tried to do was to negate it. We asked questions: we sought answers. Answers in the form of words. But why? Why this preference for decidability? This preference for what the ethnomethodologists call 'formulation'? With saying in as many words, what it is all about? Three possible observations follow:

> *First*, to formulate is to attempt to *bring it all together*. To pin it down. To see it, or tell it in one place and at one moment. *Second*, it has the effect of re-creating, performing, a particular kind of *authority*. The authority of the word. Or better, the authority of the word when it issues from the mouth, perhaps the pen, of an authority. An authority, that is, as a location. A specific place. A point. A point guaranteed by special access to truth, and perhaps to the guarantees of method. Or, as Foucault suggested, a func-

tion. *Third*, it is also, or so all our studies of the textures of power/knowledge suggest, *all in vain*. Or better, perhaps, a delusion. For it *is* possible to bring things together, to make the knowing at a single point. But this is only possible if the distributed processes that have led to, performed, that heroic authority are all deleted. Which means that conclusions and précis are effects that delete their grounding in the inconclusive.[16]

At this point we are left with a problem, a problem of attitude. It is, indeed, a restatement of the division in attitude between modernism and postmodernism. One attitude says that:

- it would be better to seek to pull things together; that it would, for instance, be better to convert mimes into words;
- it would be better to bring things to the point, and make authorities or authority locations, even though we know that this cannot ever be achieved;
- it would be best to rest knowing upon (as it were) the deferral of deferral.

An alternative attitude is to ask what knowing might be if it were instead to celebrate – or at least come to terms with – its chronic heterogeneity and deferral.[17] This, of course, is a postmodern attitude. Perhaps the choice, or the contrast looks something like this:

Table 4.1

Pull things together	Dispersal
Conceal dispersal	Explore dispersal
Reduce tension	Accept tension
Make a central authority	Refuse a central authority

Like all contrasts and binary lists, this table is flawed. Or, to put it another way, it is biased in favour of the clarity and concentration of modernism. The need to collapse matters to consistency, to see them as a whole. But perhaps we can escape this insistence on the ubiquity of concentration. Perhaps we can say instead that there is a *tension* between concentration and dispersal, which is also a tension between simplification and complexification; a tension between enacting and talking, telling it as it is. But then to note the fact of a tension, of a difference, does not necessarily convert into contradiction, or indeed, the need to make a choice. That tension can be lived, is a form of knowing.[18] And the tensions *between* simplification and complexification are forms of knowing.

Story 3

Three days of the summer school have passed. We have been working together. Talking formally and informally. This morning we are talking – that is to say, I am talking – about a house designed by the architect, Frank Gehry. It is the house in which he lives in Santa Monica. I have never been there and have never seen it. The most that I have done is to look at pictures and read descriptions of it. As, for instance, in Frederic Jameson's book, *Postmodernism, or, the Cultural Logic of Late Capitalism* (1991). Indeed, we are in the process of working through a version of Jameson's analysis. So what does he say?

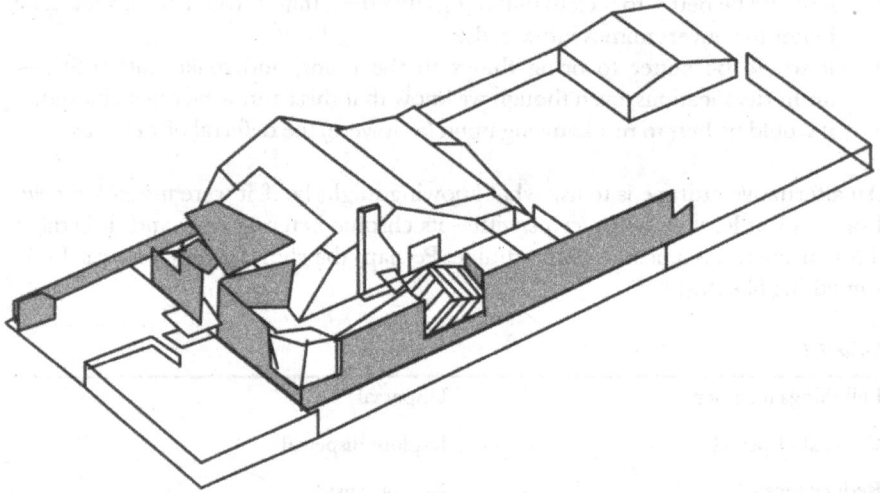

Figure 4.1

Well, to talk about it at all we need first to talk about what the house is 'like'. To offer a description of it. A tension, to be sure, between talking and acting. Anyway, we have looked at one or two photographs of the house. It looks chaotic, full of odd angles and pitches, blank walls, wire-netting, something that looks like corrugated iron. So it does not look like a house at all, at any rate, not like the kind of house that you or I might live in. So much for the photos. Now I am starting to point to some of the structural features of the house. To do this, I follow Jameson by putting up an isographic drawing. This looks down, in a cutaway mode, from somewhere – or is it nowhere?[19] – diagonally above and to the front. First, I draw attention to the fact that at the core of the house there is another house. This is what Americans call a 'tract house'. Perhaps it was built in the 1930s. At any rate, it is a perfectly ordinary house. It has an 'ordinary' pitched roof, identifiable features such as vertical windows, doors and a chimney. And, if we follow Jameson in his written description, we learn that in the tract house there is an upstairs and a downstairs, and that at least some of the rooms – in particular those that are upstairs – are matter-of-fact little boxes, with windows and doors.

Next, again following Jameson, I point to the way in which there is a 'wrapper' around the core of the house. This is an addition designed by Frank Gehry. It means that what was a small original house has been converted into something much larger. But more important, the wrapper is utterly different in style. Some of the differences are clear from the photos. The wrapper is at odd angles. It is not very easy to tell exactly what is happening from the isographic drawing (and it is no easier looking at the photographs), but the roof pitches are all 'wrong', so too are the angles of many of the walls. Furthermore, the wrapper has blown holes in the tract house. There are places where the old walls have disappeared, and rooms combine the rectangular volumes of the old structure with the exotic shapes of the new. Perhaps it is easier to decipher some of the *contents* of the rooms: when one of the photos was shown somebody said, 'well, at least that's the kitchen'. And, indeed, it was possible to discern a work surface with a fitted cooker and what might have been a refrigerator. But, even though the contents of the kitchen look conventional, they are lodged under an extravagant glass and wood ceiling at a steep angle. This gives a view of a further part of the wrapper, which is also at different and rather odd angles and is made of wire-netting, as if it were part of a tennis court. A kitchen in a space that makes less sense.

We talk about all of this. In particular, about the isographic drawing. I am saying that this is a 'postmodern' house. I am saying (but am simply following Jameson), that it is impossible to sum up. It is not possible to get an overall feel of it. 'Hah', says someone sceptically, 'the *humans* may live in a postmodern house, but the cars don't!'. We all look back at the drawing, and sure enough, at the top we find that the cars live in a little pitched-roof garage with doors: an arrangement that speaks of utter conventionality. Or, if you prefer the term, 'modernity'. I show another overhead transparency as there is a further step in Jameson's argument. We have this juxtaposition between two houses: a tract house on the one hand and the wrapper on the other. But, what is the relationship between the two? The answer is that it is possible to set this up as an opposition: to imagine some kind of contradiction. For instance, one could imagine a list like this:

Table 4.2

tract house		wrapper
classic materials		junk
simple volumes		complexity
inside/outside	OPPOSITION?	no inside/outside
form		formlessness
first world		third world

In which case one would end up with a story about inconsistency. About incoherence. About the way in which things do not fit together. A house where the pieces crash up against one another in conflict. But this possibility is not what interests Jameson most. His concern is different. He wants to explore nonbinary logics in which things do not come together. So his suggestion, like ours above, concerns the question of tension. There is, he argues, a tension between the two parts of the house. There is a continual movement between them, which means that despite the fact that we (and he) describe it in this way, he does not see two houses. He does not see a tract house on the one hand and the wrapper on the other. Rather he imagines a single house that is also in a constant state of tension, of oscillation; a house that does not come to rest, that cannot be centred, summed up into an effect that does not move, that cannot, in particular, be represented in a flat photographic perspectival form which allows everything that is important to be seen all at once. Jameson's particular argument is that the house represents the irreducible interdependence, the constant movement and exchange, between the first world (the tract house) and the third world (the junk wrapper). One form of tension. But it is also another kind of movement, of strain, of displacement. This is because it can also be imagined as a way of knowing the irreducible interdependence, that is also a constant movement, between the experience of 'lived reality' and the shifting, chaotic and hyperreal networks of global capitalism, between lived experience and the social world that exists, as it were, out there. So, his argument is that the person moves through the house, never summing it all up, never bringing it all together, never reducing it to a point, which brings him to what for me is his punch line: 'Frank Gehry's house is to be considered the attempt to think a material thought' (Jameson, 1991: 129). So, in Jameson's understanding the house is a *technology for thinking*. It is a method for thinking the new kinds of thoughts that are needed if we are to apprehend the reality that the world has become around about us as a result of the operations of global capitalism: a new material method for the process that he calls 'cognitive mapping'. The house *is* a thought.

Commentary 3

Jameson's problem is a version of our problem. It is about the materialities of knowing: the materialities of knowing in tension. For he is asking the question: *what is it to know, if it is not possible to draw everything together onto a flat surface?*, if it is not possible to imagine knowing as an interaction between a surface and an eyeball that sees it all, that moves at will across that surface. How might one make maps, representations, in a world where versions of Mercator's projections no longer – or, perhaps more subtly, no longer claim to – sum it all up?[20] His answer is that knowing is displaced from a *result* to a *process*, from *knowledge* to *knowing*. It is displaced from *two dimensions* to *three*. For instance, from the textual to the architectural and from the moment when knowledge is achieved as a stable link between the eye and a surface (which is, or so it seems, the model to which modernism aspires) to the tension implied in the acknowledgement of deferral.

Perhaps, then, the argument looks like this – although by now we know enough to be very cautious of the clarity and the reduction in tension that is the effect of drawing tables such as these.[21]

Table 4.3

Text or photography	Architecture
Two dimensional	Three dimensional
Concentrated	Distributed
Centred	Decentred
Seen	Lived
Can be overseen	Cannot be overseen
Resolves tension	Exists in tension
Static	Involves movement

Tension, movement, the passage of time, the lumpy and material distribution of the process of knowing, these are the keys. In his world the process of thinking material thoughts – for instance architecturally – never comes to rest. And it does not, at any rate primarily, exist within the head, or somewhere between the eyes of a head and a dominated surface. Rather it is achieved in the movement of the body through places. A body that necessarily exists in tension. In tension with its material surroundings. Take note of that: a body that *necessarily* exists in tension.[22] And in movement.

Jameson is doing something important. He is echoing Derrida. He is trying, as I interpret him, to shift our understanding and appreciation of deferral. He is trying to shift us from the understanding of tension that has driven the models of knowing dominant in the West, at least since the Enlightenment. He is trying to shift us from a teleological appreciation of the character of tension to one that accepts, indeed embraces, its irreducibility.

Perhaps it is like this. In teleology it is imagined that knowledge derives from the *reduction* of tension. It subsists, then, in a distinction between means and ends. Knowledge is an end that may be achieved if matters can be summed up, brought to a point, brought together. It is something that will have been achieved once relative stability is attained. Which means in practice, to be sure, that movement is necessary. For the Enlightenment project, the modern project, is all about movement: movement through genius, through method. Progress. Accretion. 'Technical' adjustment. But the character of this movement is particular. It is movement which will reduce tension to achieve the state of rest we are used to calling knowledge: the state of rest that is the effect of bringing things together. Movement, then, is a means that has been distinguished from the ends: the ends of knowledge.

The alternative preferred by Jameson also has to do with moving, but perhaps it is movement of a different kind – not teleological movement, movement directed to an end state. For in the alternative, movement is irreducible – not a means, but rather endless. So knowing resides, not as a state in which things have been brought to rest as a satisfactory and integrated whole, but as . . . but as what? Here Jameson makes an interesting move. Uncertain whether he wishes to push the logic of tensions to its farthest point, he writes:

> What would be the mark or sign, the index of a successful resolution for this cognitive but also spatial problem? It could be detected, one would think, in the quality of the new intermediary space itself. . . . If that space is meaningful, if you can live in it, if it is somehow comfortable but in a new way, one that opens up historically new and original ways of living . . . then, one would think, the dilemma, the aporia, has been resolved, if only on the level of space itself.
>
> (Jameson, 1991: 128–9)

New forms of subjectivity. New forms of living. New forms of bodily integration – no doubt less cognitive and more aesthetic or emotional in character – these are the tentative suggestions he offers for imagining success or otherwise in postmodern knowing.[23] Which is, indeed, one form of resolution – and one which, like its Enlightenment predecessor, is interestingly centred around the experiences of the body.[24] One which amounts to a novel mode for seeking to reduce the tension of knowing. But, no doubt, there are alternatives to Jameson's solution. For instance, as scholars in STS or organization theory we might ask how comfortable(!) we feel about the way in which he privileges the body, the human as against the inhuman.[25] And we might press the argument about stress one stage further by suggesting that knowing is located in the tensions within the materialities of movement; the strains that are linked through movement and displacement; the pressures that subsist between materials, materials that do not reduce to one another; in short, that knowing is decentred performance of material heterogeneity.

Afterword

Living tension. Living in tension. The strain between tension and tension-reduction. The tug between complexification and simplification. Between drawing things together and the acknowledgement of deferral. Between movement as teleology, located within a mean–ends scheme, and movement as essential, an irreducible set of connections between materials that cannot be reduced. Between centred knowledge and decentred knowing. Between authority and distribution. These are the kinds of issues – dare I say it, tensions? – which have come to shape our problems, shape our thoughts, after meta-narrative.

So what should we make of this? These tensions? I am extremely hesitant.

Because if meta-narrative is dead, then the age of method, the age of legislation, is also coming to an end.[26] Legislation and method are monarchs that do not rule. Or they lay claim to empires when at best they exert a tenuous control over short-lived principalities. So the most I would do is to offer a few thoughts on what we might make of the materialities of knowing.

The first is this. Since centralization, authority, simplicity and the search for a few foundational principles are celebrated – and have for a long time been celebrated – perhaps there are contingent reasons to recommend a counter-celebration: a celebration of complexification. Not because complexification is right and simplification is wrong. Not even because it is possible to embrace complexification without recourse to simplification. But rather because complexification has for so long been the subordinated movement.[27] Which means, a second thought, that there is perhaps some local merit in tending to perform complexification and (in particular) deferral. In imagining ways of performing tension, of rendering the unfinished character of knowing more visible. And this is what I have tried to do in the present text. I am located in a text. As an author. Perhaps as an authority. And you are located within that text as a reader. But, within the limitations of this performance – limitations that generate powerful forms of simplification, that tend to draw things together – I have sought to complexify and defer. In two ways. First through a form of reflexivity: in the building of rhetorical moves that uncover movement and deferral in rhetorics which might otherwise appear as fixed, as given. For instance, by observing that the construction of a history of modernism and postmodernism, the arraying of authorities such as Marx and Lyotard, the use of texts and lecture rooms, all of these are contingent and local authority achievements rather than facts, methods, or causal chains, given in the order of things.

Second, I have also tried to imagine other materialities of knowing. This is why I have talked of mime. And why I have asked in what sense mime, as a form of knowing, might be said to be incomplete. For mime, or at least the mime at the summer school, created a tension, a tension that we sought to reduce through formulation. Through telling in as many words, what it was all about. But, or so the argument implies, there was nothing wrong with mime, nor indeed the tensions that it created. We might have lived with those tensions. Lived them as a form of knowing. Instead of which we used words. Words which seemed to deny, to conceal, their dependence on deferral, on tension. Words which, interestingly, *appeared* to draw it all together in a way which the mime did not. But words that were no different from the mime they replaced. Words which could not, could *never*, draw it all together.

Other materialities of knowing. I talked of two. Mime, and architecture. But there are so many other possibilities. Potential models proliferate: intelligent systems; networks; cybernetics; cyberspace; cyborgs; biotechnologies; and theories of the immune system. Or materialities such as music; theatre; film; video; art; design; dance; the city; the mathematics of chaos; the space of exhibition. Or spiritualities such as: silences; apprehension of the deity; the goddess; or mystery. Or the political such as: rainbow alliances; partial connections. All of these and no doubt many more.[28]

There are so many possibilities. For if we start to think about the decentring of knowing by imagining the tensions that might be performed within and between materialities the list is endless. So we must select. Select our materials. Select our material tensions. Try to make sure that we are not overwhelmed by the complexities. Which means that we will sometimes, as is unavoidable, strain towards simplicity. Offer a paper. A form of words. Create a figure or a table. Something that draws it all together. In the knowledge that the security that this provides, the moment of rest, is indeed but a *moment*. A moment of concealment. An illusory stasis. In the knowledge that our heterogeneous concerns with the materialities of knowing have made – and will make – their own particular contributions to the end of discipline, the end of method, the end of guaranteed universality. For we live after meta-narrative. The authority of the centre is dead.

Postscript

When we were planning the summer school I talked with the organizers, and we agreed that I should offer an introductory lecture. An introductory lecture which we called, 'Did the modern fail?' Something that would orient the students. Allow them to see what the summer school was about. A lecture which would bring things together in a summary manner. That might act as a narrative, like the programme notes we read at the opera. That would make it easier to see the general lines of debate. That would link it, in as many words, with other narratives. That would make the links quickly. As they say, efficiently. In a somewhat general manner. That would, for instance, unambivalently point to the ambivalence of the postmodern. That would, as I now see it, reduce tension. That would make it possible to say what had been done. That the students might take away. That would, in a word, offer a perspective on modernism and postmodernism.

And that lecture worked. That is, it worked well. And badly. Both.

Acknowledgements

I am grateful to the Institut de Sociologie des Communications de Masse and the Institut de Linguistique et des Sciences de Langage at the Université de Lausanne for the invitation to prepare and present this chapter to a workshop held in Lausanne on 7–9 December 1994; to the organizers of the workshop on 'Action, Language and Structure', held in Trondheim on 30–31 May 1995, for a similar invitation; to the organizers and especially to the participants of the 1994 Dutch Science, Technology and Society summer school on '(Post)modernism and STS' for the opportunity – indeed the necessity – to reflect critically on the character of authority and authorship after certainty; and to the following friends and colleagues for their intellectual support and friendship: Ruth Benschop, Robert Cooper, Michel Callon; Bruno Latour, Annemarie Mol, Rolland Munro, Marilyn

Strathern and Sharon Traweek. A version of this chapter is to be published in translation in *Arr: Idéhistoriske Tidsskrift*.

Notes

1. See Jean-François Lyotard (1984).
2. This is an argument developed further in Jean-François Lyotard and Jean-Loup Thébaud (1985).
3. See Karin Knorr-Cetina (1991, 1992, 1995a, 1995b).
4. See Traweek (1988).
5. See Cooper (1986, 1987, 1989a, 1989b) and Cooper and Burrell (1988).
6. On the 'silencing' of technicians: see Shapin (1989); of women and blacks: Haraway (1992), Said (1978), Singleton and Michael (1993) and Star (1991); of Jews in Nazi Germany: Bauman (1989); of androids, see Haraway (1990); of nonhumans, see Callon (1986), Law (1991), Latour (1993) and Mol and Mesman (1996). (I place 'silencing' in quotation marks because the word tends to imply that the silenced both exist and have an innate voice of their own, that is given in the order of things. Some of these authors would, indeed, tend towards this view, but others, particularly those influenced by the semiotics of post-structuralism, would not.)
7. The phrase is drawn from Latour (1990). Note that the distinction between principles and practice is itself indeterminate, or better, complex like a fractal. See Mol and Berg (1994).
8. This is not a new problem, in former times being known as the 'problem of relativism'. However, it has achieved recent prominence in the debates around postmodernism. Note the additional argument: if the speaker is understood then she has also, or so the argument runs, traded on and shared general conditions of intelligibility. For a summary of these debates see McLennan (1992).
9. Norbert Elias, unnoticed by many of those writing in science, technology and society, generated a nondualist sociology of the performance of the textures of subjectivity and objectivity. See, for instance, Elias (1983). Erving Goffman's work on the textures of role is also important. See, for instance, Goffman (1968).
10. See Latour (1990).
11. See Law and Mol (1995).
12. See Latour (1988a).
13. And, at any rate for me, in particular from that extraordinary contemporary classic, *Discipline and Punish* (1979).
14. The classic study of laboratory practices – and indeed of the structure of scientific texts – is arguably that of Latour and Woolgar (1979). See also Ashmore (1989). On the performance of scientific organizing and management, see Law (1994) and the anthropological study by Traweek (1988).
15. Undecidability: a term which derives from Derrida and is linked to his concern with *différance*, the process of endless deferral, and hence endless tension, within which language resides. See Derrida (1981).
16. Note that this argument has been developed, albeit in different vocabularies, in a number of different locations. It is, or so it seems to me, implicit in Kuhn's insistence on the importance of exemplars in science (Kuhn, 1970; Barnes, 1982). And in the Wittgensteinian sociology of scientific knowledge (see Barnes, 1977; Collins, 1985). It is also a point developed by the ethnomethodologists. They talk of the indexicality of terms – that is, how they are irreparably dependent on their context for their meaning. This indeterminacy is locally overcome in the process of reflexivity which includes 'formulation', or saying in as many words what has been said or done. But it is, of course, not possible to say what has been done in as many words, at any rate in any

ultimately grounded or literal way. The classic text in this tradition is surely Garfinkel (1967). For an extended study in science, technology and society studies, see Lynch (1985).
17 A point explored in Law and Mol (1994).
18 A point beautifully explored by S. L. Star (1991) in her paper where she talks about the 'high-tension zone'.
19 The 'view from nowhere': a trope taken from feminist writing, and in particular in this context from Donna Haraway's socialist-feminist attack on the 'god-trick' which claims to see everything, despite being located nowhere in particular. See Haraway (1991b). Note the similarity between this kind of cartography and the art of describing developed in Dutch painting. See Alpers (1989) and Benschop and Law (1995).
20 The mention of Mercator is more than a literary flourish. Jameson draws a precise parallel between the argument about the Gehry house and the invention of navigation. He writes: 'cognitive mapping in the broader sense comes to require the coordination of existential data (the empirical position of the subject) with unlived, abstract conceptions of the geographical totality' (1991: 52).
21 Note that the table conceals an important distinction between the textual – the narrative that (indeed) moves us – and the optical co-presence of the visual, as in photography. I am grateful to Ruth Benschop and Rolland Munro, both of whom have insisted on the importance of this point. The table, like earlier tables, also lapses, if that is the appropriate word, into two-dimensional optical co-presence in order to make a point that is precisely about that which cannot be overseen.
22 Like the pragmatic entrepreneurs at Daresbury Laboratory, who know that they have imperfect knowledge, and even know that their knowledge will always remain imperfect (Law, 1996).
23 An argument developed in a different, psychoanalytic idiom by Ehrenzweig (1993). I am grateful to Bob Cooper for this reference.
24 I am grateful to Mike Savage who first pointed out to me that Jameson's resolution has strong overtones of theoretical humanism.
25 He writes that there must be a relationship between 'abstract knowledge and conviction or belief about the superstate and the existential daily life of people ... or else we are altogether in science fiction without realizing it' (Jameson, 1991: 128). But by now in science, technology and society studies we are dealing in science fiction: the inhuman of Lyotard (1991), the decentred cyborgs of Haraway (1990), or the monsters that I have elsewhere written about (Law, 1991).
26 Zygmunt Bauman (1987) contrasts the 'legislators' of modernity with 'interpreters' of postmodernity.
27 This argument was made in the course of discussion by Annemarie Mol, another resource person at the summer school discussed in this chapter. I am most grateful to her for allowing me to make the point here.
28 To be sure, the list is limitless. For thoughts about intelligent systems see Lyotard (1991), and the work of Cooper (1992; 1993); on silences see Jabès (1989); on cyborgs see Haraway (1990) and also Cooper and Law (1995); on the immune system see Haraway (1991a). Marilyn Strathern (1991) draws the notion of 'partial connection' from Donna Haraway and explores it at length in her book. On dance, see Cussins (1994), and on museums, Bouquet (1995). For a comparison of regions, networks and fluids, see Mol and Law (1994). On networks, see Callon, Law and Rip (1986), Callon (1991), and Latour (1993); on connections with politics, see Harvey (1989); Keith and Pile (1993); and the papers collected in *Configurations* (1994). On chaos theory, see Hayles (1990).

Bibliography

Alpers, S. (1989), *The Art of Describing: Dutch Art in the Seventeenth Century*, London: Penguin.
Ashmore, M. (1989) *The Reflexive Thesis*, Chicago, IL: Chicago University Press.
Barnes, B. (1977) *Interests and the Growth of Knowledge*, London: Routledge & Kegan Paul.
—— (1982) *T. S. Kuhn and Social Science*, London: Macmillan.
Bauman, Z. (1987) *Legislators and Interpreters: On Modernity, Postmodernity and Intellectuals*, Cambridge: Polity Press.
—— (1989) *Modernity and the Holocaust*, Cambridge: Polity Press.
Benschop, R. and Law, J. (1995) 'Representation, Distribution and Ontological Politics', paper presented at workshop on the Labour of Division, Keele University Centre for Social Theory and Technology (23–5 November).
Bouquet, M. (1995) 'Displaying Knowledge: the Trees of Haeckel, Dubois, Jesse and Rivers at the *Pithecanthropus* Centennial Exhibition', in M. Strathern (ed.) *The Uses of Knowledge: Global and Local Relations*, London: Routledge.
Callon, M. (1986) 'Some Elements of a Sociology of Translation: Domestication of the Scallops and the Fishermen of Saint Brieuc Bay', in J. Law (ed.) *Power, Action and Belief: a new Sociology of Knowledge? Sociological Review Monograph* 32, London: Routledge & Kegan Paul, 196–233.
—— (1991) 'Techno-economic Networks and Irreversibility', in J. Law (ed.) *A Sociology of Monsters? Essays on Power, Technology and Domination, Sociological Review Monograph* 38, London: Routledge, 132–61.
Callon, M., Law, J. and Rip, A. (eds) (1986) *Mapping the Dynamics of Science and Technology: Sociology of Science in the Real World*, London: Macmillan.
Chia, R. (ed.) (1998) *In the Realm of Organization: Essays for Robert Cooper*, London: Routledge.
Collins, H. M. (1985) *Changing Order: Replication and Induction in Scientific Practice*, London: Sage.
Configurations (1994) vol. 2 (1) (Winter), special issue on 'Located Knowledges: Intersections Between Cultural, Gender and Science Studies'.
Cooper, R. (1986) 'Organization/Disorganization', *Social Science Information*, 25/2, 299–335.
—— (1987) 'Information, Communication and Organization: a Post-structural Revision', *The Journal of Mind and Behavior*, 8/3, 395–416.
—— (1989a) 'The Visibility of Social Systems', in M. C. Jackson, P. Keys and S. Cropper (eds) *Operational Research and the Social Sciences*, New York: Plenum, 51–9.
—— (1989b) 'Modernism, Postmodernism and Organizational Analysis 3: the Contribution of Jacques Derrida', *Organization Studies*, 10/4, 479–502.
—— (1992) 'Formal Organization as Representation: Remote Control, Displacement and Abbreviation', in M. Reed and M. Hughes (eds) *Rethinking Organization: New Directions in Organization Theory and Analysis*, London: Sage, 254–72.
—— (1993) 'Technologies of Representation', in P. Ahonen (ed.) *Tracing the Semiotic Boundaries of Politics*, Berlin: Mouton de Gruyter, 279–312.
Cooper, R. and Burrell, G. (1988) 'Modernism, Postmodernism and Organizational Analysis 1: An Introduction', *Organization Studies*, 9/1, 91–112.
Cooper, R. and Law, J. (1995) 'Organization: Distal and Proximal Views', *Research in the Sociology of Organizations, Vol. 13*, Greenwich, CT: JAI Press, 237–74.
Cussins, C. (1994) 'Ontological Choreography. Agency for Women Patients in an Infertility Clinic', in A. Mol and M. Berg (eds) *Differences in Medicine: Unravelling Practices, Techniques and Bodies*, New York: Duke University Press.

Derrida, J. (1981) *Dissemination*, trans. B. Johnson, Chicago, IL: Chicago University Press.
Ehrenzweig, A. (1993) *The Hidden Order of Art*, London: Weidenfeld & Nicholson; 1st edn, 1967.
Elias, N. (1983) *The Court Society*, Oxford: Basil Blackwell.
Foucault, M. (1969) 'Qu'est-ce qu'un auteur?', *Bulletin de la Société Française de Philosophie*, 63, 73–104.
—— (1979) *Discipline and Punish*, trans. A. Sheridan, Harmondsworth: Penguin.
Garfinkel, H. (1967) *Studies in Ethnomethodology*, Englewood Cliffs, NJ: Prentice-Hall.
Goffman, E. (1968) *Asylums: Essays on the Social Situation of Mental Patients and Other Inmates*, Harmondsworth: Penguin.
Haraway, D. (1990) 'A Manifesto for Cyborgs: Science, Technology and Socialist Feminism in the 1980s', in L. J. Nicholson (ed.) *Feminism/Postmodernism*, New York: Routledge, 190–233.
—— (1991a) 'The Biopolitics of Postmodern Bodies: Constitutions of Self in Immune System Discourse', in D. Haraway, *Simians, Cyborgs and Women: The Reinvention of Nature*, London: Free Association Books, 203–30.
—— (1991b) 'Situated Knowledges: the Science Question in Feminism and the Privilege of Partial Perspective', in D. Haraway, *Simians, Cyborgs and Women: the Reinvention of Nature*, London: Free Association Books, 183–201.
—— (1992) *Primate Visions: Gender, Race, and Nature in the World of Modern Science*, London: Verso.
Harvey, D. (1989) *The Condition of Postmodernity: An Inquiry into the Origins of Cultural Change*, Oxford: Basil Blackwell.
Hayles, N. K. (1990) *Chaos Bound: Orderly Disorder in Contemporary Literature and Science*, Ithaca, NY: Cornell University Press.
Jabès, E. (1989) *The Book of Shares*, Chicago, IL: University of Chicago Press.
Jameson, F. (1991) *Postmodernism, or, the Cultural Logic of Late Capitalism*, Verso: London.
Keith M., and Pile S. (eds) (1993) *Place and the Politics of Identity*, London: Routledge.
Knorr-Cetina, K. D. (1991) 'Epistemic Cultures: Forms of Reason in Science', *History of Political Economy*, 23, 105–22.
—— (1992) 'The Couch, the Cathedral and the Laboratory: on the Relationship between Experiment and Laboratory in Science', in A. Pickering (ed.) *Science as Practice and Culture*, Chicago, IL and London: University of Chicago Press, 113–38.
—— (1995a) 'How Superorganisms Change: Consensus Formation and the Social Ontology of High-energy Physics Experiments', *Social Studies of Science*, 25, 119–47.
—— (1995b) 'The Care of the Self and Blind Variation: an Ethnography of the Empirical in Two Sciences', in P. Galison and D. Stamp (eds) *The Disunity of Science: Boundaries, Contexts and Power*, Stanford, CA: Stanford University Press.
Kuhn, T. S. (1970) *The Structure of Scientific Revolutions*, Chicago, IL: University of Chicago Press.
Latour, B. (1988a) *Irreductions*, published with B. Latour, *The Pasteurization of France*, Cambridge, MA: Harvard University Press.
Latour, B. (1988b) *The Pasteurization of France*, Cambridge, MA: Harvard University Press.
—— (1990) 'Drawing Things Together', in M. Lynch and S. Woolgar (eds) *Representation in Scientific Practice*, Cambridge, MA: MIT Press, 19–68.
—— (1993) *We Have Never Been Modern*, Brighton: Harvester Wheatsheaf.
Latour, B. and Woolgar, S. (1979) *Laboratory Life: the Social Construction of Scientific Facts*, Beverly Hills, CA and London: Sage.

Law, J. (1991) 'Introduction: Monsters, Machines and Sociotechnical Relations', in J. Law (ed.) *A Sociology of Monsters? Essays on Power, Technology and Domination, Sociological Review Monograph* 38, London: Routledge, 1–23.

—— (1994) *Organizing Modernity*, Oxford: Basil Blackwell.

—— (1996) 'Organizing Accountabilities: Ontology and the Mode of Accounting', in J. Mouritsen and R. Munro (eds) *Accountability, Power, Ethos and the Technologies of Managing*, London: International Thompson Business Press.

Law, J. and Mol, A. (1994) 'On Hidden Heterogeneities: the Design of an Aircraft', Keele University and the University of Limburg: mimeo.

—— (1995) 'Notes on Materiality and Sociality', *The Sociological Review*, 43, 274–94.

Lynch, M. (1985) *Art and Artifact in Laboratory Science: a Study of Shop Work and Shop Talk in a Research Laboratory*, London: Routledge & Kegan Paul.

Lyotard, J.-F. (1984) *The Postmodern Condition: a Report on Knowledge*, trans. G. Bennington and B. Massumi, Manchester: Manchester University Press.

—— (1991) *The Inhuman: Reflections on Time*, trans. G. Bennington and R. Bowlby, Cambridge: Polity Press.

Lyotard, J.-F. and Thébaud, J.-L. (1985) *Just Gaming*, trans. W. Godzich, Manchester: Manchester University Press.

McLennan, G. (1992) 'The Enlightenment Project Revisited', in S. Hall, D. Held, and T. McGrew (eds) *Modernity and Its Futures*, Cambridge and Oxford: Polity Press and Open University Press, 327–77.

Mol, A. (1991) 'Wombs, Pigmentation and Pyramids: Should Anti-Racists and Feminists Try to Confine "Biology" to Its Proper Place?', in J.J. Hermsen and A. van Lenning (eds) *Sharing the Differences: Feminist Debates in Holland*, London and New York: Routledge, 149–63.

Mol, A. and Berg, M. (1994) 'Principles and Practices of Medicine: the Coexistence of Various Anaemias', *Culture, Medicine and Psychiatry*, 18, 247–65.

—— (1994) *Differences in Medicine: Unravelling Practices, Techniques and Bodies*, New York: Duke University Press.

Mol, A. and Law, J. (1994) 'Regions, Networks and Fluids: Anaemia and Social Topology', *Social Studies of Science*, 24, 641–71.

Mol, A. and Mesman, J. (1996) 'Neonatal Food and the Politics of Theory: Some Questions of Method', *Social Studies of Science*, 26, 419–44.

Pickering, A. (ed.) (1992) *Science as Practice and Culture*, Chicago, IL and London: University of Chicago Press.

Reed, M. and Hughes, M. (eds) (1992) *Rethinking Organization: New Directions in Organization Theory and Analysis*, London: Sage.

Said, E. W. (1978) *Orientalism: Western Conceptions of the Orient*, London: Penguin.

Shapin, S. (1989) 'The Invisible Technician', *American Scientist*, 77, 554–63.

Shapin, S and Schaffer, S. (1985) *Leviathan and the Air Pump: Hobbes, Boyle and the Experimental Life*, Princeton, NJ: Princeton University Press.

Singleton, V. and Michael, M. (1993) 'Actor-networks and Ambivalence: General Practitioners in the UK Cervical Screening Programme', *Social Studies of Science*, 23, 227–64.

Star, S. L. (1991) 'Power, Technologies and the Phenomenology of Conventions: on Being Allergic to Onions', in J. Law (ed.) *A Sociology of Monsters? Essays on Power, Technology and Domination, Sociological Review Monograph* 38, London: Routledge, 26–56.

Strathern, M. (1991) *Partial Connections*, Savage, MD: Rowman & Littlefield.
—— (ed.) (1995) *The Uses of Knowledge: Global and Local Relations*, London: Routledge.
Traweek, S. (1988) *Beamtimes and Lifetimes: The World of High Energy Physics*, Cambridge, MA: Harvard University Press.

Part II

LOGICS OF ORGANIZING

5

FROM BOUNDED SYSTEMS TO INTERLOCKING PRACTICES: LOGICS OF ORGANIZING[1]

José Malavé

Introduction

The postulation of boundaries separating organizations and environments imposes, from the start, a definite strategy in approaching organizational phenomena. Phenomena are to be separated into distinct categories: internal and external, endogenous and exogenous, controllable and uncontrollable. A common response to failures in noticing key factors, or providing solutions to problems, is to blame the researcher's lack of skill in collecting, handling or interpreting the data. Less frequent is the attempt to look behind the framework in use. The assumption of boundaries has been the basis for constituting the organization as an entity – a system – and thus focusing analyses on its internal properties. The present chapter begins by inquiring into the foundations of the systems theory of organization: from Thomas Hobbes' use of the concept of system to twentieth-century system models of organization. Summary expositions of the systems theory of organizations (for example, Scott, 1987), though leaving unsolved the theoretical problem of boundaries, offer suggestions for managing them 'in practice'.

By following one of Robert Cooper's ideas: 'Organization as an active process of displacement or transformation denies and defies such categories as inside and outside; it is more like a process that travels along sociotechnical networks' (1992: 262) – an exploration of network approaches, as potential alternatives to the systems approach, is undertaken here. Two main traditions of network analysis – the social and technical perspectives – and its application in organization studies are briefly discussed. It is argued that traditional network analyses are unable to provide the looked-for alternative to the systems approach. For the sense of process – the work – vanishes in the representation of flat 'nets'.

Law and Callon's (1988) analysis of sociotechnical networks suggests a way of approaching the study of organization, in Cooper's terms, as 'a process that travels along sociotechnical networks'. This requires the recognition of the social and technical character of organization; not simply to look for a way of coupling two separate elements, but to understand what the social and the technical share. A common feature of tools and words – the possibility of endlessly repeating ways of representing and transforming the real – provides a key to understanding the sociotechnical character of organization. Since the idea of sociotechnical networks does not refer directly to the precise nature of process involved in organization (but to its 'avenues', so to speak), it seemed necessary to introduce the notion of transformation-displacement networks, which tries to capture what organization as a process would consist of. A *transformation-displacement network* (TDN) may be defined as a series of ongoing processes formed by the interlocking of repeatable actions (whether performed by humans or nonhumans) through which a practice becomes an enduring feature of the real. Two methodological implications of this idea are introduced: TDNs lack absolute beginnings or ends – any delimitation derives from a particular analytical concern – and the analysis of TDNs requires a topological rather than Euclidean approach. Instead of a logic of distance and measurement (as in traditional analysis), a logic of displacement and transformation is required where emergence and dissolution of such forms as bounded organizations are to be thought of as transitory folds and unfolds of an historical field.

A TDN approach might lead to a certain dilemma: either organizations as bounded entities are bound to dissolve or, simply, the approach cannot explain their presence. It might be argued that the solution of the inside–outside problem, in terms of folds and unfolds, lacks a consistent explanation of the closure and the boundaries. The next section explores a way of accounting for the boundary condition in process terms. Floyd Allport's event-structure theory (1940, 1954, 1955, 1962, 1967) suggests a way of understanding the closure of organizational structures as a case of 'event-structuring'. A structure's closure is a probabilistic rather than a deterministic problem. It requires a probable density of events. But boundaries traced according to this theory might not coincide with those of a firm, or any other example of organization. An extension of the original hypothesis of event-structuring is then introduced in order to account for the object of organization theory. This leads to the recognition that organization theory, as a particular way of representing a class of phenomena, could be analysed like any other practice, and its persistence as another case of event-structuring.

The modernization of social theory

According to the *Oxford English Dictionary* (OED), *system* means: 'A set or assemblage of things connected, associated, or interdependent, so as to form a complex unity; a whole composed of parts in orderly arrangement according to some scheme or plan'. Likewise, *organization* means: 'The action of organizing, or condition of being organized, as a living being. . . . The action of organizing or putting into systematic form; the arranging or coordinating of parts into a systematic whole'. The meanings of system and organization thus resemble each other. But organization has a specific referent: a living being. The conflation of both meanings would be complete if it were possible to represent a 'living being' as a system: a whole composed of parts according to some plan. An illustration of such a possibility is provided by Hobbes' *Leviathan* (1991). Interestingly, the OED's earliest reference to the word system was drawn from *Leviathan*, published around 1650.

Hobbes' purpose in writing *Leviathan* was to design a scheme or plan convincing enough, and subject to constraints imposed both by nature and God, for the attainment of order. His solution to this problem has posited an object for social scientific inquiry, and followed what, in contemporary terms, might be called a simulation procedure:

> For seeing life is but a motion of Limbs, . . . why may we not say, that all *Automata* (Engines that move themselves by springs and wheels as doth a watch) have an artificiall life? . . . *Art* goes yet further, imitating that Rationall and most excellent worke of Nature, *Man*. For by Art is created that great LEVIATHAN called a COMMONWEALTH, or STATE (in latine CIVITAS) which is but an Artificiall Man.
>
> (Hobbes, 1650 [1991: 9])

The resources Hobbes employed in solving his problem were those provided by traditions he belonged to as inheritor and participant. Like many others of his time, Hobbes was attracted by two currents: scepticism regarding men and praise of accounting as both an exercise of reason, and a way of countering the uncertainty and unreliability human nature introduces into public affairs.

Hobbes' starting-point was a common recognition: men will be inevitably led to controversies about their accounts. Against the alternatives of 'coming to blows' or leaving controversies undecided, an agreement is needed in order to have an arbitrator or judge. But his proposition is not to be reduced to one of a contract. What should be noted is his emphasis on the need for a visible power, a 'terror' of power. For '[c]ovenants, without the Sword, are but words', and 'the question is not of promises mutuall, where there is not security of performance' (Hobbes, 1650 [1991: 102]). Saying that Hobbes used a biological metaphor would also be inexact. Hobbes' metaphor was representation itself: the metaphor of theatre.

> a *Person*, is the same that an *Actor* is, both on the Stage and in common Conversation; and to *Personate*, is to *Act*, or *Represent* himselfe, or an other; and he that acteth another, is said to beare his Person, or act in his name. . . . And then the Person is the *Actor*, and he that owneth his words and actions, is the AUTHOR: In which case the Actor acteth by Authority.
>
> (Hobbes, 1650 [1991: 112])

Strategically, Hobbes presented authority as something given to the actor, an authorization to act, by a public which is created in the same act. The question is, then, how enduring the representation can be, or how long the play can last. His answer is that the artificial man should have an artificial eternity. But, the artificial man was, 'not only subject to violent death, by foreign war; but also through the ignorance, and passions of men, it hath in it, from the very institution, many seeds of a naturall mortality, by Intestine Discord' (Hobbes, 1650 [1991: 153]). So dramatic a conclusion is another instance of representation. The opposition between order and disorder reveals Hobbes' strategy: contrasting an assumed state of nature – a chaotic state which should be terrifying for modern, civilized men – with the peace and protection attainable through the maintenance of a theatre of power.

Leviathan is a model of argumentation and exposition of a system of ideas – a myth in the Platonic style (Oakeshott, 1975b). The representation of order emerging from chaos, the creation of a social order, provided a foundation for modern social science, and an inexhaustible source of problems too. Social theorists are still struggling, for instance, with the distinction between the artificially designed and the naturally emergent. The introduction of the idea of a social system is a sufficient condition for regarding Hobbes' work as a key step in modernizing theoretical reflection on social organization. However, contemporary readers of *Leviathan*, looking for Hobbes' concept of system, may feel something of a disappointment: no more than ten pages, and a simple definition of the term 'system' at that. But, a closer look at this definition might reveal certain interesting details:

> Having spoken of the Generation, Forme, and Power of a Commonwealth, I am in order to speak next of the parts thereof. And first of Systemes, which resemble the similar parts, or Muscles of a Body naturall. By SYSTEMES; I understand any numbers of men joyned in one Interest, or one Businesse. Of which some are *Regular*, and some *Irregular*.... Of Regular, some are *Absolute*, and *Independent*, subject to none but their own Representative: such are only Common-wealths.
>
> (Hobbes, 1650 [1991: 155])

Apart from the definition of a system as an assembly of individuals, still a basic or intuitive notion, it is interesting to note Hobbes' distinguishing of similar and organic parts of the commonwealth. In an extensive literature on *Leviathan*, this distinction has received no attention, as far as a preliminary review has been able to discover (Baumrin, 1969; Bertman, 1981; Callon and Latour, 1981; Gauthier, 1969; Goldsmith, 1968; Hampton, 1988; McNeilly, 1968; Mintz, 1962; Oakeshott, 1975b; Pye, 1988; Skinner, 1972; Strauss, 1966; Tuck, 1989; Watkins, 1973). This also applies to the notion of system, with the exception of a comment by Goldsmith – 'The theory of personation provides a general explanation of "systems" – organized groups, or "bodies politic". The unity of a system is the unity of its representative' (1968: 159) – which reveals his understanding of Hobbes' method.

Similar are those parts of the commonwealth which have the same nature and functional character, hence the examples of muscles in a positive sense, and 'apostemes' in the negative (Hobbes, 1650 [1991: 165]). Corporations and other 'bodies' share a common feature with the commonwealth: all of them consist of assemblies of people. Commonwealths are particular cases of systems: those which are absolute and independent. *Leviathan* might well have been entitled: *The Social System*. If Hobbes' chapter on systems seems too short, it should be remembered that what was said of commonwealths might be applied to other (similar) systems. *Similar* is also a technical term in geometry: similar are triangles, for example, different in size but with the same shape. Hobbes' regard for geometry is well known: 'It was the discovery of geometry which set him off in quest of science' (Goldsmith, 1968: 10). Besides, the procedure of spatial representation, the use of triangles as a device for dealing with different kinds of practical problems, was another of the Renaissance's rediscoveries. A knowledge of mathematics and geometry was a definitive feature of the intellectual equipment of Renaissance man (Baxandall, 1991). The definition of systems, in such spatial terms, may have served Hobbes as a way of indicating not only the common character of the commonwealth and other assemblies of people, but also the required attention to their properties in constructing and dealing with them – hence his division of systems into regular and irregular. To be regular meant both maintaining shapes and following rules. Regular systems were subordinated to the sovereign who authorized them, and constituted them with 'letters', 'patents that may be read'.

A distinctive feature of Hobbes' concept of system is its spatial character as a representation, along with the Renaissance appreciation of proportion and regularity. The notion of system was articulated in terms of an object with certain geometric properties, a body: 'The Word *Body*, in the most generall acceptation, signifieth that which filleth, or occupyeth some certain room, or imagined place' (Hobbes, 1650 [1991: 269]). In this sense, Hobbes introduced a research programme for social science. From then on, the definition of a system – the positing of an object by following a procedure of spatial representation – would become the starting-point or the foundation of social scientific inquiry. The application of the systems approach to the explanation of social phenomena constitutes an inherent feature of modernity. Such an approach corresponds to a particular form of life in which boundaries, levels, compartments, and functions, are 'natural' elements of the social order, inscriptions which define the horizons of meaning and sense.

Social scientists have been criticized for adopting the notion of system from the natural sciences. Such a criticism overlooks the more general phenomenon of the institutionalization of rules for modern science. As Rapoport (1968: 452) indicated, the word system is used 'as a program or direction in the contemporary philosophy of science'. Rapoport made a distinction between two kinds of system: those in which elements and how they are related have to be discovered, and 'technological systems' whose structure 'is completely known, since such systems are designed by men' (1968: 457). What kind of system is the social scientist dealing with? Was Hobbes discovering or designing? It might be argued that all systems are, in a sense, 'technological' resulting from a previous work of representation. In this sense, the problem comes to the same thing: framing a set of phenomena. And, for social scientists, at least from Hobbes' times, this is familiar territory.

Talcott Parsons' work provides a good example of the implementation of this programme. He derived the distinctive feature of the social system from a certain syllogism: living systems are open systems, a social system is a living system, therefore a social system is an open system. The minor premise is the basis of the structural-functional analysis: 'the dependence of the organism on its physical environment for nutrition and respiration is . . . the essential basis of the famous concept of *function* as it applies to social systems, as to all other living systems' (Parsons, 1968: 460). But the social system does not have direct contact with either the physical environment or with 'ultimate reality'. Ultimate reality refers to a general ordering according to a cybernetic hierarchy of control; a modernized version of the theological interpretation of the world, in which the sensory is controlled by the suprasensory. In fact, for Parsons, '[r]eligion . . . remains the "master system" in the cybernetic sense' (1968: 468).

The object Parsons was simulating is insinuated in the following statement:

> The self-sufficiency of a society is a function of the balanced *combination* of its controls. . . . This includes the *cybernetic* aspect of control by which systems high in information but low in energy regulate other systems higher in energy but lower in information. . . . Thus, a programmed sequence of mechanical operations (e.g. in a washing machine) can be controlled by a timing switch using very little energy compared with the energy actually operating the machine's moving parts or heating its water.
>
> (Parsons, 1966: 9)

While in Hobbes' time the prime example of automata was a watch, and the regulated motion of its parts, Parsons could latterly refer to a formidable washing machine whose operations could be controlled with a minimum of energy. However, both of them reached, in the end, a similar conclusion. The artificial man was unable to secure its immortality, and the control system was unable to attain full command: the social system could not be 'completely immune to the kind of political opposition which can lead to the disruption of its basic solidarity' (Parsons, 1968: 464). Neither book-keeping nor cybernetics seem to be able to cope with men's unreliability. But there is an important difference. For Parsons, the disruption of the system's basic solidarity became an example of differentiation in the political subsystem, and thus a theme for further elaboration, rather than a dramatic manifestation of weakness. This kind of optimism resembles that of a mathematician who 'thinks inside a society that has triumphed over noise so well and for such a long time that he is amazed when the problem is raised anew'

(Serres, 1983: 68). Modern social theory found in the concept of system a way of representing a desirable state of order, by following a procedure of spatial representation of a certain body in analogy to mathematical forms. Such a programme would be followed by organization theorists.

Organizing as systematizing

Philip Selznick's (1948) pioneering paper contained an exposition of the nature, problems, and possibilities of organization theory. The paper's intention was to deal with a difficulty in the traditional notion of organization: the 'organizational paradox'. For Selznick, the traditional point of view conceived of formal organization as the structural expression of rational action. The paradox arises when it is recognized that there are 'nonrational' dimensions of behaviour unaccounted for by formal structures which, at the same time, are indispensable for the system's persistence: 'that which is not included in the abstract design (as reflected, for example, in a staff-line organization chart) is vitally relevant to the maintenance and development of the formal system itself' (Selznick, 1948: 25). Selznick solved the paradox by conceiving of the organization as an adaptive system capable of surviving and evolving, because of the dynamism introduced by the reciprocal influences of divergent interests.

Selznick's formulation of the opposition between rational and nonrational, formal and informal, provided the basis for a 'dynamic' theory of organization. His methodological proposition emphasized the testing of empirical generalizations about organizational conditions, and excluded consideration of accidents or external conditions regarded as historical events. It would be acceptable to state, as Barnard (1975) did, that the 'innate propensity' of organizations to expand is a function of an inherent stability of incentives. For in such a way the terms would remain at the organization level. Selznick illustrated what could be expected from a fruitful generalization with the hypothesis of 'co-optation' as an organizational 'self-defensive' mechanism. The purpose was to appropriate a field, which amounted to a call to action for a generation of scholars.

Peter Blau proposed the following answer to the question of how an organization comes about: 'An organization comes into existence when explicit procedures are established to coordinate the activities of a group in the interest of achieving specified objectives' (1968: 297–8). Thus, organizing means establishing procedures, whether by a group for themselves or by one group on behalf of another. Before the organization's appearance, what exists is an emergent social structure, exchanges and competitions, forces, attempts to exercise power, and so on. After the establishment of procedures there begins the story of a deliberately established social structure. The task of research consists in describing organizations, and explaining observed variations of organizational characteristics. That would be the basis for a genuine theory of organizations, strategy as the only way of producing such a theory.

Two main currents of organization studies developed from these approaches:

in-depth case studies (following Selznick's approach), and comparative studies (following Blau's). Selznick and Blau coincided in the identification of the source of 'scientifically relevant' problems: the opposition between the formal and the informal, the planned and the emergent. What Selznick's and Blau's programmes for organization theory share can be found in a previous work which systematized social phenomena in these terms. After Hobbes' seminal formulation, it was Max Weber who formalized the task of 'systematizing' in terms of the meaning of action.

The articulation of a theory of organization required the possibility of distinguishing between particular organizations and organization in general. In this sense, it might be said that *organization theory* began when Weber defined an organization as 'a system of continuous purposive action of a specified kind' (1947: 151). For Weber, the problem faced by the sociologist is that those cases in which the meaning of action is conscious and explicit are rather exceptional. But, this 'difficulty need not prevent the sociologist from systematizing his concepts by the classification of possible types of subjective meaning' (Weber, 1947: 112). His idea of rationality had a situational, rather than psychological, sense: the actor's behaviour is to be analysed in terms of a constructed situation. For example, in the case of a money economy, Weber stated: 'The "pure" expression of this situation leaves the individual trapped within the market a choice between only . . . two alternatives: "teleological" accommodation to the "market" or economic ruin' (in Jacobs, 1990: 562). The rationale for constructing situations consists in exhausting the possibilities, or degrees of freedom, for individual action, and reducing them to clear, unambiguous statements. The action is rational insofar as it fits a model. Values, purposes, or rationality, were all classifying categories with no foundational properties.

But this last aspect of Weber's legacy was not completely accepted by his followers. Parsons (in his 'Introduction to Weber', 1947: 29) criticized Weber's 'inadequate attention to psychological problems'. And, Weber's methodological position notwithstanding, the search for psychological explanations became a focus for organization theory. Parsons' own reliance on generalizations drawn from group experiments provides, finally, a clue to understanding how organization theory became a research field for social psychologists. It is, therefore, no surprise that a further development of the systems theory of organization appeared in a book entitled *The Social Psychology of Organizations* (Katz and Kahn, 1966).

For Katz and Kahn, the basic framework for a theory of organization should be that of the system's functioning: input-process-output-feedback. The system's self-regulation became expressed in terms of controlling entropy by means of feedback mechanisms. By recalling the second law of thermodynamics, Katz and Kahn formulated the problem of organization theory as one of explaining the capability of organizations, as open systems contained within a larger system, of countering the tendency to entropy. The task of organizing would be to avoid the uniformity of energy distribution inside the larger system. It is a kind of inverse image of the one suggested by Boulding (1956). Instead of surviving because of a tendency to become isomorphic with its environment, as Boulding proposed, the system has to transform the environment into an image of itself. The task is more complex than that of an adaptive system – controlling a washing machine, for example.

The question is, how will the system be able to do this? At this point the psychological content of the model comes to the fore. This can be appreciated in the discussion of the system's boundaries. Although Katz and Kahn refer to boundaries in different ways throughout the book (barriers to membership, energy differentials, breaks in activities), ultimately the boundary condition is a psychological one.

> By passing the boundary and becoming a functioning member of the organization, the person takes on some of the coding system of the organization, since he accepts some of its norms and values, absorbs some of its subculture, and develops shared expectations and values with other members.
>
> (Katz and Kahn, 1966: 228)

There is a certain circularity in this theory: the organization's existence depends on its members' perceptions which, in turn, depend on their passing through its boundaries. A process of absorbing a certain way of perceiving is postulated, through which the system ensures the attainment of order. But what the boundaries consist of is not explicitly determined. According to Katz and Kahn, organizations differ in terms of the degree of permeability of their boundaries. There are organizations whose boundaries are so sharply defined that it is not a matter of individual decision to enter or to leave. Such a definitiveness of boundaries seems to be related to the system's size and self-sufficiency. The thermodynamic requirement of organizing is to be satisfied through the organization's ability to appropriate the world and transform it, by imposing values, expectations, codes.

Another formulation of the systems model attempted to define boundaries in terms of breaks in ongoing activities. According to Miller and Rice (1973), by conceiving the system in terms of activities (those required for transforming inputs into outputs), the deduction of its boundaries should be straightforward. They noticed, however, a difficulty in matching a criterion of inclusion–exclusion (the sense of boundaries as a membership condition) with that of a discontinuity in ongoing operations. But they did not solve the problem. A solution was suggested by Emery and Trist (1981) who, looking for a way of coupling the social and technical components of systems, defined the technical component as 'belonging' to an enterprise. Such a definition formally locates input–output points, but does not explain discontinuities in process terms.

Organizational literature contains a variety of strategies for managing boundaries, which have been grouped in two general kinds (Scott, 1987): buffering (protective artificial closing), and bridging (changing the boundaries). These practices suggest that something cannot be easily contained within the systems framework. Scott solves the problem of defining organizational boundaries, by deducing them from the notion of collectivity: 'All collectivities – including informal groups, communities, organizations, and entire societies – possess, by definition, boundaries that distinguish them from other systems' (1987: 171) . The boundary condition thus becomes a matter of fact, by definition. In spite of its power to bring about a coherent world picture, the system approach has been unable to account for its own foundation: the system's boundaries. Perhaps its power resides in its ability to maintain and conceal such a mystery.

Organizing in the mode of systematizing, as a particular way of representing a certain order, becomes understandable by analysing the boundary's role: 'Attention to the divisionary nature of the boundary reveals that the work of organization is focused upon transforming an intrinsically ambiguous condition into one that is ordered' (Cooper, 1990: 172). The development of the systems theory of organization, and the adoption of openness as a basic feature of systems, has undoubtedly contributed to revealing certain complexities of the real. But – even recognizing their permeability, transitoriness and, even, fuzziness – boundaries remain indispensable in order to depict a clearly specified object. Is there any other way of understanding organization?

Network analysis as a research tool

'Organization is best depicted as a network, and the mathematical theory of networks derives largely from certain branches of topology and abstract algebra rather than from analysis, which underlies classical mathematics' (Rapoport, 1968: 458). A network approach provides an ideal opportunity for thinking of organization in terms different from those of a systems approach: in terms of interlocking and extending relations through a widely defined domain, rather than in terms of the states and properties of clearly delimited entities. But the transition from analysis to topology has proved to be a difficult one. This section presents some uses of networks in social science in general, and in organization studies in particular. The question is whether these applications provide a viable alternative to the systems approach or not.

Network analysis in social science

Perhaps the most imaginative application of the concept of network in analysing social organization can be found in Jacob Moreno's work. His book's title, *Who Shall Survive?* (1934 [1953]) refers to what he was looking for: the social laws of natural selection. Moreno found a way of answering his question by analysing configurations drawn from sociodynamic studies. The data took on a revealing significance when portrayed in the form of sociograms – diagrams of expressions of attraction, indifference and rejection among individuals – which revealed these phenomena's structural features. Analyses could thus go beyond static distributions towards the apprehension of an evolving structure.

Moreno found that social structures exhibited a certain independence from the individuals' motivations: they appeared as 'chains' that linked individuals according to different criteria (vocational or religious, for example), regardless of the boundaries of any social aggregate. Moreno attempted to represent a social structure which, although related to a physical space, becomes detached from it, adopts different forms, and transforms the very sense of unity of that space. He translated social theory into the language of *topology* by using such ideas as boundaries, maps, surfaces, traversability, and the like. But this way of representing social phenomena has been hard to visualize in spite of the efforts made by Moreno and some of his followers (e.g. Lewin, 1936), who attempted to develop a topological social science. The later history of networks in social science will show the reduction of networks to nets, depicted within a system frame. A recent review of the field of social network research has summarized the dominant trend: 'Moving away from the use of the concept of a social network as a sensitizing metaphor and towards its development as a research tool, . . . to interpret the behavior of actors in light of their varying positions within social structure' (Marsden, 1990: 436).

A current technique in the field of operational research, network analysis has also been used to represent organizing as a technical problem. Instead of individuals, as in social network analysis, the points or nodes of the network represent events. An event is defined as a binary situation (e.g. Beer, 1964): either activities represented by the network's lines or arrows are accomplished or not. Two activities meet at an event, when the beginning of one of them presupposes the completion of the other. A popular application of this way of analysing networks is the Program Evaluation and Review Technique (PERT), developed for the 'Polaris Fleet Ballistic Missile System' in 1958 (Archibald and Villoria, 1967). Complex projects could thus be easily represented and critical elements, such as deadlines and costs, easily taken into account. With the aid of computers, the technique has been improved and complicated by adding constraints or contingencies (related to time or resources), and a more explicit consideration of probabilities.

These developments in network analysis constitute the workfield of a rather small community of engineers and mathematicians, because of their high levels of specialization and sophistication. In addition, the separation between the technical and the social as independent domains accounts for the almost insignificant impact of this tradition of network analysis on organization theory, which has remained mostly the domain of social scientists. The representation of a project as a purely technical problem artificially neglects its social character and implications. But the representation of the purely social artificially neglects the technical content of organization.

JOSÉ MALAVÉ

Network analysis in organization studies

The application of network analysis to the study of organizational phenomena is now a growing tradition, although not as well-established as that of systems analysis. In fact, references to networks in the organizational literature are still to be found within systems-framed expositions of organization theory (e.g. Scott, 1987; Perrow, 1986). However, a growing number of network-based research is now claiming for theoretical elaboration (see, for example, Thompson *et al.*, 1991). Here, examples of the application of network concepts in organization studies are presented, by distinguishing analyses of intra- and interorganizational networks.

Studies of *interorganizational networks* focus on problems deriving from relations between the organization and its environment: adaptation, survival, and control. In general, these studies adopt a social perspective – lines connecting individuals. Perhaps the most developed tradition of network analysis in the study of interorganizational arrangements has been the study of interlocking directorates, e.g. Mizruchi (1982), Stokman, Ziegler and Scott (1985). The term 'interlock' refers to the line which connects the same individual in two different organizations. For example, when a bank's executive becomes a member of two companies' boards, the connection between the companies is an *induced* interlock, while connections between each company and the bank are *primary* interlocks.

The starting-point remains the same systems-framed picture of organizations. But these studies focus on the network's constitution and properties. Samples of organizations are selected according to network configurations; and, by excluding isolated cases, resulting networks represent the connections between the largest and most powerful organizations. By following a longitudinal method, a study by Stokman, Van der Knoop and Wasseur (1988) attempted to portray a network's evolution and stability: permanence of lines, broken and reconstituted interlocks, and so on. Financial connections, for instance, would reveal the way configurations come about, change or endure. And, in fact, strong positive correlations between financial participation and interlocking were reported. Unfortunately, the authors' analysis limited itself to a systems-framed explanation of interlocking as an organizational adaptive mechanism, and findings were interpreted in terms of co-optation: 'companies try to acquire greater control of their environments by recruiting leading persons of surrounding large firms in their board' (1988: 205).

Studies of *intra-organizational networks* generally use a contingency-theory approach: studying relations between exogenous – age, size, technology – and endogenous variables representing interactions within the organization. The following shows how findings can be made coherent with traditional assumptions, by *purifying* the content of social interaction. A study by Shrader, Lincoln and Hoffman (1989) on the determinants of organizational structure used network concepts for operationalizing Burns and Stalker's (1961) mechanistic–organic dichotomy, and for testing contingency hypotheses. Such concepts were found better suited to this task than such traditional measures as centralization, formalization, and differentiation. However, it was also asserted that formal structures (defined in traditional terms) take precedence over network structures. It was found, for example, that increase in size leads to increase in differentiation, centralization and formalization which, in turn, leads to decrease in density, connectivity, and symmetry. Data were gathered from a population of private nonprofit agencies providing services to troubled youth in a large midwestern metropolis in the USA. Correlations supported the hypotheses. The authors found, however, contrasting correlations between centralization and symmetry, depending on the nature of the network concerned: nonsignificant negatives in the communication network, and significant positives in the referral network. 'Referral' is here a technical term: the referral of clients from one section of the staff to another. Why were they dealing with two different networks? By separating communications from referrals, they attempted to analyse a *pure* social network: 'client referral relations, to a greater degree than communications, will be conditioned on the exogenously-determined attributes and needs of clients, thereby attenuating the effects of organizational variables' (Shrader, Lincoln and Hoffman, 1989: 54).

Network analysis has become confined within the systems frame by reducing itself to placing figures onto a plane: spatial attitudes in a social perspective, spatial time in a technical perspective. This strategy of representation reduces networks to 'flat nets' which neglects the sense of active work, the sense that something is going on. This result might be due to the separation of the social and the technical as independent professional domains, which leaves researchers with abstractions that can be easily handled but are devoid of content.

Technology and organization

In order to develop an approach to the study of organization as a process, it seems necessary to start thinking of technology in terms wider than those of machines. Everyday life shows how inextricably related are techniques and languages, technical changes and social arrangements, uses of technologies and ways of representing the real. A way of understanding the concept of technology can perhaps be found in Heidegger's paradoxical idea that 'the essence of technology is by no means anything technological' (1977: 4), but a way of revealing through which the real appears as what is at hand, ordered, ordinary. In his reading of Heidegger's work, the Italian philosopher Gianni Vattimo (1991) indicates the complexities involved in such an idea of technology: the connections between metaphysics, humanism, and technology. Michel Serres' (1983) story of Thales' theorem provides a revealing trace of such a complex phenomenon: '[Thales] stops the course of the sun at the precise instant of isosceles triangles; he homogenizes the day to obtain the general case.... What [Thales' mathematics] announces, for the first time, is a philosophy of representation, dominating both the pure diagram and its dramatization beneath the torches of the solstice' (Serres, 1983: 87).

The theatrical idea of dramatization brings to light a basic character of technology: to produce a representation and reproduce the conditions for its repetition. The pure diagram expresses a metaphysics of repeatability. The story of Thales' theorem, and of a philosophy of representation that still dominates diagrams and dramatizations, illustrates the convergence in a single piece of work of technology, humanism and metaphysics. Perhaps all of them were simultaneously expressed with a single word in Ancient Greek. Perhaps the word *techne* conveyed a more complex meaning than *technique*. But those forgotten meanings seem to remain with us.

'Everything is technology': the historian Fernand Braudel (1985: 334) uses such an assertion to stress the relevance of the smallest details of everyday life for understanding how civilizations remain within certain constraining horizons: by repeating successful ways of doing things. The phrase also refers to his recognition that an attempt to focus exclusively on material things cannot be carried too far: 'In fact, our investigation takes us at this point not simply into the realm of material "things", but into a world of "things and words"' (Braudel, 1985: 333). He was actually trying to understand the phenomenon of the confinement of everyday life inside the walls, so to speak, of things and words within which it repeats itself. Such a phenomenon may, in fact, be understood by analysing the relationship between words and tools: 'Both of these involve the same detachment from the immediate context; in both cases a temporality and an order emerge which are *sui generis* and which are superimposed on natural temporality and order' (Castoriadis, 1984: 229).

This is another way of expressing the point made by Serres in his story of Thales' theorem. But, the idea of detachment summarizes the effect attained by means of representation: a way of acting at a distance, while transforming the real. Words and tools share the possibility of introducing a temporality and an order. What is not yet clear is precisely how they emerge, and are superimposed. (It should be added that the idea of a 'natural temporality and order' might be misleading, since it would amount to presupposing or looking for a certain origin.) An answer to that question can be found in Serres' idea: the possibility of repetition or 'dramatization'of forms of detached manipulation is what explains the emergence and superimposition of those particular temporalities and orders. Using words and tools possesses a character of *repeated detachment* through which the real reveals itself as what is at hand, ordered, ordinary.

Technology and organization can be thought of as instances of the same phenomenon: an enduring way of representing which reveals and imposes an order and a temporality by ensuring the possibility of endless repetition of such revealing and imposition. Cooper (1992) has analysed the relation between organization and representation by highlighting three aspects of modern technology: remote control, displacement, and abbreviation. By converting force, power, and things into information, modern technology offers the required conditions of detached manipulation. In fact: 'Administrators and managers, for example, do not work directly on the environment but on models, maps, numbers and formulae which represent that environment' (Cooper, 1992: 257). Particular forms of *detached manipulation* are a matter of historical contingency. Think, for instance, of the difference between the techno-organization put to work in the Portuguese's development of oceanic navigation in the fifteenth century (Law, 1986), and the contemporary enterprise of populating outer space with satellites and space stations. But both projects share the features highlighted by Cooper. In both, the unknown is transformed into charted routes, the distant into the immediate, the complex into the simple and measurable.

Transformation-displacement networks

The idea that organizing processes travel by imposing particular orders and temporalities can be derived from a simple fact: the repetition of ways of speaking and doing things. Thus:

> Material life . . . presents itself to us in the anecdotal form of thousands of assorted facts . . . little facts which do, it is true, by indefinite repetition, add up to form linked chains. Each of them represents the thousands of others that have crossed the silent depths of time and *endured*.
> (Braudel, 1985: 560)

Transformation-displacement networks (TDN) can be viewed as those chains which, formed by the repetition of everyday facts, link themselves and endure. And it is in this sense that organization can be understood in process terms: as the development and the strengthening of those chains. It should be evident that the expression network refers here both to a work and (not only) to a net.

Towards a definition of transformation-displacement networks

A starting-point for the definition of TDNs can be found in the idea of 'sociotechnical networks', as used by Law and Callon (1988). The qualification 'sociotechnical' was, for them, a way of 'underlining the simultaneously social and technical character of technological innovation' (1988: 285). Although not explicitly defined in their work, the meaning of 'sociotechnical network' can be derived from the idea of 'sociotechnical scenario'. An engineering project constitutes a sociotechnical scenario in the sense that it contains a technical objective, the way of reaching it, and a representation of how the social world would look through its implementation. A sociotechnical scenario constitutes, for Law and Callon, a 'putative' sociotechnical network, a design for an ideal world: 'and it is easy to design ideal worlds. The problems arise when it becomes necessary to mobilize or create the actors that will play these parts' (1988: 287).

Sociotechnical scenarios differ from the diagrams used in traditional network analysis. The sociological character of engineering work, pointed out by Law and Callon, might be as striking for sociologists as for engineers; since both of them work on abstractions belonging to different realms. But, by using network analysis, both sociologists and engineers share a way of representing the real. However, the diagrams used by engineers are nearer to the idea of a putative sociotechnical network than those used by social scientists. The abstraction of the social removes interaction from the tools, materials, and even learning processes related to activities. In an engineering project, actors can still be found in a state of heterogeneity regarding their nature. Two differences should be noted. Sociotechnical networks can be visualized as sequences of activities represented by lines, without reducing them to an exercise of plane projection. And they can be bounded, but the boundaries result from the need for telling a story, since there are no absolute beginnings or ends. Engineering diagrams not only specify all possible paths, but also specify the best one. In their ideal world there is no place for encounters.

The idea of TDNs has its inspiration from that of sociotechnical networks, but is more concerned to indicate the kind of process involved rather than the network's nature. TDNs are meant to refer to the organizing processes themselves rather than to the (sociotechnical) avenues they travel on, as Cooper (1992) originally put it. TDNs represent what can be found 'beneath' organizational boundaries. If the boundary condition were erased a miscegenation of organization and environment would be found. Thus, instead of an idea of exchange, what is needed is a notion of transformation and displacement, of practices which transform-displace and are transformed-displaced by other practices. By relaxing the boundary condition, a transition from a notion of organization as a *boundary-maintaining system* to one of organization as a *network-strengthening practice* is prompted. A TDN can be defined as a series of ongoing organizing processes formed by interlocking, repeatable actions (whether performed by humans or nonhumans) through which a way of representing becomes an enduring feature of the real.

Methodological requirements for a transformation-displacement network approach

The experience of 'talking' with a computer is now an everyday fact for many people. When analysed as a part of a TDN, this experience becomes embedded in complex sequences of *events and associations* from which appropriated behaviours of both individuals and machines result. A methodological requirement for a TDN approach can be introduced as follows: understanding particular behaviours (whether of humans or nonhumans) requires putting them into a 'story', where they can be recognized as occurrences contingent on other occurrences (Oakeshott, 1975a). An example of this kind of story can be found in Latour's (1987) study of science:

> If you proposed to build a 16-bit computer to compete with DEC's VAX 11/780 machine I'll know who, when and where you are. You are West at Data General in the late 1970s. I know this, because there are very few places on earth where anyone has the resources and the guts to disaggre-

gate the black box DEC has assembled and to come up with a brand new make of computer.

(Latour, 1987: 138–9)

The understanding of organizing processes requires an approach sensitive enough to the ways in which displacements and transformations of human and nonhuman actors occur along certain networks or circuits. Such an approach should be able to provide an intelligible form to those displacements and transformations by translating them into a story.

TDNs might be represented as diagrams but their analyses require a qualitative rather than quantitative approach. This implies substituting a logic of *displacement and transformation* for the traditional logic of distance and measurement. This is a second methodological requirement. However, adopting such a different logic faces some obstacles. Topological concepts – because of their 'speculative' character – are not included in the formal training of social scientists and engineers. The very idea of speaking in different terms would appear as a deviation. Curiously enough, when it is necessary to deal with problems of uncertainty and ambiguity, with those situations which reveal the instability and fissures of the 'real world', the language used is precisely that qualitative and speculative language of traversability, inclusion, mutual arrangement, and so on. This recalls one of those paradoxical drawings of Escher's in which certain features, which should not normally be shown simultaneously in the same world, are nevertheless presented as such.

One of the curiosities which can be found in certain topological forms (the Moebius strip, for example) is the confusion of inside and outside. When trying to follow a path which is clearly on one side of the strip, the observer strangely ends up on the other. The surprised observer has always been on the same 'side', which folds and unfolds, so producing the illusion of border. Such an illusion, as well as those associated with other 'impossible' objects, may suggest that certain phenomena cannot be accounted for by a traditional logic. Thus, by expressing the curious relation between inside and outside, in topological terms, the inside would be a 'folding' of the outside. Both of them would be in permanent contact, and the external would be homologous to the internal (Deleuze, 1988).

The organization's inside might be thought of, in this sense, as an environmental fold or, to use Cooper's expression, as a 'pocket of externality folded in' (1989: 487) . The systems-framed notion of organizational functioning, as one of exchanges, would be replaced by one of transformations and displacements through which such folds emerge. Emergence and dissolution of organizations would become transitory folds and unfolds of an historical field. Understanding the inside as a fold of the outside would distinguish a TDN approach, methodologically speaking, from a system approach, in which disappearance of boundaries corresponds to the system's 'death', in a biological sense (Parsons and Bales, 1953: 92). Maintaining boundaries is a matter of life or death, in a system approach, for accepting changes of forms would imply losing the stability of distances and measurements. In a TDN approach, a system 'death' would mean an unfolding, a relaxation of a transitory loop in the course of an ongoing process, due to intersections or inclusions of organizing processes.

This point can be illustrated with those cases of factory closures which show how, after an immediate period of difficulty, different skills, products, or markets are developed. Perhaps, it can be argued, in cases of the obsolescence of specific assets there is no easy way of finding profitable alternative uses. However, there are good examples of the transformation of industrial activities using quite specific equipment, procedures and skills, as a consequence of changes in market conditions or technological innovations. A well-known example is the experience of some Swiss watchmakers who, facing the invasion of the Japanese into their traditional industry, successfully changed to producing different products — heart pacemakers. Should these cases be analysed as deaths, resurrections or agonies?

The question is, how can organizing processes be traced? Although there is no single answer, a general indication can be provided: only when the repeated exercise of a practice is achieved can it be said that an organizing process is taking place. In this sense, the study of organizing processes may be conceived as one of analysing practices. Foucault (1988b) referred to his own method as one of analysing practices; practices being understood as those 'places' where ways of doing and speaking meet and interconnect, and which 'possess up to a point their own specific regularities, logic, strategy, self-evidence, and "reason"' (1988b: 102–3). In order to approach the study of organizing processes, the methodological strategy would consist in identifying the actors and their trajectories, connections, and encounters that concur in constructing those places. Such a strategy can be illustrated with Latour's (1988) story of the Pasteurian project as an example of a way of tracing TDNs for analysing organizing processes.

This story refers not only to Pasteur's work inside his laboratory, but to a multiplicity of actions which Latour named a 'network of gestures and skills' (1988: 53): a collective enterprise in which Pasteur and the hygienists' movement played as important a role as other actors, including the microbes. Latour's use of this notion illustrates an attempt to specify a concept for the multiple elements of a practice. Some examples of this network of gestures and skills may provide insights into how the practice of 'pasteurization', a remarkable case of organization in nineteenth-century France, took place:

- Taking blood samples from infected animals.
- Inscribing the microbes' answers in homogeneous, alphanumerical terms.
- Using statistics, and comparing death rates of vaccinated and nonvaccinated animals.
- '[T]he *theatre of the proof*... such dramatized experiments that the spectator could see the phenomena' (1988: 85).
- The hygienists' 'support of laboratories, and even the continual praise of the "great Pasteur"' (1988: 52).
- Developing antidiphtheria vaccination.

- Disinfecting midwives' hands.
- Building of drains.
- Sterilization of milk.
- Generalizing vaccination.
- Establishing methods for purifying water.
- Legislation 'on the basis of advice given by this new profession, scientific hygienism' (1988: 56).

What followed was the routine maintenance of a regime of practices, represented in the Pasteur Institute, sanitary organization, regulations, policing, and so on. A lesson Latour drew from this story is that practices develop from other practices: 'Order is extracted not from disorder but from orders' (1987: 161). Previously well-established practices of farmers, midwives, physicians, etc., were transformed and displaced by the new 'Pasteurian' practices. Thus, another methodological requirement for a TDN approach is to start understanding current, ongoing practices, no matter how primitively or irrationally they might be presented.

Another example of transformation-displacement of practices can be found in a case study of the introduction of advanced materials (Willinger and Zuscovitch, 1988). Japanese firms started producing ceramics when the metal industry was still expected to maintain its dominant position in the market for ceramics in thermo-mechanical applications (engines, turbines). Their strategy was to gain industrial control of ceramics production by developing new production techniques. The very introduction of new materials and production processes would, sooner or later, influence the path of technological development in that industry. The case illustrates the incremental process through which the introduction of the new materials took place, along with its economic implications. This can be appreciated in the following excerpts from Willinger and Zuscovitch's (1988) study:

> The designer will typically insert a new piece made of new materials in *existing technical devices* and the new item will have to match up to the old ones. For example, some parts such as piston heads will use new ceramics in an otherwise metallic engine. . . . This piece-by-piece substitution process implies that the R & D will have to handle compatibility properties, and *complementarity* links are created between old and new materials. Through this incremental process learning occurs. As scientific and technical problems are progressively solved, new processing techniques are elaborated and thus knowledge and know-how are created, skill networks and industrial standards emerge, scale economies appear, and cost reduction along with it. During the 'step-by-step' substitution periods, firms search and, consciously or not, relax the technical constraints of the 'old' optimal solution. As the process goes on, knowledge concerning advantageous reconception opportunities is gained. When the field of such

opportunities is sufficiently opened, a qualitative jump becomes possible on the technical level as well as on that of economic performance.

(Willinger and Zuscovitch, 1988: 242–4)

This case gives a good idea of how a new practice progressively develops, by inserting itself within already established practices. This is a transformation-displacement story. Whether the Japanese will control the market for advanced materials or not is not the problem here. But, certainly, they have been developing the 'skill networks', and ensuring the possibility of repetition of their laboratory representations. This story also confirms that orders and temporalities do not simply emerge, but result from a piece-by-piece, step-by-step process through which little facts add to each other to form enduring practices which displace-transform previous ones. Such processes are not effortless or costless, but require the accumulation and mobilization of resources needed for constructing and supporting certain theatres in which representations are to be produced and reproduced.

An objection to the transformation-displacement networks approach

It might be objected that, by applying a TDN approach, organizations as bounded entities are bound to disappear or dissolve, amidst series of processes or stories which lack the clear and stable structure attributed to empirical organizations. It might be answered that, in any case, such an approach provides a better grasp of the real. For example, information technology is transforming traditional organizations into networks where highly skilled people work in relative isolation, and, therefore, the concept of organization as a bounded entity would be of no use in this world. But this 'realist' standpoint would lead, in turn, to disregarding the practical need for a graspable object – the organization – through which concepts, categories and theories become coherent with current practices. Such a 'realist' view will then be confronted with a dilemma. If the approach rendered unnecessary such entities, it would be possible to produce stories in which they appear as remnants of past language games, without any guiding authority. If not, it should be recognized that the approach lacks a consistent explanation of the boundary condition.

A way of solving this apparent dilemma may be found by understanding how a probably perishing object (the organization as a bounded entity) comes into existence and acquires a certain structural stability. This requires that we neither dissolve current categories nor appeal to an extraordinary ability to get in touch with things. It requires that we explain how a structure appears by starting from a series of ongoing processes. In a sense, this implies a return trip to the systems frame. But the starting-point would be an *ongoing* process instead of an already existing entity, and resulting boundaries could or could not coincide with those we call a firm, a government agency, or indeed any other form of organization. The next section is devoted to outlining a way of accomplishing this task.

Organizing as event-structuring

By assuming that the structural features of organizing can be explained in terms of the conditions for the repeated exercise of practices instead of attributing properties to certain objects, the task consists of analysing ongoing processes and accounting for the assembling of structures from other structural elements. This section consists of an exposition and discussion of Floyd Allport's theory of event-structuring, based upon his works on this theme from 1940 to 1967. This theory will be shown to be particularly suitable for: (1) explaining a structure's occurrence in terms of the repetition of ongoing processes; (2) defining boundary conditions in process terms; and (3) explicating a structure as an assemblage of other structures, which follows the idea that order, instead of emerging from chaos, is built from other orders.

Elements of event-structure theory

Allport's theory stands against two current assumptions: 'It has been assumed either that structures are fortuitous, endlessly varied, and inexplicable, or else that the quantitative laws and equations will always suffice, in principle, to explain them whenever they need explaining' (Allport, 1955: 622). Quantitative aggregation cannot explain structures; for quantities are the amounts in which the structure is seen to operate and, therefore, presuppose its existence. With respect to another common procedure, resorting to the notion of agency, Allport remarked that it implies postulating a being that uses certain means in achieving a goal, and that 'here we are likely to fall back upon anthropomorphic descriptions or tautologies' (Allport, 1967: 2).

Such concepts as organism, group, corporation, are all based upon the idea of agency. Moreover, observations are expressed in terms of acts of certain agents and their consequences: 'the corporation is said to pay its debts, the committee is said to decide a question, and a government or state to agree to a treaty, adopt a foreign policy, maintain its honor, or declare war' (Allport, 1940: 417). Allport's concept of structure departs from the traditional strategy of simulating bodies or organisms: 'We are not dealing with a structure composed of anatomical units or bodies.... Instead, we are dealing with dynamic elements, with ongoing processes and events. Events are given a relatedness, a structure, by the ongoings that connect them – and so we have a "structure of events". Ongoings are also connected by the events; the structure is really one of ongoings *and* events' (Allport, 1955: 616). In Allport's 'kinematic' conception, the structure consists of organized patterns of segments of behaviours, not of individuals and their purposes. This is remarked on in his introduction of the condition of 'invariance': 'If they exist at all, they are *invariant* through changes of magnitude, number, or dimension.

Neither can they, as such, be teleologically or functionally defined, since they are invariant with respect to all changes of purpose as well as the absence of purpose' (Allport, 1967: 16).

The first kind of element – ongoings – consists of a form of motion through time and space; whereas the second kind – events – represents points of contact, encounter, or junction. Events are occurrences linking ongoings. For simplicity, an event is usually referred to in the singular. But, actually, a large number of elementary events must occur for a macroscopically observable 'event' to be able to occur. Allport introduces the concept of 'event-regions' – places in which events may or may not occur – for conveying the idea of multiplicity and the need for probabilistic considerations: 'There is a weighted probability, but not a certainty, that events will occur in what we have called the event-regions. . . . Statistical considerations and the notion of "probable density" of events are here brought into play' (Allport, 1955: 641).

The idea that order does not simply emerge from disorder, but presupposes the existence of previous orders, provides a key to understanding the coming into being of a structure: 'If structure is to be conceived as organization, then organization has to be pervasive throughout all the parts or "subwholes" of the aggregate' (Allport, 1955: 617). Allport is referring here to the explanation of perceptual phenomena. But this reference has a particularly interesting implication. He criticized topological theories of perception for their way of solving the inside–outside problem:

> In topological field theory a questionable strategy for solving the inside–outside problem was found to be employed in the device of 'everting' the contents of the 'inside' field, thus avoiding the essential structuring problem and producing a model that lacked consistency. . . . Yet because of these very limitations, we become the more clearly aware of the kind of aggregating or structuring principle that is needed.
>
> (Allport, 1955: 618)

This suggests that conceiving the inside as a fold of the outside would simply avoid the structuring problem, but also that such a topological view contributes to the understanding of the kind of problem to be solved. In this sense, Allport's theory would provide a required extension of the TDN approach, by analysing the conditions for the occurrence and persistence of a structure's closure.

In Allport's theory, closure is defined as the completion of cycles of ongoings and events. What has to be shown is how and why ongoings come back to the starting region. A process is usually thought of as a linear advance towards a goal, which 'seems more suited to the paradigm of teleology' (Allport, 1967: 6). However, re-entrance is also a crucial aspect of an ongoing. Think, for example, of the first manned lunar landing. The success of the whole enterprise did not reduce to putting a man on the moon. It could not be simply taken for granted that the spacecraft would return. This had to be *ensured*, as a condition for the closure of such a structure. Common examples are the factory's need for workers returning every day at a precise time to repeat their jobs, or the church's need for people returning every Sunday to religious services. The closure can be understood as the transformation of networks into structures. Graphically, this might be represented as a bending of networks which produces the loops identifying the cyclical character of ongoings. Allport (1955) illustrated this idea in relativity-theory terms:

> The curving or self-closing character of the elementary ongoings ... which, in accordance with that theory, is *more* curving in regions of 'matter' or 'greater density of the field', is a feature that is believed to bias the probability towards a density of event-occurrence in the event-regions that is greater than that which would be produced by randomness or chance.
>
> (Allport, 1955: 647)

Thus, the structure's occurrence is the effect of certain biasing conditions which reduce or control randomness, and which ensures the availability of a required density of events. This can be illustrated with the point made by Stinchcombe (1965 [1986]) that the coming about of particular 'organizational inventions' depended on the availability of certain sociotechnical conditions:

> the unbureaucratized craft-subcontracting structure of the construction industry is particularly suited to the highly variable work load of the industry, the varied nature of its products, and to the fact that the work that has to be done at a particular site varies a great deal depending on the stage of the process of building which has been reached.... As soon as the social structure of early modern cities was appropriate for the development of this form, special-purpose organizations for construction were 'invented'.
>
> (Stinchcombe, 1965 [1986: 206])

Stinchcombe's analysis of the construction industry shows that certain conditions must be present for the occurrence of particular structures and their distinctive features. The idea that a structure cannot be built except out of other structural elements implies that a structure cannot be defined in isolation: 'There is always "tangency" with other structures somewhere' (Allport, 1954: 289). A structure is built from ongoings and events contributed by other (tangent) structures. Its occurrence is the result of the positive (reinforcing) or negative (inhibiting) consequences of other structures' contributions. Allport's theory suggests that structuring processes go hand in hand with destructuring processes. Structuring and destructuring can be thought of as displacements or transfers of density through which the completion of a cycle of ongoings and events is precluded in one place and facilitated in another. These are not instantaneous or automatic, but slow, trial-and-error processes. The case of the introduction of ceramics in thermomechanical applications, referred to above, shows the structuring of a new ceramics-based industrial configuration, which implies destructuring a metal-based one, as a slow, step-by-step process.

The definition of higher order structures as assemblages of lower order ones is crucial for understanding the inside–outside problem: 'When a higher order is thus attained, the lower-order "parts" (substructures), which previously had only their own "inside" meaning, now acquire also an "outside" meaning through their role within the larger, more inclusive, structure' (Allport, 1955: 661). Thus, the *boundary condition* could be defined in terms of the closure of cycles of ongoings and events, when the structure is analysed from the perspective of the completion of an inclusive structural format. Boundaries result from accumulation processes through which tangencies become assimilated, as it were, to an inside. The structuring of an inside space implies a shortening of cycles; and, therefore, a higher probability of encounters can be expected, along with a decrease in time, resources, and number of ongoings required (Allport, 1967). This is a consequence of the structure's occurrence, and cannot be taken for granted as systems theory does. Although an affinity can be noted between both event-structure and systems theories, Allport stated a basic difference between his and the systems approach: 'We make no assertion about society as a whole, nor do we assume that it is all a grand event-system. We assume, in fact, no ultimate unity of the social order' (Allport, 1940: 433).

A discussion of event-structure theory

Event-structure theory implies a departure from traditional ways of representing: '"Bodies" or "things", as such, disappear in event-structure theory; we think, instead, with kinematic concepts that are abstract and geometric, but always denotably testable in principle' (Allport, 1955: 664). At the same time, for Allport the event is 'a part of nature and capable of objective observation' (1955: 624). This reveals a particular difficulty in Allport's theory: maintaining an observational language, without using such referents as bodies and things.

In solving this problem, Allport found some support in relativity theory, at the price of introducing the problem of the observer's position. By discussing the problematic feature of the event as a discontinuity without a break in any physical continuance, Allport referred to the observation that objects come to near-points due to space–time curvatures, while continuing their trajectories, and that the observers see only 'a dichotomy that separates the fact of approach from the fact of recession' (Allport, 1955: 624). Thus, it is necessary to account for a phenomenal experience through which the event's occurrence, and with it the structure's closure, could be 'denotably testable'. Now the possibility arises that what appears as a structure, from a certain position, is actually a part of a larger structure which is out of the range of the observer's experience. This might be the case when the cause of organizational phenomena were explained by different researchers as being inside or outside certain boundaries. For example, what appears as an organization's low performance, bottlenecks, or corruption, may be operational features of a larger structure. Researchers might be led to explain or invoke an arbitrary closure, whether by resorting to an agent or by taking for granted the existence of an entity.

This discussion seems to lead to a certain philosophical dilemma: either the event has an ascertainable presence or not. According to Derrida (1973), instead of looking for a presence, the event should be thought of as a 'simulacrum', as something whose appearance is disguised in the form of disappearance. This sense of displacement beyond physical recognition implied by the concept of event has been expressed by Lyotard (in an interview with Van Riejen and Veerman) as follows: 'the event ... never stops retreating, because it is never there' (1988: 300). But the search for a pure event, as Foucault asserted, 'leads to thought in an absolute sense' (1988a: 178). This would lead the inquiry too far from the local problem of how certain features of the world appear and endure. What is needed here is a way of understanding a 'vast construction site of traces and residues' which, as Vattimo (1991: 161) has said, can be reduced neither to an 'iron cage' of total administration nor, in the opposite, to a 'glorification of simulacra'. If searching for the event's place in nature leads to the difficulty of accommodating the event's elusiveness within an observational language, searching for a pure event would lead towards an ideal world where metaphysical categories appear inverted – instead of presence, simulacrum; instead of beings, mimes. The difficulty, for understanding structural phenomena, seems to be one of thinking of incomplete wholes, simultaneously enduring and vanishing presences.

A way of addressing the problem of thinking of the structuring event as something that seems to vanish in its own occurrence consists of conceiving the event as an instance of 'appropriation': 'The gift of the presence is the property of Appropriating' (Heidegger, 1972: 22). Structuring, as appropriation, occurs when an ongoing process becomes appropriated and represented in a certain enduring way. This idea of appropriation can be appreciated by analysing science as ongoing activity, and its institutional appropriation:

> research is not ongoing activity because its work is accomplished in institutions, but rather institutions are necessary because science, intrinsically as research, has the character of ongoing activity.... More and more the methodology adapts itself to the possibilities of procedure opened up through itself. This having-to-adapt-itself to its own results as the ways and means of an advancing methodology is the essence of research's character as ongoing activity. And it is that character that is the intrinsic basis for the necessity of the institutional nature of research.
>
> (Heidegger, 1977: 124)

This necessity becomes the basis for a certain inversion of terms: science 'is' what the institution presents. The analysis of this institutional structure as appropriation reveals a tension between the ongoing and the institutional character of research.

Research activities are, in a sense, irreducible to the boundaries of the university as a structure of bodies, or anatomical units. Moreover, science's enduring presence depends on such a structure of ongoings, rather than on the university *per se*.

The seemingly contradictory features of structures – their simultaneously enduring and vanishing presences – may be metaphorically understood in terms of Vattimo's analysis of the work of art: 'The techniques of art . . . can be seen as stratagems . . . that transform the work of art into a residue and into a monument capable of enduring because from the outset it is produced in the form of that which is dead' (1991: 86). Hobbes' call to avoid the dissolution of Leviathan, due to the ignorance and passions of men, illustrates these kinds of stratagems for producing a monument from perishing materials; hence its still persuasive power.

The structure's probable existence might now be thought of as indicating less a problem of calculus, through which a feature of nature could be established, than its peculiar character of weakness and persistence as an instance of appropriation, as a play between boundedness and boundlessness. This does not mean the death of any organization. Instead, by thinking of organizations and of bounded entities in general, as weak or perishing beings, the possibility arises of accounting for their earthly existence which is inevitably one of deterioration, or convalescence as Vattimo would have said. The next, closing section is devoted to analysing the techniques and stratagems through which a probably perishing object – the bounded organization – persists and endures.

Organization theory as a case of event-structuring

Bounded organizations can be understood as instances of appropriation, in which networks of ongoing activities become represented in the form of assemblies of individuals with boundaries defined in terms of membership. Such a way of representing is 'dramatized' in the form of an academic discipline: the disciplined elaboration of a discourse about certain objects called organizations. The following statement is illustrative of this kind of discourse: 'Organizations in a structured field . . . respond to an environment that consists of other organizations responding to their environment, which consists of organizations responding to an environment of organizations' responses' (DiMaggio and Powell, 1983: 149). The analysis of this case of event-structuring should start by identifying certain techniques and stratagems through which the representation of organizations as bounded entities endures and its dramatizations become institutionalized.

Mary Douglas' (1987) analysis of institutions shows how they acquire their particular strength or persistence: 'Here, it is assumed that most established institutions, if challenged, are able to rest their claims to legitimacy on their fit with the nature of the universe' (Douglas, 1987: 46). Moreover, Douglas' analysis suggests that institutions endure by disguising the event of their own constitution. Thus: 'the effort to build strength for fragile social institutions by grounding them in nature is defeated as soon as it is recognized as such. That is why founding analogies have to be hidden and why the hold of the thought style upon the thought world has to be secret' (Douglas, 1987: 52).

There is a connection between Douglas' analysis of institutions and event-structure theory. For Douglas, institution building requires the accumulation of a certain density of events: 'This is indeed how we build institutions, squeezing each other's ideas into a common shape so that we can prove rightness by sheer numbers of independent assent' (Douglas 1987: 91). These numbers of independent assent are the quantities in which the structure is seen to operate, and which gives a proof of its existence. But, as Allport would have said, an institution cannot be defined in isolation. In Douglas' terms: 'a theory that is going to gain a permanent place in the public repertoire of what is known will need to interlock with the procedures that guarantee other kinds of theories' (Douglas, 1987: 76). Douglas called this condition the 'principle of coherence', and elaborated the following implications: (1) a theory should be compatible with already-naturalized political values; (2) prevailing institutions save the theory's proponents the task of justifying their classifications; and (3) 'we should relate what is shared in our mental furnishing to our common experience of authority and work' (Douglas, 1987: 98).

The recognition of the institutional character of organization theory leads the analysis to the context where it becomes a discipline, a professional domain. Samuel Weber (1982) has summarized the basic features of the professional as follows:

> A professional was – and is – a specialist who lives from his work, who has undergone a lengthy period of training in a recognized institution (professional school), which certified him as being competent in a specialized area; such competence derives from his mastery of a particular discipline, an esoteric body of useful knowledge involving systematic theory and resting upon principles.
>
> (Weber, 1982: 66)

Another element of Weber's argument is particularly important for the point to be stressed here: 'professionalism is construed not merely as "a set of learned values", as an integral system, but also and most important, as a set of habitual *responses*' (ibid.). This disciplining condition of professionalism has a direct relevance to the construction of a discipline's particular discourse. This can be illustrated with an example drawn from managerial education, which shows that character of institutionalization described by Douglas (1987) as 'squeezing thinking'.

Henry Mintzberg (1990), in referring to the Harvard Business School's tradition of strategic management, has noted a strong relationship between the model of strategy formation and the case study method. It is not fortuitous that this tradition, as Mintzberg recognizes, had provided a vocabulary and framed strategic management as the search for a congruence between external opportunities and internal capabilities. The following is a sample of the typical instructional situation: 'Bear in mind that time is short: the external environment must be assessed, distinctive competencies identified, alternate strategies proposed, and these evaluated, all before class is dismissed in 80 minutes' (Mintzberg, 1990: 187). Anyone who has taken a course in a business school anywhere will be familiar with this. This tradition of theorizing and teaching serves to suggest how organization theory becomes institutionalized: by producing taken-for-granted facts which simplify life and appeal to a constructed common sense. The structuring process consists here in narrowing conceptual pathways towards the principles of the discipline – the body of knowledge which distinguish the practice of a particular profession. The biasing conditions operating in this case may be called, following Weber (1982), conditions of 'imposability':

> by focusing upon the conditions of possibility and impossibility of systems, what has been neglected is what I would call the conditions of *imposability*, the conditions under which arguments, categories and values impose and maintain a certain authority, even where traditional authority itself is meant to be subverted.
>
> (Weber, 1982: 60–1)

Such conditions, interpreted in terms of event-structure theory, increase the density of certain events – Douglas' numbers of independent assent – making possible the persistence of a structure – organization theory as a discipline. It is not necessary to invoke states of mind, forces, or agents, for explaining in noncircular terms the occurrence of such a structure. What has to be recognized is the persistence of a practice, and the conditions for its repetition. The meaning of organization as a bounded entity is to be sought less in a certain state of nature, or in a conceptual property of systems, than in such practices as teaching, research and publishing.

Note

1 This chapter seeks to contribute to the understanding of a distinctive feature of organizational phenomena – the interlocking of practices – which is disregarded in the traditional representation of organizations as bounded systems. A great deal of inspiration for writing it has been drawn from Robert Cooper's (e.g. 1990) highlighting of the role played by imposed frames in representing and understanding organizational phenomena. Organization theory's positing of a bounded entity – 'the organization' – as its object of study indeed has become a frontier for organizational knowledge. The central question is how an approach to the study of organization as process, irrespective of boundaries between organizations and environment, can be developed. The chapter explores and discusses one way of solving this problem. It draws heavily on the work presented as the author's doctoral dissertation at Lancaster University (Malavé, 1992).

Bibliography

Allport, F. H. (1940), 'An Event-system Theory of Collective Action', *Journal of Social Psychology*, 11, 417–45.
—— (1954) 'The Structuring of Events', *Psychological Review*, 61/5, 281–303.
—— (1955) *Theories of Perception and the Concept of Structure*, New York: Wiley.
—— (1962) 'A Structuronomic Conception of Behavior', *Journal of Abnormal and Social Psychology*, 64/1, 3–30.
—— (1967) 'A Theory of Enestruence (Event-Structure Theory)', *American Psychologist*, 1–24.
Archibald, R. D. and Villoria, R. L. (1967) *Network-Based Management Systems (PERT/CPM)*, New York: Wiley.
Barnard, C. (1975) *The Functions of the Executive*, Cambridge, MA: Harvard University Press.
Baumrin, B. H. (ed.) (1969) *Hobbes's Leviathan: Interpretation and Criticism*, Belmont, CA: Wadsworth.
Baxandall, M. (1991) *Painting and Experience in Fifteenth-Century Italy*, Oxford: Oxford University Press.
Beer, S. (1964) *Cybernetics and Management*, New York: Wiley.
Bertman, M. A. (1981) *Hobbes: The Natural and the Artifacted Good*, Berne: Peter Lang.
Blau, P. M. (1968) 'Theories of Organization', *International Encyclopedia of the Social Sciences*, New York: Macmillan and The Free Press.
—— (1974) *On the Nature of Organizations*, New York: Wiley.
Boulding, K. E. (1956) *The Image*, Ann Arbor, MI: University of Michigan Press.
Braudel, F. (1985) *The Structures of Everyday Life*, New York: Harper & Row.
Burns, T. and Stalker, G. M. (1961) *The Management of Innovation*, London: Tavistock.
Callon, M. and Latour, B. (1981) 'Unscrewing the Big Leviathan', in K. Knorr and A. V. Cicourel (eds) *Advances in Social Theory and Methodology*, New York: Routledge.
Castoriadis, C. (1984) *Crossroads in the Labyrinth*, Brighton: Harvester Wheatsheaf.
Cooper, R. (1989) 'Modernism, Postmodernism and Organizational Analysis 3: the Contribution of Jacques Derrida', *Organization Studies*, 10/4, 479–502.
—— (1990) 'Organization/Disorganization', in J. Hassard and D. Pym (eds) *The Theory and Philosophy of Organizations: Critical Issues and New Perspectives*, London: Routledge; 1st published in *Social Science Information*, 25/2, 299–335, 1986.
—— (1992) 'Formal Organization as Representation: Remote Control, Displacement and Abbreviation', in M. Reed and M. Hughes (eds) *Rethinking Organization: New Directions in Organization Theory and Analysis*, London: Sage, 254–72.
Deleuze, G. (1988) *Foucault*, trans. S. Hand, Minneapolis, MN: University of Minnesota Press.
Derrida, J. (1973) *Speech and Phenomena*, trans. D. Allison, Evanston, IL: Northwestern University Press.
DiMaggio, P. J. and Powell, W. W. (1983) 'The Iron Cage Revisited: Institutional Isomorphism and Collective Rationality in Organizational Fields', *American Sociological Review*, 48, 147–60.
Douglas, M. (1987) *How Institutions Think*, London: Routledge.
Emery, F. E. and Trist, E. L. (1981) 'Sociotechnical Systems', in F. E. Emery (ed.) *Systems Thinking*, Harmondsworth: Penguin.
Foucault, M. (1988a) 'Theatrum Philosophicum', in D. F. Bouchard (ed.) *Language, Counter-memory, Practice*, Ithaca, NY: Cornell University Press.

—— (1988b) 'Questions of Method: an Interview with Michel Foucault', in K. Baynes, J. Bohman and T. McCarthy (eds) *After Philosophy*, Cambridge, MA: MIT Press.
Gauthier, D. P. (1969) *The Logic of Leviathan*, Oxford: Oxford University Press.
Goldsmith, M. M. (1968) *Hobbes's Science of Politics*, New York: Columbia University Press.
Hampton, J. (1988) *Hobbes and the Social Contract Tradition*, Cambridge: Cambridge University Press.
Heidegger, M. (1972) *On Time and Being*, New York: Harper & Row.
—— (1977) *The Question Concerning Technology and Other Essays*, trans. W. Lovitt, New York: Harper & Row.
Hobbes, T. (1650) *Leviathan*, Cambridge: Cambridge University Press, 1991.
Jacobs, S. (1990) 'Popper, Weber and the Rationalist Approach to Social Explanation', *The British Journal of Sociology*, 41/4, 559–70.
Katz, D. and Kahn, R. L. (1966) *The Social Psychology of Organizations*, New York: Wiley.
Latour, B. (1987) *Science in Action: How to follow Scientists and Engineers through Society*, Milton Keynes: Open University Press.
—— (1988) *The Pasteurization of France*, Cambridge, MA: Harvard University Press.
Law, J. (1986) 'On the Methods of Long-distance Control: Vessels, Navigation and the Portuguese Route to India', in J. Law (ed.) *Power, Action and Belief: a New Sociology of Knowledge? Sociological Review Monograph* 32, London: Routledge & Kegan Paul, 234–63.
Law, J. and Callon, M. (1988) 'Engineering and Sociology in a Military Aircraft Project: a Network Analysis of Technological Change', *Social Problems*, 35/3, 284–97.
Lewin, K. (1936) *Principles of Topological Psychology*, New York: McGraw-Hill.
McNeilly, F. S. (1968) *The Anatomy of Leviathan*, London: Macmillan.
Malavé, J. (1992) 'Systems, Networks and Structures', unpublished Ph.D thesis, University of Lancaster.
Marsden, P. V. (1990) 'Network Data and Measurement', *American Review of Sociology*, 16, 435–63.
Miller, E. J. and Rice, A. K. (1973) *Systems of Organization*, London: Tavistock.
Mintz, S. I. (1962) *The Hunting of Leviathan*, Cambridge: Cambridge University Press.
Mintzberg, H. (1990) 'The Design School: Reconsidering the Basic Premises of Strategic Management', *Strategic Management Journal*, 11, 171–95.
Mizruchi, M. S. (1982) *The American Corporate Network 1904–1974*, Beverly Hills, CA: Sage.
Moreno, J. (1934) *Who Shall Survive?*, New York: Beacon, 1953.
Oakeshott, M. (1975a) *On Human Conduct*, Oxford: Oxford University Press.
—— (1975b) *Hobbes on Civil Association*, Oxford: Basil Blackwell.
Parsons, T. (1966) *Societies*, Englewood Cliffs, NJ: Prentice Hall.
—— (1968) 'Social Systems', *International Encyclopedia of the Social Sciences*, New York: Macmillan and The Free Press.
Parsons, T. and Bales, R. (1953) 'The Dimensions of the Action-space', in T. Parsons, R. Bales and E. Shils (eds) *Working Papers on the Theory of Action*, New York: The Free Press.
Perrow, C. (1986) *Complex Organizations*, New York: Random House.
Pye, C. (1988) 'The Sovereign, the Theater, and the Kingdom of Darknesse: Hobbes and the Spectacle of Power', in S. Greenblatt (ed.) *Representing the English Renaissance*, Berkeley, CA: University of California Press.
Rapoport, A. (1968) 'General Systems Theory', *International Encyclopedia of the Social Sciences*, New York: Macmillan and The Free Press.
Scott, W. R. (1987) *Organizations: Rational, Natural and Open Systems*, Englewood Cliffs, NJ: Prentice Hall.

Selznick, P. (1948) 'Foundations of the Theory of Organization', *American Sociological Review*, 13, 25–35.
Serres, M. (1983) *Hermes: Literature, Science, Philosophy*, Baltimore, MD: Johns Hopkins University Press.
Shrader, C. B., Lincoln, J. R. and Hoffman, A. N. (1989) 'The Network Structure of Organizations: Effects of Task Contingencies and Distributional Form', *Human Relations*, 42/1, 43–66.
Skinner, Q. (1972) 'The Context of Hobbes's Theory of Political Obligation', in M. Cranston and R. S. Peters (eds) *Hobbes and Rousseau*, New York: Doubleday.
Stinchcombe, A. L. (1965) 'Social Structure and the Founding of Organizations', in A Stinchcombe (ed.) *Stratification and Organization*, Cambridge: Cambridge University Press, 1986.
Stokman, F. N., Van der Knoop, J. and Wasseur, F. W. (1988) 'Interlocks in the Netherlands: Stability and Careers in the Period 1960–1980', *Social Networks*, 10, 183–208.
Stokman, F. N., Ziegler, R. and Scott, J. (1985) *Networks of Corporate Power*, Cambridge: Polity Press.
Strauss, L. (1966) *The Political Philosophy of Hobbes*, Chicago, IL: University of Chicago Press.
Thompson, G, Frances, J., Levacic, R. and Mitchell, J. (eds) (1991) *Markets, Hierarchies and Networks*, London: Sage.
Tuck, R. (1989) *Hobbes*, Oxford: Oxford University Press.
Van Riejen, W. and Veerman, D. (1988) 'An Interview with Lyotard', *Theory, Culture and Society*, 5, 277–309.
Vattimo, G. (1991) *The End of Modernity*, Cambridge: Polity Press.
Watkins, J. W. N. (1973) *Hobbes's System of Ideas*, London: Hutchinson.
Weber, M. (1947) *The Theory of Social and Economic Organization*, New York: The Free Press.
Weber, S. (1982) 'The Limits of Professionalism', *Oxford Literary Review*, 5/1–2, 59–79.
Willinger, M. and Zuscovitch, E. (1988) 'Towards the Economics of Information-Intensive Production Systems: the Case of Advanced Materials', in G. Dosi, C. Freeman, R. Nelson, G. Silverberg and L. Soete (eds) *Technical Change and Economic Theory*, London: Pinter.

6

ON THE RIM OF REASON

Rolland Munro

Things as they are, are changed upon the blue guitar
(Wallace Stevens)

Introduction

Organization theorists are mesmerized by various forms of a segmentation thesis. Selznick (1948, 1966), for example, differentiated between formal and informal systems. Dalton (1959: 3) puzzled over the gap between 'official and unofficial' ways of doing things. The Tavistock researchers set up a division between a technological organization (equipment and process layout) and a work organization (people and their tasks). The 'new institutionalists' de-couple formal structure, with its highly rationalized appearance, from actual organizational practice. The 'guru quacks' champion a 'strong' corporate culture over formal modes of accounting control. And, more recently, Roberts (1991) has theorized a duality between hierarchical and social forms of accountability. The colouring in of key distinctions ranges variously, but the picture of the organization as segmented remains.[1] This chapter explores this recurrence of organization theory in the form of dualisms. Indeed, I want to go further and contest a 'world picture' which seems, increasingly, to identify the formation of dualisms *as* theory. While clearly not every dualism takes on the status of theory, organization theory might be caricatured as an archaeological site in which none of the competing dualisms making up 'organization theory' ever become abandoned, either from the textbook or from everyday practice.

I want to begin more specifically by questioning the current status of one particular artefact, the organization chart. Once a centre-piece of administrative theory, the organization chart was one, albeit simple, way of picturing formal organization. However, the organization chart has come to be seen as a mere paper representation of formal lines of authority or accountability. Instead of being read as the most potent symbol in organizations, the organization chart has become increasingly marginalized as window dressing. This is not just to see things in the eye of the sociologist, for whom the organization chart has long been little more than an expression of wishful thinking, a persistently failing attempt to superimpose hierarchy on social interaction; or, more provocatively, a Weberian attempt to impose rational thought over human emotion. Even the managerialists, in giving their attention to empowerment, core values, team-building, de-layering and business process re-engineering, also appear to be caught in a new commercial agenda (Munro and Hatherly, 1993) that accords scant attention to rank.

The organization chart seems now virtually abandoned on all sides.[2] This gives me some pause for thought. An earlier marginalizing of this formal device undoubtedly provided an antidote to a trivial story of power: the administrative dogma that equated power with organization rank. But what are the benefits once the managerialists themselves have moved on? If the 'new managerialism' (Ezzamel, Lilley and Willmott, 1994) now champions the so-called soft variables, then the attendant danger, as I will argue, is to overlook the importance, practical and theoretical, of devices like the organization chart. In the 'new managerialism', not everything is as it seems, and in trivializing the chart as merely symbolic, we may overlook ways in which its potency is being revitalized.

Of a more general concern is this framing of organization theory around its dualisms. In opposition to a reliance on dualistic thinking, I want to suggest how formal material, like the organization chart, interpenetrates everyday social interaction. Once we understand the different ways in which all informal occasions are mediated by formal material and devices, we can proceed without making dualisms foundational to organization theory. This much is clear. There is, in truth, no formal, or informal, merely material and circumstances with which we produce such differences as *effects*. We need to stop thinking in terms of the dualisms being separate, or even overlapping, systems and begin investigating how it is that actors help create 'occasions' as either formal or informal.[3]

But I am also asking a different question. I am asking what happens when the dualisms become stabilized as artefacts of organization practice. Should we now begin to see the distinction between formal and informal less as a topic and more as a resource? My concern here is not one of purifying organization theory, but rather of following the theories as artefacts as they enter and alter practice. So this is the question: has not this organizing of theory in the form of dualisms itself become something of a device: one that is operated on not only by managers, but by all organization participants? In illustrating this theme, I will explore the possibility that the organization chart is at its most potent when it is being made most recessive. Once our conceptions of organization theory are more clear, I will then go on to suggest some relations between dualisms and a 'world picture' of theory.

Hierarchy and interaction

Read one way, an organization chart is a series of lines that connects particular parts of the organization. As an image of connectedness, it delineates what is being brought together. Read in another way, however, the chart depicts a set of 'gaps'. In this reverse image, that of division, the chart is instructing what is to be 'held apart'. It incites us over what is to be *made* (and kept) different.

As an image of connectedness, the organization chart, then, is also an image of division. What is to be linked, brought together, also has to be rendered apart. Of course, lines of division vary. In a functional organization, for example, production arrangements are symbolized as separate from customer service. Maternity wards may be separated off from acute medical care. Or, in a more integrated structure, product division A is symbolized as a separate business unit from product division B. Geriatric wards may be kept distinct from paediatric units, each with their own consultants, and so on.

Considered together, therefore, the organization chart is a matter of di-vision. Adopting Cooper's formulation, there are two visions, each vision an 'intrinsic component' of the division (Cooper, 1989: 51). Hence, the two readings of the chart, either as connection or as division, depend on whether one makes the lines or the gaps, the 'intrinsic component'. Whether an organization chart is read as a 'bringing together', or a 'rendering apart', depends on which vision is being made the 'figure' and which vision is being made the 'ground'; which vision is made 'proximal' and which 'distal' (Cooper and Law, 1995).

The first reading of connection is traced through the 'line', the vertical run of connections that superimpose hierarchy on various parts. In defining *hierarchy*, Cooper suggests: 'In hierarchy, it is recognized that systems, social or otherwise, are structured around binary oppositions (e.g. good-bad, male-female) in which one of the terms dominates the other' (Cooper, 1989: 52). Cooper, with Derrida in mind, is clearly offering a more general definition than that associated with an organization chart. Nevertheless, the reliance on binary oppositions remains embedded in different possible readings of the chart: supervisor–supervisee, superior–subordinate, purchaser–provider, accountee–accountor, and in that, one term is positively valued and the other is negatively valued, the same consequences appear to follow: 'we are not dealing with a peaceful co-existence of a *vis-à-vis*, but rather a violent hierarchy. One of the two terms governs the other (axiologically, logically, etc.), or has the upper hand' (Derrida, 1981: 41). One term governs the other. Indeed, in returning Derrida's definition to the familiarities of the organization chart, an association with the potential for violence seems overfamiliar. People do lose jobs. Some bosses do make the life of their subordinates unbearable.

This brings us to the second reading: the 'gaps', the gaps that appear where no connections have been ruled in; the gap between purchasing and production, between sales and service, or between one plant and another plant. Or, the gap between rehabilitation care and wards devoted to acute medicine, or the gap between teaching and research. The spaces in the horizontal frame in which social interaction appears ruled out.

So what about interaction? Cooper, again following Derrida, defines *interaction* as a continuous double movement within the binary opposition. Cooper continues: 'In fact, the relationship between the apparently opposing terms is really one of mutual definition in which the individual terms actually inhabit each other' (Cooper, 1989: 52). One effect of this mutual definition is such that the positively-valued term (for example, superior) is defined only by contrast to the negatively-valued second term (for example, subordinate). This contrast is where a potential for 'slippage' lies. A mutuality of definition makes any basis for contrast 'undecidable'. In 'interaction' the individual terms give way to a 'process where opposites merge in a constant *undecidable* exchange of attributes' (Norris, 1987: 35). Interaction is a process, therefore, that goes beyond a fashionable discussion of 'fractals' (Wagner, 1991). It is not just that the shoreline is 'fuzzy', an indistinguishable mud of sand and water. In that each term is co-constituting of the other, there is a subtle process of sociality at work here, one that involves persons 'rendering' terms apart. We will return to this matter of sociality in a moment but, ahead of this, we turn to explore the 'logics' of division.

The logics of division

In introducing his terms 'hierarchy' and 'interaction', Cooper too readily treats Derrida's analysis as if it existed as a binary division. This is unfortunate, for Derrida's (1982) hostility to a founding dualism is captured in the impossibility of his own term *différance*, a hybrid of the terms 'to differ' and 'to defer'. Cooper's own terms come close. There is, of course, an aspect of hierarchy in the idea of 'to differ' and, in treating interaction as undecidable, Cooper also captures something of the notion 'to defer'. But what Cooper fails to stress is a 'reserve' we need to put on his own explanatory terms. Just as 'to differ' spills over into 'to defer', and vice versa, so the terms that make up the contrast between 'hierarchy' and 'interaction' need to be thought of as also existing in 'interaction'. In this respect, what Cooper omits to underline is that hierarchy is already a di-vision. Within the concept of hierarchy there are two visions, where, as already noted, each vision is an 'intrinsic component' of the di-vision. In any hierarchy, there are two terms, each in interaction with the other. But this is not, conventionally, what we see. What we see is the appearance of one term governing the other. The potential for 'slippage' is obviated. Insofar as hierarchy requires a binary opposition, such as good–bad or superior–subordinate, that binary opposition is already, and irredeemably, caught within 'interaction'. We may better consider this complexity as the effect of what Cooper (1989) calls the two logics of division. First, there is a *division of labour*. This is a most familiar logic. As terms, for example, hierarchy and interaction can be considered to exist in a division of labour, each term taking in what the other does not.

In this way, the distinction of hierarchy and interaction may itself be read as a binary opposition – with, say, the managerialists and the sociologists each hierarchizing one term, hierarchy or interaction, as governing the other. There is, however, a further complexity. Within this logic, hierarchy can be seen to be a device for bringing back together that which the division of labour has already made separate. Considered as a mode of ordering, then, hierarchy brings together parts of the organization. It is hierarchy which 'joins'.[4] But these are parts that are also, and at once, the fractured effects of a division of labour. Along the horizontal 'gaps', work may have been allocated on the basis that some activities are, for example, concerned with drug prescription and that other activities are concerned with delivering the drugs to patients. Vertically, work may have been allocated on the basis that some work, say, is supervisory and other work is task-oriented. In traditional organization charts, the vertical is the device for bringing the horizontal segments back together. As Cooper remarks, the division of labour is 'where the emphasis is placed on the specialization of skills and occupations *in an hierarchical framework*' (Cooper, 1989: 51, emphasis added). So there is a pattern of recursiveness to be explained.

This brings me to the second logic of division. This is related to the creation of 'gaps', the making and keeping of things apart. We can think of this as what Cooper calls, incisively, a *labour of division*. Unfortunately, Cooper's specific remarks here are overly brief, adding little more than the idea that this is a 'differentiation process', a process that he also describes as 'social' (1989: 51). I want to go on here to suggest that Cooper's emphasis on the 'labour of division' follows interaction, rather than hierarchy. The labour of division is the social process of rendering apart. This labour is continuous and unremitting. It is never fixed or certain since, as mentioned above, there is a 'constant *undecidable* exchange of attributes'. Terms, for example like consumption and production, exist in mutual definition of each other, so they have to be 'rendered apart'. Horizontally, I labour to recognize what is, for example, design work, that which sets specifications, and what is delivery work, that which meets specifications. Vertically, I am able to recognize that some work is deemed to be, for example, strategic and that other work is taken as operational. Similarly, and recursively, the terms 'hierarchy' and 'interaction' may be also understood as being in a 'continuous double movement'. In order to act as a binary opposition, the terms hierarchy and interaction have to be continuously forged out of a process that merges them. To differ is also to defer, and deferral necessitates making a difference. The opposition of hierarchy and interaction has to be created and reproduced against this '*undecidable* exchange of attributes'. Attempts to define terms are always partial and provisional (see also Strathern, 1991). Within language in use, there is no fixed division of labour. Rather, through an unending 'labour of division' there is a constant creation and reproduction of each dualism. Within the binary opposition of hierarchy and interaction, each term *becomes* necessary: each props the other up. It should be clear, from the foregoing example, that we do not ever have a choice between tracing the lines or excavating the gaps, between a vision of hierarchy or a vision of interaction, between a division of labour and a labour of division. Without the line there are no gaps. Without the gaps, there are no lines. Just as each 'vision' is dependent on the other, so each 'logic' of division depends on a coexistence of the other.

Inclusion and exclusion

We are ever on the rim of reason, in di-vision. But it is its peculiarity that reason never seems this way. A constant obviation of the potential for 'slippage' not only installs one reading over another. It annuls a sense of interaction and creates and reproduces an appearance of hierarchy. The labour of division, as constant, as unremitting, is 'forgotten'. Instead we ontologize the division of labour. We fix on segmentation effects, the division, and forget the labour.

Since the early experiments of the Gestalt psychologists, we have of course become familiar with inversions in the hierarchy of figure and ground. What is taken as proximal one moment can be taken as distal the next (Cooper and Law, 1995). But inversion is not the same as undecidability. Only by insisting on undecidability can philosophers like Heidegger or Cooper *write* on the rim of reason. The point here seems similar to Derrida (1978: 31–63) who, in his close reading of Descartes, shows that Descartes' moment of truth, his momentary escape from the *logos* depends on his momentary indifference to whether he is thinking truth or thinking madness. All we can do, if we want to *appear* monofocal, appear logical, is make our readings conform to our chosen perspective: *as* an observer, or *as* a participant; *as* a managerialist, or *as* a sociologist. In this respect, what Derrida, and others, refer to as the 'logos' may be understood as an *obligation*. The obligation of the logos is to obviate one reading in favour of the other. This matter of obligation (the suppression of 'slippage' at its very moment of use) brings me to the issue of belonging. Where there are sides, where, say, the organization chart represents us, as belonging here, or belonging there, then we have to know where we stand. We have to see the world *from our position*. We have to take sides. We feel called upon and the call is always to obviate one reading in favour of the other. And, as always, it seems as if there are only two sides to take. For example, if we were to position ourselves as managerialists, our reading might depict *inclusion*. For the managerialist, the organization chart advertises who, or what, is to be included where. Although it seems banal to spell it out, the chart 'places', say, the plant managers in line with the production director; or the ward manager as reporting to the nursing director. In this case, the chart can be understood to be merely affirmative of a narrow form of belonging, emplacement. It underlines normal channels for a descent of authority and, with this, emphasizes those responsibilities for reporting which are already known. However, other relationships need not be so self-evident.

A different reading, that of belonging, might be based around the theme of *exclusion*. The organization chart also instructs each of us over who, or what, is to be excluded from where. Exclusion, as Douglas (1975) has pointed out, gets to the heart of the relations between knowledge and belonging. In this respect, the organization chart can be understood to act as a ritual artefact for emplacement, mediating acts of knowing and acts of belonging. In a functional organization, for example, the chart is expressive of different territories. Anyone from marketing would feel this as soon as they stepped inside a plant in most organizations, certainly as they were structured up to five or ten years ago in the mid to late

1980s.[5] Of course feelings of exclusion are not *only* a consequence of an organization chart. Other matters than emplacement enter into the processes of filling out a sense of belonging. Indeed, these matters, like unofficial culture, may appear to make more sense of people's feelings of exclusion. And no doubt interpreting formal placement as an 'exclusion' seems banal, especially in the context of a simplistic functional structure. But, in the context of more complex structures, as I hope to show, much more is at stake.

Are we fish or fowl? In moments of doubt, and these are ever present in matters of belonging, the chart offers itself, symbolically, as a shared expression. As a shared expression, one that is kept in constant play even when not on show, the organization chart is more than an incantatory device through which relative positions can be affirmed. It is, as with all ritual devices, potentially transformative. My accomplishing a difficult mission can be read as underlining your wisdom in entrusting me to go ahead. You giving me friendly advice might also be interpreted as a case of my subordinate bringing information for me to act on. What is interesting is the extent to which each of us can help the other *feel* the occasion to be formal or informal.

The labour of division, the rendering of terms as contrasts, relies on the 'slippage' as a resource that affords its own obviation. The transformations are endless. As David Clare, president of Johnson and Johnson, argues:

> If a manager insists on a course of action and we (the executive committee) have misgivings, 9 times out of 10 we will let him go ahead. If we say no, and the answer should have been yes, we say, 'Don't blame us, it was your job to sell us on the idea and you didn't do that'.
>
> (Anthony, Dearden and Bedford, 1989: 502)

As I often remark, hierarchies are mechanisms for transmitting credit upwards and divesting blame downwards. But to speak so is to rely on a shorthand that too easily reifies the organization chart *as* a hierarchy. As an example of what Cooper is talking about in terms of interaction and mutuality, we can recognize some of the background to David Clare's comment. In terms of accountability, it is first and foremost a senior manager's responsibility to listen. The interest, then, is in how senior managers might divest themselves of this responsibility. Once senior executives of a company like Johnson and Johnson express misgivings on everything, they create circumstances in which their responsibility to listen is turned into a responsibility for the subordinate to tell them sufficiently well. So forcing subordinates to 'sell' to them becomes precisely a paradigm case of the senior directors doing *their* job.

To summarize the earlier discussion, it is worth remembering that hierarchy is only one 'component' of a di-vision. What I want to stress here, however, is how acts of knowing, inclusion, also become acts of belonging, exclusion, and vice versa. As in the Johnson and Johnson example, being placed as a subordinate can entail being positioned in particular ways over knowledge, expertise and accountability. And more. In order to belong, to be included in interaction *as* a manager, as a member of the group of managers, one *has* to know. The difficulty is that matters of belonging and matters of knowing also exist in mutual definition; they too are intrinsically undecidable.[6]

Travelling in advance

As a ritual artefact, the organization chart might be expected to be of interest to sociologists, especially for those with a continuing interest in bureaucracy. But this is not usually so.[7] Focusing, they suppose, on everyday interaction, the sociologist wants to know only what *social* relations are being reproduced and distorted. Their (mis)reading of the social as interaction *minus* technology informs them, they suppose, of the asymmetries in power relations. But, by investing power as causal to social relations, by looking at interaction *as* asymmetries, it is as if they assume some 'have' power and others do not. Thus, although appearing to disregard hierarchy, they actually re-instantiate it. Old dualisms perpetuate.

The sociologist's reliance on reading everyday interaction for relations of power is not a method peculiar to sociologists. Quite to the contrary, this is, as a matter of method, something on which the 'new managerialism' also relies. Being competent in reading everyday interaction for relations of power becomes constitutive of 'membership'. To ensure one is included in the group of 'real' managers (as distinct from being classed as, say, a 'glorified supervisor'), members may become complicit in making rank recessive. And once in play, the matter becomes a self-fulfilling prophecy. The more rank is made recessive, the more interaction becomes 'instrumental' in finding out relations of power. The more interaction becomes 'instrumental' in finding out relations of power, the more rank can be made recessive. So with these possibilities in mind, I do not see the sense in overlooking the capacity, within interaction, for persons making a continual return to notions of rank. For, in that the chart advertises inclusion and exclusion, it also advertises inclusion and exclusion daily to those engaged in the day-to-day. As a shared expression, the organization chart is already active. A reading of the lines of inclusion and a reading of the gaps of exclusion is already part of any interaction. Some qualifications are necessary here. First, to say that the organization chart prefigures interaction is not the same as to say that it freezes interaction *as* hierarchy. Nor is it to suggest that its propensity to set up one reading rather than another inheres solely within a process of socialization. It is to say, instead, that its potentiality *travels* ahead of each and every interaction. The chart is always 'in advance' (Cooper, 1993: 284). Second, to say that the organization chart 'travels' is not quite, as will become clearer later, to suggest that it is of the same status as the 'immutable mobile' that Latour (1987, 1993) has developed from John Law's (1986) example of maps used by the Portuguese navigators. The organization chart has something of this quality, but it is not only a representation of space. The relationships exhibited can also be understood as particularly affecting 'spaces' of representation (Munro, 1993). Existing in interaction, 'lines of authority' are interpretations that constantly have to be materialized and dematerialized. As interpretations, their materiality is different, much more provisional and hence less 'durable' than the more ostensibly physical examples to which Latour (1991) attends.

This travelling *in advance* bifurcates 'within' spaces of representation, depending on whether we need to know our 'standing' (hierarchy), or argue our belonging (interaction).[8] With respect to the specifics of the organization chart, I am arguing, therefore, how aspects of the formal can have their effect in the informal. Just as the opposite is true. In a strict sense of formal accounting relations, for example, people do not *belong* to any other space than that to which they are 'officially' accorded. They do not belong, that is, at least in any sense other than as an intermediary, a transient being who has to justify her/his presence for as long as she remains in another part of the organization. And while a nurse from the maternity ward might accompany a mother to the operating theatre, she/he may do so as a comfort, someone to hold the mother's hand. Similarly, although a production engineer from product division A might enjoy visiting a plant in product division B, he or she remains transient. As a visitor, they cannot stay beyond the duration of their mission; their time 'belongs' elsewhere.

Whether it is over our standing *vis-à-vis* the organization chart, or our emplacement in interaction, there is an 'undecidable' exchange of attributes. What I want to press is that devices like the organization chart enter, however recessively, into this undecidability. The organization chart travels in ways that have no respect for the borders of different spaces in a dualistic thinking. Although formal in design, neither placement nor status can be contained within the space of the formal.

Indeed, what I want now to go on to argue is precisely that contemporary management techniques *rely* on formal devices interpenetrating the informal. This is the condition of possibility that facilitates the contemporary manager's trick of bracketing out rank at the very moment when they most rely on it. Importantly this happens in ways that sustain a dualism, rather than overcome it. To illustrate the richness at work here, I now turn to some specific field examples.

Charting the field (1)

Any binary 'opposition', such as hierarchy and interaction, or formal and informal controls, or an official and unofficial 'culture', is an effect. As something that is produced and reproduced, its very stability has to be explained, not relied on as a causal agent. One way of explaining these stabilities is to examine organization practice in detail. Not, I should stress, to merely add detail. In its elimination of difference, a mere collection of items seeks no more than confirmation of a prior theory (Popper, 1963). Such a move is self-sealing. Rather we need to work towards the detail of a writing that is sufficiently rich in its diversity as to provide its own explanation.

In setting up my ethnography of the Bestsafe company (Munro, 1995a), I drew on the organization chart initially for structuring interview material; material intended to serve as background to the prolonged periods of participant observation that followed later. In so much as I was interested in gleaning organizational 'accounts', especially in the form of stories, I figured that interviewing across seven levels of hierarchy would create a sufficient range of subordinate–supervisor pairings over which I could cross-check manager 'stories'. As my time in the field developed, especially during the long periods of participant observation, I became aware that the pattern of most intense loyalties also lay along the grid of subordinate–supervisor relationships: I say 'aware' advisedly, not only because this finding greatly surprised me, but because these relations were not enunciated in any explicit way. No one made claims about being loyal to their superiors, whether in the interview material or in the day-to-day. Indeed, relations with superiors were described in a quite casual manner, and not at all as relations of fealty. Further, their claims to me that they enjoyed considerable 'autonomy' fitted neatly with later observations of a virtual absence of explicit instructions by superiors. Yet, despite this apparent confirmation of the formal being decoupled from actual organizational practice, the extent to which the 'line' governed conduct gradually became clear.

Around a pattern of presences and absences, I was able to reconstruct a pattern of kinship among the operating managers that traced a patrilineal descent of authority back to an attenuation of 'access' by their head of division. Good 'access' was read by the beneficiary, and his or her colleagues, as indicative of a manager doing something right. In these circumstances, delegated authority could be tentatively assumed, without it ever having been explicitly given. Similarly, difficulties with access implied disapproval over current 'delivery'. Even where the offender seemed recalcitrant over changing his or her priorities, others could 'read' the exclusion for what it symbolized, an absence of delegated authority, and amend their priorities accordingly. Lines of authority seemed at their strongest, then, when relations of hierarchy were least evident.

I call this system 'managing by ambiguity'. Unusually today, there was within Bestsafe almost no reliance on formal accounting measures. This had led me to expect more explicit leadership, or at least a 'strong' culture. But neither of these two matters were present in ways discussed in other ethnographies, nor was strategy ever discussed or communicated. Indeed, instructions, particularly over what might constitute 'delivery', were almost entirely absent; rather than be given top down, instructions were almost always being inferred bottom up. Likewise authority was almost never granted top down, but also had to be inferred, in interactions, from the piecemeal gossip among one's neighbouring managers. It surprised me to see how much hierarchy was actually strengthened by this absence of explicit instructions. Indeed, I am tempted to trace the success of Bestsafe to this deferral, this apparent abdication of 'power over' in favour of the processes of interaction. Rather than legislate over difference, undecidability was left in the hands of those best able to resolve it, at least beforehand. Once events began to speak for themselves, operating managers could of course be called to account for going the wrong way. Why had they not taken the obvious path, the way that retrospect had made much more clear? Actually this kind of reckoning seldom happened face-to-face. Instead, it was as if events 'spoke for themselves' over who was making the grade – who was gaining the identity of being 'someone who delivers'. While much of the detail is missing from this gross abbreviation of the study, it should be sufficient to suggest that power relations were both an effect of interaction, as the sociologists argue, and that rank affected how to 'do' managing, as the managerialists suppose. When we stop being the dupes of our own dualisms, we can see how artefacts, such as that of the organization chart, come to be drawn into a process of interaction. This point requires some further comment.

In examining the detail of organization practice, we can look to see how people are managing their everyday use not only *as* hierarchy, but in ways that keep *making* hierarchy happen when it is apparently nowhere to be seen. Thus, the general point I am making should not be reduced to one of paradox. Certainly there is an air of paradox in the idea that strong systems of command and control work best without commands. But this is only paradoxical if we hang on to our dualisms and unnecessarily equate hierarchy with notions of command and control. At a sufficient level of detail, most so-called paradoxes, I suspect, dissolve. This is not quite to argue that the dualisms themselves dissolve. Just that the requisite level of detail arrives when we understand how the work conducted by each aspect of a binary opposition interpenetrates and intermeshes with each other. This was certainly the case with Bestsafe, when it became clear how all aspects, formal and informal, official and unofficial, hierarchical and social, worked together.

Charting the field (2)

The formal is as steeped in 'interaction' as the informal. In Cooper's formulation, interaction is always inclusive of hierarchy as a 'component'. Indeed, in terms of providing material for an 'extension' of self (Munro, 1996a), the formal offers a rich source of artefacts for identity work. This is where the sociologists have been negligent. In a disdain for what they take to be a managerial perspective, they overlook a different story. Feelings of belonging cannot just be relegated to the unsurveilled passages of the informal, the unofficial, the social. At least the social in its attenuated form; as something pure and distinct from the smell of anything formal or official.

The second example I want to draw on comes from what Cohen (1992) calls post-fieldwork fieldwork. Having studied the effects of a purchaser–provider regime being introduced into a district council, I went back to re-examine an earlier study of the Worldbest company (Munro, 1996b). This retrospective analysis suggested various ways in which the organization chart, if implicitly, had actually been redrawn. Even if no one is ready to place plant managers directly under someone called a marketing director, changes to lines of authorization and flows of accountability can signal a different structure: one that *excludes* the possibility of the production division simply dumping on the marketing division all that it makes. Indeed, it was more or less this reverse relationship of a 'make and sell' policy that I found to be the case in Worldbest. This reversal will take a moment's explanation.

Prior to its take-over by Goodadverts, marketing was conducted separately within each unit that produced the 'brand' for sale in world markets. Subsequent to the take-over, the distribution outlets moved from being twenty-five per cent owned by Worldbest to seventy-five per cent owned. At the same time, through the creation of a system of 'internal' markets, marketing and sales were repositioned as a single (monopolistic) purchaser from the plants. In my first analysis, I had assumed that this talk of markets was just 'intended' strategy. I saw the abandonment of a formal structure of product divisions as merely dressing up a temporary centralization, one designed to ensure short-term control. At the time I saw no particular connection between a statement of ideals and the 'enactment' (Weick, 1977, 1979) of a long-term strategy. But I recognize now that it was a mistake to think that a de-coupling of marketing and production merely marked a return to a traditional functional structure. In that the plants have, first, to bid against each other in order to act as providers and, second, to audit themselves on 'quality, service, flexibility and cost', this is a deliberate transposition of previous arrangements. First, in a simulation of the market, line management in production is being subordinated within the 'horizontal' relations of purchasers and providers. In that the marketing arm in the role of purchasers is able to select among the 'bids' and set the specifications, there is an official hierarchization of previously more horizontal relations. Second is the sustained and persistent 'rubbishing' of the previous system as 'old company', which I had initially mistaken for drum-beating by the new managers. Certainly the top managers of Worldbest, especially those sent in by Goodadverts, were openly attacking the 'old culture' set up by the product divisions. But, although I could detail the new rhetoric which put the systems of the previous company under a sustained attack *as* old culture, I saw no substance in the new rhetoric. My sense of things at the time was that traditional mores would outlast and undermine the paraphernalia of core values (quality, cost, flexibility and service) and the concomitant 'technology' of nonfinancial measures being created to support these. But, and here is the point, the traditional mores of social interaction were not being attacked as if there were an unofficial culture: the traditional mores were being attacked as if these related directly to *formal* systems. The matters under attack, such as the 'brand loyalty' of the 'old' organization and its lack of a 'sense of markets', were being traced by the new managers to an organization that had been previously driven by accounting numbers. So, suddenly, it is as if there is no segmentation thesis, as if there are no dualisms, and, in a sense, the new managers are right. I began to make sense of their talk of markets only when I began to recognize that it was not the organization chart, but what it 'advertises' that was under attack. It was traditional *readings* of the organization chart that were being treated as an enemy.

In a revision that is as reminiscent of David Clare's words, reported earlier, senior managers positioned themselves *as if* they knew more strategy, but not in ways that go on to insist that they should disseminate this. Rather, in ways that are similar to the approach taken at Bestsafe, it is up to the operating managers to find their 'instructions' themselves. With the formal channels blocked off, operating managers were turned towards the 'interaction' of the informal. If the managerialists had ever lagged behind the sociologists in their appreciation and reliance on the informal, they had caught up and, indeed, were now ahead.[9]

In terms of the earlier analysis of Cooper's work we should certainly expect to find a division of labour between formal and informal channels, and so on. But to settle on the requisite level of detail is to say more than we should understand the 'function' of each, or even go on to identify which aspect 'governs' the other. We should also expect to find a labour of division perpetuating each and every dualism: a sociality that is bound within a division of labour, but a sociality that is also, and always, overcoming its 'constant *undecidable* exchange of attributes'.

Within any sociality, it is the undecidable that is being organized. But so, too, do formal relations enter into this undecidability, reshaping its form between who is to 'bid' and who is to decide: between who is to find the 'instructions' and who is to judge their efficacy and over who is to listen, and when, and who is to be made responsible for making others listen. For example, the question 'who listens?' seesaws between expectations about being silent in order to receive instructions and expectations over speaking up first so that the senior manager has the opportunity to defer judgement. Think of the reserve that comes merely from turning the reply of 'yes' into 'I hear what you say'. These examples suggest we have to check continually to see exactly how each term of a binary opposition mutually inhabits the other. We have to find out how each aspect of a so-called dualism is working in a 'continuous double movement'.

Discussion

Seen not as a mere representation of space, but as a device for stabilizing 'spaces' of representation, the organization chart is an example, perhaps the grossest example, of the reversal that Heidegger addresses in his essay, 'The Age of the World Picture' (1977a). Inverting the usual idea of pictures as representations of the world, Heidegger's theme is that the world is made to resemble its representations: 'world picture, when understood essentially, does not mean a picture of the world but the world conceived and grasped as picture' (Heidegger, 1977a: 129). This is the vital point of representation, it is always a re-presentation. The world is not only being pictured within interaction, it becomes conceived and grasped *as* picture.

Things are changed upon the blue guitar. To re-semble implies also a reassembly. As Cooper says, 'world picture' means 'the world is made into a vast construction site of detached and controllable representations' (1993: 288). But, this is perhaps to overstate matters, for re-assembly is not all. The terror is not only a mechanization of the world understood as 'out there reality', the terror is also in a mechanization of the world understood *as* 'picture'. Where people, from the

Victorian father to the president of Johnson and Johnson, insist on truth being responsive to their delineated authority.

In his analysis, Heidegger was concerned with how 'we' become like our representations. So this, too, enters into the undecidability. Thus, Heidegger's theme captures not just the real being made in the image of the ideal. Real and ideal also constitute a further binary opposition. A construction of reality is never literally just that, a construction of the real. Again, as we saw before, the apparently opposing terms of the real and the ideal mutually define each other. In constructing the world, it is being re-turned, made to conform with our representations of it, as it should or could be. In this re-turning of the world to picture that makes stable the picturing of the picture. This is the potential for horror.[10] What I am suggesting is that the organization chart is just such a mechanization. It is precisely its stability that makes it transportable across 'spaces' of representation: a stability that makes hierarchy seem first fundamental, then natural and, finally, normal. Nevertheless, as I stated before, the organization chart should not be conceived of as an 'immutable mobile'. Certainly, it travels 'in advance'. But, today, for purposes of understanding contemporary managing techniques, this offers only part of the picture. In its variations on the segmentation thesis, organization theory not only pictures the world made up of binary divides. In so picturing them, it orders the dualisms of organization theory as a 'standing reserve' (Cooper, 1993: 283). This is now discussed.

Heidegger views technology as transforming everything into being ready for production, a standing 'in advance'. In the examples of my fieldwork given above, I have been concerned to contest the traditional view that suggests that a world that can be 'represented' in dualisms. Far from dualisms acting in opposition to each other, to shape and colour the world, the dualisms themselves form part of this standing 'in advance' – this re-turning of the world to 'picture' that Heidegger analyses as a circumnavigation of modernity. Effects such as formal and informal channels work to augment and support each other, and especially so when we have come to regard each as a 'failing technology'. As soon as the formal channel fails in its standing 'in advance', the informal channels can act as a 'standing reserve'. As soon as the intended strategy fails, the 'enacted' strategy moves in. As soon as the official culture packs up, the unofficial can be relied upon. As soon as hierarchical forms of accountability become closed, more social forms take over. Or so it would seem, so let us go back over this argument more carefully.

The notion of people themselves becoming part of a 'standing-reserve' is certainly in line with Heidegger's own reasoning. Indeed, in his essay on technology, Heidegger sees this turning of people into a standing-reserve as the 'supreme danger':

> As soon as what is unconcealed no longer concerns man even as object, but exclusively as 'standing-reserve', and man in the midst of objectlessness is nothing but standing-reserve, then he comes to the very brink of a

precipitous fall, that is, he comes to the point where he himself will have to be taken as standing-reserve.

(Heidegger, 1977b: 308)

Everyday interaction, the 'social' to which the sociologist has been so romantically held captive, has, for Heidegger, become a mere standing-reserve. The idea is, of course, both true and palpable nonsense. We owe it to Foucault's (1970, 1977, 1991) work to have made much more explicit how it is that these 'other' spaces have their own forms of governance. The informal, the enacted, the unofficial, the 'social' are no such thing. They are all 'spaces' of representation governed by discourse effects. Possibly, although this is another argument, they are spaces of 'saying', rather than 'seeing' (Cooper, 1993; Munro, 1993; Latimer, 1994). But they all are spaces in which accounts, re-presentations, are travelling ahead of interaction, narrowly understood. In hierarchy and in interaction, in our division of labour and in our labour of division, in our inclusions and in our exclusions, these are all 'spaces' of representation; spaces in which our sociality, in all its dualisms, can be considered as more than making up a 'standing-reserve'. Following Heidegger, the 'social' is always caught up in the 'technological'. So we can think this matter differently. For none of this is to say that devices like the organization chart, even when in use, will be dwelt on endlessly. Quite the opposite may appear to be the case. As Giddens (1984) remarks, power is at its most effective when 'running silently'. Just as with sanctions, which seem to work best when used least, so the 'component' of hierarchy in the organization chart may be at its most effective when it is at its most recessive.

This is the twist in the tale of contemporary managerialism; the inversion that Heidegger and others have not anticipated. Once the 'informal', the 'everyday', the 'official', and the 'social' are governed through discourse effects, and have become a form of 'standing-reserve', it makes more sense for these to be positioned front-stage, evocative of a new democracy in organizing. Thus, the inversion, the re-positioning of the informal, the everyday as standing 'in advance' and the keeping of the 'formal' and the 'official' as back-up. Organization can feed off the informal and the everyday in ways that leave the 'economic' and 'the exceptional' increasingly as a *standing-reserve.*

It is just this inversion in the story of managerialism that is suggested by my field studies. Contrary to its stereotype, contemporary managerialism does not proceed, top down, through the formal, the official, the hierarchical, dragging the informal, the unofficial, the social, behind it. Nor, as the sociologists might have it, do managers ride on the informal, the unofficial, the social – with all their attendant apparatus of the formal, the official and the hierarchical merely floating on these. Both forms exist, but not separately. They exist, mutually, in 'interaction'. It is always tempting to argue that there are no separate spaces today, no dualisms. But a de-differentiation is always only partial; 'spaces' of representation for membership work feed on the old adage that there is no smoke without fire. They preserve difference at the same time as deferring it.

Hierarchy seeming absent, therefore, need not be confused with a lack of presence. However obviated, its presence can easily be re-called. For example, within everyday interaction, if someone 'forgets' his place, his 'emplacement' (see also Weber, 1990) as a subordinate, the superior can *make* the component of hierarchy present. She can re-call the organization chart to view with a gesture. Or make hierarchy re-present itself, by referring, say, to her responsibility to pass on her subordinate's account to her own superior. Or, by casually mentioning the appraisal that she should conduct next month. Or by questioning the expenses form her subordinate has left her to sign. Or by sitting on her subordinate's budget request.

Conclusion

The question of division animates the work of Robert Cooper. And it is by keeping division *as* a question that his writings become so valuable in keeping organization theory from its own managerialism. Where other theorists espouse new divisions, Cooper has opened up this process of differentiation as a question. Where others seem content to prescribe arrangements, top down, whereby this or that must be kept as distinct from that or this, Cooper has held up to view similarities in organizing strategies across the institutions of language, technology and social science. Where others have sought to close down organization theory as the study of organizations, particularly business organizations, Cooper has held out for a more general study of organizing.

Following Cooper, we have to stop adopting dualisms as administrative solutions to a search for organization theory. Instead, we can re-learn to 'see' organizing as it happens *through* the dualisms. This I take to be Cooper's (1993) crucial insight for organization theory: *no vision without division*. It is through dualisms, Derrida's binary oppositions, that we make up the world. Further, if more problematically, we can follow Cooper in recognizing how every division is also a di-vision. One 'component' of this is that we 'see' the world through the 'world pictures' that we produce and reproduce. The other 'component' is that, in making up identity and difference, we are also ordering and reordering the world through 'saying'. If Cooper is right in his formulation of division as di-vision, then there are no fundamental divisions and organization theory's quest to find its fixed point is over. There is never one fixed point in which to move the world, but an interplay of endless dualisms.

Cooper's contribution is critical in that it challenges conventional wisdom in at least three respects. First, divisions, such as that between culture and process, have come to represent the shape of organizations. They act as a 'world picture' of organizations. Indeed, it is no exaggeration to suggest that dualisms come to represent the modern organization: organizations, to be organizations today, incorporate rational *and* irrational conduct, information *and* gossip, cognitive *and* emotional behaviour, espoused *and* shared values. But this does not make them paradoxical; it merely means that we have to work harder to understand that dualistic theories are already at work as 'world pictures' within organizations.

Second, this picture of organizations as dualistic has helped partition the area for study between, say, the managerialists and the sociologists. The picture of organizations as dualistic facilitates a tidy division of labour, whereby the managerialists' black box culture and the sociologists bracket off the more technical processes like accountancy. These arrangements of convenience help, of course, to perpetuate theories of social action that are narrowly humanistic and exclude technology as *other*. In rethinking social theory we have to do more than pay lip service to technology as prosthetic and understand, instead, how differences in technology create differences in feelings of belonging.

Third, dualisms seem to *organize* theory. As well as representing organizations, dualisms come to picture theory as organized in particular ways. In that dualisms start to look foundational, 'division' comes to represent theory as its 'essence'. Dualisms take on the form of being the very *nature* of theory. The endless range of dualisms comes to organize theory itself *as* dualistic. This intimate tie between conceptions of theory and perceptions over what is 'organized' requires some further comment.

In line with Cooper's post-structuralism, what I have been suggesting is that much of a current appearance of paradox can be traced back to the effect of organizing theory on a foundation of dualisms. A basic point here, and it is an old argument of the ethnomethodologists, is to stop impaling the study of organizing on our own divisions, either as managerialists or as sociologists. Since Garfinkel (1967), the ethnomethodologists have argued that we have to see the 'methods' by which members make up their organizational practice. These methods, it has always been assumed, will be highly specific to each particular organizational practice. To be sure. But we need not stop there, *as if each organizational practice actually is water-tight from every other organizational practice*. To think so is to be culturally duped. In contrast to the relativism which insists on difference as ontological, I am suggesting that members draw on dualisms and divisions *as if* they were specific and foundational to their organizational practice. The 'technology' of membership work, I suggest, lies in how members make (their) dualisms appear as both specific and yet foundational.

It is in this spirit of inquiry, rather than as a surrender to their entrenchment, that I suggest it is a serious mistake to attempt to flatten the dualisms in which organization theory stands replete. Just as we cannot afford to take paradox as foundational, so we cannot simply have a 'bonfire of the dualisms' (Law, 1994). This is especially the case if, as I have just suggested, the 'technology' of membership work is for members to make (their) dualisms appear both specific and foundational. Where this is so, as researchers, we have to examine *how* members draw on dualisms and when to understand how they instantiate their practice, first, as the *same* as other members and second as *different* from every other organizational practice. Indeed, we can go just one step further and suggest that, far from the world being founded on dualisms, the world is moved *through* dualisms. As researchers of organizations, we can best understand who is moving whom, not by recourse to theories of domination, but by being able to elucidate which dualisms are being brought into being to elicit movement, and when.

To elucidate this idea, I have been suggesting that the organization chart is one device that is drawn on by members for making divisions, one that travels 'in advance' of interaction. Indeed, I suspect that it is only by attending to devices like the organization chart, its appearance and disappearance in accounts, its presence and absence in interaction, that we can learn about aspects of belonging that go beyond the narrow scope of lines of authority and responsibility. But the organization chart is only one device, and of necessity a particularly gross resource for pre-figuring divisions. There are many others that come to mind, particularly the profit and loss account with its equally troublesome division between revenue and cost.

I have given much attention to the organization chart to illustrate how, instead of looking to theory to stand 'in advance' of our representations, we had much better look at how such theories are already circulating as organizing devices. Instead of looking for a dualism to act foundationally, we can understand dualisms as organizing devices travelling 'in advance' of practice and facilitating members turning the world towards themselves as 'picture'.

So where does the formal and the informal, the official and the unofficial, stand in all this? Certainly organizing devices, such as the organization chart, could animate the informal as a 'standing-reserve', as Heidegger fears. My particular concern, however, has been to capture how these organizing devices animate sociality in ways that manufacture differences between the formal and the informal, the official and the unofficial. So it becomes as likely that the new managerialism works rather in reverse, letting the formal act as 'standing reserve'. But, and here is the catch, without theory going ahead, we no longer can expect to know which is formal and which is informal, what is intended and what is enacted, what is official culture and what is unofficial, what is hierarchy and what are social forms of accounting. This is all being decided, partially and provisionally, in the labour of division, in the here and now.

Notes

1 The consequent 'crisis' for organization theory stemming from its generation of dualisms has met with a varying response. In a popular mood which Tom Peters captures as that of 'thriving on chaos', a recent tendency has been to encourage managers to celebrate the dualisms. More often than not, researchers are also being asked to embrace paradox and contradiction as empirical fact, rather than critically examine these as anomalies in our reasoning. In this respect, Law's (1994) systematic attempt to 'make a bonfire' of the dualisms looks more appealing, but carries with it an implicit resort to hierarchy. Methodologically, the dictum, 'there are no dualisms', could be as problematic as a position which insists that 'there are only my dualisms'.
2 There are many stories of the organization chart being abandoned. Sometimes these are of the form 'that it changes too fast'. In other organizations, its absence excites

people into working backwards to establish their rank from other devices such as the presence of windows, the number of ceiling tiles and the model and make of car.

3 The idea of making 'occasions' of things is Garfinkel's (1967) (see also Latimer, 1994) and is crucial to a full appreciation of 'membership work'. None of this is to say therefore that dualisms between formal and informal controls, technical and social systems, or official and unofficial cultures, are unimportant for understanding how organizing works today. Quite the opposite. Knowing the nuances for, say, staging formality and informality is, following Goffman (1958), integral to organizing. However, a competence in slipping between the staging posts of any dualism also relies on a 'slippage' within the dualisms themselves. Dualisms, as will be discussed, are not all that they seem. They are not, for example, entities that we can rely on to provide explanation. To the contrary, as stable effects, dualisms are themselves something to be explained.

4 Hierarchy may be understood as also having a 'centralizing', and hence a controlling, process. This is to suggest that 'control' also involves a censoring of interaction and, with this, mutuality.

5 Within companies, concepts, such as integrated manufacturing or producing to order, are much in vogue. These attempts to make production responsive to 'the market' have certainly changed relations between production and marketing in that products are produced less on a 'make and sell' basis. The complex relations here are further elaborated later in the text.

6 Elsewhere, following Garfinkel (1967), I have shown how membership work simultaneously calls for 'accounts' and is enacted through a giving of 'accounts' (Munro, 1993, 1994, 1995b).

7 The new institutionalists take note of features like 'clear lines of authority', which they see as legitimating devices decoupled from 'actual organization practices' (DiMaggio and Powell, 1983). However, reading these devices *as* formal not only 'decouples', it purifies the informal – as if there could be organizational practices devoid of the formal. This is not to say that sociologists in general suppose interaction to be 'pure' since, as is now discussed, social relations are assumed to be shot through and through with 'power'.

8 Spaces of representation do not need to be thought of as literally separate. Possibly they only bifurcate in the sense of configuring in the following way: status, and also self-identity, is a hierarchy of representations around the axis of self *to* other; while belonging and membership, identity work, is an interaction of self *as* other.

9 The above examples, as with much of my work, come from business organizations that consider themselves 'excellent'; they have outstanding reputations for managing and outstanding track records of profits and growth. But the basic point I am making about understanding contemporary organization arrangements remains; any segmentation or de-coupling is far more sophisticated than we have suspected.

10 A sense of the horror for Heidegger is suggested by a passage in the manuscript of a 1949 lecture where Heidegger writes: 'Agriculture is now the motorised food industry – in essence the same as the manufacturing of corpses in gas chambers and extermination camps, the same as blockading and starving of nations, the same as the manufacture of hydrogen bombs' (in Bernstein, 1991: 130). As Bernstein comments, 'Heidegger's "cool" comparison of motorized industry, mass extermination and manufacturing bombs is not . . . some grotesque lapse or incidental "insensitive remark"; it is a necessary consequence of the very way in which Heidegger characterizes Gestell [enframing]' (1991: 131). Despite this insight, Bernstein goes on to condemn Heidegger for this analogy, as it suggests to Bernstein an indifference to individual suffering which he finds damning. It would seem to me that if Heidegger is at fault, it is for putting truth first; the same fanaticism to which Bernstein seems equally fated in *insisting* on putting

suffering first. As the utilitarian dilemmas suggest, questions of truth and suffering are not reducible to each other.

Bibliography

Anthony. R. N., Dearden, J. and Bedford, N. M. (1989), *Management Control Systems*, Homewood, IL: Irwin, 6th edn.
Bernstein, R. J. (1991) *The New Constellation: The Ethical-political Horizons of Modernity/Postmodernity*, Cambridge: Polity Press.
Cohen, A. P. (1992) 'Post-fieldwork Fieldwork', *Journal of Anthropological Research*, 48, 339–54.
Cooper, R. (1989) 'The Visibility of Social Systems', in M. C. Jackson, P. Keys and S. A. Cropper, (eds) *Operational Research and the Social Sciences*, New York: Plenum, 51–9.
—— (1993) 'Technologies of Representation', in P. Ahonen (ed.) *Tracing the Semiotic Boundaries of Politics*, Berlin: Mouton de Gruyter, 279–312.
Cooper, R. and Law, J. (1995) 'Organization: Distal and Proximal Views', *Research in the Sociology of Organizations, Vol. 13*, Greenwich, CT: JAI Press, 237–74.
Dalton, M. (1959) *Men Who Manage*, New York: Wiley.
Derrida, J. (1978) *Writing and Difference*, trans. A. Bass, London: Routledge & Kegan Paul.
Derrida, J. (1981) *Positions*, trans. A. Bass, Chicago, IL: University of Chicago Press.
—— (1982) *Margins of Philosophy*, trans. A. Bass, Hemel Hempstead: Harvester Wheatsheaf.
DiMaggio, P. J. and Powell, W. W. (1983) 'The Iron Cage Revisited: Institutional Isomorphism and Collective Rationality in Organizational Fields', *American Sociological Review*, 48, 147–60.
Douglas, M. (1975) *Implicit Meanings: Essays in Anthropology*, London: Routledge & Kegan Paul.
Ezzamel, M., Lilley, S. and Willmott, H. (1994) 'The "New Organization" and the "New Managerial Work"', *European Management Journal*, 12, 454–61.
Foucault, M. (1970) *The Order of Things: An Archaeology of the Human Sciences*, trans. A. Sheridan, London: Tavistock.
—— (1977) *Discipline and Punish*, trans. A. Sheridan, London: Allen Lane.
—— (1991) 'On Governmentality', in G. Burchell, C. Gordon and P. Miller (eds) *The Foucault Effect: Studies in Governmental Rationality*, Hemel Hempstead: Harvester Wheatsheaf.
Garfinkel, H. (1967) *Studies in Ethnomethodology*, Englewood Cliffs, NJ: Prentice Hall.
Giddens, A. (1984) *The Constitution of Society*, Cambridge: Polity Press.
Goffman, E. (1958) *The Presentation of Self in Everyday Life*, Edinburgh: University of Edinburgh Social Sciences Research Centre.
Heidegger, M. (1977a) 'The Age of the World Picture', in *The Question Concerning Technology and Other Essays*, trans. W. Lovitt, New York: Harper & Row.
—— (1977b) 'The Question Concerning Technology', in *Martin Heidegger: Basic Writings*, ed. and trans. D. F. Krell, New York: Harper & Row.
Latimer, J. (1994) 'Writing Patients, Writing Nursing: the Social Construction of Nursing Assessment of Elderly Patients Admitted to an Acute Medical Ward', Ph.D thesis, University of Edinburgh.
Latour, B. (1987) *Science in Action: How to follow Scientists and Engineers Through Society*, Milton Keynes: Open University Press.

—— (1991) 'Technology is Society Made Durable', in J. Law (ed.) *A Sociology of Monsters? Essays on Power, Technology and Domination, Sociological Review Monograph* 38, London: Routledge, 103–131.

—— (1993) *We Have Never Been Modern*, trans. C. Porter, London: Harvester Wheatsheaf.

Law, J. (1986) 'On the Methods of Long-distance Control: Vessels, Navigation and the Portugese Route to India', in J. Law (ed.) *Power, Action and Belief: a new Sociology of Knowledge? Sociological Review Monograph* 32, London: Routledge, 234–63.

—— (1994) *Organizing Modernity*, Oxford: Basil Blackwell.

Munro, R. (1993) 'Just When You Thought It Safe to Enter the Water: Accountability, Language Games and Multiple Control Technologies', *Accounting, Management and Information Technologies*, 3, 249–71.

—— (1994) 'Calling for "Accounts": Monsters, Membership Work and Management Accounting', proceedings of the fourth Interdisciplinary Perspectives on Accounting Conference, University of Manchester (11–13 July).

—— (1995a) 'Managing by Ambiguity: an archaeology of the Social in the Absence of Management Accounting', *Critical Perspectives on Accounting*, 6, 433–82.

—— (1995b) 'Governing the New Province of Quality: Autonomy, Accounting and the Dissemination of Accountability', in H. Willmott and A. Wilkinson (eds) *Making Quality Critical: New Perspectives on Organizational Change*, London: Routledge, 127–55.

—— (1996a) 'Extension, Exchange and Identity: the Consumption View of Self', in S. Edgell, K. Hetherington and A. Warde (eds) *Consumption*, Sociological Review Monograph Series, Oxford: Basil Blackwell.

—— (1996b) 'Facing the Future: the New Internal Strategy and the New Management Accounting', in R. Berry and D. Otley (eds) *Performance Measurement and Control*, London: CIMA.

Munro, R. and Hatherly, D. (1993) 'Accountability and the New Commerical Agenda: Reworking Accountability Towards the Self-Audit', *Critical Perspectives on Accounting*, 4, 369–95.

Norris, C. (1987) *Derrida*, London: Fontana/Collins.

Popper, K. (1963) *Conjectures and Refutations: The Growth of Scientific Knowledge*. London: Routledge & Kegan Paul.

Roberts, J. (1991) 'The Possibilities of Accountability', *Accounting, Organizations and Society*, 16, 355–68.

Selznick, P. (1948) 'Foundations of the Theory of Organization', *American Sociological Review*, 13, 25–35.

—— (1949) *TVA and the Grass Roots: A Study in the Sociology of Formal Organizations*, New York: Harper & Row; repr. 1966.

Strathern, M. (1991) *Partial Connections*, Baltimore, MD: Rowman & Little.

Wagner, R. (1991) 'The Fractal Person', in M. Godelier and M. Strathern (eds) *Big Men and Great Men: The Personification of Power*, Cambridge: Cambridge University Press.

Weber, S. (1990) 'The Vaulted Eye: Remarks on Knowledge and Professionalism', *Yale French Studies*, 77, 44–60.

Weick, K. (1977) 'Enactment Processes in Organizations', in B. Staw and G. Salancik (eds) *New Directions in Organizational Behavior*, Chicago, IL: St Clair, 267–300.

—— (1979) *The Social Psychology of Organizing*, Reading, MA: Addison-Wesley, 2nd edn.

7

UTILITIES, TOYS AND MAKE-BELIEVE: REMARKS ON THE INSTRUMENTAL EXPERIENCE

Jannis Kallinikos

> Time present and time past
> Are both perhaps in time future
> And time future contained in time past
>
> (T. S. Eliot, *Four Quartets*)
>
> There is no such thing as a logical method of having new ideas
> (Karl R. Popper, *The Logic of Scientific Discovery*)

The rule of rationality

To refer to the ubiquitous presence of what March and Olsen (1989) call anticipatory-consequential models of choice in contemporary systems of production and administration seem almost trite. In many diverse guises, such models have always assumed a central place in modern social doing and thinking. The basic picture is one in which individuals and organizations are portrayed as omniscient and consistent entities. They know their own preferences very well and have little difficulty in knowing how they will feel and what they will prefer in the future. They can anticipate the future, assign probabilities to future consequences and then choose and act by relating preferences to consequences. The picture is not substantially different in the models which seek to bypass the reductionist orientation intrinsic to theories of choice, and to underscore the significance of systemic rationality. Structural change and environmental adaptation can admittedly raise problems of significant complexity, but these are seen as ultimately reducible to technical issues that can be managed by proactive and calculative human intervention (e.g. Thompson, 1967; Aldrich, 1979).

Little wonder, then, that this picture has been subjected to penetrating criticism over the last thirty years or so. An interesting contrast emerges, however, between the rich theoretical and philosophical debate concerning the foundation of rational models on the one hand, and the impoverished versions that are usually encountered in the 'mundane' or 'practical' disciplines which purport to account for the managing and controlling of everyday goal-oriented activity, on the other. In many areas of the administrative sciences and, even more in practice, the contradictions and plurality of the issues relating to the rational consideration of the world seem to have faded and dissolved into a secular and often tacit version of instrumentality. In such a version of formal organization everything is to be subordinated, accounted for and justified by resorting to a notion of efficiency, calculated, it is claimed, in terms of the least costly means in the service of pre-established ends.

The persistence and centrality of rational models of choice and action, whether of reductionist or systemic flavour, certainly seem very strange in light of the comprehensive and keen criticism they have received over almost the entire spectrum of the social sciences. Many reasons could perhaps be invoked to account for the prevailing situation. While anticipatory-consequential models of choice and functionalist theories of formal organization can be criticized and found inadequate in many respects, it is not easy to suggest viable alternatives. Could the management of the contemporary world be handed over to contingency, accident or indeterminacy? The most likely answer is no, even though it could be thought that such a reaction merely reflects a cultural bias. However, the ontological and epistemological foundations of modernity and industrialism cannot be ignored or easily changed overnight.

Another pertinent cluster of possible reasons relates to the fact that most of the criticisms raised against the anticipatory-consequential models of choice and functionalist theories of organizational action have evolved as a counter-reaction to the models of man propounded by many variants of the rational view of social and economic organization (see, e.g. Lindblom, 1959; March, 1988; Sen, 1987; Simon, 1959). But counteraction can incur a high cost, in that the questions it ponders tend to assume the character of anti-questions. There is an intrinsic danger of reacting to a set of issues which have been framed by interests and preoccupations other than one's own. The technicalization of the ethical-political issues facing organizations and their reduction to something that can be framed in terms of risk and uncertainty (Tsivacou, 1996) provides an example of the curtailed voice of counteraction. The assumption that social incidents not conforming to an ideal type of rational action could be viewed as deviations or even aberrations from this type seems to have had an uncanny influence on social theorizing.

It would of course be possible to reject the idea of rationality altogether and to claim that organizations do not behave as prescribed by rational models of choice and action. In this view, the rational, consequential models would be no more than parochial exercises, the leftover relics of rational illusions anchored in the Enlightenment and the early days of modernity. Organizations would be rather chaotic, characterized by unpredictable events arising from the human qualities of forgetfulness, unreliability, emotionality, factionality and so forth. While this could certainly be the case, such an interpretation fails to account for the pervasive presence of all kinds of rationally grounded models in organizations, or for the regular and recurrent ways in which many people conduct their everyday work. To view these as purely symbolic, in the sense of an epiphenomenon deprived of any substantial value, amounts to bypassing the question. The symbolic value of the pervasive presence of rational models is their implicit yet fundamental capacity to structure human experience, and there is no point in treating the symbolic value as a secondary phenomenon that fulfils an embellishing or even simply a legitimating role.

Here, I think, lies one of the greatest fallacies in much social theorizing in general, and in organization theory in particular, namely, that social practices directed at the production of utilities can be evaluated in terms of the *model of truth*. However, formal organizations are not concerned with reflecting the way humans are and the way they function; rather they construct or implicate models of man, forms of actorhood which constitute the *canon*, the normative yardstick against which individuals judge the appropriateness – not the truth value – of their actions. There is no universal and transhistoric model of man which instrumental experience fails to take into account, although there may be human characteristics encountered in other contexts of the contemporary, highly differentiated lifeworld, to which the instrumental preoccupation of formal organizations may be averse. Anticipatory-consequential models of choice and action, and the instrumental experience they are inextricably bound up with, should therefore be interpreted not as scientific statements but as normative devices which produce, rather than reflect, reality and truth (Foucault, 1977; Lyotard, 1984, 1991).

To be sure, no normative or prescriptive statement is devoid of descriptive content which can, after all, be tested against what is often referred to as facts or real states of the world. However, to evaluate normative statements against the model of truth is to commit a category mistake and to confuse one language game – e.g. 'the university should be open on Monday' – with another – e.g. 'the university is open on Monday'. If I am right, then the confusion of normative with descriptive statements can account for the resistance which all versions of the rational choice and action models have shown to the massive criticism directed against them. For such criticism has, by and large, been irrelevant or misplaced, insofar as it has exchanged organizational models of a rational bent for scientific statements, and has then blamed them accordingly for failing to account for the plurality, the complexity and the extension of the world (humans included). Despite notable differences this seems to be the implicit or explicit moral offered by such diverse theorists as Argyris (1964), Lindblom (1959, 1977), March and Olsen (1976, 1989), Pfeffer (1981) Schein (1980), Simon (1959), Mouzelis (1967) and Silverman (1970). It may sound cynical, but the normative orientation of rationality reflects other priorities than the creation of organizational models and schemes that truthfully map the complexity of humans and the social world.

The profound consequences of failing to discern the predominantly normative orientation of rational models, have meant that the evaluation of instrumental experience has always been predicated upon a relationship moving *from* the actor (individual or collective subject) *to* the world. Such a relationship is ultimately grounded in a wider, fundamental asymmetry, i.e. that between subject and object (Cooper, 1983, 1989b). To privilege the subject in this way amounts to always taking the ensemble of intentions and preoccupations that make up this subject as a point of departure. The relationship always runs in one direction, i.e. from the subject to the world. Although framed in terms of risk and uncertainty, the problem is basically conceived as one of extension. The metaphor is one of exploration. Accumulated knowledge is supposed to improve the possibilities for the effective conquest of the extension of the world. Knowledge constantly enlarges the subject's conquering eye and expands its vision. Intentions and goals can therefore be changed or restructured in light of increasing knowledge and greater visibility, but the relationship between the eye and the world, between subject and object remains basically unaltered. No wonder then that the subject as such, and the way the subjectness of subjects is constructed, have remained outside the concerns of organization theory and outside much of social theory as well. The normative character of rational models of choice and action has been largely overlooked.

It is my contention that the analysis of instrumentality cannot escape the critical questions of *who* this subject is, and whether and how *its own constitutive characteristics* participate in the construction of instrumental worlds. A positive answer to this last question inevitably undermines the agent's controlling, exogenous and consequently stabilizing position, and creates a context in which the very notion of instrumental or goal-rational action acquires a new meaning. Deprived of their privileged position, subjects can be seen as constructing, just as much as being constructed by, the very processes over which the instrumental worldview assumes them to be in full control (Cooper, 1986, 1989a, 1989b; Weick, 1979a, 1979b). Thus, making the subject an intrinsic part of the analysis necessarily reframes all questions relating to the privileged status of the ends–means distinction. It also calls into question a number of other basic distinctions such as those between intention and action, planning and execution and goal – and value – rationality.

A general framework for reapproaching these central questions is perhaps provided by *play*. Detached from the dominant connotations of fun and pleasure, play can be regarded as a *mode* of organizing activities rather than a particular and limited set of activities (Miller, 1973). As a general schema of organizing activities, play violates the fundamental organizational recipe of instrumentality epitomized in the rigid separation of means from ends, of subject from object. Play seems to be able to reframe these relationships, and to provide important insights into the complex concatenations which the subject–world, ends–means interactions imply (Kallinikos, 1989; March, 1976; Miller, 1973; Weick, 1979a). More particularly, its dissociation from the subjective states of fun and pleasure and its conceptualization as a mode of organization contains the promise of transcending the anthropological view of both play and action, and – to make use of an old idea that has recently become fashionable again – of 'decentring' them from the notion of the subject or agent in a transcendent or exterior and controlling position.

Play thus emerges as a challenging alternative framework for the investigation of the complex processes whereby social agents, while planning and acting, may themselves become the objects of planning and action (Erikson, 1978). However, the exploration of the forms whereby the normative content of rational models is associated with the subjectness of organizational agents makes it necessary to re-examine the foundations of the instrumental worldview. It is extremely important in this context to ascertain the ways in which the descriptive content of rational models of choice and action fail to accomplish what it claims. The normative status of such models emerges more clearly, in relation to the questions raised by such failure. It is worth noting here that an overwhelming amount of the criticism of rational models has been unable or unwilling to pay attention to the way the playful character of human language and signification takes part in the construction of instrumental worlds. To do so would actually amount to recognizing the immanent role of the subject in the process, and the immense complexity of the issues involved.

The knowledge deficit can always be reduced. The answer to a problem construed in these terms is clear most of the time: more knowledge creates the conditions for informed action and better technological applications. But what would the answer be if the failure to meet the instrumental ideal could be traced not to the knowledge deficit – which can after all be remedied from without – but to the very *constitution* of the entity that attempts to construct the instrumental worlds? I would like to reapproach these questions, putting more emphasis on imagination, language and signification and connecting these with the questions raised by the normative orientation of rational models. Thus, the main thrust of this chapter is directed towards re-examining in some detail the 'fundamentals' of the instrumental order, and reinterpreting the limitations of its descriptive content in the light of its primarily normative purposes. Even if the description of the world entailed by such models is simplistic or idealized, it can perhaps be tolerated or even encouraged in view of its disciplinary (in the Foucauldian sense) effects.

Instrumentality, planning and make-believe

Instrumentality refers to the material and social organization by means of which human beings produce utilities of any kind under conditions where the efficient articulation of means to ends is supposed to reflect the former's total subordination to the latter. The selection and efficient organization of means is guided and produced by a goal or end-state prior and exterior to these means. The *primacy of the outcome* is then a major feature of the consequentialism of instrumentality, but one that must be supplemented by the requirements of *consistency* in preferences and acts and the *rational deduction* of means from ends (March, 1976, 1981). Instrumentality is not exhausted by its unambiguous orientation towards goal accomplishment, but demands also a consistent and rational or optimal selection and organization of the means leading to goal accomplishment. While the very existence of an end-state or imagined outcome constitutes a fundamental requirement of instrumentality, the actual question of the content or the values sustaining the end-state remains outside its concerns.[1] What counts is the definite separation and the rigid exteriority of means to ends or, to use another language, of planning to execution. Such a stance asserts, more or less explicitly, that instrumental results can only be appraised and evaluated from the point of view of goals pertaining to particular and well-delimited contexts of accomplishment.[2] Goals intrinsic to other contexts or ethical considerations only create complications, leading either to infinite regress – goals are evaluated by other goals *ad infinitum* – or to the reintroduction of values and politics into the realm of instrumental action.

Both empirical evidence and theoretical reflection suggest that this idealized picture is hard to sustain. At the risk of considerable simplification, I would like to group the counteractions to instrumentality into three distinct intellectual traditions. The first, concerned with the effects of the *unconscious* and comprising psychoanalytically inspired studies of work groups and organizations, suggests that instrumentality's three core assumptions are reversed and perverted by the human being's emotional and regressive tendencies operating in the dim, murky and uncontrollable area of the unconscious (e.g. Bion, 1961; Jaques, 1955; Kets de Vries and Miller, 1984). The second tradition centres around *cognition*'s conditioning effects on instrumentality. The limited cognitive capacity of human beings, coupled with the differentiation and plurality of contemporary life, interact to produce a number of constraints on the capacity of social actors to pursue optimal means–ends organization and to meet the ideal description of instrumentality (Lindblom, 1959; March and Simon, 1958; March and Olsen, 1976; Simon, 1959). Cognitively inspired theories strongly question the assumption of the primacy of goals, and show that consistency and rationality have but a partial grasp on the behaviour of social agents. Finally, the last of the three traditions draws on the notion of power. While it keeps intact the idea of individual rationality, it views collective action as inherently *antagonistic*. Markets and organizations, seen as inhabited by actors driven by incompatible interests, have been portrayed in the liberal tradition as compromising and bargaining systems (Cyert and March, 1963; Pfeffer, 1981), or in the radical Marxist inspired tradition as instruments of domination (e.g. Braverman, 1974).[3]

In one way or another the notions of the *unconscious*, the *cognitive* and the *antagonistic* have considerably enriched our understanding of instrumental processes. All three seem to be moving towards incorporating characteristics of the subject into the analysis of goal-oriented activity. Yet there is a tendency in all of them to relegate such characteristics to the status of *limits* or *constraints*, to which instrumental action is subject. Constraints condition but do not alter the hierarchical character of the subject–object relationship implied by instrumentality. Thus, according to Bion, the reality-attuned work group triumphs over the regressive and obstructive tendencies of the unconscious, while in March and Simon's (1958) view rationality emerges as a fundamental, albeit conditioned, social principle. In the latter authors' widely known term, rationality is but bounded. Finally, the notion of power questions the neutral character of instrumentality but not its ontological status. It is in this respect that I have already referred to them as anti-perspectives, treating them as having grown out of basic concerns and questions originally pondered within the realm of the instrumental and the rational view of social organization. In a sense, all three react to an idealized vision of instrumentality and all propose qualifications to this ideal. Their contribution seems to shape a discourse whose agenda has been determined by the priorities of a rational vision and by the attempt to accommodate conspicuous aberrations from an ideal type instrumentality.

The re-examination of the status of the conceptual strategies and operations that allows social agents to objectify the world and to instrument prearranged and predictable sequences of acts may produce a different picture of instrumentality. Instrumentality has always been based on the separation of means from ends and the hierarchization of the relationship between the two (Cooper, 1989b). Means will always be deduced from ends. The effectuation of such a project calls for the social and spatio-temporal differentiation of activities into planning and design activities on the one hand, and execution on the other. Planning partly coincides with the institutionalization of goal-setting activity, and always implies the spatio-temporal delimitation and detachment of planning activities from immediate involvement in consequentiality. To plan always means to turn away from action.

However, in relation to execution and the consequent flow of activity, plans appear at the same time as *ends* and as abbreviated representations of *ends–means relationships* in a projected time. Running ahead of time is always an act of imagination, albeit conditioned by different technologies of prediction. Despite the aura of realism surrounding the activity of planning and the attempt to place and justify it by resorting to a consequential and utilitarian rhetoric, plans and plotted decisions are no more than simulations, i.e. rehearsals and experimentations with alternative combinations of materials, technologies and acts in an imagined future, a projected time. Unless these plans are arrested and determined by a 'higher' set of goals or a realm of necessity imposing itself upon the activity of planning they are destined to remain a 'utilitarian make-believe' (Goffman, 1974: 59), an experimenting and playing with alternative courses of action in a projected scene. Plans and plotted decisions are themselves real, but their content is as yet a fiction or prediction to be brought into being only with the passing of time and very often – as life confirms – in a partial and incomplete fashion.[4]

The attempt to divest and dissociate planning from make-believe produces certain interesting paradoxes. One such alternative, namely to conceive plans as means deducible from a series of predictable and calculable operations of 'higher' goals, implies in principle the denial of the activity of planning and decision-making. For these activities are inextricably bound up with the ambiguity, randomness and unpredictability to which they owe their existence. In a wholly recurrent and transparent world there is nothing to plan or decide about. Planning as the management or objectification of time attempts to transform uncertainty and ambiguity into probabilistic expectations of means–ends relationships. But such a process cannot be understood or captured in terms of a series of deducible calculations. Like any other simulation it constructs the objectness of the world, as we shall soon see, by relying on a set of conceptual operations which are essentially metaphoric and which defeat explication solely in terms of calculation. But the attempt to ground the consequentiality of planning in a set of exterior or prior goals creates yet further problems and faces the prospect of infinite regress whereby a set of plans – ends–means relationships – always has to be accounted for and determined *ad infinitum* by a 'higher' system of goals that always lies 'beyond'. Infinite regress is an obvious consequence of refusing to conceive the world in terms other than those implied by the polar distinctions of means and ends. The two options left by instrumentality's assertion of goals anterior and exterior, and its simultaneous refusal to account for their content in terms of values, are infinite regress or play, fantasy and make-believe. For obvious reasons social values are a conceptual category foreign to instrumentality.

Even more paradoxical is the attempt to account for the instrumental character of planning by having recourse to factors intrinsic to the particular contexts to which instrumentality applies. The attempt to dissociate planning from make-believe and to motivate its usefulness by reference to a rhetoric of realism – i.e. to evaluate it against the truth model – makes the consequential flow of activity appear to be justifying the content of planning, reversing thus the hierarchical order of instrumentality. Plans appear as copies of the world, thus losing again what ought to characterize them, i.e. the simulation of instrumental relationships in a projected time. The attempt to anchor planning in reality, by way of the massive fabrication of future states by widely available technologies of anticipation and prediction (means), does not change the situation. Even in this case means produce and fabricate ends, rather than the other way round (Tsivacou, 1996). It seems almost ironical that, once separated, means and ends appear as recalcitrant and difficult to freeze into univocal and hierarchical relationships. The distinguishing mark of instrumentality (i.e. the distinction of means from ends) also contains the seeds of the conditions of their definite dissociation as well. Once separated, means seem to be able to take on a life of their own and to be detached from their 'embedment in consequentiality' (Goffman, 1974: 59).

Plans and plotted decisions can thus be seen as contrived in a series of actions that are cut off from what is usually conceived as the consequential flow of activities. Thus detached and dissociated from the tight cause–effect sequences of the consequential order, and without being embedded in any wider contexts of actions and goals, plans cannot but appear as aimlessly simulated stories of future events, a kind of 'utilitarian make-believe'. The stabilization of the procedures of planning and their reliance on different technologies of writing and notation, do not alter this fundamental condition (Kallinikos, 1990; Kallinikos and Cooper, 1996; Tsivacou, 1996). Writing exhibits no lesser fabricating capacity than other signifying conventions, although it certainly imposes its own particular way of fabricating future relationships (Derrida, 1976, 1978; Goody, 1986; Ong, 1982).

Compared with oral forms of communication, the analytic predilection of writing may convey an aura of objectivity and factuality. Organizational relationships conveyed by written forms can be inspected, cross-examined and verified in various ways. Even so, writing falls short of expectations when it is evaluated against the truth model and needs to be understood as a major disciplinary technology (Cooper, 1989a; Kallinikos, 1996b).

Relationships comparable to those which plans and decisions bear to actuality may be said to obtain between other types of activities commonly assumed to be governed by a strict means–ends calculus. Research and development, for example, appear as simulated production. Obviously research and development are not subject to the same organization as the group of activities they simulate; rather they detach a set of functions or roles from their 'embedment in consequentiality' and their subordination to clearly defined goals, with the intention of rehearsing and exploring novel uses and alternative combinations into which these functions and roles may enter. Similarly, practice and training is simulated work which follows the spatio-temporal organization implied by work albeit modified in certain important respects, i.e. consequences are decoupled and the objects of training are very often surrogates (Goffman, 1974). Such activities, as planning and decision-making contain a strong element of pretension, possessing an *as if* quality and representing performances, are often ritualized, of a series of acts kept distinct and apart from real-life imperatives.

Plans, play and metaphor

The paradoxes epitomized by such polar distinctions as ends versus means or planning versus execution emerge even more clearly when the instrumental vision is contrasted with play. As noted above, the idea of pleasure and fun usually associated with play cannot say anything about play as a mode of organization. Pleasure and fun both describe the feelings and attitudes that may arise as the result of play, but they fail to analyse play as a particular mode of producing and organizing activities. Nor can the notion of utility be used as a criterion for distinguishing between instrumental activity and play. For utilities can be and often are produced playfully. Only the three fundamental requirements of instrumentality together (March, 1976) – i.e. the pre-existence of a goal, rationality and consistency – can provide adequate criteria for distinguishing between the predictable and prearranged character of instrumental worlds and the evasiveness of play. Yet these fundamental requirements do not seem to be met by planning and goal-setting and the other group of activities mentioned above. They all seem to be delimited and clearly distinguished from the background of the activities and events that appear to be embedded in consequentiality, and to be organized in a way that possesses formal affinities with play.

However, while practice and training and laboratory research could be said to bear the conspicuous mark of metaphor, resulting in the temporary relaxation of the rules characterizing the simulated realms, planning and goal-setting appear to involve a more complex and ambiguous set of activities. The detachment from consequentiality in this last case does not just assume the character of the temporary relaxation of consequential rules and the search for alternative ones; rather, planning seems to be concerned with the fabrication of roles and relationships and the delineation of the terms that will lead to the future materialization of the depicted relationships. Yet such a fabrication does not really have an object or a state model, an already existing set of relationships to lean on, e.g. work, production processes, and so on. Little wonder that planning always departs from the nexus of prevailing relationships that it seeks to transpose, albeit in a modified form, into the future. Yet these relationships do not form an integrated realm or model as in the case of training (work) or laboratory research (production process). It would seem that in the case of planning the simulating and the simulated realm coincide in a way that tends to blur the clear separation of the model from the process of modelling, i.e. ends from means – a situation that makes planning appear even closer to play and make-believe. But these comments demand some explanation.

A principal attribute of planning is its attempt to master ambiguity and the unpredictability of interdependent action by riding ahead of time. In this respect planning could be said to differ radically from play and from the immersion of play in the present. But these are differences in intentions or dispositions which do not necessarily bear on the mode in which planning and play are organized. Planning and play do seem to share certain fundamental characteristics which deserve serious consideration. Neither planning nor play can occur unless the world can be rehearsed, i.e. enacted and described in *many alternative* ways. This basic condition of *plurality*, from which play and planning evolve, coincides with signification. It is only because the world can be posited and described through human artefacts that it (the world) can be posited and described in many alternative ways. It is by virtue of being posited and described in many alternative ways that the world can be negated, confirmed, contradicted, dissimulated, and so on.

It is only against the background of a fundamental distinction between sign and referent that plurality emerges and play becomes possible. For, unless the message-bearing entity (i.e. a phonetic or graphic sign, an object, a motion) is allowed to have an equivocal relationship to what it stands for, there is no possibility of signifying or playing. A simpler way of saying this, perhaps, is to construe the message-bearing entity as referring at least to two things or states under conditions that do not clearly specify when it refers to one or the other (Kallinikos, 1992, 1993). Play emerges from the very ambiguity which allows one referent to be exchanged with the other.[5] The discrimination thus implied between sign and referent, name and thing, representing and represented, led Bateson (1972) to conclude that play may have marked an important step in the evolution of communication. In his pioneering work, play emerges as a transfiguration of combat or fight made possible by the capacity to affirm and negate, to equate simultaneously and differentiate separate contexts of experience. The primary model of fight, whose organization play emulates, is dissipated at the very moment it is posited.[6]

It is to just such an original or basic experience of *simultaneous equating and differentiating* of distinct realms of experience that Bateson (1972) sought to trace the emergence of metaphor. His view seems to coincide with what Ricoeur (1977) referred to as the interaction theory of metaphor whereby meaning is produced by the friction or tension between the juxtaposed realms. Ricoeur contrasts this view of metaphor with what he calls the substitution theory of metaphor, in which one sign or set of signs from one context is inserted in the place of signs from another context. The substitution theory of metaphor, according to Ricoeur, seems unable to account for the generation of new meaning, since a paraphrase of the meaning that results through substitution, i.e. through metaphor, can take us back to the meaning of the 'original' or replaced sign. Substitution theory thus dissolves the irreducibility of metaphor into a passive action of exchange of two signs derived from different contexts. However, new meaning emerges out of the interstices, as it were, of the juxtaposed realms, due to the constant tension generated by the transposition of a word or sign into an alien context.

Planning shares with play, and all symbolic mediation, this equating and differentiating of the signifying and signified realms. Yet, to conceive plans as metaphors runs counter to dominant views on planning, and seems to violate the stipulated conditions of rationality and consistency that are so fundamental to the instrumental experience. As I will maintain below, rationality and consistency are not undermined only by the inability to scan and classify the extension and plurality of the world into comparable means–ends chains (i.e. the cognitive constraints implied by bounded rationality), but also by metaphor's irreducibility to single and separable signifying entities and its resistance to reification and deliberate manipulation. Metaphor does not and cannot exist in the precise and literal world of instrumentality. Separability – disjointedness – and hierarchical differentiation are properties of logic, not of metaphor. The very activity of planning is possible only because of the construction (affirmation) of a set of relations and rules projected into the future and the simultaneous negation of their reality, following from the recognition that plans are no more than assumptions about future states. It is because such a conceived and vicariously instrumented set of activities cannot yet exist – hence the notion of simultaneous affirmation and negation – that makes planning both meaningful and possible. In such a fusion of imagination and reality (Hirschmann, 1984), the notion of linear time appears as if it has been created only to be dissolved again.[7] Goals and plans exist because humans behave *as if* they were capable of leaving the present.

The diffusion of planning conventions and prediction technologies, observed by the institutional school of organization theory (e.g. Jepperson and Meyer, 1991), does not alter or contradict this basic condition. It transforms, perhaps, the *ad hoc* original creativity of planning into a routine duplication of a passive imitation. But imitation itself bears the indelible marks of metaphor and play and is in any case far removed from the ideal conditions of instrumentality. The most elementary act of planning, Kenneth Burke (1978) remarked, such as 'I shall gather some wood, to build a fire' involves a process which he referred to as metaphorical or analogical extension or transposing actual or imaginary experiences into the future. In Burke's own words:

> The attempt to fix argument by analogy as a distinct kind of process, separable from logical argument, seems increasingly futile. The most practical form of thought that one can think of, the invention of some new usable device, has been described as analogical extension, as when one makes a new machine by conceiving of some old process such as the treadle, the shuttle, the wheel, the see-saw, the wedge, etc., carried over into some sets of facts to which no one had previously felt that it belonged. . . . 'Carried over' is itself as etymologically a strict translation as you could get of the Greek word 'metaphor'.
>
> (Burke, 1978: 18–19)

Even if planning and policy-making are detached from consequential involvement and are marked by the playful and imaginary element in human signification, the question still remains of the contexts that are embedded in rigid, consequential networks. It would seem that the tight cause–effect sequences that characterize consequential networks impose their own coordinative requirements. It is a well-established assumption in current organization theory that the appropriate functioning of organizations and bureaucracies necessitates a set of supportive functions – provided by planning and administration – that ensures the undisturbed and smooth unfolding of core actions as repeatable, determinate and prearranged sequences of steps (Mintzberg, 1979; Pondy and Mitroff, 1979; Thompson, 1967). In such an account, core actions emerge as embedded in rigid means–ends sequences, designed in advance and calculated to ensure the maximum efficiency of means in the service of pre-established ends. This is instrumentality's official rhetoric, and in such a quasi-mechanical universe there is, it would seem, no room for play or make-believe.

However, upon close examination, consequential networks seem to posit a number of interesting paradoxes and impasses. The pre-existence of a goal or a system of goals demands that the outcome of the consequential process is appraised and evaluated with reference to goals. Consequentiality refers to a prearranged or expected chain of causes (means) and effects (ends) that are intrinsic to the set of activities that make up the consequential context. Each step is related only to adjacent steps through a logic entailing a calculus of causes and effects. But the instrumentality of the whole process cannot be evaluated by the logic of adjacent causality, for this would necessarily lead to suboptimization. Instrumentality means that the final outcome of the consequential process must be evaluated against the overall goal of the system to which the consequential process is supposed to belong. The consequential flow of activities is thus inextricably connected with the conceptual output of planning. In an interdependent world, planning must be able to resolve the problem of internal optimization in the face of potentially conflicting subgoals, as well as the immense and perhaps impossible problem that the effects of all other constellations of ends–means external to the system can be known and managed in ways that preclude interference with the functioning of the system.

The requirements of consistency and rationality always assume that the conceptual output of planning is capable of answering the question 'What would be the effect on the satisfaction of other wants if this particular means were not used for satisfaction of one given want?' (Weber, 1947: 162), and also of effectively separating and controlling the factors and the circumstances involved. This, it is assumed, is how the problems of optimization and closure are solved in the ideal world of instrumentality. Both problems are essentially more insidious than this, however, and can be related – as noted above – to the notion of bounded rationality (March and Simon, 1958). Yet they cannot be reduced or attributed to it. The limited cognitive ability of humans poses a technical problem whose solution can be vastly improved by using the immense calculative capacity of digital machines. The problems of closure and optimization – identical in a sense with those of rationality and consistency – are not simply problems of *extension* but also, and primarily, of *constitution*, due to the intrinsic semantic plurality, interdependence and ambiguity of human action and signification and to the irreducibility of metaphor into single and manipulable entities. I suggest that the problems of internal optimization and closure could also arise in a limited cognitive universe which does not meet the principles of semantic unambiguity, disjointedness and differentiation (Kallinikos, 1992, 1993).[8]

Language and instrumentality

The metaphoric character of planning and the paradoxes surrounding the consequential nature of what are envisaged as its core activities inevitably raise the question of the ontological status of instrumental worlds. There is a widespread belief that the forward-looking and quasi-fictional character of plans or plotted intentions still obeys a logic that is subordinate to the harsh reality imposed by the demands of consequential networks. Imagination and experimentation with alternative uses or courses of action could even at best enjoy only a temporary relaxation from the cold facts of market competition and profit-making and the technological requirements imposed by the management of complex systems. These are well-known scenarios echoed by many prominent scholars. Marcuse (1955), in particular, has delineated the contradictions inherent in the requirements of capitalist production and the advance of civilization on the one hand, and man's inclination for spontaneous and playful activity on the other. Even such a pioneering work on play and culture as that of Huizinga (1949) could be read as implying that man's path through history is marked by the successive expulsion of playful elements from social and cultural life. Weber's (1947) concern with rationalization might also be interpreted in a similar fashion.

It cannot be denied that the world could be interpreted in this way, and there is both strength and insight in such an interpretation. In effect, such an analysis superimposes the social upon the technical understanding of instrumentality. The infinite regress consequent upon instrumentality's rendering of the world as a vast field of means and ends is replaced by the prevailing nexus of interests and values which are thereby assumed to arrest the never-ending substitutions of means and ends and to legitimate their particular outcomes. However, this is not evidence of the independent ontological status of instrumental action, nor does it testify to the prior and exterior impact of such action upon the social and cultural sphere. To single out a particular realm of social life designated as 'instrumental', and to ask about its effects on social life, by no means implies any unambiguous causality. Only a realm of necessity relating to the means of life reproduction could perhaps motivate such a mechanical causality (Arendt, 1958), and in fact modernity has never confronted such a question.

The conception of the world implied by the bipolar distinction of an instrumental and a noninstrumental realm cannot therefore be attributed to any natural necessity. Such a distinction can certainly be justified and partly explained by invoking social values and conventions. But values and conventions lack any ultimate cognitive foundation or origin (Castoriadis, 1987; Derrida, 1976, 1978). Values and norms are ethical categories that cannot be tested against facts. They are certainly embedded in webs of historical necessities but they cannot be reduced to them. The instrumental conception of the world, what passes as efficient or instrumental, is itself inconceivable without the networks of values and significations employed by humankind. The attempt to attribute to instrumentality a prior or independent ontological status, appears increasingly futile in the context of postindustrial affluence. Instrumentality has far-reaching effects upon contemporary life, but such effects have to be attributed to the instrumental conception of the world and the values and significations coinciding with and accompanying it, not to some prior and independent realm designated as instrumental. As Castoriadis (1987) has acutely pointed out, the instrumental vision of the contemporary world is inextricably bound up with webs of imaginary significations that, despite the aura of realism, permeate modern technology and institutions. In his own words:

> To treat a person as a thing or as a purely mechanical device is not less but more imaginary than claiming to see him as an owl: for not only is the real kinship between a man and an owl incomparably greater than it is with a machine, but also no primitive society ever applied the consequences of its assimilations of people with things as radically as modern industry does with its metaphor of the human automaton.... The bureaucratic universe is permeated through and through with the imaginary.
>
> (Castoriadis, 1987: 157–8)

The reduction of the world to an infinite and calculable series of means–ends reflects the attempt to suppress the ethical-normative character of instrumentality and to clothe it in a rhetoric of necessity and realism that helps to legitimate the preoccupations of the instrumental worldview. An inevitable concomitant is not only to bypass the question concerning its normative effects, but also to leave out of account the ways in which the ambiguous character of language and signification impinge on the conception and construction of instrumental worlds. The unpredictability contingent upon the subject–object interaction under conditions where neither dominates is thus ignored or delegated to other disciplines. The exclusion of language and narrative knowledge coincides with the hierarchization and stabilization of the subject–object relationship and the subordination of the object to the requirements of the subject as noted in earlier chapters (Cooper, 1983, 1989b). The above-mentioned problems of optimization and closure are therefore solved by avoiding the plural semantic constitution of language and signification.[9] The meaning of formal or propositional knowledge has to be understood against the background of the separation and hierarchization of the subject–object relationship that thus creates rather than reflects the conditions of rationality.

And yet, as we have seen, the conception of a goal, so fundamental to the instrumental experience, is always the conception of a signified state which is made possible by the capacity of signification to project itself into the future and to rehearse alternative states of the world. Such semantic plurality is essential to meaning and signification and yet it has to be curtailed and closed by the ontological, epistemological and ethical monism of instrumental calculation. In this respect, instrumental relationships might be said to resemble literal meanings in their selection and realization of univocal relationships. Both are singular realizations of much broader systems of potentialities – language and action – which exist not despite, but thanks to, humankind's signifying capacity. Instrumental relationships, like denotative meanings, might be said to arise out of the successive closure of ambiguity and plurality. Yet such a closure needs what it denies or attempts to close, and can only occur against the background of ambiguity and plurality.

Propositional (literal) knowledge and instrumental (univocal) action have always, and for obvious reasons, been connected with one another. Each presupposes and enhances the other. Yet both are enveloped by the wider systems of language and action. The introduction of the latter into the analysis of instrumental experience implies the reconsideration of the subject as an immanent part of the instrumental processes. The subject as the bearer of intentions does not simply fail to account for the complexity and extension of an external world, but is constantly betrayed and perverted by its own defining characteristics, i.e. the elusive, playful and partly uncontrollable nature of signification. The ambiguity and open texture of language always evade its 'identitary' (stabilizing identity) or propositional dimension (Castoriadis, 1987) and elude the project of cross-contextual semantic stability.

The open texture and complex semantic organization of natural language clearly indicate that neither bounded rationality nor the insights stemming from the paradigms of the unconscious and the antagonistic, actually dispense with the assumed centrality of human agency, in that the cognitive, the unconscious and the antagonistic are treated as external constraints and prolegomena rather than as intrinsic and active conditions of human action (Cooper and Fox, 1990). The open texture and inherent ambiguity of language and signification imply that things always escape the definite categorizations of a human agent who is always implicated in the production of calculable objectifications. Such an agent no longer responds to the conditions surrounding him/her, *subject* to constraints, but acts on the basis of what constitutes him/her: an unconscious, a cognitive structure, a class or group affiliation, a language, a history, a culture. Human action unfolds as the play, – the nonarrested dance – of these forces, not in spite of them. Individuals and social units are no more than flexible architectures of constraints, as it were (Kallinikos, 1995a).

Organization theory has certainly provided us with rich empirical evidence of the complex relationships involved between intended and realized states of being, between instrumentality's predictable and prearranged worlds and the unexpected nature of actual outcomes (e.g. March and Olsen, 1976; Meyer and Rowan, 1977). Such evidence is essential to the substantiation of the issues discussed here. Although always interpreted from the horizon of incomplete knowledge and as a problem which ultimately can be traced back to boundedly rational individuals, evidence of an instrumental world far distant from that of ideal instrumentality is ample. As March and Olsen (1989) noted, particular events can be: 'Predictable or even subject to manipulation but neither the processes nor the outcomes appear to be closely related to the explicit intentions of actors.... Intention is lost in context-dependent flows of problems, solutions, people and choice opportunities' (March and Olsen, 1989: 14).

Expedients, makeshifts and fabrications

Central elements in the ideas presented above are captured in Lévi-Strauss' (1966) well-known account of the *bricoleur*, whose work methods and procedures the great anthropologist juxtaposed and contrasted with those of two other archetypal figures, namely the *engineer/scientist* and the *artist*. The *bricoleur* described by Lévi-Strauss as a tricky generalist, an idiosyncratic craftsman typical of the early days of industrialism, undertakes to accomplish whatever is demanded of him. He has at his disposal no more than a limited and shifting repertoire of tools, techniques and already applied choices which have been left over in one form or another from previous solutions and uses, individual or collective. The elements making up the *bricoleur*'s instrumental set, specialized to a certain extent, are kinds of quasi-tools, allowing him a range of different applications. But they never reach that level of specialization which tends to conform to a single, closed and definite use. Rather than being intentionally made to fulfil a specific purpose, these quasi-instruments betray in their shape and their functions the marks and traces of the *bricoleur*'s random confrontations and involvements with diverse puzzles and projects.

Each future project adds a new context in which the *bricoleur* can test the ability of his instrumental set. Through improvization and the ongoing restructuring of the relationships existing between his tools, techniques and ideas, the *bricoleur* may indeed be able to achieve surprising results as he goes on exploring the possibilities of his instrumental resources. It is just through tinkering and experimentation that his conceptual and material resources reveal their silent and hidden potentialities: 'A particular cube of oak could be a wedge to make up the inadequate length of a plank of pine or it could be a pedestal. . . . In one case it will serve as an extension, in the other as material' (Lévi-Strauss, 1966: 18–19). By constant interrogation of what has been achieved in the past, earlier solutions and functions are recalled into the present and recombined and reframed to fit novel projects, to form an organization of means from which new solutions are to emerge. In this last case, the accomplished solutions may deviate considerably from those initially needed or conceived, and may reflect a compromise between the ability of the *bricoleur*'s instrumental resources and the requirements of the project.

The *bricoleur*'s work can therefore be conceived as an extensive yet limited series of substitutions, whereby previous solutions, i.e. ends (signifieds), are turned into means (signifiers) and vice versa (Lévi-Strauss, 1966: 21).[10] In such an account the relationships between means and ends appear as interdependent and symmetrical rather than separate and hierarchical. A set of anterior relationships makes up a pool of potential solutions and significations which, loosely conditioned by the requirements of the novel project, are carried over and tested, transfigured and changed, to meet the perceived challenge of the project. The equating and differentiating of separate contexts thereby implied, the carry-over and turn (trope) of a signified into a signifying realm, show how conception and planning are implicated in instrumentation and accomplishment and can be said to follow the playful and slippery track of metaphor.

It is evident that the emphasis is on the *bricoleur*'s contingent, inductive and playful style of work, whereby his means and ideas are not subordinated to, nor can be unambiguously derived or dictated from, a prior and exterior system of goals – a procedure reserved for the deductive and rational character of the *engineer/scientist*'s work. By contrast, Lévi-Strauss argues, the *bricoleur* is not concerned only with accomplishment and execution. Each project simply provides an occasion for reanimating past solutions and testing their validity and extension into the present, a particular context for experimenting and tracing the otherness of his instrumental resources and of their potential uses and applications. Means and ends represent a pretext only, an interface upon which the *bricoleur* unfolds his technical and imaginative capabilities.

However, there is also a sense in which the *bricoleur*'s imaginative search appears much more bounded and constrained than that of the *engineer/scientist*. The number of substitutions or permutations into which the *bricoleur*'s elements can enter has its upper limit in the finite and highly interdependent universe of his instrumental resources and previously applied solutions. A change in one element usually demands the reorganization of the whole instrumental set. The previously applied solutions constitute the population of potential signifiers. Thus in the history and applications of his instrumental set the *bricoleur* confronts his own limits. By contrast, the *engineer/scientist* is portrayed as potentially capable of transcending his limits, of breaking with history and past applications, a capability that results from the *engineer/scientist*'s conceptual resources, his involvement in the transparent and abstract world of concepts as opposed to the *bricoleur*'s obscure and idiosyncratic percepts and signs.

The abstract and transparent constitution of concepts transcends the spatio-temporal limits of percepts and gives the *engineer/scientists* the ability to achieve considerable control and inspection over the contingencies that lie far beyond the context of immediacy. In Lévi-Strauss' structuralist version, concepts are seen as capable of entering into a greater number of permutations with other concepts. Percepts always signify by means of affinity or similarity between the sign and the referent, between the message-bearing entity and what it stands for. But designation by similarity or any other kind of intrinsic relationship is excessively constraining in that it is always tied to immediate contexts. Concepts break with similarity and context-embedded or indexical signification and introduce formal relationships far beyond the limited spatio-temporal coordinated of immediate contexts (Cooper, 1992).[11]

Against the background of these observations, the *engineer/scientist* is seen as more capable of reflecting on and breaking with previous discourses or applications, of detaching himself from his cultural inheritance and his embeddedness in the contingent and particular. Instead of constantly interrogating a set of particulars, the *engineer/scientist* seeks to enter the transparent world of universals. Concepts, as opposed to mere signs are free from cultural contamination (Lévi-Strauss, 1966: 20). The interface between these two figures is reserved for another archetypal figure, namely, the *artist*. There is no doubt that we are looking at ideal figures. Lévi-Strauss himself draws attention to the idealized characteristics of his own description. He construes the differences as being of degree rather than of kind.

Reduced to its basic elements, Lévi-Strauss' rigorous and highly suggestive comparison of the *bricoleur* and the *engineer/scientist* largely coincides with what Lindblom (1959) saw as the difference between the *rational-comprehensive* method and the method of *successive-limited comparisons*, between rational and incremental decision-making and foundational and experiential knowledge. However, I have tried in this chapter to question such distinctions or, more accurately, their character and effects. It is not a question of denying the existence of formalized and codified knowledge or even the production of utilities by methods that recount, albeit imperfectly, the rational or instrumental story, but of reinterpreting their status and effects. On closer examination the claims made as regards the *engineer/scientist* appear as fictive as those made about instrumentality. The power of both should be sought in effects other than, or additional, to those associated with the adequate or accurate description of the world, i.e. the truth model.

In yet another way, as we have seen, abstraction and formalization emerge from the hazy background of the linguistic description of the world. Just as numerical abstraction is inconceivable without concepts, so conceptual formalization depends on the 'raw material' supplied by natural language. Concepts exist only in a linguistic universe, in networks of other concepts and linguistic signs, in relation and contradistinction to which they acquire their shifting semantic boundaries. Semantic boundaries are simply local and temporary accomplishments destined to be infiltrated by and dissolved into the ongoing restructuring of a living language (Kallinikos, 1992). The transparency of the concept and the sociohistorical contamination of the sign is a consequence of seeing instrumentality as being concerned only with the comprehensive and definite transformation of the natural and social world into a vast field of means and ends. As I have noted several times, such an interpretation is incapable of keeping track of the very process of subjectification and its ambiguous and unpredictable character. In the relationship thus reversed, the instrumental project and the *engineer/scientist* can be seen, as Derrida has pointed out, as an expedient and fabrication of the *bricoleur*. Let us give the last word to him:

> The notion of the engineer who supposedly breaks with all forms of *bricolage* is therefore a theological idea; and since Lévi-Strauss tells us elsewhere that *bricolage* is mythopoetic, the odds are that the engineer is a myth produced by the *bricoleur*. As soon as we cease to believe in such an engineer and in discourse which breaks with received historical discourse, and as soon as we admit that every finite discourse is bound by certain *bricolage* and that the engineer and the scientist are also species of *bricoleurs* then the very idea of *bricolage* is menaced and the difference in which it took on its meaning breaks down.
>
> (Derrida, 1978: 285)

Subjects and objects: some concluding remarks

It would seem, then, that instrumentality does not exist except as an ideal, a horizon along which instrumental consciousness attempts to achieve the universal categorization of things and actions into functional singularities. And yet, deprived of these expectations, the instrumental ideal would appear as something of a paradox – or indeed as a vice – if it were not involved in constitutive complicity with the very *subjectness* of subjects that is assumed to command the construction of instrumental worlds. Instrumentality in general, and its different applications in particular, is not simply concerned with the categorization and emplacement of resources into functional relationships governed by the rule of optimality. Important as it is, such a project implies a subject – an ensemble of interests and preoccupations, and a body of knowledge and operations – that is itself constructed, developed and modified as it continues to construct and realize its instrumental vision. Efficiency, if such exists, arises more from the coordinative advantages conferred by established ways of doing things, the indigenous economies of normativity, than from the accurate description and anticipation of an exogenous and independent world.

In its most general form, instrumentality constitutes a worldview, an ontology which provides the general principles for constructing the modern forms of actorship, a very particular way of 'being human which means the realm of human capability as a domain given over to measuring and executing' (Heidegger, 1977: 132). It is only natural, then, that the different applications of instrumentality are not exhausted in a relationship whose direction is *from* the subject *to* the world, but an opposite movement *from* the world *to* the subject is entailed. The exteriority and the dominant position of the subject can be seen simply as a strategy or guise, which helps to solidify the fragile and recalcitrant character of human action and signification. The ambiguity and unpredictability inherent in human action and cognition are arrested by the institution of divisions and are structured and mediated by the transparent objectifications of instrumental worlds (Cooper, 1989a, 1993; Cooper and Fox, 1990). This objectified world becomes a mirror on the surface of which the 'subject' recognizes its own 'sovereign' image and acts accordingly. The frailty of human action and cognition thus acquires stability and consistency in time and space (Arendt, 1958).

Note that the notion of bounded rationality is predicated upon the first of the above relationships, i.e. the one directed from the subject to the world. This is why it interprets instrumentality as no more than imperfectly realized, and social action as being boundedly rational. Yet the same relationship can be approached from the opposite direction, i.e. from the world to the subject. Rationality thus emerges as the *outcome* rather than the *a priori* principle of human action, coinciding with the invention and institution of boundaries and limits.[12] This seemingly Foucauldian argument draws, in our case, on Winnicott's (1971) account of play as the basic form of ontogenesis, i.e. the construction of individual identity. In Winnicott's view, play provides the social and conceptual space that mediates and structures the transition from the illusions of infancy to the shared reality of others. The early not-me experiences of objects establish the otherness of the world and of others, securing and reinforcing the self and its sense of identity separable and apart from others. However, not-me experiences under conditions of play are inescapably bound up with the plurality of the objectness of objects, i.e. the constitution of playful acts along plural and rehearsable tracks. Play coincides with the opening of a mediating or *intermediate* space in which the objectness of objects can be explored, rehearsed and built up. Such a process implies a subject which acquires its self-awareness and learns about itself by learning about its objects.[13]

Play, as Winnicott (1971) recognizes, is not a temporary or transitory state which ends with childhood; rather, it is a permanent human condition in which subject and object interact in open and symmetrical terms, which tend to produce unexpected outcomes whose significance goes both ways, i.e. from subject to object and vice versa. Similarly, the fabrication of instrumental worlds can be said to turn back upon its fabricators, whose values and identity it somehow solidifies and reproduces. In this sense, instrumental rationality is always involved in some kind of constitutive complicity with particular forms of actorship, which it silently implicates and reproduces. Instrumental action can thus be seen as double-edged. Work appears like work only from the horizon of an already accomplished subjectivity, e.g. worker, owner, and so on. Yet this same phenomenon appears like play as soon as the processes of subjectification (i.e. the making of identity) are taken into account. For in this case the subject has to be deprived from its superior position, becoming – at least partly – the object of its objects, driven and directed by them as much as it drives and directs them (Cooper, 1989b).

Notes

1 This is akin to Weber's (1947) well-known distinction between value-rationality and goal-rationality.
2 This is a controversial claim that creates a number of interesting paradoxes. Let us simply note here that it is the rule of optimality itself that indirectly implicates comparisons across different contexts of accomplishment. Optimal organization cannot be known unless alternative constellations of ends–means are taken into account and compared. The question that arises, then, is how the relevant constellations of ends–means are known. In most cases, this question cannot be answered unless one arbitrarily delimits one's efforts to a limited and manageable number of alternatives.
3 A fourth current of reactions to rational approaches is represented by the recent emergence of neo-institutional approaches (e.g. Powell and DiMaggio, 1991). New institutionalism is not, as the name might indicate, a uniform school of thought. A significant number of institutional contributions re-echo earlier concerns and analytical strategies, albeit clothed now in different terms. They could quite easily be redistributed to join the rational approaches of systemic orientation, or the three reactions outlined in the chapter. However, genuine institutional contributions (e.g. Friedland and Alford, 1991; Jepperson and Meyer, 1991; March and Olsen, 1989) raise questions that are largely coextensive with those I seek to address here. The same holds true for a number of other recent approaches in organization theory, which draw on what is sometimes referred to as *postmodernist* discourse and which many associate with the name of Robert Cooper. But since the term is often associated with every kind of oddity and Cooper himself is very ambivalent about it, a few words of caution are necessary. There is no doubt that the term *postmodernism*, like other central terms in the history of organization theory such as power, system, environment and culture, has been abused in various ways. Most unfortunate is the superficial treatment of complex questions covered under what looks like a proper postmodern vocabulary. It would be most regrettable were Cooper's deeply insightful work to be associated with such parroting. Cooper's serious attention to the continental intellectual climate goes back to the 1960s and his first seminal work to reflect these preoccupations, i.e. 'The Open Field', appeared in the journal *Human Relations* (1976), long before postmodernism became a fashion in North America and the UK.
4 It would perhaps appear unfair or even irrelevant to attempt to evaluate instrumentality by reference to the content of goals, since such an attitude tends to blur the distinction between goal-rationality and value-rationality. However, as noted above, it is the claim to optimization that raises this issue. Also, the requirements of rationality and consistency force the examination of the status and the stated anteriority of goals. 'Unreal' or posterior goals are obviously incapable of guiding the efficient organization of means, and violate the ideal conditions of instrumentality.

5 Eco (1976) and Erikson (1978) note that lying and signification and, by extension, politics presuppose this fundamental plurality and ambiguity, and Bateson (1972) classifies deceit, histrionics and threat in the same group of phenomena as play.
6 Ritual, in particular peace-making ceremonies, also implies the semblance of a fight where the defeated tribe restores the power and prestige balance through the opportunity to defeat, during the ceremony, the dominant tribe (Bateson 1972).
7 It is to such a fusion of imagination and reality, of present and future time, of means and ends, that Hirschmann (1984: 91) appeals in order to explain a significant portion of human activities unaccountable by conventional economics: 'Activities such as the pursuit of truth, beauty, justice, liberty, friendship, love, salvation' defy analysis in terms of means and ends and are best described by 'a certain fusion (and confusion) between *striving* and *attaining*. In other words, an important part of the motivation for striving comes from the conviction that one already has attained it' (1984: 91, emphasis added). Hirschmann nicely describes here the important and surreptitious working of metaphor.
8 For a fuller treatment, see the first two chapters in Kallinikos (1996a).
9 Models of anticipatory-consequential choice have their paradigmatic roots in the economic and perhaps the political science tradition of methodological individualism. Recall from the preceding chapter that such a paradigm is inimical to anything that can be said to pre-exist and structure individual preferences and estimates. I shall not deal with this question here (but see, for example, Kallinikos, 1995b, 1996a). Suffice it to say that in this void social world the institution of language exists only as a simple medium which mediates preferences. It is transparent and subordinate to the individual will of the independent actor.
10 It is Lévi-Strauss himself who conceives of means as signifiers and ends as signifieds.
11 For a fuller treatment of this topic, see my analysis of Italo Calvino's fiction, *Invisible Cities*, in Kallinikos (1995a, 1996a).
12 This argument owes much to my personal conversations with Robert Cooper. Arguing for the importance of conceiving limits as an immanent and constitutive part of human action, Cooper has often quoted the US poet Charles Olson's dictum that: 'Limits are what any of us are inside of'.
13 This is just one possible road to self-awareness and self-identity, perhaps coinciding with modernity and its ontological and epistemological premises. Human history and the contemporary world attest to other alternatives as well (see Heidegger, 1971).

Bibliography

Aldrich, H. (1979), *Organizations and Environments*, Englewood Cliffs, NJ: Prentice Hall.
Arendt, H. (1958) *The Human Condition*, Chicago, IL: University of Chicago Press.
Argyris, C. (1964) *Integrating the Individual and the Organization*, New York: Wiley.
Bateson, G. (1972) *Steps to an Ecology of Mind*, New York: Ballantine.
Bion, W. (1961) *Experiences in Groups*, London: Tavistock.
Braverman, H. (1974) *Labor and Monopoly Capital*, London: Monthly Review Press.
Burke, K. (1978) 'Rhetorics, Poetics and Philosophy', in D. Burks (ed.) *Rhetoric, Philosophy and Literature*, West Lafayette, IN: Purdue University Press.
Castoriadis, C. (1987) *The Imaginary Institution of Society*, Cambridge: Polity Press.
Cooper, R. (1976) 'The Open Field', *Human Relations*, 29/11, 999–1017.
—— (1983) 'The Other: a Model of Human Structuring', in G. Morgan (ed.) *Beyond Method: Strategies for Social Research*, Newbury Park, CA: Sage, 202–18.
—— (1986) 'Organization/Disorganization', *Social Science Information*, 25, 299–335.

—— (1989a) 'The Visibility of Social Systems', in M. C. Jackson, P. Keys and S. A. Cropper (eds) *Operational Research and the Social Sciences*, New York: Plenum, 51–9.

—— (1989b) 'Modernism, Postmodernism and Organizational Analysis 3: the Contribution of Jacques Derrida', *Organization Studies*, 10/4, 479–502.

—— (1992) 'Formal Organization as Representation: Remote Control, Displacement and Abbreviation', in M. Reed and M. Hughes (eds) *Rethinking Organization: New Directions in Organization Theory and Analysis*, London: Sage, 254–72.

Cooper, R. (1993) 'Technologies of Representation', in P. Ahonen (ed.) *Tracing the Semiotic Boundaries of Politics*. Berlin: Mouton de Gruyter, 279–312.

Cooper, R. and Burrell, G. (1988) 'Modernism, Postmodernism and Organizational Analysis 1: an Introduction', *Organization Studies*, 9/1, 91–112.

Cooper, R. and Fox, S. (1990) 'The Texture of Organizing', *Journal of Management Studies*, 26, 575–82.

Cyert, R. M. and March, J. G. (1963) *A Behavioral Theory of the Firm*, Englewood Cliffs, NJ: Prentice Hall.

Derrida, J. (1976) *Of Grammatology*, trans. G. Spivak, Baltimore, MD: Johns Hopkins University Press.

Derrida, J. (1978) *Writing and Difference*, trans. A. Bass, London: Routledge & Kegan Paul.

Eco, U. (1976) *A Theory of Semiotics*, Indianapolis, IN: Indiana University Press.

Erikson, E. H. (1978) *Toys and Reasons*, London: Marion Boyars.

Foucault, M. (1977) *Discipline and Punish*, trans. A. Sheridan, London: Penguin.

Friedland, R. and Alford, R. R. (1991) 'Bringing Society Back In: Symbols, Practices and Institutional Contradictions', in W. Powell and P. J. DiMaggio (eds) *The New Institutionalism in Organizational Analysis*, Chicago, IL: Chicago University Press.

Goffman, E. (1974) *Frame Analysis*, New York: Harper & Row.

Goody, J. (1986) *The Logic of Writing and the Organization of Society*, Cambridge: Cambridge University Press.

Heidegger, M. (1971) *On the Way to Language*, trans. P. D. Hertz, New York: Harper & Row.

—— (1977) *The Question Concerning Technology and Other Essays*, trans. W. Lovitt, New York: Harper & Row.

Hirschmann, A. O. (1984) 'Against Parsimony: Three Easy Ways of Complicating Some Categories of Economic Discourse', *The American Economic Review*, 74, 89–96.

Huizinga, J. (1949) *Homo Ludens: A Study of Playful Element in Culture*. London: Routledge.

Jaques, E. (1955) 'Social Systems as Defence Against Persecution and Depressive Anxiety', in M. Klein *et al.* (eds) *New Directions in Psychoanalysis*, London: Tavistock.

—— (1976) *A General Theory of Bureaucracy*. London: Heinemann.

Jepperson, R. L. and Meyer, J. W. (1991) 'The Public Order and the Construction of Formal Organizations', in W. W. Powell and P. J. DiMaggio (eds) *The New Institutionalism in Organizational Analysis*, Chicago, IL: Chicago University Press.

Kallinikos, J. (1989) 'Play and Organizations', in M. C. Jackson, P. Keys and S. A. Cropper (eds) *Operational Research and the Social Sciences*, New York: Plenum.

—— (1990) 'Techniques of Notation and Behaviour', Working Paper 1990/9, Department of Business Studies, Uppsala University.

—— (1992) 'The Significations of Machines', *Scandinavian Journal of Management*, 8/2, 113–32.

—— (1993) 'Identity, Recursiveness and Change: Semiotics and Beyond', in P. Ahonen (ed.) *Tracing the Semiotic Boundaries of Politics*, Berlin: Mouton de Gruyter.

—— (1995a) 'The Archi-tecture of the Invisible: Technology is Representation', *Organization*, 2/1, 117–40.
—— (1995b) 'Cognitive Foundations of Economic Institutions', *Scandinavian Journal of Management*, 11/2, 119–37.
—— (1996a) *Technology and Society: Interdisciplinary Studies in Formal Organization*, Munich: Accedo.
—— (1996b) 'Predictable Worlds', *Scandinavian Journal of Management*, 12/1, 7–24, special issue on writing, rationality and organization.
Kallinikos, J. and Cooper, R. (eds) (1996) 'Writing, Rationality and Organization: an Introduction', special issue of *Scandinavian Journal of Management*, 12/1, 1–7.
Kets de Vries, F. R. M. and Miller, D. (1984) *The Neurotic Organization*, San Francisco, CA: Jossey-Bass
Lévi-Strauss, C. (1966) *The Savage Mind*, London: Weidenfeld & Nicolson.
Lindblom, C. E. (1959) 'The Science of Muddling Through', *Public Administrative Review*, 19, 78–88.
Lindblom, C. E. (1977) *Politics and Markets*, New York: Basic Books.
—— (1981) 'Comments on Decisions in Organizations', in A. Van de Ven and W. Joyce (eds) *Perspectives on Organizational Design and Behavior*, New York: Wiley.
Lyotard, J.-F. (1984) *The Postmodern Condition: A Report on Knowledge*, trans. G. Bennington and B. Massumi, Manchester: Manchester University Press.
—— (1991) *The Inhuman: Reflections on Time*, trans. G. Bennington and R. Bowlby, Cambridge: Polity Press.
March, J. G. (1976) 'The Technology of Foolishness', in J. G. March and J. P. Olsen (eds) *Ambiguity and Choice in Organizations*, Oslo: Universitetsförlaget.
—— (1981) 'Decisions in Organizations and Theories of Choice', in A. Van de Ven and W. Joyce (eds) *Perspectives on Organizational Design and Behavior*, New York: Wiley.
——. (1988) *Decisions and Organizations*, Oxford: Basil Blackwell.
March, J. G. and Olsen, J. P. (1976) *Ambiguity and Choice in Organizations*, Oslo: Universitetsförlaget.
—— (1989) *Rediscovering Institutions*, London: The Free Press.
March, J. G. and Simon, H. A. (1958) *Organizations*, New York: Wiley.
Marcuse, H. (1955) *Eros and Civilization*, Boston, MA: Beacon Press.
Meyer, J. W. and Rowan, B. (1977) 'Institutionalized Organizations: Formal Structure as a Myth and Ceremony', *American Journal of Sociology*, 83, 440–63.
Miller, S. (1973) 'Ends, Means, and Galumphing: Some Leitmotifs of Play', *American Anthropologist*, 75, 87–98.
Mintzberg, H. (1979) *The Structuring of Organizations*, Englewood Cliffs, NJ: Prentice Hall.
Mouzelis, N. (1967) *Organization and Bureaucracy*, London: Heinemann.
Ong, W. (1982) *Orality and Literacy: The Technologizing of the Word*, London: Routledge.
Pfeffer, J. (1981) *Power in Organizations*, London: Pitman
Pondy L. R. and Mitroff, I. (1979) 'Beyond Open Systems Models of Organization', in B. M. Staw (ed.) *Research in Organizational Behavior*, London: JAI Press.
Powell, W. W. and DiMaggio, P. J. (eds) (1991) *The New Institutionalism in Organizational Analysis*, Chicago, IL: Chicago University Press.
Ricouer, P. (1977) *The Rule of Metaphor*, Toronto: University of Toronto Press.
Schein, E. H. (1980) *Organizational Psychology*, Englewood Cliffs, NJ: Prentice-Hall.
Sen, A. (1987) *On Ethics and Economics*, Cambridge: Cambridge University Press.
Silverman, D. (1970) *The Theory of Organizations*, London: Heinemann.

Simon, H. A. (1959) 'Theories of Decision-making in Economics and Behavioral Science', *American Economic Review*, 49, 253–83.
Thompson, J. D. (1967) *Organizations in Action*, New York: McGraw-Hill.
Tsivacou, I. (1996) 'The Written Form of Planning', *Scandinavian Journal of Management*, 12/1, 69–98.
Weber, M. (1947) *The Theory of Social and Economic Organization*, New York: Oxford University Press.
Weick, K. (1979a) *The Social Psychology of Organizing*, Reading, MA: Addison-Wesley, 2nd edn.
—— (1979b) 'Cognitive Processes in Organizations', in B. M. Staw (ed.) *Research in Organizational Behavior*, London: JAI Press.
Winnicott, D. W. (1971) *Playing and Reality*, London: Tavistock.

8
NEGATION AND IMPOTENCE

Pippa Carter and Norman Jackson

> The essential political problem for the intellectual is ... that of ascertaining the possibility of constituting a new politics of truth. The problem is not changing people's consciousnesses – or what's in their heads – but the political, economic, institutional regime of the production of truth.... It's not a matter of emancipating truth from every system of power (which would be a chimera, for truth is already power) but of detaching the power of truth from the forms of hegemony, social, economic and cultural, within which it operates at the present time.
>
> (Foucault, 1980a: 133)

Introduction

On the Hill of Tara, legendary seat of the High Kings of Ireland, stands the remnant of a supposed stone cross which carries an enigmatic effigy with horned ears and crossed legs. An eminent historian asserted that 'It would be dangerous to try to explain it' (Ronan, cited in MacGowan, 1993: 39). This statement raises the interesting question of why any knowledge should be dangerous. The danger might be epistemological, getting the facts wrong, but the historian immediately goes on to suggest that 'it symbolises the triumph of Christianity – the harnessing of the devil' (ibid.). That the eminent historian in question was a Catholic priest makes this explanation unsurprising, though the grounds for it do not seem obvious on the artefact itself. But the explanation suggests that the danger he referred to is danger to the soul, like the danger from eating the fruit of the tree of knowledge of good and evil, that for this reason some things are better left not known. Ignorance is bliss (the special happiness of heaven). Wherever there is orthodoxy, heterodoxy is dangerous. The idea that there are categories of knowledge which are dangerous is not exclusive to theology, but is a feature of all societies, even our own enlightened one.

The focus of this chapter is on the known and the not-to-be-known of organization(s). We argue that there are things which can be said and things which cannot be said and seek to address the question of what it is that cannot be said, and why. Taking the theme of negation, we explore the organization of knowledge about organization(s) to argue that the failure of the dominant mode of such knowledge to solve (organizational) problems is a direct consequence of the dichotomy between acceptable knowledge and unacceptable knowledge. Negation is characterized as the repository of all alternatives to that whose certainty has been affirmed. The ways in which negation has been denigrated, both culturally and epistemologically, are explored, not least in the context of its semantic connections with uncertainty and disorder. But, since we live in a world which is infinitely ambiguous and uncertain, the pursuit of certainty through order can be seen as not merely ineffectual but itself creating impotence in solving problems. The potential of negative thinking to overcome these limitations, and the relation to power/knowledge in which negation stands, are explored. These considerations are located in characterizations of organizations and of organization theory, which are necessarily broad. Both are seen as underwritten, explicitly or implicitly, by the defining assumption that improving efficiency is the ultimate goal to which all other considerations must tend. This efficiency is to be measured by profit, although, since the link between efficiency and profit is imprecise, the use of surrogate measures is prevalent.

Modern society is characterized by unquestioning commitment to the idea of progress. Implicit within the idea of progress is the sense of constant, continuous and inexorable advancement towards some unspecified, but easily recognisable, utopia. Few would, in general, dispute the desirability of utopia although unspecified, and different in both nature and means of achievement in different epochs. The key feature of contemporary utopianism is that its achievement depends on the perfectibility of organizations. Post-World War Two experience in the UK has seen enormous commitment to the idea of the role of government to facilitate and encourage optimization of organizational configurations, through totalizing interventions at both macro levels (for example, based on the profound belief in the value to this aim of the privatization of all organizations irrespective of function) and micro levels (for example, the deregulation of constraints on *laissez-faire* organizational practice) – the political and managerial worlds complementing each other in what Mészáros (1989: 85) calls a 'reciprocal authentication'. Clearly, the realization of such policies as paths to utopia is a matter of ideology rather than of quintessential truth (see, for example, Hutton, 1995). Nonetheless, they are presented as truth and, as such, resist question. Knowledge production commits itself to furthering organizational perfectibility within the context of this supposed truth as episteme. Yet organizations demonstrate a stubborn resistance to achieving perfection, in spite of all the incitement towards it, remaining characterized by unregenerate problems both old and new. And the problems of the 'human condition' remain remarkably constant: poverty, ignorance, disease. Although in the late twentieth century the technology to resolve such problems is available, they do not go away. Their resolution is no longer an issue of technology, but is one of organization.

One of the effects of any version of the true path to utopia becoming constituted as the one best way is the delineation, *a priori*, of possible solutions to problems, which are defined by ideological appropriateness. Potential solutions which do not dovetail with the dominant belief systems are inadmissible. Even though there is almost epidemic definition and description of problems, there is only one set of solutions that can be administered to them. Yet not only are organizations not approaching perfectibility, the evidence seems to point in exactly the other direction. This can be seen at various levels, from the collapse of large financial institutions due to mismanagement or fraud to the increasing recognition that working in organizations is likely to be physically and psychologically unhealthy. The fundamental contradiction between the dream and the practice is neatly summarized by Foucault: 'We have institutions administering shortages, whereas we are in a situation of superabundance' (1988: 326). This can be demonstrated at many different levels. For example, despite abundant available resources for education and health care, such resources are increasingly being diverted into the management of rationing supply; in the labour market, while organizational practice is to reduce demand for labour, political practice is to exhort people to work, and unemployment is used to punish (e.g. Gorz, 1989) – and, since wages remain the principal source of income for most people, everybody is punished: if we have a job, we experience downward pressure on earnings and upward pressure on the amount of work to do because of shrinking numbers of people doing it, but if we do not have a job we are excluded both from social structures and from the means of generating our own survival; technology is increasingly used to reduce demand for labour and the benefits of technology translate directly into loss of income, so a smaller workforce supports a larger inactive sector to the disadvantage of both (Hutton, 1995). But the way we think about organizations and the specific significance we give them as paths to happiness does not allow us a way out of this impasse. The episteme itself is profoundly sterile: while failing to offer solutions it also effectively denies other possibilities. A compelling description is offered by Adorno, of whom Buck-Morss (1977) noted that he:

> never gave up his characterization of society as fragmented, discontinuous . . . , and in a state of disintegration; . . . he simply added to it the opposite idea, that it formed a closed, air-tight system, that '*the total organization of society through big business and its omnipresent technology has . . . taken unbroken . . . possession of the world and imagination*'.
>
> (Buck-Morss, 1977: 85)

More recently, Derrida has said, of the apparent triumph of capitalism over socialism, that its stridence seeks 'to disavow, and therefore to hide from, the fact that never, never in history, has the horizon of the thing whose survival is being celebrated (namely, all the old models of the capitalist and liberal world) been as dark, threatening and threatened' (1994: 52).

Something and nothing

The concept of the 'thing' denotes that which is, which exists. The primary definition of thing, however, relates to assembly, court, parliament. Both senses have traces in ancient Norse languages, and the primary sense is still represented in modern usage by names such as Storting and Tynwald, the Norwegian and Manx parliaments respectively. Things are that which exist, which can be subjected to scrutiny, which can be talked about. Things to be talked about are *matters* for discussion: things *matter*, and matter is both *topic* (the thing to be talked about) and *material*; material is both having real existence, substance, and being relevant, important (and substance has the same connotations). Thus that which can be talked about has both *form* and *significance*. Thing-ness is constituted by our awareness, is that which is thinkable (thing-able?) and, given its derivations, achieves substance through articulation – it is constituted by language. In opposition to this, no-thing is that which cannot be brought to mind, which cannot be talked about, which has no substance, which does not matter. In this sense, nothing is zero, the void – to be a-voided, empty, a vacuum, vacuous (and vacuity is absence of action). Nothing is the unknowable, and thus the uncertain, that which is to be feared.

> To write, read, talk about Nothing, or to believe in it, or to claim, as Socrates did, to know nothing, is to sit close to the obvious possibility that one is involved in the ultimate unreality of signifying not Nothing but no thing.
>
> (Rotman, 1987: ix)

Things are also referred to as goods. Goods are also good – positive, beneficial, desirable, worth some-thing, have value. While not linked etymologically, theologically God is Good. The devil, however, is, etymologically, slander, scandal, devaluation, speaking against the truth, denying go(o)d, denying what is, and: 'to talk of something being no-thing, to give credence to that which was not and could not be in God's world, was to risk blasphemy or heresy' (Rotman, 1987: 4).

The deification of what is (presence) and the diabolization of what is not (absence) is a strong theme in the Judeo-Christian tradition, reflected in the simple binary split between good and evil, between Christ and Antichrist. Denial of the revealed truth in Christ is seen as the ultimate sin: 'He is Antichrist that denieth the Father and the Son' (First Epistle General of John). The force of such characterization is that denial was not a sin which one could lightly choose to commit: given the severity of the sanctions which attended denial it was not, in the normal course of events, a possible act. All good was embodied in Christ, who was only good, and all bad in the devil who was, by the same token, only bad. Because there can be no good in denial then denial must be repressed, for our own good.

This is characteristic of all dominant ideologies. Obvious examples can be cited in the totalitarian regimes of the twentieth century, where great effort was devoted to the repression of denial. But it is also characteristic in much less extreme cases, for example, the response to dissenters in our own society which humiliates, disdains and cries betrayal. So immanent is this response to denial that it can be applied to anyone who dissents from authority, such as, in the organizational context, whistle-blowers. In some liberal democracies it is literally illegal to deny the Holocaust. But, however morally and politically worthy the spirit of this prohibition may be, the repression of denial clearly does not result in its absence. Denial is not unthinkable; it is only unspeakable. Marcuse (1968) suggested that the mind and the soul are potentially the only sites of autonomy, and so, although it may be possible to stop people saying it, it is not possible to stop them thinking it. Thus the repression of denial is an issue of power, not one of cognition. Of course, it is quite possible to influence what is thought, even to influence the capacity to think, (e.g. through education), but it is not possible, ultimately, to control *what* people think. Orwell (1954) convincingly demonstrated the problems of trying to make people love Big Brother, of making people love the received wisdom about what is.

The point about 'thing' and 'nothing' is not that 'nothing' is unthinkable, but the danger should it be said, for, once said, 'nothing' becomes 'some-thing'. While a concept remains unsaid, it is impotent. This is the rationale for the processes of exclusion from the discourse described by Foucault (e.g. 1971, 1974). In recognition that it is not possible (in Western liberal democracies) literally to prevent articulation, the discourse defines what, legitimately, can be said, who can say it and how it can be said, and sustains these rules through the exercise of power. Thus while those excluded from a discourse can speak, what they say can be treated as immaterial because it does not conform to the rules. The discourse is the order of things. Beyond the discourse is no-thing. A function of the discourse, therefore, is to repress denial.

To deny is to be negative, both in its literal sense of being oppositional in refusing to accept what is and in its acquired sense associated with badness. Thus to say a person is being negative does not just mean that they are denying some thing, but also implies a qualitative criticism, that they are being unconstructive, defeatist, curmudgeonly. Ideologically and culturally, language – and thus psyche – are steeped in the assumption that positive is good, negative is bad, positive is active, negative is passive, positive is presence, negative is absence. But, dispossessed of such ideological and cultural accretions, a negative is merely a relational concept. Negation, in the sense of denial, only refers to the refusal to accept or affirm the veracity of a prior statement, and thus is always a response to something which has gone before: a thing cannot be denied until it has first been posited. Denial, therefore, is always denial *of* some-thing. To posit some-thing is to make a claim for truth. Claims for truth can be either hypotheses or statements of fact. A hypothesis invites denial as part of the process of testing its truth content, and so presupposes that negation is a necessary element of establishing truth, facts, and so on. But where statements of fact reflect conditions of power there is no invitation to disbelieve, to doubt. Things posited are *de facto* positive, i.e. good. Thus to deny or negate becomes bad. There is no reason in logic why this should be so, unless those with access to power are only capable of stating truth, upon which history alone must cast doubt. Negation is bad because it is a challenge to power itself. But this would only be tenable if power were equated with goodness and truth. As it is, to deny the positive does not carry any *necessary* implications of badness or falsity. A positive statement is a variety attenuator. It condenses all possibilities into those contained in the statement and definitively represses those excluded. To negate a positive statement is merely to restate the case for other possibilities, to re-present that which it sought to repress. Issues of truth and goodness are not related to positive and negative, but lie in another realm. Positive and negative are simply relational conditions, not matters of content.

This point can be illustrated by analogy with a power battery. By convention batteries have positive and negative terminals. Manifestly, it is not possible to claim that the positive terminal is good, the negative one bad. More importantly, both are essential and equally effective. One could not choose to eliminate the negative terminal. It does not produce worse electricity than the positive terminal. Indeed, without it there would be no electricity at all. What is necessary for a battery to function is the relation between these two poles. (It is also interesting to note that, conventionally, positive is symbolized by '&+;' (more) and negative by '&-;' (less) – put this way, it is obviously nonsense to claim that more or less are intrinsically good or bad.) The case of the battery is directly analogous to the binary nature of understanding. At a primary level, understanding depends on the distinction of what *is* from what *is not*. The identity of any concept depends fundamentally upon its difference from every concept which it is not. In this sense positive and negative are not qualitative but simply indicators of difference. As with all binary systems, both are necessary. If every statement or definition had no negative form it would be meaningless to state it – if there were no possibility of Big Brother not loving us, it would be pointless to state that he did. It is well established that recognition of the binary nature of the world is necessary for survival in it. The ability to recognize and understand difference, the ability to mediate difference, is a prerequisite of living in the world – we are, *tout court*, organisms which function through appreciation of difference. Binary systems only exist when they contain difference. If difference were to be expunged by the elimination of one part, the system itself would be eliminated. The ideological and cultural accretions to the negative present as a desirable state a condition of the elimination of difference. Yet such a state, even if it could be desirable, cannot be possible: as with the battery, social existence requires the relational conditions of positive *and* negative.

Typically, positive and negative are conceived as diametrical oppositions. However, even in binary systems, positive and negative are oppositional, rather than opposites. This could be illustrated by reference to the etymology of positive and negative. Positive derives from 'place', but negative does not derive from 'remove' or 'displace', it derives from 'deny'. When we distinguish between what is and what is not, what is not is not the opposite of what is, but everything which it is not. Thus, for example, no physical object has an opposite, it merely has difference. The negative, therefore, is much more than the mirror of the positive, it contains all difference, all repressed possibilities. In the most common binary notation, 1 and 0 – the thing and the no-thing – these are not opposites. The one, that which is, is distinguished from the zero, the void, everything which is not. The conventional pejorative significations associated with zero, of the unholy, chaos, infinitude and formlessness can be counter-posed to what Rotman (1987: 105) calls 'the generative, infinitely proliferative principle' of the zero. The zero, that which is not the 1, the negative, is the sum of all possibilities beyond the 1. It is the condition of heterogeneity.

From difference to différend

Nonetheless, there is a sense in which negation is conventionally seen as having positive value, in its connotation of opposition. Thus, for example, there is wide acceptance that states in which there is no legal opposition should be seen as dangerous, not least at the level of individual freedom. In some ways, geo-political developments over the last several hundred years can be seen as shaped by attempts to combat the obstacles in the path of development towards enlightened society represented by absolute power. The overthrow of absolute monarchies has been mirrored in the twentieth century in the overthrow of totalitarian regimes. The legal ability of one person, or group of people, to define for all what is good and bad, true and false, right and wrong, is almost universally regarded as evil: 'power tends to corrupt, absolute power corrupts absolutely'. However, not only is the right to dissent seen as a check on the ability of the one or the few to dominate, it is also seen as having positive benefits in furthering justice, equity, humanity, not to mention knowledge.

A fundamental value is placed on a simple pluralist principle, whereby all voices have an equal right to speak in their own interest, and from which condition a compromise can be hammered out in debate which will represent, at least, utilitarian benefit. A more sophisticated approach does not just accept the existence of a *de facto* pluralism, but structures this into a formally adversarial model for the representation of interests, such as the legal system, or, more generally, a parliamentary model where things are discussed. Benefits are held to accrue from such a process which can be seen as representing a form of dialectic intended to, and expected to, generate a state of dynamic equilibrium through which society progresses. Informed debate between opposing interests is seen, on one hand, as providing effective counter-weights against the excesses of those with power and, on the other hand, through the process of debate and reflection, as being synergetic, expansive, in developing new thinking and new solutions – the ideal of creative conflict. The functioning of this ideal system is seen as safeguarded by the installation of various feedback loops which trigger awareness when any part of the system veers towards excess. The model is operative at many levels, for example, at the sociopolitical level (e.g. parliament), at organizational levels (e.g. collective bargaining), and at the level of discursive formation (e.g. intra-paradigmatic debate).

Notwithstanding the deep-rooted belief in the need for dissent to be voiced, the formalization of procedures for this to occur and the faith in the intrinsic value of the pluralist model, this ideal is far from being realized – or, we would suggest, capable of being realized. It is a model in which dissent, or negation, can only be reactive: it is always a response to the affirmation which has already been stated. In this context, then, negation is inevitably defined by the agenda presupposed in the initiating statement – it does not have, and cannot have, an agenda of its own. Critique is, in essence, parasitic upon that which is criticized. The pluralist model as a means of recognizing the relevance of dissent and formalizing its potential to operate is only an ideal. In practice, the extent to which interests are represented, whose interests are represented, and by whom, is a function, not of the legitimacy or other value of those interests, but of the acquisition of means to be considered part of the debate – in other words, of power. The function of pluralist debate is to establish the competitive market between interests which is resolved by power, rather than to establish which interests have the most merit or potential to do good, however defined.

Within the pluralist model, once an interest has achieved the power to be represented, all other interests accept its legitimacy on this basis. Thereby such an interest also achieves the power to define the terms of the debate, and other interests are represented, to a greater or lesser extent, by opposing it, demonstrating *its* merits and failings, defining their own merits and failings in the context of the powerful interests rather than as intrinsic to a genuine alternative. As Adorno and Horkheimer (1979) note, even against its intention, such critique becomes incorporated. Formal opposition is, thus, inevitably incorporated into the agenda of the interests with the most power and the debate becomes monological. What is not accepted into that agenda becomes illegitimate and excluded from the forum. Once that situation is established, mechanisms for repressing such other dissent can also be established and invoked – examples in the UK political system which have been so treated include trades unionism, environmentalism, whistle-blowing, and so on. Eventually, unincorporated dissent can be characterized as destructive, anarchic, unrealistic, even unpatriotic, and an ethos emerges whereby unauthorized negation is not just marginalized and trivialized, but culturally disapproved, even proscribed.

These outcomes are the natural outcomes of the pluralist model. The role of a formalized opposition in such a model is not to challenge the status quo but to maintain it. The model is naive in that it fails to take account of the role of power in pursuit of interests. What is needed properly to represent alternatives is a form of negation which is capable of transcending such incorporation, a form in which negation is not merely a reaction to some orthodox discourse, but is a rejection of the totality of that discourse, including its formalized opposition. Such a form of negation would be the sum of all possibilities outside the authorized discourse, which are, thereby, repressed.

There is a popular association between negation and the concept of the antithesis, in the essentially Hegelian dialectical movement – the dynamic triad of thesis, antithesis and synthesis. Although both pluralism and this form of dialectic represent similar processes, there are important differences. While pluralism, in its ideal form, represents a system for containing and managing contradictions, it is not teleological, in the sense that these contradictions are not expected to be resolved. The Hegelian dialectic, however, purports to represent a method of resolving contradictions which will lead to some concept of truth. Whereas pluralism seeks to maintain contradictions, the Hegelian dialectic seeks to resolve them, not in a Kuhnian sense, by the triumph of one over another through better 'explanatory power', but in the sense of a synthesis of 'micro-truths' contained within both thesis and antithesis. However, like pluralism, the problem with this is, as Adorno (1973a) argued, that the antithesis can only respond within the context of the agenda of the thesis. Since the synthesis contains some element of truth in both thesis and antithesis, it is a fundamental requirement that both speak of the same thing. Where there is no acceptance of the topic of the thesis there can be no (Hegelian) dialectic. A negation which refuses to accept the ontology of the thesis remains nondialectical.

The shortcomings of the Hegelian dialectical movement have been widely identified. In particular, Adorno and Horkheimer (1979) argued that the thesis with which negation, in the form of the antithesis, is supposed to oppose is so totalizing and totalized that there is nothing in it with which genuinely negative thinking can engage. It is already so exclusive that negation can only proceed on the basis of accepting, *a priori*, its assumptions and agenda, leaving as the only possibility a sort of nibbling away at the edges. They argued that, therefore, in contemporary society, negation in the context of a Hegelian dialectic is already emasculated before it is even uttered. Even the concepts through which it can be articulated are colonized, defined, by the positive thesis – as Adorno said, in another context, 'The words become terms of the jargon [of authenticity] only *through* the constellation that they negate' (Adorno, 1973b: 7, emphasis added). Equally relevant is that the tendency of the Hegelian dialectic is, inexorably, towards synthesis. This is inevitable because of Hegel's insistence on the relationship between reason and reality – the real is rational and the rational is real. For Hegel, the role of thought is to explain reality, the search for truth, its discovery being, presumably, at the point where reason and reality coincide. But for Adorno and Horkheimer, the role of thought – most particularly of negative thinking – was not just to describe reality but also to change it. Adorno (1973a) argued that the synthesis proposed by Hegel was simply unachievable. The reason for this was because of contradictions inherent both in society and in thought: 'reason and reality did not coincide . . . (the) antinomies remained antinomial, but this was due to the limits of reality rather than reason . . . because the contradictions of society could not be banished by means of thought, contradiction could not be banished within thought either' (Buck-Morss, 1977: 63). The thrust of both these arguments is that the whole dialectical process inevitably takes place within a particular set of values and assumptions. The dialectic does not, and cannot, provide a means to break out of, or even to challenge, those values and assumptions because it merely describes the process of progression of ideas: the dialectic is a method, not an epistemology.

A parallel concern to the general examination of the limitations of the Hegelian dialectic within the critical theory of the Frankfurt School was to describe and explain the ways in which the set of values and assumptions of the thesis became totalizing to the extent that their negation must either accept them as a basis for debate or, if it rejects them, locate itself outside that debate. Thus, for example, Marcuse sought to identify the intellectual and cultural trends which had produced a society characterized by total administration. In an introduction, written in 1965, to his essays *Negations*, written before the Second World War, he commented on the rapid development since then of totalization in Western societies. He said:

> Today total administration is necessary, and the means are at hand; mass gratification, market research, industrial psychology, computer mathematics and the so-called science of human relations. These take care of the nonterroristic, democratic, spontaneous-automatic harmonisation of individual and socially necessary needs and wants, of autonomy and heteronomy. They assure the free election of individuals and policies necessary for this system to continue to exist and grow. The democratic abolition of thought which the 'common man' undergoes automatically and which he himself carries out (in labour and in the use and enjoyment of the apparatus of production and consumption), is brought about in the 'higher learning' by those positivistic and positive trends of philosophy, sociology, and psychology that make the established system into an insuperable framework for thought.
>
> (Marcuse, 1968: xix)

The 'trends' which make totalization possible Marcuse identified, *inter alia*, as commodification and commercialization, 'the systematic organisation of needs and wants, including intellectual ones' (ibid.), technocratic rationality and the colonization of language, and surplus repression. These, according to Marcuse, characterized a society in which the potential for genuine negation was fundamentally repressed. As Adorno and Horkheimer had put it: 'There is no longer any available form of linguistic expression which has not tended towards accommodation to dominant currents of thought; and what a devalued language does not do automatically is proficiently executed by societal mechanisms' (Adorno and Horkheimer, 1979: xii). Adorno famously believed that 'after Auschwitz' speculative discourse had reached a point beyond which it could not go. The particular characteristic of speculative discourse is that it is affirmative. The force of the affirmative voice was to be understood as the negation of negation, and the affirmation led to Auschwitz. Lyotard (1988), however, argues that the reason why Auschwitz has this silencing effect is, rather, that there is a lack of an affirmative language with which to describe it. It can only be described vicariously, since those who might affirm it, who knew and experienced it, who were its victims, are not alive to articulate it. Even the empirical evidence which would confirm its existence was itself destroyed. Dependence on affirmation leaves this problem insoluble. Understanding, therefore, cannot be seen solely in terms of this affirmation of identity. Lyotard develops this with his concept of the *differend*. He gives as an example of the *differend*:

> the case where the plaintiff is divested of the means to argue and becomes for that reason a victim. . . . A case of differend between two parties takes place when the 'regulation' of the conflict that opposes them is done in the idiom of one of the parties while the wrong suffered by the other is not signified in that idiom. . . . The differend is signaled by this inability to prove.
>
> (Lyotard, 1988: 9–10)

This incommensurability between the affirmative and its negation is what is masked by the dominance of the language of affirmation, which reduces the 'victim' to silence. Although silence itself can signify denial indeterminately.

This is profoundly different to dialectical negation because the negation in the differend is not in any sense linked to the affirmation. Indeed, it is by definition separated from it by the incommensurability of their languages. Even where each understands the language of the other, it is not possible for that language to be used to express the victim's 'essence' – Lyotard uses the example of a labour tribunal, where the dominant language expresses labour as a commodity, while the 'labourer' expresses it as labour power. As Bataille (1988) says: 'The weak are fleeced, exploited by the strong, who pay them with flagrant lies. But this cannot change the overall results, where individual interest is mocked, and where *the lies of the rich are changed into truth*' (Bataille, 1988: 74, original emphasis).

The effect of such totalization is a context in which a dominant interest constitutes itself as rational. Therefore, any negation of it as irrational, in which dissent is seduced by desire for the commodities which it is claimed will bring about betterment, and in which these forces have achieved such acceptance that ambiguity, uncertainty and questioning of them, produces a deep sense of anxiety. The status quo has become, in Foucault's term, *normalized*. Yet, under such circumstances, negation becomes even more necessary. But it must be both dynamic and able to stand outside the totalizing normality. Marcuse's own concluding comments to his Introduction express this clearly:

> More than before, breaking through the administered consciousness is a precondition of liberation. Thought in contradiction must be capable of comprehending and expressing the new potentialities of a qualitatively different existence. It must be capable of surpassing the force of technological repression and of incorporating into its concepts the elements of gratification that are suppressed and perverted in this repression. In other words, thought in contradiction must become more negative and more utopian in opposition to the status quo.
>
> (Marcuse, 1968: xxvi)

Illegitimizing negation

Within the conventional disciplines, whatever method of knowledge production is preferred and/or adopted, there is an important implicit assumption which underlies the pursuit of knowledge, that the generation of knowledge moves us inexorably towards, if not Absolute Truth, at least more perfect understanding. This itself is conventionally underlaid by the conviction that there is an intimate cause/effect relationship between knowledge and change – that is, that change in the social world is epistemologically driven, and that the achievement of increasingly perfect understanding is an intrinsic requirement for progress. Thus the drive to generate more and more knowledge and to remove all impediments to understanding are essential to the achievement of utopia. However, it has already been suggested that knowledge is only in part a function of epistemology, and that epistemology itself is a function of a dominant value system, an episteme. It is on this basis that a fundamental element of the critique of knowledge offered by the critical theory of the Frankfurt School is that this knowledge is not knowledge *per se*, but bourgeois knowledge. Feminists, however, criticize it as male knowledge, blacks criticize it as white knowledge, homosexuals criticize it as heterosexual knowledge, and so on. In general, conventional prevailing forms of knowledge have been characterized as first-world, male, white, Anglo-Saxon, heterosexual, Protestant, liberal knowledge rather than as generalizable knowledge (as it claims to be). What is significant in this context is less the substance of such critiques than that they represent a claim that there is a dominant body of knowledge which excludes certain interests (rather than subsuming them), and that those interests are thereby disempowered and marginalized. The very possibility of such criticisms argues that knowledge is not merely an accumulation of ideas, theories, facts, etc., transcending all interests, contributing unidirectionally to general progress, but that it is multifaceted, both in what it contributes to and in how it functions, for example, in maintaining asymmetries of power.

In a more recent formulation of the Frankfurt School tradition, Habermas has developed the conceptualization of this relationship between knowledge and power, particularly in terms of the distortive effects on understanding resulting from the influence of power relations, arguing that 'true' knowledge can only be achieved in the absence of power. However, Foucault argued that knowledge and power are inseparable. Indeed, once it is recognized that knowledge is only possible through the mediation of language, this seems an inevitable conclusion at any level of analysis, since language always represents processes of prioritization and repression of meaning which reflect interests. As Barthes aphoristically stated, 'Language is never innocent' (1967: 22), and Lyotard, similarly, noted, 'Language is not meant for telling the truth' (1977: 96). The ability to prioritize meaning is an act of power. Foucault's concept of discourse, however, argues much more than this. It is a description of the ways in which claims to truth are made and the immanence of power in legitimating truths through structures which define, in advance, who can make such claims, how they must be made, and what they can be about. It is power which defines what is true. It thus effectively represses negation because, although we may legitimately argue about whether a particular fact is true, questions about the *meta-truth* which power has defined are ruled out, are by definition inadmissible. Such questions can only be asked *outside* the discourse, where, by the same token, they can be ignored.

The general point is reinforced by Derrida (1994: 53), who argues that three apparatuses of the discourse act in concert to maintain its hegemony, the political, the intellectual and the media cultures, which 'communicate and cooperate at every moment towards producing the greatest force with which to assure the hegemony' of capitalism. Derrida notes that the discourse of academia is 'relayed by the academic and commercial press, but also by the media in general' (ibid.). This academic use of popular media is nowhere more prevalent than in organization theory, where management gurus appear on television and video, and in popular literature, communicating their wares. However, the case of organization theory is unusual because, whereas, for example, popular history is aimed at a lay audience, popular management is aimed at practising managers as well as at lay people, and this not only informs but also helps shape organizational practice. Derrida sees such 'discursive domination' through 'techno-mediatic power' as conditioning and endangering democracy.

Foucault (1974) has argued that the pursuit of knowledge has never been, and could not be, guided by the gradual accumulation of truths towards some great whole which would represent, in its totality, the rubric for progress, but that it is, and must be, problem-centred, i.e. represents some interest which is to be served. At one level this interest is the problem to which a solution is sought, but at another level it is that which is constituted as legitimate by the discourse. Thus, pursuit of knowledge is problem-centred in terms of the problems which are defined as acceptable within the discourse. What is sought is not a solution *per se*, but a solution which fits the conceptualization of interests which is considered to be appropriate. Not all solutions are admissible, only those which fit some prior definition of what is admissible. Thus the process of negation *within* the discourse already accepts the rules of the discourse and so is defined by it. As Foucault suggests, 'the good old "logic" of contradiction is no longer sufficient, far from it, for the unravelling of actual processes' (1980b: 164). What difference would it make, he asks, if the prisoners ran the panoptical tower, rather than the guards? And he answers, none . . . unless there were to be some further purpose to the operation – in our terms, a different discourse. What this implies is that negative thinking cannot hope to become effective by becoming legitimate within the established discourse. It cannot try to change the discourse by making new knowledge because what moves the discourse is not knowledge but power. To be accepted into the discourse is to accept existing power relativities and to lose, or give up, the potential to challenge that power. Yet, as already noted, negation in its fullest sense concerns itself with all alternatives which are excluded by this power, the possibilities of all things not articulated by the discourse. Negation, therefore, is bound to place itself outside the established discourse, to construct a discourse of its own.

The capitalist regime of truth

Foucault points out that what he calls the regime of truth 'is not merely ideological or superstructural; it was a condition for the formation and development of capitalism' (1980a: 133). By any measure, organization, work and management must be seen as essential ingredients of this development of capitalism. But, equally clearly, knowledge of organization, work and management as experienced in contemporary society is defined by what is acceptable to this regime of truth. In this sense, the conventional form of knowledge about organizations is not organization theory *per se*, but organization theory within the capitalist regime of truth. The problem on which this knowledge is, ultimately and inevitably, centred is the efficiency of capitalism as a socioeconomic system. The fundamental notions of the nature and role of organizations are defined by their role in the efficiency of capitalism. This has become translated into the (relatively) unchallenged assumption that the problem which organization theory has to solve is the efficiency of organizations. The history of organization theory is the history of the development of techniques designed to contribute to the achievement of efficiency. The elements of applied organization theory and behaviour, such as scientific management, theories of motivation to work, theories of leadership, of structure, of work design, of decision-making, of strategy, and latterly human resource management, total quality management and all their derivatives, have all had as their object increase in efficiency. And, because capitalism defines the regime of truth, the equally unchallenged assumption is that efficiency represents, is measured by, profitability – witness the inadmissibility of any solution, however perfectly formed epistemologically, which costs more than it generates. (This is not to say that the acceptable solutions do actually increase efficiency, even in terms of profitability, not least because there is often no way of knowing what contribution to profitability they have made.)

The existence of negation within this discourse is evidenced by the detailed and interminable – i.e. unresolvable – arguments about which technique best serves the interest of efficiency, whether job enrichment is better than job simplification, charismatic authority better than rational-legal authority, organic structures better than mechanistic ones, participative management styles better than authoritarian management styles, psychological incentives better than financial incentives, and so on. The limits of these debates are established *a priori* because, once negation enters into debate on such issues, it has already accepted the terms and conditions of what is real and rational. That the desired end point is efficiency is not open to question. What organization theory amounts to is a constant refinement of features of organization, work and management which are already established, already present, therefore positive and therefore good.

It is not particularly contentious to point out, however, that a difficulty with this body of knowledge about organizations is that it is characterized by apparently unregenerate issues, which have been identified as problems and for which conventional theory has claimed the ability, and the authority, to provide solutions. These issues occur at all levels of analysis. Some of them have been consistent throughout the history of modern organizations, such as the problem of what these days is called motivation to work (or often simply, motivation, on the basis that motivation and motivation to work are the same thing). Within the capitalist regime of truth it is a firmly held conviction that 'workers' must be encouraged to perform adequately, as defined by management – what, e.g. McGregor (1960) described as *the ideal* of getting people to put forth adequate effort for the achievement of organizational objectives. The nature of such encouragement has varied over time but, basically, falls into one of two types, seduction or coercion. Sometimes attempts have been made to buy compliance with material incentives, at others to release some supposed inner desire to work by creating the 'right' conditions for that desire to be fulfilled, or, in the contemporary case, to elicit compliance through fear. That none of these techniques had been successful definitively in inducing the sort of compliance that is desired is hardly a matter of dispute. However, motivation to work remains an obsession with both managers and management academics, and enormous amounts of money and effort are devoted to it, although to no avail. Other kinds of unregenerate problems are perceived to be more recent phenomena such as the experience of stress at work. In this case there are, in fact, very few attempts actually to solve the problem, the tendency being rather, in recognition of the detrimental impacts on efficiency, to try to teach people how to cope with stress – perhaps implicitly claiming that such effects are inevitable. Again, a whole 'industry' has grown up around such issues. Yet other kinds of problem are associated with the impact of organizations on society in general, and may have a long pedigree or be more recent, e.g. unemployment or pollution. The approach to this type of issue is rather different to the previously mentioned cases. That they are impacts of organizations on society is not in dispute, in terms of the production of knowledge about organizations, they have not generally been considered part of its remit, and have been defined as social rather than organizational problems.

The unregenerate quality of these 'problems' arises not from the failure to address their 'solution', but from a fundamental conflict between the 'problems' and the discourse within which it is attempted to 'solve' them. As already suggested, this discourse works on the presupposition that its role is to improve efficiency in organizations. The 'problems' are defined as factors which impinge on efficiency, but the possibility that any realistic 'solutions' might themselves conflict with efficiency, especially in terms of its measure, profit, is inadmissible. Thus, for example, the so-called problem of motivation to work is, and always has been, a euphemism for concerns about productivity. It is not really a concern with motivation to work at all, but, even if it were, the 'solutions', as has been demonstrated by state-of-the-art theories of motivation to work, would almost inevitably conflict with pre-defined concepts of efficiency and with profit. If proposed solutions are ruled inadmissible because they conflict with profit, then consideration of what such solutions are intended to solve is irrelevant. The same case can be noted with regard to stress at work. It is recognized that stress has dysfunctions for profit, but also that any genuine solution to the problem would have even greater dysfunctions. For example, if stress is caused by overwork in some form or other, an obvious solution might be to reduce the amount of work done on an individual basis, perhaps by employing more people. Since this, again, is an inadmissible solution, the response is stress management – not stress itself seen as the problem, but rather its impact on efficiency. In the case of issues such as unemployment and pollution, these are problems which are, *a priori*, ruled out of relevance in terms of organization theory, because they are direct consequences of the emphasis on efficiency and profit. Organizations are allowed to export such problems onto society at large, which, it can then be claimed, is not part of the arena of knowledge about organizations.

The difficulty for the normalized discourse of organization theory is three-fold. First, it is only an article of faith that the issues with which it concerns itself do restrict efficiency, rather than, for example, that the way efficiency is conceptualized may be problematic. Second, both problems and proposed solutions are allowed, thereby, only a very limited range of acceptable definitions, because of the 'capitalist regime of truth'. Third, their history as issues suggests that the definitions offered may only be rhetorical devices, since on one hand, there is really only one problem to which the discourse addresses itself, and on the other, they thus have only a narrow range of specification for inclusion in it. Discursively, the issues of admissibility are more important than any problem or solution which may be adduced. Given this clearly there are many problems, even as defined by the discourse, which cannot be solved within it.

Negative capability

It is because the 'positive' or 'affirmative' thesis is biased towards particular sectional interests that negation is both necessary and has to place itself outside the dominant discourse. But the very conditions which make negation necessary also act as obstacles to its realization – the totalizing, normalized character of the discourse itself makes opposition to it difficult. The complexity of this normalized totality is profound, but the examples of socialization, ideology and existential anxiety may be briefly cited as indicators of this difficulty.

The role of socialization in any society is to produce members of that society who will contribute to its reproduction. Within capitalist societies, therefore, we can expect that the myriad forces of socialization will be directed towards developing citizens who will, more or less willingly, contribute to whatever is seen as required for the continued success of capitalism as a socioeconomic system. As Marx and Engels pointed out in the *Manifesto of the Communist Party* (1848), the ruling ideas of any epoch are those of the ruling class. The longer that capitalism sustains its dominant position, the more difficult it becomes to challenge its regime of truth, the more totalizing, normalized and monological that regime of truth becomes. Not only are we not trained or encouraged to think negatively, but we are encouraged by all our training to reinforce what is, and what is is, therefore, good.

The very language we use is replete with the repression of all that is negative. Negation beyond the limited sense of antithesis becomes alien. All we learn subscribes to the idea that knowledge proceeds by the appropriation of certainties and the elimination of doubt. Knowledge is the penetration of the darkness of ignorance, opinion, mystique, with the light of reason: clarity replaces confusion, sense replaces nonsense. Truths are revealed, prejudices dispelled, we move slowly but inexorably towards total knowing. To negate this is heretical.

Related to this is ideological commitment to the perpetuation of the system. Some of this commitment is active, is positive support for the system, and some is passive, in that it simply does not question. However, the system itself is proactive in reinforcing both these aspects of ideological commitment, in presenting itself as the provider of those things which we have been 'taught' to desire (see, for example, Deleuze and Guattari, 1984). Thus we come to believe that, whatever the problems, the system 'delivers the goods', what Marcuse (1986) called 'happy consciousness'. The more ideological commitment we experience, the more difficult it becomes to question. Ideology attenuates doubt. But beyond this are other issues of psychological resistance to questioning. On one hand are anxieties about survival: the world is a dangerous place, partly because of its uncertainty, and if we can reduce that uncertainty, either in 'real terms' or in terms of a believable illusion, we can believe it is safer. On the other hand are anxieties about identity. In the case of knowledge producers, particularly in the Western traditions of such activity, such identity is profoundly linked to the belief that knowledge represents truth and certainty. To abandon this belief is to abandon all basis for authority and to threaten identity itself.

It was a popular government slogan in the UK in the 1980s that 'there is no alternative', which even acquired the status of recognition by acronym, TINA, alone. This slogan represented the claim by those with power that it was bootless even to consider the question of alternatives to their ideology, since none was even conceivable. The willingness of the electorate to re-elect the proponents of this political ideology demonstrates some considerable success in their persuasion to accept this assertion. Perhaps what TINA symbolized was the reduction of uncertainty, and the acceptability of relinquishing the responsibilities of freedom, to be informed and to make decisions which reflect social responsibilities as well as responsibility to the self, to question. But, as Foucault points out, there are always alternatives. No development is inevitable, but is always chosen, which implies the prioritization of one course of action over others which are rejected, for whatever reason and whether or not that is acknowledged. These developments include, not just practical action, but, more generally, other ways of defining problems and solutions. That it may be difficult to do does not constitute reason to abandon the attempt. Perhaps all that is required to start the process is an effort of imagination, and the recognition that questions about received wisdom can be asked. And, in what is conventionally referred to as the world of the imagination, the arts, there are many traces to be found to stimulate the impulse to imagine alternatives.

Traditionally and historically, the arts have represented a particular repository of 'alternative thinking', as witnessed by the attention of various social theorists who seek to draw attention to the potential for such negation to be expressed. Thus, for example, Marcuse (1986) talks about art in terms of the 'Great Refusal', although there is much variation among writers, about the re-forming potential of the arts. Nonetheless, their significance as a possible reservoir of negation, and as possessing the potential to disrupt what is, has been widely recognized and has made the arts an arena subject routinely to control by those with power. Sometimes some kinds of art are literally proscribed, more often the arts are simply marginalized and/or commodified. Such responses have varying degrees of success in limiting oppositional potential, but cannot utterly repress it – to be orthodox, the orthodoxy must distinguish itself from what is not orthodox.

The poet John Keats, writing to his brother in 1817, identified what can be seen both as an unorthodoxy, and as a quality which epitomizes a way of thinking which resists certainty, a quality he called negative capability: 'And at once it struck me, what quality went to form a man of Achievement.... I mean *Negative Capability*, that is when man is capable of being in uncertainties, mysteries, doubts, without any irritable reaching after fact and reason' (Keats, in Foreman, 1901: 49–51, original emphasis). The poet Charles Olson, who took this concept of negative capability, together with Heraclitus' dictum that 'man is estranged from that with which he is most familiar', as the theme of his *Special View of History* (1970), argues that, to be no longer estranged from what is most familiar, we have to be negatively capable. Negative capability for Olson is counterposed to and counterposes power. He argues:

> There is no limit to what you can know. Or there is only in the sense that you don't find out or you don't seek to know. There is no truth at all, of course, in the modern velleity (the lowest degree of desire) that you can't know everything. It is literally true that you *have* to know everything. And for the simplest reason; that you do, by being alive.... [But] when either perfection or form is achieved, it is already imperfect or less than the necessary form by the very fact of coming into its own existence: it has pushed the limit of possibility by its own achievement. (Here, by the way, is the only allowable meaning of progress.)
> (Olson, 1970: 29)

Negative capability, according to Jones, 'silently confronts the rest of the world's Positive Incapacity' (1969: 19) (impotence).

There is, possibly, a link here to Lyotard's (1994) use of Kant's concept of negative presentation. The discursive rules which prioritize affirmation, identity, the empirical, have the result that knowledge which negates this affirmation is divested of a language with which to present itself. Recognition of this negation, Lyotard argues, opens up an infinite space of possibilities, and this space is also the only space in which it is possible to approach 'the sublime' (Kant). In order to 'think' about the sublime it is first necessary to abandon finitude – affirmation, thing-ness

– the sublime is boundaryless. Even having done so, however, the sublime remains unpresentable. There is no example which can comprehend it, not least because to do so would be to give it identity, to bound it, and the sublime would thereby escape, exceeding its example. Nonetheless, it is possible to cognize traces of the sublime, and these traces Lyotard calls negative presentation. The negation which Lyotard proposes makes possible the world of nonidentity. To negate an affirmation is to recognize indeterminacy. In its denial, negation does not necessarily propose a different affirmative, but opens up the realm of all possibilities which the affirmation has denied. (There may also be some faint resonance, in a different realm of analysis, with 'the philosophy of no' proposed by Bachelard. See, for example, Lecourt, 1975.)

Escape from the dominant discourse is not merely to replace it with another set of theories equally chasing scientific certainty, since any-thing which claims completion, perfection, by its own claim pushes out the 'limit of possibility'. Thus the very desire for certainty is only its own prison, its own constraint. Escape from its clutches leaves the way open for developing an understanding rooted in the everyday experience of doubt and disorder, of living with *un*certainty. Rather than a 'training' which teaches us that anxiety can only be eliminated when we know for certain, we need to learn to live at ease with uncertainty. Uncertainty is not a pathological condition amenable to therapy but is the normality of infinitude. The pursuit of certainty within a framework of the possibility of achieving it leads inevitably to inflexibility and to the failure to recognize opportunities, potential benefits, other solutions to problems, and solutions to other problems, offered by the very ambiguity and uncertainty that are so feared. It is also self-defeating. Trying to create certainty as an antidote to anxiety in a world inherently uncertain is doomed to failure.

Uncertainty is not to be lived with as a punishment, but embraced as the only truth. Living in a world of uncertainty requires us to abandon the props which give the illusion of certainty and, at the same time, to recognize that human action can lead to failure as well as to success. But, in such a case, failure is not to be associated with inadequacy but to be treated as a learning point, to be seen as a real experience which can be turned to affirmative value. Negative capability opens up a world of possibilities denied by the rules of inclusion and exclusion enforced by the dominant discourse. It diverts energies from supporting and reinforcing a system, which is flawed into exploration of possibilities which are declared inadmissible only within a particular regime of truth. It is a means to recover the wider arena of what is possible. Negative capability is an initial requirement for negation. To discover why this may be so we can turn to the world of cybernetics.

Negative potential

Boulding (1978) notes that the tendency of systems towards increasing disorder, entropy, seems to be at odds with the evolutionary tendency to become increasingly complex. He suggests that one way to understand this paradox is to see entropy as *negative potential*. This emphasizes a diminishing potential for order in a system. Evolutionary developments thus need to be seen as islands of order made possible by increasing disorder elsewhere. These potentialities of the system may be renewed by a sort of iteration, but the outcome will always be a different configuration. Boulding illustrates this with the example of the reproductive process, where new islands of order are created but never with exactly the same characteristics of order as the creators. Using this as an analogy for organizations, negative potential suggests that within any system there are myriad possibilities for its reconfiguration, and that the abandonment of the already configured releases energies to be used for other purposes. Such other possibilities, however, cannot be realized when the focus of energy is directed towards maintaining the status quo. Furthermore, what the alternatives are is not to be specified *a priori*, but are a function of what is possible. By implication, the presence of real contradictions in society, such as those identified by Adorno and others, can only be dissolved in terms of real possibilities.

It is increasingly recognized in some kinds of contemporary theory that certainty is no more than an illusion, and therefore that its pursuit is a waste of time and effort. The uncertainty that Keats suggests we need to accept and embrace could be seen in terms of this tendency to increasing disorder addressed by Boulding. This would suggest that living with uncertainty is not a matter of choice but one of necessity. To resist disorder by claiming to be able to order it is never to be more than a very temporary achievement. In the longer term it is both futile and destructive. Not only that, but the concepts of negative capability and negative potential permit us to see this increasing disorder as also re-presenting increasing opportunities.

Organizations are configurations of people which are designed, in general terms, to produce synergy. If we could hypothesize a population without organization, such a population would be characterizable as exhibiting maximum disorder, maximum entropy. But, at the same time, as Bateson (1973) points out, this condition would also exhibit maximum flexibility, i.e. the maximum potential for different ways of organizing. Once a particular organizational form has been configured – once an island of order has been created (which in Bateson's terms represents specialization and in Boulding's terms represents the evolutionary tendency) – in this section of the population flexibility is lost. Maintaining this order requires the creation of negative entropy, which is to forego negative potential. As Bateson comments, 'flexibility is to specialization as entropy is to negentropy' (1973: 473). In order to maintain negative entropy, inputs to the system, i.e. information, are necessary. Bateson identifies two characteristics of information: on the one hand, it is 'the difference that makes a difference' (1973: 351) and, on the other, it excludes alternatives.

This can be illustrated in the context of formal organization. Once created, if left alone it will tend to develop increasing levels of disorder, but this can be combated by a learning process which allows negative entropy to be created. One obvious source of this negative entropy is organization theory which, over its existence, has produced a series of knowledge claims (information) which oppose the tendency to disorder, allowing the system to maintain its identity. However, as this information is reactive – its purpose is to solve perceived problems (to reduce increasing entropy) in the organization – it tends to create ever more specialization in the system, by removing variety, and at the same time, increases the amount of control, both present and required, to maintain this specialization. Increasing amounts of energy are needed within the system to sustain this control and so decreasing amounts of energy are made available to be devoted to the production of useful outputs. Information, in this sense, is only concerned with system maintenance, and has no 'interest' in the purpose of the system. It is because of this that systems exhibit tendencies to become autopoietic, a state where the maximum amount of energy is devoted to system maintenance, rather than to the production of outputs (coming from the earlier cited comment of Foucault on devotion to administering scarcity in a situation of superabundance). Autopoietic systems in this sense are ultimately self-destructive, since it is production of outputs which contribute to system maintenance, in a healthy system.

It was previously suggested that the purpose of capitalist organizations is to be efficient, and that organization theory is geared to providing techniques to increase efficiency. Increasing efficiency, in these terms, means that for a given level of output there is a reduced input. A particular form of this in recent years has been manifested in organizations shedding labour. Organization theory's informational contribution to this has been the concepts of downsizing and delayering (the difference). This 'truism' leads to action in organizations which results in relative contraction of labour inputs (that makes a difference). But, as the pool of labour is reduced, the possibility for alternative actions is also reduced (increased specialization, loss of flexibility).

Another term which can be used to describe the selection of a particular configuration for organizations is opportunity cost. In that all forms of organization are purposeful, a particular form excludes the possibility of organizing differently, either for the same or for different purposes. This is an example of what we have previously described as exclusionary ways of defining problems and limiting the admissibility of solutions. The opportunity cost is the loss of negative potential. Once energy has been used in the system, it can never be recovered. Using up negative potential to sustain the status quo, simply to defend it from increasing entropy, or disorder, has two major consequences. On the one hand it is used to attempt to achieve the unachievable, to increase order. On the other hand, that negative potential is no longer available for possible redefinitions and reconfigurations, admitting different definitions and different solutions. Where there are soluble problems which cannot be dealt with by the existing configurations of order, their solution must lie within the arena of negative potential. Negative potential is the arena of all possible solutions not already configured, and repressed by the solutions which are configured.

'The work thing'

We have suggested that negation acknowledges that present conventional ways of understanding, however totalizing they may seek to be, do not encompass all possible definitions and solutions, and that it offers the opportunity to recover all such possibilities defined, *a priori*, as inadmissible by these conventional understandings. Negative capability describes a way of understanding the world and negative potential provides a way of describing what can be understood – what is, at present, described as the no-thing. The point is not to prescribe in advance what alternatives might be tried, since the first step is to uncover what those alternatives might be. There are many traces to be found, clues to both the process and what it might produce, but these exist by definition, outside the dominant discourse of organization theory.

We live in a society which has the technical capacity to solve problems, but which apparently lacks the will to do so. In other words, there is a profound impotence in our normal(ized) ways of understanding and organizing. Thus, for example, we have a wage-labour economy, in which the ability to survive depends upon income earned by those working, but this economy fails to provide enough work for all who need it and, at the same time, exhibits a strong reluctance to pay many of those who have jobs a living wage. Since labour is so closely linked to income as the means to purchase the benefits of society, exclusion from the ability to acquire the necessary income also excludes from such social benefit. On a global scale, the problems of want, ignorance and disease remain intractable – the so-called advanced industrial societies overproduce and destroy the surplus while, elsewhere in the world, people starve. This is what Bataille (1988) refers to as the accumulation, appropriation and squandering of resources. Social and organizational problems are endemic and, whatever level of analysis is chosen, the system seems to be failing.

It is not that such problems go unnoticed but rather that, because analyses which address them reject the dominant definition of efficiency, they are inadmissible to the discourse of the capitalist regime of truth. For example, Gorz (1989) argues that we have increasingly become defined as workers (rather than as human beings) at a historical moment when there appears to be an absolute decline in the demand for labour. This signifies a contradiction. Modern development in wealth creation processes has reduced the demand for labour, for the first time in human history, in that all necessary wealth can, apparently, be created with a quantity of labour far less than the pool available. At the same time, both intellectual and managerial understandings of organization have effected a profound attenuation of the enormous variety of humanity, to the point when we are defined purely in terms of our utility to the wealth-creation processes, as no more than producers and/or consumers. Managerially, the situation is exacerbated by the expressed belief that, in spite of defining survival in terms of a wage-labour economy, work organizations have no absolute responsibility to provide levels of remuneration necessary for such survival, as witnessed by the abolition of the UK Wages

Councils, the use of zero-hours contracts, the debilitation of collective bargaining, deterioration of terms and conditions of employment and official sanctioning of continuous downward pressure on wages. Thus recognition that organizations are the almost exclusive source of income in a wage-labour economy is withheld. Intellectually, through organization theory, this condensation of people into workers has been substantiated by, for example, the characterization of people as resources, as in *human resource* management – resources being things to be used, exploited. Understandings of people as people have disappeared: organization theory has little to say about the totality of the life of 'workers', economically, socially or psychologically – 'in general a capitalist society reduces what is human to the condition of a *thing*' (Bataille, 1988: 129, original emphasis). Both in theory and in practice, organizations have succumbed to the temptation to become, in Bateson's terms, ever more specialized, and, thus, ever less flexible, rather than more so, as claimed.

This contradiction can be summarized: at a moment when the centrality of labour is declining there is, *for ideological reasons*, an increasingly dominant understanding of labour based on its scarcity. That such understanding is selective is not difficult to show. Thus, for example, the move to 'Japanize' industry is focused exclusively on labour practices, while the same strictures are not applied to capital, such as applying a much lower acceptable rate of return on investment and its deferred realization as growth rather than its immediate appropriation as dividend, even though, as Hutton (1995) notes, too high profit targets and short-termism are endemic problems in the UK economy. Japan also recognizes overwork as an industrial disease (with ten thousand attributable deaths per year), yet in the UK labour intensification is driving up the length of the working week. The drive to labour intensification has been dutifully legitimated by organization theory in its role as the discourse of prescriptive knowledge about work organization. One might begin to wonder, however, about claims to expertise when a recent longitudinal study reported that refuse collectors were better predictors of economic performance than finance ministers, company chairmen/women or Oxford students (*The Economist*, 1995: 98). This, perhaps, suggests that expertise has more to do with discursive acceptability than with knowledge *per se*.

Equally, the kind of solutions proposed by Gorz (1989), such as the abandonment of the work ethic, the idea of work as a good in itself and the 'ideology of hard work', the need to detach work from income and to accept the sharing out of available work, have many implications for addressing the myriad dysfunctions of work and of unemployment which could be explored but are simply inadmissible to the discourse, because they are ideologically inappropriate, irrespective of whether they have potential value. Whether or not such ideas might 'work' is irrelevant in the face of their challenge to the hegemony which the discourse represents and serves. Because of such exclusions the experience of work and the conditions, both local and global, in which it occurs are, ultimately, left untouched. Brendan Behan said that 'a job is death without the dignity'. Baudrillard talks about 'labour as slow death' (1993: 39). It might be suggested that the organization and management of work, both in theory and in practice, are peculiar as professional activities in that, in their impact on people, their operation is directed to emiseration rather than to amelioration.

An organization theory which has seen its role as one of increasing the efficiency of capitalism both as a practice and as a socioeconomic system has, ultimately, said very little about organizations, even in those areas to which particular attention has been paid. There are no conclusive theories of motivation, leadership, structure, culture, and so on. Incidentally, it may have taught us a lot about dominating people, but that was not its overt purpose. It is a knowledge 'which aims to reduce its object to the condition of subordinated and managed things' (Bataille, 1988: 74) . And, whatever it has done, it has not addressed the fundamental issues about what it means to organize and how organization is accomplished. It could be argued that it is hardly meaningful, let alone informative, to talk about organizations (plural) until we understand what is meant by organization (singular). While this issue is now beginning to be addressed, such work remains firmly outside the dominant discourse since it does not contribute to capitalist notions of efficiency. Such work is, thus, a prime example of what negation implies: it draws *nothing* from, and relates to *nothing* in, the dominant mode of organizational thinking. This dominant mode fails to solve increasingly pressing problems, indeed exacerbates them. Redefinition of problems and, thereby, of admissible solutions can, therefore, only be pursued fruitfully outside this discourse. It may be that such a process of negation will turn out something akin to a Sartrean detotalization, in that it is unpredictable and unknowable because wholly different to what is, now. Yet we have argued that only negation will redeem potence.

Acknowledgement

One major influence that Robert Cooper has had on our thinking is recognition of the imperative of negation. His way of addressing the subject of organization is, in many ways, the embodiment of negative thinking. Insofar as this chapter represents an exploration of negative thinking, it is suffused with connections with his work. As such, it seems inappropriate to identify these connections in the conventional way, e.g. by referencing. Those familiar with his work will recognize the connections. We hope they will stand as an acknowledgement of his influence on our work.

Bibliography

Adorno, T. W. (1973a) *Negative Dialectics*, trans. E. B. Ashton, London: Routledge & Kegan Paul.

—— (1973b) *The Jargon of Authenticity*, trans. K. Tarnowski and F. Will, London: Routledge & Kegan Paul.

Adorno, T. W. and Horkheimer, M. (1979) *Dialectic of Enlightenment*, trans. J. Cumming, London: Verso.
Barthes, R. (1967) *Writing Degree Zero*, trans. A. Lavers and C. Smith, London: Jonathan Cape.
Bataille, G. (1988) *The Accursed Share*, vol. 1, trans. R. Hurley, New York: Zone Books.
Bateson, G. (1973) *Steps to an Ecology of Mind*, London: Paladin.
Baudrillard, J. (1993) *Symbolic Exchange and Death*, trans. I. H. Grant, London: Sage.
Boulding, K. (1978) *Ecodynamics*, London: Sage.
Buck-Morss, S. (1977) *The Origin of Negative Dialectics*, New York: The Free Press.
Deleuze, G. and Guattari, F. (1984) *Anti-Oedipus: Capitalism and Schizophrenia*, trans. R. Hurley, M. Seem and H. R. Lane, London: Athlone.
Derrida, J. (1994) *Spectres of Marx*, trans. P. Kamuf, London: Routledge.
The Economist (1995) 'Garbage in, Garbage Out' (3 June), 9, 98.
Foreman, G. B. (1901) *Complete Works of John Keats*, vol. 4, Glasgow: Gowers & Gray.
Foucault, M. (1971) 'Orders of Discourse', trans. R. Swyer, *Social Science Information*, 10, 2, 7–30.
—— (1974) *The Archaeology of Knowledge*, trans. A. Sheridan, London: Tavistock.
—— (1980a) 'Truth and Power', in C. Gordon (ed.) *Michel Foucault: Power/Knowledge*, London: Harvester Wheatsheaf.
—— (1980b) 'The Eye of Power', in C. Gordon (ed.) *Michel Foucault: Power/Knowledge* London: Harvester Wheatsheaf.
—— (1988) 'The Masked Philosopher', in L. D. Kritzman (ed.) *Michel Foucault: Politics, Philosophy, Culture*, New York and London: Routledge, 323–30.
Gorz, A. (1989) *Critique of Economic Reason*, trans. G. Handyside and C. Turner, London: Verso.
Hutton, W. (1995) *The State We're In*, London: Jonathan Cape.
Jones, J. (1969) *John Keats's Dream of Truth*, London: Chatto & Windus.
Lecourt, D. (1975) *Marxism and Epistemology*, trans. B. Brewster, London: New Left Books.
Lyotard, J.-F. (1977) 'The Unconscious as Mise-en-Scène', in M. Benamou and C. Caramello (eds) *Performance in Postmodern Culture*, Madison, WI: Coda Press.
—— (1988) *The Differend: Phrases in Dispute*, trans. G. Van den Abbeele, Manchester: Manchester University Press.
—— (1994) *Lessons on the Analytic of the Sublime*, trans. E. Rottenberg, Stanford, CA: Stanford University Press.
MacGowan, K. (1993) *The Hill of Tara*, Dublin: Karnac Publications.
McGregor, D. (1960) *The Human Side of Enterprise*, New York: McGraw-Hill.
Marcuse, H. (1968) *Negations*, trans. J. J. Shapiro, London: Free Association Press.
—— (1986) *One-dimensional Man*, London: Ark Paperbacks.
Marx, K. and Engels, F. (1848) *Manifesto of the Communist Party*, trans. S. Moore, Moscow: Progress Publishers; repr. 1965.
Mészáros, I. (1989) *The Power of Ideology*, London: Harvester Wheatsheaf.
Olson, C. (1970) *Special View of History*, Berkeley, CA: Oyez.
Orwell, G. (1954) *Nineteen Eighty-Four*, Harmondsworth: Penguin.
Rotman, B. (1987) *Signifying Nothing: The Semiotics of Zero*, London: Macmillan.

9

RE-COGNIZING THE OTHER: REFLECTIONS ON A 'NEW SENSIBILITY' IN SOCIAL AND ORGANIZATION STUDIES

Hugh Willmott

Introduction

'Social science is not the study of social action per se, but the study of *method*' (Cooper, 1983a: 218, original emphasis).[1] This claim departs radically from the prevalent, common sense understanding of social science as the provider of more reliable, objective reports of the phenomena that are deemed to comprise the social world. For it encourages us to re-cognize how our knowledge of action is always mediated by the methods that render that action accountable as action. In this way, Robert Cooper alerts us to, or re-minds us about, the reliance of social scientific production of knowledge (for example, about organizing and organization) *upon the methods for generating such knowledge,* including our favoured method of determining which method is capable of producing (more) accurate knowledge. Or, as he puts it: 'method is our language for engaging reality . . . the structure of method is the major means of understanding the social world' (Cooper, 1983a: 218).

Robert Cooper's work has made an important and sustained contribution to what might be termed the 'reflexivization' of social and organization studies. Substantively, his analyses extend from the problematization of key concepts, such as alienation (Cooper, 1983b), through post-structuralist analyses of organization and technology (e.g. Cooper, 1990, 1992, 1993) to an exploration of the relevance of postmodern discourse, and especially the writings of Jacques Derrida, for organization studies (Cooper and Burrell, 1988; Cooper, 1989a). These writings have consistently provoked reflection upon what is assumed to be 'obvious' or 'natural' but which, when subjected to critical scrutiny, turns out to be arbitrary and problematical.[2] In turn, this opens up a space for reflection upon how what, through a process of reflection, is now viewed as arbitrary has been rendered authoritative or taken for granted; and, relatedly, how a process of personal and social transformation might be promoted and embraced that is informed by post-structuralist thinking, so that social change moves beyond replacing one arbitrary authority (for example, theism, religion) with another (humanism, science).

This chapter circles around a number of Robert Cooper's concerns as reference is made to contributions from the fields of sociology and philosophy,[3] as well as organization studies. The chapter offers a loosely connected set of reflections upon issues that are pivotal for the production and dissemination of knowledge in these fields. Its intention is to contribute to an ongoing process of debate upon these issues rather than to provide any kind of definitive, integrated or conclusive exposition of them. It concludes by providing an assessment of the strengths and limitations of Robert Cooper's current thinking.

From organizational analysis to the methodic organization of analysis

Since the publication of Silverman's *The Theory of Organizations* (1970), at least,[4] recurrent doubts have been cast upon the capacity of the established (positivist) structure of method to appreciate the constricted and powerful qualities of organization.[5] Doubts voiced by Silverman about the monopoly and adequacy of orthodox organization theory were subsequently appropriated, amplified or extended by Child (1972), Clegg (1975) and, most influentially, by Burrell and Morgan (1979).[6] Despite its shortcomings (see Willmott, 1993), Burrell and Morgan's *Sociological Paradigms and Organisational Analysis* (1979), in particular, has supported and promoted a greater awareness of, and attention to, the ways in which our knowledge of organizations is governed by 'normalized criteria' of knowledge production rather than by the empirical topics of its analysis. It has nonetheless served to encourage an understanding of how accounts of organizations/organization/organizing are products of the organizing activity of their authors, such that:

> it becomes impossible to disentangle the content of organization studies from the theory or methodology that frames it. By this logic each statement about system or organization is not merely a piece of information about a particular subject matter but – significantly – the statement 'produces' what it denotes.
>
> (Cooper, 1990: 197)

Instead of generating *analyses of organization* that assume its objects to exist 'out there', waiting to be captured by the tools of the social scientist, analysis is informed by the *reflexive understanding* that *the (methodical) organization of analysis* (for example, within different paradigms) is productive of what we know (see Willmott, 1977, 1995). During the past decade or more there has been a significant enrichment – or disarray, depending upon one's favoured structure of method[7] – of organization studies as the attention of a growing number of analysts has turned to the methodic reasoning that constitutes topics of studies and guides the organization of their analyses.

It is perhaps worth stressing that the concern to reflect upon how different methods, or ways of thinking, are productive of different knowledges, encompasses a much broader conception of the nature and significance of 'method' than discussions of method presented in most research method(ology) textbooks. What Cooper means by method is not to be equated with an explication of the theories and techniques that aspire or claim to capture different aspects of social reality (for example, Morgan, 1986). Rather, Cooper's conception of method serves to problematize the separation of subjects (observers) and objects (observed), together with the aspirations and claims associated with knowledge whose authority rests upon an assumption of this separation. Despite being problematical,[8] the distinction Cooper makes between social science as the study of social action and the study of method (see above) is invaluable. Otherwise, social science can easily become mesmerized by what Habermas (1972) terms 'the illusion of pure theory' – an illusion that acts to conceal how seemingly authoritative scientific statements are not sharply distinguishable from the common sense reasoning which informs processes of scientific knowledge production.[9]

A new sensibility

Robert Cooper has been in the vanguard of contemporary efforts to encourage and enable students of organization and organizing to problematize, 'deconstruct' and think beyond established ways of making sense of organization and organizing. To this end, he has drawn attention to how our knowledge of organization is framed by 'method' – an endemic and powerful, yet often unacknowledged or silent, partner in the process of knowledge production. Most recently, a distinction between 'distal' and 'proximal' ways of thinking has been advanced to highlight how knowledge is the product of such methodic ways of representing experience:

> The *distal* stresses boundaries and separation, distinctness and clarity, hierarchy and order. The *proximal* manifests implication and complicity, and hence symmetry, equivalence and equivocality. . . . The distal organization is a definable system with a strong boundary. For instance, the traditional distinction between organization and environment is a distal conception. So is the idea that organizations are 'things' that can be measured. By contrast, proximal thinking views organizations as mediating networks, as circuits of continuous contact and motion – more like assemblages of organizings.
> (Cooper and Law, 1995: 239, emphasis added)

In everyday language, the terms 'organization(s)' and 'organizing' broadly express these two kinds of thinking. Typically, the term 'organization(s)' conveys the *distal* understanding that certain, discrete entities called organizations exist 'out there';

and that these organizations can be studied in whole or in part as objects that possess distinctive characteristics or 'variables'. This formulation is an expression of what Chia (1996) has termed 'being-realism'. In contrast, *proximal* thinking attends to the way in which all 'organizations' comprise diverse ongoing and open-ended activities. Whatever boundaries or variables are identified, they are understood to be constructed, arbitrary and unstable rather than reflections of the world 'out there'. Whereas distal thinking encourages an understanding of knowledge as something like a map of a comparatively well defined 'out there' reality, proximal thinking articulates and promotes an appreciation of the precarious and incomplete processes of constituting our sense of the 'out there'; and, in doing so, it reveals any taken-for-granted sense of the 'out there' to be the product of a particular, distal form of thinking, or structure of method, rather than something which exists *sui generis*. It exemplifies what Chia (1996) has called 'becoming-realism'.

Cooper's questioning of the authority and self-understanding of the established distal structure of method, which articulates the dominance of distal thinking, is symptomatic of what Giddens (1979) has termed the breakdown of 'the orthodox consensus' in social science. One of the two principal pillars of this orthodoxy, Giddens argues, rests upon assumptions about the logical form and likely achievements of social science.[10] More specifically, this pillar is constructed upon (a) functionalism which assumes that the organization of social systems can be explained in terms of their functional consequences for the *pre-servation* of order; and (b) naturalism which assumes that 'the logical frameworks of natural and social sciences are in essential respects the same' (ibid.: 237). As the hegemonic grip of functionalist and naturalist thinking has slackened, alternative currents of thought have developed and strengthened in the social sciences (Giddens, 1976) and subsequently in the field of social and organization studies (Alvesson and Willmott, 1996). As early as 1976, Bernstein characterized this shift as a 'new sensibility' when he observed that:

> The initial impression one has in reading the literature in and about the social disciplines during the past decade or so is that of sheer chaos. . . . There is little or no consensus – except by the members of the same school or sub-school – about what are the well established results, the proper research procedures, the important problems, or even the most promising theoretical approaches to the study of society and politics.
>
> (Bernstein, 1976: xii)

As a philosopher of social science, Bernstein has been more attentive to the variety and 'chaos' of the field than those who have continued to beaver away within particular disciplines or theoretical schools, largely unconscious of, indifferent to or sheltered from other ways of determining 'proper procedures, important problems and promising theoretical approaches' (ibid.).[11] But, equally, current conditions – and not least the destructive consequences of capitalist expansionism fuelled by the technological application of scientific knowledge (for example, the car culture) and its role in the generation and identification of risk – are productive of experiences and awareness that problematize the authority of this knowledge. As Giddens (1991) has observed,

> Modernity's reflexivity refers to the susceptibility of most aspects of social activity, and material relations with nature, to chronic revision in the light of new information or knowledge . . . *the reflexivity of modernity actually undermines the certainty of knowledge, even in the core domains of natural science.*
>
> (1991: 20–1, emphasis added)

It would, of course, be foolish to submit that an attentiveness to the *interdependence* of researcher and researched and, in particular, the role of method in the constitution (as contrasted with the accumulation) of knowledge, is an entirely modern phenomenon.[12] However, in recent decades, there has been a strengthening of 'the new sensibility' which has challenged the possibility and the rationality of founding scientific inquiry upon the assumption of 'any permanent division between observation and theory' (Bernstein, 1988: 172). Even in the natural sciences, where the objects of study cannot readily 'act back' upon the researcher, 'the new physics' has radically challenged the assumption of a separation between observer and observed (see Cooper, 1987: 414). In the new physics, *what* is observed is understood to depend upon *how* it is observed. Or, as Capra (1983) has articulated this understanding:

> The crucial feature of quantum theory is that the observer is not only necessary to observe the properties of an atomic phenomenon, but is necessary to bring about these properties. . . . *In atomic physics the sharp Cartesian division between mind and matter, between the observer and the observed, can no longer be maintained.*
>
> (1983: 77, emphasis added)

This post-Cartesian understanding, as Capra goes on to note, has profound implications for our conception of science and, relatedly, for any aspiration to develop a more rational society. It questions the coherence of the belief that a unified Scientific Method can (eventually) provide objective and reliable knowledge of the world. Relatedly, it doubts the claim that scientific knowledge can ever be value-free since the assumptions of the observer inevitably condition what is observed.[13]

As long as a traditional Cartesian ontology is assumed, there occurs what Cooper has characterized as 'a seduction of knowledge by the empirical world' (Cooper, 1983b: 718) – a seduction that is a condition and consequence of 'the rise of positivism in social science' (ibid.). However, if value-freedom is a myth, then scientists are morally as well as intellectually responsible for their research; and knowledge that enjoys the soubriquet of 'science' is recognized to be *the product of a moral and political process* rather than a product of dispassionate procedures undertaken by impartial experts.[14]

Normal service will be resumed: or will it?

Many social scientists and organizational analysts remain largely untouched and unmoved by the 'new sensibility' (sometimes dubbed 'postmodernism'). They have continued to assume the adequacy, and to privilege the authority, of forms of analysis that assume that its topics exist 'out there'; and that there is little that is problematical about identifying and measuring 'relationships between variables defined in terms of the [analyst's] world-taken-for-granted' (Silverman, 1970: 226).[15] Others have been disturbed by 'the new sensibility' and sought to restore order by professorial fiat. Pfeffer (1993), a leading North American organization analyst, has urged his colleagues to accept the imposition of a consensus about what is authoritative (or at least to manage the appearance of it) in order to restore their status in the marketplace for ideas and funding. A decline in their status and fortunes is attributed to the emergence of the new sensibility. But it might equally, and more persuasively, be ascribed to the hostage to fortune created by earlier inflated claims to objectivity – a hostage that they now seek to rescue from the diversification of social scientific activity.

According to Pfeffer, it is only through the creation of a ruling elite whose members zealously dictate the fundamental questions, enforce a set of research standards and generally defend the boundaries of acceptability that 'orderly development' of 'scientific knowledge' can be resumed. However, as Cannella and Paetzold (1994) have observed, Pfeffer's proposal disregards critiques of the traditional ontology as it immunizes the production of authoritative knowledge from anything but friendly, self-serving incremental comment. In response to Pfeffer's call for tighter, elite control over 'organizational science', Cannella and Paetzold (1994) have cuttingly remarked that:

> A consensus such as that called for by Pfeffer requires blind faith and unquestioning adherence to a dogma decreed to be 'true' by the elites of our field. . . . The concept of progress in knowledge is best achieved when there are critics among us who constantly push us to reassess our assumptions and refine our theories.
>
> (Cannella and Paetzold, 1994: 337)

Those who have become disenchanted with the relevance and value of the structure of method embraced – whether naively, heroically or cynically – by Pfeffer and his fellow travellers have been more concerned to reassess its assumptions than to propose refinements. Coupled with the challenges of the 'new physics', it is becoming increasingly difficult to deny that the meaning attached to a concept or variable is 'constituted *a priori* in the self-evidence of the primary life-world' (Habermas, 1972: 304). In which case, if the very concepts and reasoning deployed by the (social) scientist are deeply and inescapably rooted in an historically and culturally conditioned process of identifying and interpreting this world, much greater attention needs to be paid to *how the meaning of these concepts – such as 'individual' or 'science' – is socially organized*. Instead of assuming that such concepts describe or mirror an empirical reality, it is necessary to appreciate how they come into (social) existence – for example, by considering how the 'objects' of social scientific analysis, such as 'organizations' or 'technologies', result from a process of objectification that is dependent upon 'a particular *way of seeing*' (Cooper, 1987: 413, original emphasis) made possible by what Cooper (borrowing from the philosopher Gaston Bachelard) has termed 'phenomeno-techniques' (see below). Instead of striving to produce more distal knowledge of such entities, Cooper urges a study of 'the *a priori* meanings [such as the common sense identification of individuals – H. W.] which, through the logic of words and language, attach us to those things' (Cooper 1983b: 718). Key concepts in social science, such as 'individual' or 'organization', he argues, cannot sensibly 'be abstracted from everyday speech and used to support a theory of social behavior without first being critically examined for their ontological meaning' (ibid.: 719). Cooper thus invites us to deploy our capacity for critical thinking to reflect upon how the use of the concept of 'individual' or 'organization' *defines the reality of the world* in particular ways (for example, the individual as a discrete entity) instead of assuming that such concepts simply provide a more or less adequate reflection of empirical reality.

Technology and science as phenomeno-techniques

Technology is widely represented as a set of techniques for accomplishing particular purposes. For example, in Giddens' voluminous writings, the discussion of technology (which is revealingly scanty) is largely restricted to a consideration of the role of technological innovation in the development and expansion of capitalist economies (for example, Giddens, 1973). Were Giddens to discuss technology at any length, it may be imagined that his analysis would incorporate an appreciation of how social scientific knowledge(s) of technology feeds back into lay discourse to reproduce or transform the world that they seek to explicate. It is much less likely that Giddens would analyse technology as a way of ordering and revealing the world – which is the tack favoured by Cooper (1987).

Technology, Cooper (1987) suggests, mediates our relation to the world because, in order to make it and use it, we are required to render the world meaningful in ways that signify the relevance and value of the technology. A condition of the use of technology is the mobilization of phenomeno-techniques to (re)inscribe the world in ways that make it available and amenable to technological intervention (see also Cooper, 1993: 283, 299). For example, a condition of riding a bicycle is the (re)inscription of the world in ways that are relevant for its effective use in transporting the rider from A to B. Likewise, the operation of social technologies (for example, organizations) is conditional upon people learning and applying phenomeno-techniques that minimize indeterminacy or 'un-readiness':

knowledge of the social technologies of organizing renders people ready to function in self-disciplined ways. 'In such ordering', Cooper writes, 'people must necessarily include themselves as raw material . . . they are reinscribed as human resources' (1987: 414).

Here we find a central and recurrent theme of Robert Cooper's writings: namely, the precarious accomplishment of organization/determinacy out of disorganization/indeterminacy; and, relatedly, the chronic recurrence of the repressed as the Other (i.e. indeterminacy, disorganization, the un-ready) returns to disrupt the (sense of) orderliness. Social institutions, Cooper (1993) suggests, are organized in ways that 'make it difficult for us to think of the *un-ready* since they are continually working to structure our thoughts and thinking processes for us. Universities, schools, political programmes, religious credos, academic theories *all forbid the possibility of the un-ready*' (1993: 300, second emphasis added). Formulating the argument in this way tends to suggest that forbidding the possibility of the un-ready is actually achievable or even achieved. But it is perhaps more plausible to submit that, as we reproduce or transform social institutions, including social science, we can necessarily and routinely only *strive* to forbid, or act to impede, the un-ready (Willmott, 1986; Weber, 1987, Chap.2). This effort never fully succeeds precisely because the un-ready defies capture and control. It repeatedly returns *inter alia* in the form of 'unexplained variance' or disputed claims, and thereby fuels the renewal of efforts to pin down or tame 'the un-ready' (see, for example, Child, 1972):

> The *already* is the conversion of the indeterminate and *un-ready*. The indeterminate and *un-ready* is pure act, without name or identity, that precedes all determining thought. The *un-ready* is 'a stranger to consciousness and cannot be constituted by it . . . it is what dismantles consciousness, what deposes consciousness, it is what consciousness cannot formulate, and even what consciousness forgets in order to constitute itself'.
> (Cooper, 1993: 300, citing Lyotard, 1989: 197, original emphasis)

Here, the established self-understandings of common sense and social science are problematized by remembering what consciousness presents as the empirical reality of organizations, for example, it does not exist independently of our methodical ways of accounting for this reality. By recollecting how the 'un-ready' precedes all determining thought, it is recalled that our knowledge (for example, of organizations) rests upon the forgetting of how 'the un-ready' is at once a condition of its possibility and a recurrent threat to the authority of our knowledge. In effect, 'the un-ready' manifests itself as a disruptive, agonistic force which repeatedly exposes the precariousness of efforts to create organization/determinacy out of disorganization/indeterminacy: it 'dismantles' and 'decomposes' every effort to carve 'the ready' from 'the un-ready'. Our knowledge of 'the un-ready' is derived from its effects upon 'the ready' whose limits it repeatedly exposes. Experientially, it is felt as insecurity, anxiety and disappointment about the precariousness of 'the ready' and the anticipation or actuality of the deconstruction of 'the ready' by 'the unready'. A parallel line of analysis has been advanced by Melvin Pollner, a sociologist-cum-philosopher, who has undertaken a sustained analysis of the organization of what he terms 'mundane' reasoning.

Pollner's contribution to the new sensibility

Pollner (1987) identifies two models of knowledge generation: the mundane and constitutive models (which are broadly comparable to Cooper and Law's (1995) distal and proximal ways of thinking discussed earlier). Those operating with a mundane model, Pollner argues, simply disregard the reflexivity of knowledge production. When social scientists mobilize this model, little or no attention is paid to the ways in which common sense reasoning is used to identify and analyse the objects of investigation. Research which exemplifies the mundane model represents actors as pre-given agents 'confronting an objective, pre-given, "out there" world' (Pollner, 1987: 122). In contrast, those operating with a constitutive model conceive 'of mundane inquiry as *constructing* its world' (ibid., emphasis added), rather than simply providing more or less accurate, factual reports of its reality. From the perspective of the constitutive model, mundane inquiry is 'constitutive of the world it subsequently treats as "always already there" and by reflexive reference to which mundane inquiry knows itself as such' (ibid.).

Pollner's models also parallel the distinction Robert Cooper draws between social science as the study of social action and the study of method. When the *mundane* model is deployed, organization and organizations are analysed as if their reality were simply awaiting capture by social scientific study. This approach assumes a division between subject (for example, the scientist) and the world (for example, social action) in which reliable knowledge of the latter is produced by identifying and removing forms of 'bias' from the former. In contrast, the *constitutive* model assumes an inescapable interdependence of subject and object in which the methods of social scientists are understood to be irremediably implicated in the constitution of the social world. Instead of interrogating methods for symptoms of bias – which assumes that the methods developed for detecting bias are themselves unproblematical – there is a concern to appreciate and study how methods are deployed to produce everyday and scientific knowledge.

In the field of organization studies, Chia (1994) has illustrated this perspective in relation to the study of decision-making. Commonsensically, decision-making is understood to identify a particular, bounded domain of activity that exists 'out there' in the world. What such mundane reasoning dissembles or glosses, Chia argues, is the role of decision-making as a fundamental, ontological act of differentiating 'this' (for example, the individual or decisions) from 'that' (for example, the world or nondecisions). Or, as Chia (ibid.) puts it, decision-making is fundamentally about: 'the creating of a primary distinction, the cleavage of an empty space. . . . *Such primary incisional acts are what generate couplets such as inside/outside, part/whole, observer/observed and most importantly the is/is not thought structure*' (ibid.: 800, emphasis added). Unless the primacy of such 'incisional acts' is fully acknowledged, and this awareness then informs social scientific analyses, social scientists inevitably collude in the reproduction of a form of discourse that forgets, denies and distorts 'the complex dialectical structure that inheres in the very language we use to define the world' (Cooper, 1983b: 718). Analysis based upon the understanding that 'individuals' or 'organizations' exist as empirical entities simply takes for granted the authority of their common sense representation as discrete entities and thereby embroils the researcher in 'a false objectivism' founded upon an uncritical acceptance of the authority of common sense concepts (see the discussion of Bittner's work below).

In addition to situating the domination of mundane reason sociohistorically (coming from Cooper, 1990: 191), Pollner explores the possibilities for moving outside of the idiom of mundane reason. Within this realm it is taken for granted that there are 'objects', 'subjects' and diverse modalities which, 'mediate, deflect or separate the "subject" from the "object": "perception", "experience", "consciousness", "dreaming" and "memory"' (Pollner, 1987: 128). Pollner accepts that such terms are heuristically useful, and indeed essential, for negotiating our way in the world (including the world that is constituted through reflexive analysis). But he also highlights the value of radical reflexivity for changing our being-in-the-world (see Willmott, 1994), in addition to its contribution to exposing the precarious authority of mundane reason. I return to this theme towards the end of this chapter.

Recasting social science as the study of method

It has been noted how Robert Cooper's view, or claim, that social science fundamentally concerns the study of method rather than the study of social action, departs from established conceptions of social science. Conventional thinking has it that social scientists study the 'structures' and/or 'actions' that comprise the social world in much the same way that natural scientists study the physical world. However, as Cooper argues, this understanding is forgetful of how concepts used in scientific analysis are inescapably framed by a particular language that imbues them with meaning. It assumes that social science can provide direct access to the social world 'out there'; and, in doing so, it overlooks how this access is inescapably conditioned by the particular method, or way of seeing the world, that is embedded in the language that is used to represent and study this world.

One of the earliest articles to articulate elements of this argument in the field of organization studies was Bittner's 'The Concept of Organization' (1965 [1973]). Drawing upon the insights of Schutz (1953) and what was later dubbed ethnomethodology.[16] Bittner draws attention to how students of organization borrow concepts (for example, ideas about alternative configurations and distinctive properties of organizational structures) from those whom they seek to study. Bittner accepts that the borrowing of such concepts is unavoidable: in order to study the world, we depend upon whatever language is available to us to identify it.[17] But he questions the unreflexive use of these concepts to represent, say, the properties of organizational structures. The legitimate role of the social scientist, Bittner argues, is to examine the common sense reasoning, or methods, that generates the meaning of terms like 'organizational structure', and which mobilizes their use in particular contexts. Problematical, he submits, is the unreflexive use of common sense concepts (for example, those relating to the formal design of organizations) by social scientists to develop theories of organization:

> The point at which the use of common-sense concepts becomes a transgression is where such concepts are expected to do the analytic work of theoretical concepts. When the actor is treated as a permanent auxiliary to the enterprise of sociological inquiry at the same time that he is the object of its inquiry, there arise ambiguities that defy clarification.
> (Bittner, 1965 [1973: 265])

Here Bittner questions the coherence of analysis that draws unreflexively upon mundane reasoning which assumes that organizations and organizings exist 'out there' and that they possess properties (for example, elements of structure) that can be accurately represented or captured by scientific method. When reference is made to the actor being 'treated as a permanent auxiliary', Bittner highlights how social scientists routinely and *unreflexively* adopt actors' common sense ways of representing their reality (for example, through the use of terms such as 'organization' and 'structure'). Instead of adopting and refining such common sense concepts to study or measure the social world, Bittner commends the study of their 'methodic use', arguing that: 'The varieties of ways in which the scheme can be invoked for information, direction, justification, and so on, without the risk of sanction, constitute the scheme's methodical use' (ibid.: 272). Bittner urges social scientists to take the practical use of widely used concepts as the focus of their analysis. That is to say, he urges analysts of organization to study the occasions on which the concept of 'organization structure', for example, is (methodically) invoked by organizational members. This attentiveness to the accounting practices of common sense reasoning parallels Cooper's understanding that 'the *structure* of method is the major means for understanding the social world' (1983a: 218, quoted earlier, original emphasis). However, there are important differences, for example, ethnomethodologists, like Bittner, have tended to direct their attention to the empirical minutiae of how members of society, including social scientists, accomplish a sense of 'seeing, describing, and explaining order' (Zimmerman and Weider, 1971: 289). Zimmerman (1971), for example, has studied how employees within a public assistance organization engage in (methodic) 'judgemental work' as they organize their activities in ways that they (methodically) understand to satisfy the requirements of bureaucratic rules even though their actions may deviate from what fellow employees and scientific observers may deem to be the actions prescribed or proscribed by a given rule. Such analysis understands human action to be guided not by rules *per se* but by actors' methodical ways of 'providing for the reasonableness of viewing particular actions as essentially satisfying the provisions of the rule' (Zimmerman and Weider, 1971: 238).

In Bittner's analysis, there is also a presumption that empirical analysis can resolve theoretical disputes. Thus, towards the end of his discussion, Bittner (1965 [1973]) speculates that discourses on the formal design of organization are developed and mobilized, among other things, for purposes of gaining compliance from employees or, relatedly, to construct a sense of unity; and he concludes by suggesting that the veracity of his speculations 'is a matter to be decided by empirical research'. In so doing, he perversely reverts to, and thereby reinforces, the very 'distal' thinking, or structure of method (i.e. that research can determine how well a theory describes organizational reality), that ostensibly his article is concerned to challenge. To be clear, I am not suggesting that there is anything inherently 'wrong' or 'inferior' about undertaking empirical research as a means of questioning or advancing existing understandings. What *is* decidedly odd, though, is Bittner's unqualified and seemingly unreflexive claim that such research could 'decide' the matter of whether the concept of organization is used to gain compliance or construct a sense of unity.

Critical of this 'empiricist' tendency, which is seen to trivialize the more radical implications of phenomenological insights, Pollner (1991) has accused ethnomethodology of 'settling down in the suburbs of sociology' (1991: 370). Ethnomethodology, he contends, has become preoccupied with the production of empirical studies, to the neglect of the social and political significance of reflexivity (see, for example, McHugh *et al.*, 1974 and Mehan and Wood, 1975, discussed in Willmott, 1977). Ethnomethodologists stand accused of having appropriated phenomenological insights simply to stake out a new terrain of empirical inquiry: namely, the practical accomplishment of the practices that are productive of what is taken to be the orderly structure of the social world. In Bittner (1965 [1973]), the area of this terrain is the study of how concepts, such as 'organization structure', are practically invoked by organizational members and more specifically, the testing of his speculations about how these concepts are invoked to gain compliance from employees or, relatedly, to accomplish a sense of unity. Ethnomethodology, Pollner persuasively observes, 'approximates empirical social science' (1991: 372) to the extent that it becomes more concerned with providing seemingly authoritative (distal) accounts of how diverse social phenomena become accomplished than it is with stimulating a (proximal) appreciation of the nature and significance of reflexivity. In a way that resonates with Cooper's (1989a) interest in the work of Derrida, Pollner (1991) contends that because the attentions of radical reflexivity:

> are directed at the primordial suppositions of discourse and the conditions that constitute 'descriptions' as an intelligible possibility, radical inquiry positions itself outside of the processes and practices that create the ontological space for conventional inquiry. At the least, radical inquiry has an equivocal relation to the discursive practices of represen-

tation: it states and cancels its own findings as when Derrida (1976) crosses out the words he has written to indicate that though the text appears to be about something, it is not. Thus, radically reflexive inquiry *reneges* on findings, formulations, and accounts.

(Pollner, 1991: 374–5, original emphasis)

In principle, radical reflexivity repeatedly seeks to re-mind us that what we take to be, describe as, or scientifically represent as 'the world' is the product of arbitrary, socially organized judgemental processes – that is, particular *structures of method* – which result in the world appearing as 'this' rather than 'that'.

Arguably, whatever exists, or is deemed to exist by language, also exists before and beyond language and, for this reason, it is inherently resistant to, or subversive of, necessarily partial and divisive efforts to specify, categorize and analyse it. As Cooper observes, there is 'an intrinsic undecidability which can only be "organized" or "systematized" through an external force' (1990: 182) – a force that contrives to deny its arbitrariness and conventionality, yet is repeatedly plagued by what it strives to repress. Organization, he suggests, 'is the appropriation of order out of disorder' (ibid.: 193). However, as I have argued elsewhere (Willmott, 1986, 1994), organization is also more and less than this. Disorder, I contend, does not precede order but, rather, is a byproduct of the effort to organize or systematize. Prior to the identification of order, there is neither order nor disorder, only nothingness: 'there is not *nothing* outside of language but *no-thing*. There is no thingness about the material or social world except when comprehended through the codifying structure of language' (Chia, 1996: 37–8, original emphasis). Order and disorder are simultaneous products of efforts to organize. The effort to organize involves the creation of boundaries: it cleaves the emptiness of the unknown, or 'the unready' as Cooper (1993: 300) characterizes it, into a 'this' which derives its identity from being Other than 'that'; and it is the Other – the residual 'that' – which continuously threatens to disrupt or disorder the boundaries that have been drawn in the effort to organize.

To summarize. Shared by Robert Cooper, Chia (1994, 1996) and Pollner (1974, 1987), I have suggested, is a commitment to study the methodical production of common sense and scientific knowledge rather than social action *per se*. Cooper problematizes knowledge claims by highlighting how they appropriate 'the undecidable' (Cooper, 1990: 193). Knowledge claims to do this by contriving to provide authoritative accounts either of the 'out there' world (Pollner's mundane model; Cooper's distal thinking) or how the (common)sense of an 'out there' world is accomplished (Pollner's constitutive model; Cooper's proximal thinking). In the following section, I sketch how this understanding of radical reflexivity shared by Cooper and Pollner at once incorporates and advances upon Giddens' (1976) more familiar formulation of 'the double hermeneutic'.

HUGH WILLMOTT

The play of hermeneutics: Giddens and Cooper compared

> the subject matter [of the social sciences] has the same form as that of those who study it, so that social scientists are *already included* in the very methods of their discipline.
>
> (Cooper, 1983a: 218)

When social science is identified with the study of social action, as contrasted with the study of method, the danger is one of 'studying *things out there* instead of the *a priori* meanings which, through the logic of words and language, attach us to those things' (Cooper, 1983b: 718). If, as was argued in the previous section, concepts, such as 'organization', 'structure', 'individual' and 'difference' can never be cleansed of their everyday meaning,[18] then efforts to control common sense meanings (for example, by ascribing precise technical definitions to these concepts) are founded upon self-deception and wishful thinking.

Giddens (1976) refers to the interpenetration of common sense and scientific interpretations as 'the double hermeneutic'. Grasping the meaning of an interpretive scheme, whether it is commonsensical (for example, the concept of family) or purportedly scientific (for example, Newtonian physics or Marxism), it is understood to involve a hermeneutic process in which the distinctive claims and vision of the concept are gradually understood and accepted. The hermeneutic is 'double' because, in contrast to the objects of natural science research, 'lay' social actors are capable of incorporating elements of technical language into their own understanding so that these elements 'become integral features of that conduct (thereby in fact potentially compromising their original usage within the technical vocabulary of social science)' (Giddens, 1976: 162). For example, social scientists have endeavoured to differentiate and define (formal) 'organization' in particular ways that simultaneously draw upon common sense ideas, have sought to distance their technical definitions from common sense understandings, and have contributed to the dynamic process of renewing and extending the common sense meaning(s) of organization(s).

Giddens' concept of the double hermeneutic enables him to explore the dynamic interplay between the 'first-order' meanings of social actors and the 'second-order' meta-languages developed by social scientists. In particular, as noted above, Giddens highlights the feedback loop or 'slippage' (Giddens, 1976: 162) of the 'second-order' technical language of social science into social actors' 'first-order' world (Giddens, 1984: 284; see also, xxxii–v).[19] When exploring this interplay, he is less interested in the (methodical) structure of these meanings than in the two-way traffic between them, and especially the appropriation of social scientific formulations by lay actors. For example, it is noted that theories of the sovereign state formulated by seventeenth-century European thinkers were engaged (and continue to be so) in the everyday practical activity of organizing the modern state; and, that the (self-fulfilling) role of these ideas in constituting and rationalizing what they seek to explicate is an important consideration when seeking to account for their contemporary relevance and plausibility. But in his discussions of reflexivity and 'the double hermeneutic' Giddens largely takes for granted what Chia has termed 'the incisional, ontological act' of 'cutting and partitioning off a version of reality [for example, the reality depicted through the concept of the state – H. W.] from what has hitherto been indistinguishable' (1994: 800). Giddens' attentiveness to the play of hermeneutics is focused upon the products of this play – the interpretive schemes that are 'cut out' and their interdependence upon other schemes of interpretation. Neglected is the significance of the incisional acts or 'labours of division' (Cooper, 1989b) that are the conditions of possibility of such play.

The neglect of these conditions has consequences for how Giddens conceives and analyses the products of hermeneutical play. Consider a concept that is central to his theory of structuration and the analysis that flows from it: the human agent. For Giddens, human agency is self-evidently the manifestation of a seat of consciousness that produces purposive actions or interventions (that may nevertheless result in effects that were not intended by the agent). Agency, Giddens (1984) writes, 'concerns events of which *the individual is the perpetrator*, in the sense that the individual could, at any given phase in a given sequence of conduct, have acted differently. *Whatever happened would not have happened if that individual had not intervened*' (Giddens 1984: 9, emphasis added). In formulating his concept of agency, Giddens is at pains to stress the role of human reflexivity and purposiveness in accomplishing the acts that reproduce the social world.[20] However, it is not necessary to deny the value of Giddens' anti-functionalism (see Giddens, 1979: 2) in order to note how his conception of human agency relies upon, and leaves largely unproblematized, a common sense conception of the agent as a discrete, homogeneous entity. Of course, Giddens is not so unsophisticated as to formulate human agency as devoid of tensions and contradictions: indeed, he develops a complex 'stratification model' which incorporates unconscious motives as well as the capacity to monitor action and rationalize meaning (Giddens, 1984: 5). Yet, despite the sophistication of this model's representation of the modalities, or levels, of consciousness inhering in the human agent, Giddens conceptualizes human agency as a self-evident property, or manifestation, of more or less autonomous individuals who, in order to act, are understood to draw upon the properties of structure, such as its allocative (for example, raw materials) and authoritative (for example, ideas) resources.[21] This formulation goes some way in challenging (psychologistic) forms of analysis in which the intentions of agents are abstracted from their embeddedness in social structures. It also improves upon (sociologistic) analyses that derogate the involvement of human agency in the reproduction of these structures. Nonetheless, Giddens' theory of structuration retains and reinforces the (common sense) idea that individuals (subjects) exist separately from resources (objects) as they 'draw upon' these resources in pursuit of their purposes (Willmott, 1986, 1994).

The primary focus of Robert Cooper's reflections, in contrast, is upon the generation of meaning and, in particular, the structure of the method that is productive of both 'first-order' (common sense) and 'second-order' (social scientific) accounts. These reflections lead him to emphasize the inherent *undecidability* of social reality that is precariously ordered into seemingly discrete domains or entities whose presence is arbitrarily 'fixed' through the use of terms such as 'organization', 'individual' or 'decision'. In this way, he seeks to illuminate what Giddens assumes: the grounds, or structure, of organizing(s) that are, in effect, the conditions of possibility of the phenomena that Giddens identifies as 'the double hermeneutic'.

Consider Giddens' and Cooper's contrasting assessments of the relevance and value of Derridean post-structuralism. Giddens (1979: 28–38) complains that Derrida's analysis addresses only the play of signifiers arising from the inherent undecidability of signs, to the exclusion of their referents. Characterizing Derrida's position as 'a retreat from the object to the idea', Giddens perceives it 'to break with everything that might relate a text to an object world' (ibid.: 36). Here, Giddens makes the (common sense) assumption that 'text' and 'object world' can be unproblematically differentiated, and it is this assumption that effectively blinds him to what I take to be Derrida's central argument. Derrida's analysis does not affirm the existence of 'referents' or an 'object world' as Giddens correctly notes. But, crucially, neither does it deny them. Striving to disrupt the mundane modelling of social reality, Derrida's abiding concern is to highlight the precariousness and deceptiveness of language as a means of knowing 'objects' *qua* objects that exist independently of the 'texts', or methods, that are developed to 'read' them. Derrida's writing and, more specifically, his concept of *différance* serves to disclose how any frame of meaning acts to conceal, and not just reveal, what it purports to represent. As Cooper (1990) puts it, 'The argument that Derrida advances can be said to be essentially against the idea of a fully present reality which we normally consider the world to be, directly and unitarily available to understanding, and what is posited instead is a world that is continually deferred, postponed in space and time' (Cooper, 1990: 178). It is the operation of language – the necessary deployment of frames of meaning – made possible by the openness of *différance* that is 'responsible' for this continuous deferral. In contrast, a (Giddensian) focus upon the content and negotiation of frames of meaning operates to marginalize and devalue analyses of the grounds, or conditions of possibility, of the articulation and effects of these frames of meaning. Following Derrida, Cooper (1987) urges us to appreciate how theories and findings are the product of methods, or 'phenomeno-techniques' (Bachelard, 1934), that enable the world to be represented in 'this' way rather than 'that'.

Discussion

If it is accepted that even a value commitment to science, such as the one commended by M. Weber (1949), cannot attain a value-free mirroring of the world 'out there' (see Alvesson and Willmott, 1996, Chap. 2), then it is relevant to consider the moral and political significance of moves that are productive of knowledge and its attendant 'truth effects' (Foucault, 1980). In this section, I want to reflect upon the moral and political positions or convictions that inform a number of the elements of what I term the developing reflexivization of social and organization studies. These elements, I have suggested, include ethnomethodology and Giddens' theory of structuration as well as Robert Cooper's contributions to the study of organization and organizing. Each can be seen to make a contribution to reflexivization insofar as attention is given to: 'the vital role that interpretation plays at every stage of scientific activity and a questioning of any permanent division between observation and theory' (Bernstein, 1988: 172). Of course, it is possible and desirable to *debate* the question of the moral and political position that informs what I have termed the project of reflexivization. But it would be absurd to suggest that any definitive or unequivocal response can be provided. This is partly because, as I will argue below, the answer will differ depending upon which element of the project is investigated. But, more fundamentally, it is necessary to acknowledge that whatever response is offered, it will tell us as much, and perhaps more, about the moral and political tradition assumed by the discussant than it will about that of the author(s) under investigation. Indeed, the very identification of this issue as worthy of discussion necessarily tells us more about the tradition in which I am working (or which works me) than it does about the 'targets' of my discussion who may show little interest in, or even acknowledgement of, the features of their work that are being discursively ascribed to them.

My claim that a moral and political position or tradition is articulated, more or less explicitly, in the study of organization/organizations/organizing, arises from the understanding that any account of the world, such as those generated through study, necessarily represents the world in a partial and thus incomplete way. What such accounts do is to tempt the reader to know and share their way of making sense, if only imperfectly and fleetingly. A condition of such sharing is the taking of a more or less self-conscious leap of faith, or at least a temporary suspension of disbelief, that allows 'this' standpoint to be favoured rather than some alternative; and thus produces 'this' account rather than 'that' account.[22] This understanding leads me to interpret any contribution to the process of reflexivization as morally and politically committed because, even when it does not *directly* advise us to engage in *overtly* political action, it enables and invites us to make sense of the world in a particular kind of way that has inevitable but equivocal consequences for action or inaction. For example, I submit that contributions to reflexivization are *likely* to invite and promote a deeper scepticism about any claimed neutrality and objectivity of scientific knowledge. But, equally, for those who believe in the possibility or desirability of neutrality, etc., contributions to reflexivization are as likely to provoke a redoubling of efforts in defence of these claims as they are likely to undermine such belief. The recent furore over the spoof or parody of post-structuralist analysis published in *Social Text* (1996) provides a sharp illustration of this argument.[23]

With these provisos in mind, and especially the acknowledgment that moral and political positions are here being ascribed to what are perceived as elements of a process of reflexivization, the following conjectures are offered as a contribution to an ongoing debate about the defensibility of alternatives to so-called 'modernist' forms of analysis (for example, Cooper and Burrell, 1988; Parker, 1992, 1995; Willmott, 1996; Newton, 1996); and, more specifically, to the difficulties that 'postmodernism' poses for the grounding of claims and the guidance of action, including the claims that I make about the moral and political status of others' work.

Let us begin with Bittner's (1965 [1973]) analysis (see earlier). What is the moral and political significance of such work? In common with other contributors to reflexivization, Bittner invites us to appreciate how concepts such as 'organization' are practically invoked instead of assuming that common sense understandings or definitions of organization provide an adequate basis for their study. Bittner's approach serves to problematize the taken-for-granted meanings ascribed to concepts as he prompts us to explore how, in particular contexts, concepts such as 'organization' are deployed (for example, by organizational members) to create particular effects, such as a conjectured sense of unity. One possible effect of such analysis is to highlight how words are used to construct and sustain certain kinds of worldviews (or truths). However, in the absence of a theory that explores how the construction and reproduction of a worldview might form an integral part of a process of struggle against actual or potential alternative ways of representing the world, this approach risks becoming focused exclusively upon the empirical question of whether the concept of organization is used in the way that is conjectured. In other words, it risks the possibility of becoming preoccupied with determining the 'facts' of the matter in a way that suspends consideration of 'the vital role that interpretation plays at every stage of scientific activity' (Bernstein, 1988: 172).

Of course, once published, findings of the kind sought by Bittner are open to interpretation in the light of competing value-standpoints. Suppose that the findings of the empirical study commended by Bittner broadly confirm his hypothesis about the use of the concept organization to convey a sense of unity. These findings could then be interpreted either as confirming unitarist beliefs about organizations or as evidence of the hegemonic use of language in ascribing consensus to an institution founded upon social divisions. However, because Bittner's (ethnomethodological) approach does not engage directly with such power–knowledge issues, it is at best morally and politically neutral and, by default, it is conservative. In principle, the commitment of ethnomethodology is not to correct either 'lay' or 'scientific' theories (for example, of organization) but rather, to study how the process of making sense of the world is practically accomplished. What ethnomethodological studies have claimed, nonetheless, is that a sense of social order is routinely sustained by moral force (Garfinkel, 1967). While it would be perilous to argue that the reproduction of social order is *conditional* upon the presence of such a force (Willmott, 1994), ethnomethodological investigations do indicate that a sense of dis-order accompanied by feelings of anxiety and/or sanction arises from a breach of expectations. However, in a putatively postmodern manner, this force is *generalized* to any and every 'order'; and there is 'ethnomethodological indifference' to the basis of the moral force that pre-serves this order.[24]

Robert Cooper is also concerned with how order is accomplished. But it is the *significance* of this feat, rather than the examination of its practical achievement, that animates his concern. He is much less interested in revealing the minutiae of how any particular order is accomplished than in challenging his readers to *reflect* upon how human beings become 'engaged' with reality; and, more specifically, how structures of method render the world intelligible in particular ways. From this standpoint, I submit, pursuing empirical research (à la ethnomethodology) is comparatively unimportant because, at best, it adds to the stock of knowledge about some-thing and, at worst, it reinforces a conflation of rational, scientific inquiry with the collection of 'facts'.

Rejecting this option, Cooper's analysis seeks to illuminate how 'distinctions (such) as inside and outside, or part and whole, are not given in the order of things but are products or effects of organizing activity' (Cooper and Law, 1995: 246). This approach is inherently subversive because it does not 'simply' disclose how things are ordered, as ethnomethodology does, but shows how the distinctions upon which any order is founded are themselves the product of organizing activity. It is the concern to bring this understanding to consciousness, I suggest, that informs Cooper's identification of what I would characterize as dominant versus subversive ways of knowing the world such as the study of social action versus the study of method; and distal thinking versus proximal thinking. In each case, Cooper invites his readers to move beyond a study of how common sense thinking is accomplished so as to grasp how this thinking is structured and how it could be otherwise. Thus, commenting upon the idea of 'organizations', and to the distal thinking that supports the sense of their existence, he notes how it is,

> possible to point to boundaries for they can be *made* to exist. . . . So the distal exists – but (or so we have suggested) *it is a proximal effect*. So our argument has been that the theory of organizations privileges the distal, and tends to repress, displace, or forget the proximal. And that a theory of organization might, with profit, attend to what has been forgotten, and *explore the proximal processes that generate the possibility of the distal.*
>
> (Cooper and Law, 1995: 264, second emphasis added)

In this formulation, the dominant, distal conception of organization(s) is understood to be a routinely unacknowledged product of proximal processes – processes, that is, which are partial and precarious and are forever approached but never attained. Later in the same essay, Cooper and Law commend an approach that 'gives primacy to *proximal organizings* rather than *distal organization*' (ibid.: 271). To the extent that this invitation is accepted, the authority of distal thinking will be problematized and weakened. However, it may be asked whether, when adopting this approach, a concern to translate proximal thinking into practices and institutions that exemplify and support such thinking is incorporated and advanced. Or is the project largely, if not purely, an intellectual exercise?

In response to this question, it may be argued that the question is itself wrongheaded in assuming a separation between 'theorizing' and 'practising' – an assumption which fails to grasp how thinking and writing are themselves practices, and indeed are practices of critical importance for projects of social transformation (as the New Testament and Marx's *Capital* both testify). However, while this argument can be accepted, it does not quite deal with the contextual and embodied nature of thinking (Fay, 1987) and, more specifically, with the question of *how* proximal thinking may facilitate a unifying of mind and action *in practice*, as contrasted with showing how theory and practice are inseparably related. It is what I perceive as a reluctance, refusal or failure to engage with this issue that leads me to understand Cooper and Law's (1995) position to advance an approach to organization analysis that is disembodied and decontextualized.

In this analysis, the authority of distal thinking is undoubtedly exposed, challenged and weakened – a project that I accept is political in effect, and seemingly also in intent.[25] And yet, in the discussion of distal and proximal views of organization, the world of 'organizations' and 'organizings' is addressed only as an object of theorizing, not as an integral part of lived experience. The concern is with different kinds of thinking; and the invitation is to *think* proximally, not to explore what it might mean to *act* proximally. There *is* an interest in studying the forces that, in privileging the distal, tend to repress, displace, or forget the proximal, but absent is any apparent desire to identify, critique and transform institutional forces of repression or to release proximal praxis from their distorting influence (see Alvesson and Willmott, 1992b, 1996).

If it is accepted that what, distally, we think of as 'organizations' comprises, from a proximal standpoint, *not* sets of structures and systems with well defined boundaries but, rather, 'circuits of continuous contact and motion – more like assemblages of *organizings*' (Cooper and Law, 1995: 239, original emphasis), then a question arises about how, in *specific* historical and cultural conditions, these organizings are maintained (for example, through power relations). The problem is that Cooper and Law's (1995) discussion of distal and proximal accountings of organization is devoid of any consideration of what may loosely be termed the structuring of these 'organizings' through, say, patriarchal relations; or, relatedly, how this *structuring* might be transformed in a way that de-represses or re-members what has been repressed and forgotten. Unless this omission is corrected, it would seem that such work is also destined, like ethnomethodology, to be morally and politically conservative, although not because it has little or nothing to say that is of potentially emancipatory significance but because it is disconnected from personal/political struggles to transform self-in-society. Earlier it was noted that there are some close affinities between the work of Robert Cooper and that of Melvin Pollner. What they share, it was argued, is a concern to address the significance of reflexivity, as contrasted with an interest in cataloguing its empirical manifestations. However, whereas the focus of Cooper's work is upon 'the structure of method' or the kinds of thinking that are productive and deconstructive of our sense of the world, Pollner extends his concern to explore how we might begin to *live* in a way that is more consistent with, say, Cooper and Law's (1995) proximal thinking. Such a change demands more than simply placing a positive value upon proximal thinking or showing how proximal processes generate the possibility of distal thinking. It would, in addition, involve exploring ways of, as it were, *becoming* (more) proximal and, relatedly, identifying those conditions which either facilitate or frustrate (repress, displace, forget) this process. To put this another way, and in a way that clearly resonates with Cooper's attentiveness to organizing(s) rather than organization(s), becoming proximal would involve a radical modification of the (distal) attitude of everyday life:

> To attend to the -ing of things ... requires attending to the processes of constitution in lieu of the product thus constituted. In attending to the -ing of things one focuses on the course of activity – the form of life – which presupposes, preserves, and thereby produces the particular 'thing'.
>
> (Pollner, 1979: 253, in Preston, 1988: 12)

What, practically or experientially, might this mean? One possibility, following Preston (1988: 123, 125), is that it involves a systematic erosion and making visible of the usual reality-building processes (personal and collective) used by all groups in everyday life. In turn, this provides for the possibility of bringing about 'an existential transformation in which the problem of meaning ceases to exist', in the sense that meaning emerges from a process of becoming *rather than* being forced through a cognitive mechanism in which the 'subject' ('I') is set apart from 'object' (the 'I''s perception of the situation) and a calculation is made about how to proceed. In this experience of self, as 'becoming', Preston continues,

> The performer as intending subjectivity is eliminated in the sense that the performer is trying to do officially prescribed activities, or some idiosyncratic version thereof, that are meant to demonstrate one's particular identity. One disappears in the doing of the prescribed activity, eliminating self-consciousness.
>
> (Preston, 1988: 134)

The intensity of the engagement with the flow of becoming means that thoughts and actions are minimally cluttered and confused by conflicting interpretations or ambivalent feelings. Thinking becomes progressively embodied as the person becomes a participant in processes of becoming rather than a seemingly detached observer of the residue of a process of forgetting and repression.

Any move to embody the proximal, it is worth stressing, is not adequately understood as the product of an intention or decision to behave differently although, clearly, a more or less conscious decision to change in this way can initiate, support and sustain moves in this direction. The problem with understanding, or attributing, such change to a decision or series of decisions is that it tends to assume and reinforce the dualism of subjects and objects instead of appreciating how such changes are embedded in *socially organized processes* through which individuals become and remain involved and committed for as long as they are engaged in the processes that serve to erode the usual reality-building and ego-building practices – practices which maintain the dualism of subjects and objects as they impede openness and directness.[26]

The challenge, then, is to nurture and develop socially organized processes in which the capacity to be open and direct is valued and developed and, conversely, to transform those socially divisive institutions (for example, capitalism, patriarchy) which make individuals anxious or fearful about expressing themselves openly and directly. If the preceding analysis is accepted, then the development of *proximal practice* is contingent upon debunking experientially as well as cognitively the understanding that 'subjects' are the products of 'organizings'; and, relatedly, a transformation of these 'organizings' is a necessary condition of the development of 'subjects' who are not deluded by an exaggerated and individualistic sense of their autonomy. In Lyotard's terms, this involves a deep and lived acceptance that 'the unready', open condition of human existence 'precedes all determining thought . . . and cannot be constituted by it' (Lyotard, 1989: 197).

Conclusion

This chapter has been concerned with re-cognizing the Other, where the Other is the expression of reflexivity. Robert Cooper's attentiveness to the role of the structure of method in constituting knowledge, I have suggested, can be located in a broader stream of thinking – 'a new sensibility' – that questions the claims of traditional (Cartesian) ontology in which the Other of reflexivity is either ignored or assumed to be subdued by scientific method. Awareness of reflexivity serves to problematize the authority of whatever is taken to be self-evidently true or authoritatively known. Recognition of this Other re-minds us that what we know of the natural and social worlds, including ourselves, is conditional upon the particular method or 'paradigm' employed in the (re)production of social reality.

As awareness of reflexivity has developed, it has been addressed in a variety of ways. Ethnomethodologists have treated it as a new object or domain of empirical inquiry: they have sought to study how a (common)sense of social reality is reflexively accomplished. Others, such as Giddens, have incorporated reflexivity in theories of agency and social reproduction. In contrast, Robert Cooper has sought to appreciate the *significance* of reflexivity for appreciating and deconstructing our common sense being-in-the-world. By differentiating the study of method from the study of social action and by distinguishing 'distal' from 'proximal' thinking, his approach to re-cognizing the Other has *pointed to* the possibility of understanding and relating to the world in a radically different way. This approach has drawn attention to what is 'repressed' and 'forgotten' in established ways of thinking. However, such repression is treated as an object of intellectual curiosity, not as a matter of critique and transformation. What it lacks, I have suggested, is a theoretical framework that begins to address how power relations act within as well as upon subjects to privilege particular kinds of 'organizings'; and, relatedly, how processes of de-repression and re-membering might be fostered. One way of *being* congruent with proximal *thinking*, I have argued, would be to participate in practices and develop institutions that challenge and weaken the impulse to engage in distal thinking – thinking that ascribes to self, as an object in the world, an imaginary and contradictory sense of solidity and security.

Acknowledgement

I would like to thank Damian O'Doherty for his help in preparing this chapter.

Notes

1 The quotation is taken from the biographical details that accompany Cooper's contribution to Morgan's *Beyond Method: Strategies for Social Research*, (1983).
2 For example, these writings have challenged the (modernist) understanding of 'the human agent as the centre of rational control and understanding' (Cooper and Burrell, 1988: 91; see also 1988: 94); this posthumanist de-centring of the assumption of autonomous human agency is a more or less intended effect of such analysis.
3 Robert Cooper's writings draw continuously upon the inspiration of numerous thinkers including Bateson, Whitehead, Heidegger, Merleau-Ponty, Derrida, Lacan, Foucault, and others.
4 Silverman (1970) drew heavily upon the writings of Berger and Luckmann (1966) and Schutz (1953) to crystallize and elaborate a number of critiques, ideas and insights that had been generated *inter alia* by Gouldner (1959), Krupp (1961), Mayntz (1964), and others.
5 As Clegg has astutely observed, *The Theory of Organizations* 'spoke of no achievement in the way of research findings' but, crucially, it did take 'sociological theory seriously for the study of organizations and it articulated it in terms that were explicitly anti-positivist' (1994: 26–7).
6 To begin to understand this development would require a detailed study of the unfolding of the field and, in particular, the biographies and connectedness of key contributors, such as David Silverman, Gibson Burrell, Stewart Clegg, David Knights and Robert Cooper. It is perhaps tempting to interpret their shared interest in esoteric social theory as a form of collective psychosis in which a group of academics has become obsessed with theory or novelty at the expense of the 'proper' or 'legitimate' concerns of organizational analysis such as organizational design (see Donaldson, 1985). However, such a diagnosis simply discounts the difficulty of accepting and sustaining the agendas of a tradition when there is a loss of confidence in its foundations. At the heart of the problem, I would venture, is a broadly similar experience of disjuncture between, on the one hand, these academics' contemporary ('postmodern') being-in-the-world and, on the other hand, accounts of this 'being' and this 'world' produced by dominant, functionalist forms of organizational analysis. Such disjunctures are productive of frustration and disappointment (see Craib, 1994) – a disappointment that stimulates a search for more satisfying and/or enlightening ways of thinking than those based upon a traditional, scientistic ontology.

7 See, for example, the Pfeffer (1993) and Cannella and Paetzold's (1994) response to Pfeffer's call to crush the blooming flowers of postfunctionalism discussed briefly below.
8 The distinction between social science as 'social action' and 'method' ultimately breaks down because, arguably, 'method' is itself a form of 'social action'. It is also worth noting that the availability of (unreflective) representations of social action is a precondition for analyses that are concerned to critique or 'deconstruct' their claims (Knights, 1992).
9 These methods are traced by Habermas (1972) to knowledge-constitutive interests (in prediction and control, mutual understanding and emancipation) engendered by the cultural break from nature (Habermas 1972: 312–13). So long as the connection between knowledge and human interests is denied, Habermas contends, the illusion of pure theory is preserved. In turn, this illusion supports a fundamentalist conviction in the authority of positivist science as the sole provider of objective knowledge. In this understanding, the continuity between and mutual dependence of common sense and scientific thinking is disavowed.
10 The other pillar, Giddens (1979: 235–6) suggests, was 'the theory of industrial society' that assumed a necessary convergence and 'end of ideology' between different forms of industrial society.
11 Bernstein is perhaps inclined to highlight the chaos as a way of inflating the value of his (orderly) explanation of it.
12 Many philosophers and sages, notably those working within an Eastern tradition, have long assumed this interdependence. In the Western tradition, various branches of phenomenology, from Hegel to Merleau-Ponty, have encouraged an appreciation of how scientific concepts derive their meaning and authority from common sense preconceptions.
13 What an electron 'is', for example, is understood to depend upon whether it is interpreted as a particle or as a wave.
14 Of course, the exposure of this link does not render such knowledge false or useless. Scientific knowledge has demonstrated its productivity as well as its destructiveness – for example, by enabling all kinds of engineering projects to be undertaken. Findings based upon a traditional ontology can be accepted as 'true' *within the boundaries* that are organized (but routinely assumed to be given) by its practices.
15 It is all too tempting simply to label and reject this kind of knowledge as 'positivistic'. However, the bracketing of reflexivity about the precarious basis of any world-taken-for-granted is a necessary condition of the production of certain kinds of knowledge (see Habermas, 1972). For example, a capacity to analyse work systems so that duplicated effort may be avoided depends upon (temporarily) suspending disbelief in the variables that are identified for this purpose. Purposive-rational action based upon such a suspension remains important if only because there is a material basis to human interaction: wo/man does not live by talk alone. The problem does not reside in the generation of this knowledge *per se* but in the *self-understanding* (and associated consequences) of versions of science that are blind to the social organization, and limits, of their seemingly authoritative claims.
16 In recent years there has been a tendency to use the term 'ethnomethodology' in a loose way to describe all kinds of qualitative and ethnographic research. Arguably, however, ethnomethodology comprises a specialist form of analysis that is distinguished by its distance from all approaches that take for granted the use of common sense resources to guide and inform their identification and investigation of the phenomena that they study. Differentiating itself from folk sociology (Garfinkel, 1967), ethnomethodology seeks to explicate the common sense reasoning that enables both everyday actors and social scientists to (ethno-methodologically) represent the world as a setting of their

everyday actions or a topic of their scientific inquiries. As Zimmerman and Weider have observed:

> The ethnomethodologist is *not* concerned with providing causal explanations of observably regular, patterned, repetitive actions by some kind of analysis of the actor's point of view. He (sic) is concerned with how members of society go about the task of *seeing, describing,* and *explaining order* in the world in which they live.... Once brought under scrutiny, the 'orderly structure' of the social world is no longer available as a topic in its own right (that is, as something to be described and explained) but instead becomes an *accomplishment* of the accounting practices through and by which it is described and explained. It is in this decision to bring such accounting practices under investigation as phenomena in their own right *without presupposing the independence of the domain made observable via their use* that constitutes the radical character of the ethnomethodological enterprise.
>
> (1971: 289, 293–4, final emphasis added)

17 As Pollner articulates this point, mundane talk about any phenomenon – such as organization structure – 'is pretentious in the sense that once it has begun it tacitly assumes the always-already there structure of that which the talk-about reveals. Talk-about, by virtue of its intentional and intentionalizing (or objectivating) structures pre-delineates the nature of the domain to which it turns in that it renders the domain one which can, in fact, be talked about' (1987: 125).

18 This is impractical as the constituents of any 'cleanser' are themselves 'contaminated' by everyday meaning.

19 Giddens notes how the commitment to publication of scientific research implies openness to its utilization (Giddens, 1989). This, he observes, allows social scientific findings 'to have practical (and political) consequences regardless of whether or not the sociological observer or policy-maker decides that they can be "applied" to a given practical case' (Giddens, 1984: xxxv). In this sense, social science is inescapably involved in challenging, renewing and/or legitimizing everyday conduct.

20 This lies at the heart of Giddens' concerted attack upon functionalism (see note 10 above) in which purposes are attributed to social systems (Giddens, 1977; 1979). Social systems, Giddens writes, 'have not purposes, reasons or needs whatsoever; only human individuals do so. *Any explanation of social reproduction which imputes teleology to social systems must be declared invalid*' (1979: 7, original emphasis).

21 As Giddens puts it: 'Resources are structured properties of social systems, drawn upon and reproduced by knowledgeable agents in the course of interaction' (1984: 15).

22 Because the process of interpretation is open and 'indexical' (i.e. it is dependent upon how it is placed in context by the interpreter), the 'this' that the author recalls as what she/he intended to convey or subsequently offers as an account of the purpose of the writing is not necessarily the same as the 'this' which is read. The point, however, is that the act of writing requires a leap of faith precisely because it expresses a selective or perspectival representation of the world that involves an effort to carve 'the ready' from 'the un-ready' (see the discussion earlier in this chapter).

23 This article entitled, 'Transgressing the Boundaries: Towards a Transformative Hermeneutics of Quantum Gravity', by Alan Sokal, a physicist, purported to offer an analysis of quantum physics that exemplified and supported post-structuralist analysis. While this article made all the right noises and cited all the right authorities, it comprised, in the author's own words, when he subsequently sought to blow the whistle on post-structuralist scholarship, 'utter nonsense' which nonetheless 'sounded good and flattered the editors' ideological preconceptions' (Sokal, 1996: 19). The acceptance and

publication of this article enabled Sokal to argue that the editors of *Social Text* are willing to publish work that is not properly checked out by appropriate academic referees – for example, physicists – who would have immediately recognized it as a hoax: '*Social Text*'s acceptance of my article', Sokal declares, 'exemplifies the intellectual arrogance of Theory – meaning postmodern *literary* theory – carried to its logical extreme. No wonder they didn't bother to consult a physicist. If all is discourse and "text", then knowledge of the real world is superfluous; even physics becomes just another branch of cultural studies' (Sokal, 1996: 19). However, in order to make that kind of comment, Sokal (arrogantly) assumes the self-evidence of his own position, and seemingly can get away with it because it chimes with common sense thinking and appeals also to those who would rather not take the trouble to get to grips with post-structuralist thinking. Sokal never doubts that he/science is right: he simply points to the gullibility of the editors of *Social Text* to confirm this belief.

Fortunately, it is not necessary to believe that Sokal's article contained truth rather than utter nonsense to make the point that Sokal has sought to discredit post-structuralist analysis *not* by engaging directly with its ideas but, rather, by the more sensational method of writing and publishing a spoof to test his claim or prejudice that, in post-structuralist analysis, 'incomprehensibility becomes a virtue; allusions, metaphors and puns substitute for evidence and logic' (ibid.). Seemingly, Sokal's hoax was explicitly politically motivated by a belief that 'the self-proclaimed left' which once 'identified with science and against obscurantism' and engaged in a 'fearless analysis of objective reality' has become seduced by and entangled in 'epistemic relativism' which 'undermines the prospects of progressive social critique' (ibid.). As I indicate in the final pages of this chapter, I am also concerned about the contribution of contemporary social theory to emancipatory change. However, I am more inclined to give credit to the subversive role of post-structuralist analysis and I am critical of the political intent and effect of Sokal's ploy in polarizing evidence and logic against allusions and metaphors, as if the latter are not an indispensable component of self-styled scientific scholarship. What Sokal fails to appreciate, is that his claim to have shown that 'the emperor has no clothes' is dependent upon a tacit, unsupported assertion that science alone has the authority to determine how well *others* are dressed.

24 As Giddens has noted, this lack of interest in issues of power, and so on, explains 'the peculiarly disembodied and empty character of the reports of interactions or conversations that appear in the writings of Garfinkel and others influenced by him' (1976: 40).

25 In a personal communication, Robert Cooper has taken issue with my assessment of his position, arguing that it is mistaken to argue that 'Organization: Distal and Proximal Views' is not part of the real world of political contestation. As I reject the dualism between fact and value (Alvesson and Willmott, 1996, Chap. 2), I necessarily accept that all writing is engaged in such contestation; and, more specifically, I commend proximal thinking for its subversion of the distal view of organization. I would also like to acknowledge my debt to him for pushing me to clarify and sharpen my own thinking through an engagement with this work and his response to it. In my critique, I broadly endorse his claim that 'to think "proximally" is to think more freely, more creatively, more democratically'(letter of 25 May, 1996). And I accept that a disinclination to advertise this claim does not make it any less viable or relevant. But, I question how the kind of analysis developed by Cooper and Law, which is presumably an articulation of proximal thinking, can be of assistance in the practical, political process of changing the conditions – personal/political – that routinely impede its realization in everyday organizing practices.

26 As Chia (1994) has argued, established ideas about decision-making are predicated upon generally unacknowledged decisions to represent the world in 'this' way rather

than 'that', including the (methodic) decision to ascribe decisions ('objects') to the actions of autonomous decision-makers ('subjects').

Bibliography

Alvesson, M. and Willmott, H. C. (eds) (1992a) *Critical Management Studies*, London: Sage
—— (1992b) 'On the Idea of Emancipation in Management and Organization Studies', *Academy of Management Review*, 17/3, 432–64.
—— (1996) *Making Sense of Management: A Critical Introduction*, London: Sage.
Bachelard, G. (1934) *Le Nouvel Esprit Scientifique*, Paris: Alcan.
Berger, P. and Luckmann, T. (1966) *The Social Construction of Reality*, London: Penguin.
Bernstein, R. J. (1976) *The Restructuring of Social and Political Theory*, Oxford: Basil Blackwell.
—— (1988) *Beyond Objectivism and Relativism: Science, Hermeneutics and Praxis*, Philadelphia, PA: University of Pennsylvania Press.
Bittner, E. (1965) 'The Concept of Organization', in G. Salaman and K. Thompson (eds) *People and Organizations*, Milton Keynes: Open University Press, 1973.
Burrell, G. and Morgan, G. (1979) *Sociological Paradigms and Organisational Analysis*, London: Heinemann.
Cannella, A. A. and Paetzold, R. L. (1994) 'Pfeffer's Barriers to the Advance of Organizational Science: A Rejoinder', *Academy of Management Review*, 19/2, 331–41.
Capra, F. (1983) *The Turning Point: Science, Society and the Rising Culture*, London: Flamingo.
Chia, R. (1994) 'The Concept of Decision: a Deconstructive Analysis', *Journal of Management Studies*, 31/6, 781–806.
—— (1996) 'The Problem of Reflexivity in Organizational Research: Towards a Postmodern Science of Organization', *Organization*, 3/1, 31–60.
Child, J. (1972) 'Organizational Structure, Environment and Performance: the Role of Strategic Choice', *Sociology*, 6/1, 1–22.
Clegg, S. (1975) *Power, Rule and Domination*, London: Routledge & Kegan Paul.
—— (1979) *The Theory of Power and Organization*, London: Routledge & Kegan Paul.
—— (1994) 'Power and Institutions in the Theory of Organizations', in J. Hassard and M. Parker (eds) *Towards a New Theory of Organizations*, London: Routledge.
Cooper, R. (1983) 'The Other: a Model of Human Structuring', in G. Morgan (ed.) *Beyond Method: Strategies for Social Research*, London: Sage, 202–18.
—— (1983a) 'Some Remarks on Theoretical Individualism, Alienation and Work', *Human Relations*, 36/8, 717–24.
—— (1987) 'Information, Communication and Organization: a Post-Structural Revision', *The Journal of Mind and Behavior*, 8/3, 395–416.
—— (1989) 'Modernism, Postmodernism and Organizational Analysis 3: the Contribution of Jacques Derrida', *Organization Studies*, 10/4, 479–502.
—— (1989a) 'The Visibility of Social Systems', in M.C. Jackson, P. Keys and S. A. Cropper (eds) *Operational Research and the Social Sciences*, New York: Plenum, 51–9.
—— (1990) Organization/Disorganization', in J. Hassard and D. Pym (eds) *The Theory and Philosophy of Organizations: Critical Issues and New Perspectives*, London: Routledge; 1st published in *Social Science Information*, 25/2, 299–335, 1986.
—— (1992) 'Formal Organization as Representation: Remote Control, Displacement and Abbreviation', in M. Reed and M. Hughes (eds) *Rethinking Organization: New Directions in Organization Theory and Analysis*, London: Sage, 254–72.

—— (1993) 'Technologies of Representation', in P. Ahonen (ed.) *Tracing the Semiotic Boundaries of Politics*, Berlin: Mouton de Gruyter, 279–312.
Cooper, R. and Burrell, G. (1988) 'Modernism, Postmodernism and Organizational Analysis 1: an Introduction', *Organization Studies*, 9/1, 91–112.
Cooper, R. and Fox. S. (1990) 'The Texture of Organizing', *Journal of Management Studies*, 27/6, 575–82.
Cooper, R. and Law, J. (1995) 'Organization: Distal and Proximal Views', *Research in the Sociology of Organizations, Vol. 13*, Greenwich, CT: JAI Press, 237–74.
Craib, I. (1994) *The Importance of Disappointment*, London: Routledge.
Donaldson, L. (1985) *In Defence of Organization Theory: A Reply to the Critics*, Cambridge: Cambridge University Press.
Fay, B. (1987) *Critical Social Science*, Cambridge: Polity Press.
Foucault, M. (1980) *Power/Knowledge: Selected Interviews and Other Writings*, in C. Gordon (ed.) Brighton: Harvester Wheatsheaf.
Garfinkel, H. (1967) *Studies in Ethnomethodology*, Englewood-Cliffs, NJ: Prentice Hall.
—— (1974) 'The Rational Properties of Scientific and Common-sense Activities', in A. Giddens (ed.) *Positivism and Sociology*, London: Heinemann.
Giddens, A. (1973) *The Class Structure of the Advanced Societies*, London: Hutchinson.
—— (1976) *New Rules of Sociological Method*, London: Hutchinson.
—— (1977) 'Functionalism: Après La Lutte', in A. Giddens (ed.) *Studies in Social and Political Theory*, London: Hutchinson.
—— (1979) *Central Problems in Social Theory*, London: Macmillan.
—— (1984) *The Constitution of Society*, Cambridge: Polity Press.
—— (1989) 'A Reply to My Critics', in D. Held and J. B. Thompson (eds) *Social Theory of Modern Societies: Anthony Giddens and His Critics*, Cambridge: Cambridge University Press.
—— (1991) *Modernity and Self-Identity: Self and Society in the Late Modern Age*, Cambridge: Polity Press.
Gouldner, A. (1959) 'Organizational Analysis', in R. K. Merton (ed.) *Sociology Today*, New York: Basic Books.
Habermas, J. (1972) *Knowledge and Human Interests*, London: Heinemann.
Knights, D. (1992) 'Changing Spaces: the Disruptive Impact of a New Epistemological Location for the Study of Management', *Academy of Management Review*, 17/3, 514–36.
Krupp, S. (1961) *Pattern in Organizational Analysis: A Critical Examination*, Philadelphia, PA: Chilton.
Lyotard, J.-F. (1989) *The Lyotard Reader*, A. Benjamin (ed.) Oxford: Basil Blackwell.
Mayntz, R. (1964) 'The Study of Organizations', *Current Sociology*, 13/3, 95–156.
McHugh, P., Raffel, S., Foss, D. C. and Blum, A. (1974) *On the Beginnings of Social Inquiry*, London: Routledge & Kegan Paul.
Mehan, H. and Wood, H. (1975) *The Reality of Ethnomethodology*, New York: Wiley.
Morgan, G (ed.) (1983) *Beyond Method: Strategies for Social Research*, Newbury Park, CA: Sage.
—— (1986) *Images of Organization*, London: Sage.
Newton, T. (1996) 'Postmodernism and Action', *Organization*, 3/1, 7–29.
Parker, M. (1992) 'Postmodern Organizations or Postmodern Organization Theory', *Organization Studies*, 13/1, 1–17.
—— (1995) 'Critique in the Name of What? Postmodernism and Critical Approaches to Organization', *Organization Studies*, 16/4, 553–64.
Pfeffer, J. (1993) 'Barriers to the Advance of Organizational Science: Paradigm Development as a Dependent Variable', *Academy of Management Review*, 18/4, 499–520.

Pollner, M. (1974) 'Mundane Reasoning', *Philosophy of the Social Science*, 5, 35–54.
—— (1979) 'Explicative Transactions: Making and Managing Meaning in a Traffic Court', in G. Psathas (ed.) *Everyday Language: Studies in Ethnomethodology*, New York: Irvington.
—— (1987) *Mundane Reason: Reality in Everyday and Sociological Discourse*, Cambridge: Cambridge University Press.
—— (1991) 'Left of Ethnomethodology: the Rise and Decline of Radical Reflexivity', *American Sociological Review*, 56, 370–80.
Preston, D. L. (1988) *The Social Organization of Zen Practice*, Cambridge: Cambridge University Press.
Sokal, A. (1996) 'Throwing a Spanner in the Text', *The Times Higher Educational Supplement* (7 June), 19.
Schutz, A. (1953) 'Common Sense and Scientific Interpretation of Action', *Philosophy and Phenomenological Research*, 14, 1–38.
Silverman, D. (1970) *The Theory of Organizations*, London: Heinemann.
Weber, M. (1949) *The Methodology of the Social Sciences*, New York: The Free Press.
Weber, S. (1987) *Institution and Interpretation*, Minneapolis, MN: University of Minneapolis Press.
Willmott, H. C. (1977)'The Commitment of Sociology', Ph.D thesis, University of Manchester.
—— (1986) 'Unconscious Sources of Motivation in the Theory of the Subject: an Exploration and Critique of Giddens' Dualistic Models of Action and Personality', *Journal for the Theory of Social Behaviour*, 16/1, 105–22.
—— (1993) 'Breaking the Paradigm Mentality', *Organization Studies*, 14/5, 681–720.
—— (1994) 'Theorizing Agency: Power and Subjectivity in Organization Studies', in M. Parker and J. Hassard (eds) *Towards a New Theory of Organizations*, London: Routledge.
—— (1995) 'What's Been Happening in Organization Theory and Does it Matter?', *Personnel Review*, 24/8, 33–53.
—— (1996) '"Outing" Organizational Analysts: Some Reflections Upon Parker's Tantrum', Manchester School of Management, mimeo.
Zimmerman, D. H. (1971) 'The Practicalities of Rule Use', in J. Douglas (ed.) *Understanding Everyday Life*, London: Routledge & Kegan Paul.
Zimmerman, D. H. and Pollner, M. (1971) 'The Everyday World as a Phenomenon', in J. Douglas (ed.) *Understanding Everyday Life*, London: Routledge & Kegan Paul.
Zimmerman, D. H. and Weider, D. L. (1971) 'Ethnomethodology and the Problem of Order: Comment on Denzin', in J. Douglas (ed.) *Understanding Everyday Life*, London: Routledge & Kegan Paul.

INDEX

abbreviation 45, 46, 47
absolute monarchies 194
accidents 69; safety-critical situations 73–8
accountability 58, 80, 148–9, 152; hierarchical, and social 142
accounting procedures 151
accumulation 137, 200, 209; flexible 32; knowledge 166
Adler, N. 29
Adorno, T. W. 190, 195, 196, 197, 207
aesthetics 30, 100
affirmation 173, 197–8, 205; negation of 206
agency/agents 131, 138, 167, 169, 178, 227; causal 150
Airbus A320 crashes 74
Albertsen, N. 32
Albrow, M. 32
Aldrich, H. 57, 163
algebra 71, 120
'algorithmic compressibility' 45, 47, 59
alienation 213
Allen, D. B. 30
Allport, Floyd 112, 131, 132, 133, 134, 137
Alvesson, M. 29, 216, 228, 232
ambiguity 169, 170, 175, 177, 181, 198, 206, 223; inherent 178, 182; planning's attempt to master 172
American Standard Code for Information Interchange *see* ASCII
analysis 26, 81, 118, 133, 135, 222; coherence of 223; empirical 224; institutions 136–7; methodic organization of 214–15; modernist 230; network 112, 120–3, 125, 127, 128; post-structuralist 213; qualitative 127; scientific 222; structural-functional 116; systematic 73
androcentric assumptions 28
antagonistic notion 168, 178
Anthony, R. N. 148
anthropology 166, 178
antithesis 195, 196, 204
'apostemes' 115
appearance/disappearance 135
'appreciative inquiry' 28, 34
'appropriation' 135, 136
Archibald, R. D. 121
Arendt, H. 176, 182
Argyris, C. 27, 47, 165
Ariane 5 rocket 74, 76, 78
artefacts 142, 143, 147, 149, 188; human 172
artificial intelligence 51
artist figure 178, 180
arts 204–5
ASCII (American Standard Code for Information Interchange) 72
Ashley, D. 15
associations 126
Astley, G. 33
Atkouf, O. 30
Auschwitz 197
authorities 89–92, 94, 100–2 *passim*, 113, 147, 150, 218; abandoning all basis for 204; arbitrary 214; patrilineal descent 151; truth and 155
automata 71, 116, 176
autonomy 151, 192, 197
Ayer, A. J. 18–19

Bachelard, Gaston 3, 206, 219, 228
badness 192, 193, 194

INDEX

Bakhtin, M. 28
Bales, R. 127
Baligh, H. H. 43, 44
Barnard, C. 117
Barrett, F. J. 26
Barrow, J. 45
Barthes, Roland 199
Bartlett, C. 32
Bataille, G. 198, 209, 210, 211
Bateson, Gregory 3, 24, 52, 172, 173, 207, 210
Baudrillard, J. 68, 210
Bauman, Z. 68, 82
Baumrin, B. 114
Baxandall, M. 115
Beaumont, J. 79
Bedford, N. M. 148
Beer, S. 56, 121
Behan, Brendan 210
beliefs 17, 20, 76, 89, 189, 204, 217; constitutive 16, 21; deep-rooted 194; dominant systems 190; interlocking 15; metaphysical 27; modernist 18; unitarist 230
Bell, D. 18, 21
belonging 147, 148, 150, 152
Berger, P. 46–7
Bergson, Henri 2
Bernstein, R. J. 15, 216, 217, 229, 230
Berquist, W. 31
Bertalanffy, L. von 18
Bertman, M. A. 114
Bestsafe company 150, 151, 152, 154
Bhopal disaster 73
'Big Brother' 192, 193
binary oppositions 144, 146, 150, 152, 154, 155, 157, 191; binary notation and 193–4
Bion, W. 168
Bittner, E. 222, 223, 224, 230
Bjorn-Anderson, N. 70
black boxes 56, 127
blacks 199
blame 148
Blau, Peter 117, 118
Boje, D. 15, 26, 31
Boland, R. J. 26, 79
Boulding, K. E. 18, 207
boundaries 67–87, 111, 112, 115, 134, 136, 206, 216; acceptability 218; clear separation of 34; conceptual 4; creation of 225; defining conditions 131; invention and institution of 182; lack of consistent explanation of condition 130; maintaining 127; permeability of 119, 120; problem of defining 120; relaxing 126; semantic 181; strong 215; well defined 232
bounded rationality 17, 28, 169, 178, 182; cognitive constraints implied by 173
Bourdieu, P. 55
Bourgeois, W. V. 43
Boyacigiller, N. 29
Boyatzis, R. 18
Bradshaw-Camball, P. 26
Braudel, Fernand 124, 125
Braverman, H. 168
bricoleur account 178–80, 181
Brown, D. L. 27
Brown, J. S. 51, 52, 55, 57, 59
Brown, R. H. 15
Browning, L. 57
Buck-Morss, S. 190, 196
Burke, Kenneth 174
Burns, T. 122
Burrell, G. 15, 18, 25, 26, 68, 213, 214, 230
Burton, R. M. 43, 44

CAD (computer-aided design) 74
Calás, M. 26, 28
calculations 170, 174, 175, 177, 178
Callari, A. 15
Callon, M. 111, 114, 125
Canada 74
Cannella, A. A. 218
capability 180, 182; imaginative 179; internal 137; negative 203–6, 207, 209; technological/technical 27, 179
capitalism 175, 190, 201–3, 208, 209, 234; expansionism 216–17, 219; global 98; hegemony of 200; increasing the efficiency of 211; triumph over socialism 190
Capra, F. 52, 217
care 30
Castells, M. 68
Casti, J. 46, 50
Castoriadis, C. 46, 124, 176, 177
causality 23, 52, 150, 151, 170, 199; mechanical 176; relations 19, 149; unambiguous 176; underpinnings 33
centralization 19, 101, 122, 123; temporary 153

INDEX

certainty 189, 204, 207; knowledge 217; scientific 206
chance 76, 133
chaos 80, 82, 98, 194, 216; order from 114, 131
charts 142–3, 143–4, 146–54 *passim*
Cheal, D. 15, 21
Chen, C. C. 26
Chia, R. C. H. 26, 216, 221, 225, 227
Child, J. 17, 214, 220
Childers, P. 51
Child Support Agency *see* CSA
choices 118, 178; anticipatory-consequential models 163, 164, 165; discriminating 49; rational models 164, 166; strategic 17
Christianity 188, 191
circumscribed theorizing 32
Clare, David 148, 153
Clark, P. 17
Clarke, M. 44, 46
Clegg, S. 26, 214
closure 175, 177
codification 72, 77, 79
cognition 23, 98, 100, 157, 178; ambiguity and unpredictability inherent in 182; conditioning effects on instrumentality 168; constraints implied by bounded rationality 173; limited ability 175; quasi-formal 46, 59
Cohen, A. P. 152
coherence 15, 53, 54, 68, 91, 120, 130; analysis 223; presumptions of 79; pursuit of 77; questioned 217
Cohn, A. 76
coincidence 76
collective bargaining 194, 210
collectivities 120, 128
commodification/commercialization 197
commonwealths 113, 114, 115
communal negotiation 26
communication 4, 20, 58, 123; hierarchical model 79; master system for organization of 80; multinational organizations 33–5
compatibility/complementarity 129
complexification 95, 100, 101
complexity 68, 74, 80, 167, 177; coordinating and controlling 79; increasing 78
compliance 202, 224
composition 4

computability theory 72
computers 45–6, 69, 121, 126–7; hacking and viruses 80; hybrid networks 80; 'talking with' 126; *see also* CAD; software
Comte, Auguste 89
concepts 180, 181, 191, 192, 195; borrowing 222; common-sense 223; identity of 193; key 213; meanings 218, 219
conceptualization 166, 200, 203
configuration 19
connectedness 144
consequentiality 168, 169, 170, 171, 174; detachment from 172
consistency 167, 168, 171, 173, 175, 182
constitution 175, 221
construction industry 133
construction(ism) 29, 31, 34, 155, 177, 181, 230; individual identity 182; new worlds 30–3; social 22, 23–4; space-time 5
contexts 15–42, 72, 124, 137, 170, 173, 178; changes of, future relationships which result from 78; cultural 73; differentiating 172; discursive 49, 51; embedded signification 180; new 178; organized 44–66
contingency theories 17, 122
continuity 91
control 19, 31, 43, 152, 166, 205, 208; accounting 142; cybernetic hierarchy of 116; definitional 50; discrete, software 77; elite 218; industrial 129; internal locus of 29; market 130; remote 45, 124; safety-critical process 73, 74; sensory 116; short-term 153; social 21
conversation 20; catalytic 35; new and transformative 35
Cooper, Robert 29, 45, 68, 81, 82, 83, 111, 125, 127, 147, 149, 156, 166, 169, 170, 171, 177, 178, 180, 182, 183, 214–40 *passim*; compared with Giddens 226–8; critiques 15, 31; cybernetics 67; divisions 145, 146, 157; hierarchy 145; information shift concept 77; intellectual themes 1–5; interaction 144–5, 152; macro-organizational theories 18; ordering process 90, 120; postmodernism and organizational analysis 26; post-structuralism 67, 158, 213; relation between organization and

244

INDEX

representation 124; 'standing-reserve' 155; TDNs 126; 'world pictures' 154
Cooperider, D. 26, 28, 30, 32
'co-optation' 117, 122
Corbett, M. 51
corruption 194
credit 148
Crystal, G. 30
CSA (Child Support Agency) 49, 50, 52–3
cultural practices/life 15, 16, 23, 24, 25, 28; collectively oriented 30; company 153; generative source of meaning in 29; theory and 31
custom(s) 50, 51
cybernetics 3, 18, 67, 101, 116, 206
'cyborganization' 1, 82
cyborgs 101
Cyert, R. M. 168

Dachler, H. P. 31
Daft, R. 57
Dalton, M. 142
Dearden, J. 148
debate 194, 195, 229, 230
decision-making 19, 28, 171, 221; interactive 34; mathematical 20; rational and incremental 180; technologies of 79
decoding 79
decomposition 4
deconstruction 22, 82, 215, 221, 233; feminist strategies 28
deduction 19; rational 167
deferral 94, 95, 98, 99, 101, 145, 151, 154; acknowledgement of 100
definitions 50, 54, 114, 120, 125–6, 144–5, 230; efficiency 209; primary 191; prior 200
deformation 4
de Grazia, A. 17, 20
delayering 208
Deleuze, G. 127, 204
de Man, P. 15
democracy 200
denial 191, 192, 206
deregulation 189
Derrida, Jacques 4–5, 71, 72, 94, 99, 135, 144, 145, 147, 157, 170, 176, 181, 190, 200, 213, 224, 225, 228
Descartes, René 16–17, 147, 217
descriptions 22, 25, 27, 29, 32, 180, 224; anthropomorphic 131; linguistic 181; potentially infinite number of categories 48–9; problem 190; rigorous 70; written 97
detachment 172; repeated 124
determinism 72
dialectic 195–6, 197
dialogics 28, 81, 82
dialogues 33
Dickens, D. 26
difference 73, 77, 82, 125, 151, 159, 180, 196, 208; concept 193; consumption, conversion and coordination of 81; cybernetics of 3; preserved and deferred 156
differend 198
differentiation 116, 122, 123, 146, 157, 175, 221; context 172; hierarchical 173; simultaneous 173;
social and spatio-temporal 169; unproblematic 228
DiMaggio, P. J. 136
disasters 76
discontinuity 91, 119
discrimination 49, 51, 172
disembodiedness/disembeddedness 68
disjointedness 173, 175
disorder 72, 73, 76, 78, 82, 206; appropriation of order out of 225; increasing 207; mutual constitution of order and 90; opposition between order and 114; semantic connections with 189; tendency to 208
disorganization 31
dispersal 95
displacement 100, 102, 124, 135; *see also* TDNs
dissent 194, 195, 198
division 144, 150, 157, 159, 182; Cartesian, mind and matter 217; labour of 5, 146, 148, 154, 156, 159; logics of 145–6; sexual 80; social 230; spatial 80; system 115
division of labour 20, 145, 146, 154, 156, 158
Donaldson, L. 43
Douglas, Mary 136–7, 138, 147
downsizing 208
dramatization 123, 124, 136
dualisms 142, 143, 145, 146, 150, 152–9 *passim*, 234
Duguid, P. 51, 52, 55, 57, 59
dystopia 67

245

INDEX

Eco, Umberto 184
education 18, 27, 190
effects 5, 143, 155, 170, 176, 180, 190, 199, 230; normative 177; 'truth' 229
efficiency 164, 174, 176, 181–2; capitalist 201, 211; detrimental impacts on 202; dominant definition 209; emphasis on 203; improving 189; target-setting 58; techniques to increase 208
Ehn, P. 70
Elias, N. 91, 93
elites 218
Ellin, N. 15
embeddedness 144, 170, 171, 180, 222, 227
Emery, F. E. 119
empiricism 15, 23–4, 26, 32, 33, 44, 117, 168, 178; criticism of 224; destroyed 197; logical 18–19; 'seduction of knowledge' 217; systematic 18–20
emplacement 147, 148, 150, 181
employment conditions 210
energy 116, 118, 119, 207, 208
Engels, Friedrich 203
Engestrom, Y. 58
engineer/scientist 178, 179, 180, 181
Enlightenment 16, 20, 22, 99, 100; rational illusions anchored in 164
enrichment 28, 35
entropy 206, 207, 208
environmental conditions 17
epistemes 189, 190
epistemology 4, 164, 189, 199
Erikson, E. H. 167, 184
Escher, M. C. 127
ethics 30, 164, 176
ethnography 150, 151
ethnomethodology 222, 223, 224, 229–32 *passim*
Eurocentrism 28
European Joint Airplanes Requirements 78
evaluation 19, 174
events 126, 191; *see also* event-structure theory
event-structure theory 112; discussion of 134–6; elements 131–4; organization as a case of 131, 136–8
examples 53, 54
excellence 53–4
exclusion 119, 147–9, 152, 156, 228
expectancy theory 17
expectations 119, 154, 181; breach of 230; probabilistic 170; writing falls short of 171
expedients 178–81
experimentation 175, 179
expert systems 48
expertise/experts 15, 148, 218
explanations 23, 27, 29, 32, 49, 93; abbreviated 47; algorithmically compressible 47; consistent, lack of 130; 'grand' 73; psychological 118; theoretical 25
exploitation 67, 69, 79
extension 175
external goods 54, 58
Ezzamel, M. 143

fabrications 170, 172, 182; expedients, makeshifts and 178–81
facts 19, 45, 125, 192, 231; empirical 20
'fantasies' 79, 170
Fay, B. 232
feedback 118, 194, 226
feminism 29, 93, 199; critiques 22; deconstructive strategies 28
Feyerabend, P. K. 45
fight 172, 173
Fisch, R. 49
Fisher, M. 15
flexibility 19, 153; loss of 208; maximum 207
Flores, F. 50
focal activity 59
Fontana, A. 26
Foreman, G. B. 205
formalization 19, 48, 123, 180, 195; conceptual 181
formulation 94, 101, 117, 118, 122, 216, 226, 231; reflexive inquiry reneges on 225
Foucault, Michel 28, 90, 93, 94–5, 128, 135, 156, 165, 167, 182, 188, 190, 192, 198, 199, 200, 201, 204, 208, 229
Fox, C. 15
Fox, S. 178, 182
fractals 145
France 128
Frankfurt School 197, 199
Frascina, F. 15
Frederick, W. 20
free will 29
Fukuyama, F. 15
fun 166, 171

INDEX

function 116, 154, 171
functionalist theories 164, 216

Gadamer, H. G. 50
Galliers, R. 69
games 46, 52; 'language' 24, 130, 165; 'seductive' 28
'gaps' 144, 146, 149
Gare, A. 26
Garfinkel, H. 158, 230
Gaudel, M.-C. 78
Gauthier, D. P. 114
Gebser, J. 32
Gehry, Frank 96, 97
gender 80, 90; conflicts 28
generalizations 48, 49, 51, 61, 231; conditional 52; empirical 117; selective 55
generative theory 31–2
geometry 115
Gephart, R. P. 15, 26, 31
Gergen, K. J. 15, 26, 31
Ghoshal, S. 32
Giddens, Anthony 15, 156, 216, 219, 225, 226–8, 234
Global Leadership Competencies 18
globalization 31, 32, 79
Glorie, J. C. 43, 44
gnosis 53, 55
goals 19, 30, 49, 77, 131, 173, 177; accomplishment of 167–8; clearly defined 171; consequential process appraised and evaluated with reference to 174; exterior 179; 'higher' 168, 169, 170; primacy of 168; setting 17, 169, 171; ultimate 189
Gödel numbering 72
Goffman, E. 91, 93, 169, 170, 171
Goldsmith, M. M. 114, 115
good(ness) 193, 195, 201, 203; and evil 188, 191, 194
Goody, J. 170
Gorz, A. 190, 209
Gottdiener, M. 15
government 189, 204
Guattari, F. 204
'guru quacks' 142

Habermas, Jürgen 199, 215, 218
habitualization 46–7
Hackman, R. 17
Hage, J. 19

Haire, Mason 19
Hamada, T. 28
Hamel, G. 32
Hammersmith Hospital 74
Hampton, J. 114
Handy, C. 31
Haraway, Donna 90
Harrison, C. 15
Harvey, D. 32
Hassard, J. 26
Hatch, M. T. 26
Hatherly, D. 143
Haugeland, J. 46, 50
Hayek, F. von 52, 56
Hayles, N. K. 68, 72
hazard 73, 74, 75
Hegel, G. W. F. 195, 196, 197
hegemony 200, 210, 216, 230
Heidegger, Martin 3, 123, 135, 147, 154, 155–6, 159, 182
Heraclitus 205
hermeneutics 225, 226–8
Hetrick, W. 26
heuristics 23
hierarchy 20, 22, 79, 116, 147, 149, 151, 152; absent 157; and interaction 143–5, 156; organizational chart as 148
Hirschmann, A. O. 173
history 55, 56, 193; demise of 15; popular 200
Hobbes, Thomas 111, 113–16, 118, 136
Hoffman, A. N. 122, 123
Höpfl, H. 77
Horkheimer, M. 195, 196, 197
Hosking, D. 31
Hughes, M. 31
Huizinga, J. 175
Hunter, M. K. 51, 55
Hutton, W. 189, 210
hybridity 80, 81, 82

ideal worlds 125
ideas 114, 137, 163, 226; progression of 196; tools, techniques and 179
identity 152, 157, 208; affirmation of 198; anxieties about 204; coherent 15; concept 193; individual, construction of 182; making of 183; stabilizing 177
ideology 190, 203, 210; dominant 191; political 204
illegality 192

INDEX

illusion 127, 164, 206; certainty no more than 207; 'pure theory' 215
images 34, 48, 51, 118–19, 144; sovereign 182
imagination 175, 179, 204
imitation 173
immanence 5, 167, 177, 192
'immutable mobile' 149, 155
implementation 70, 81
'imposability' 138
'impossible' objects 127
impotence: negation and 188–212; political 90
in-one-anotherness 5
incentives 202
'incisional acts' 222, 227
inclusion 30, 119, 127, 147–9, 156
incompleteness 78, 80, 81, 82, 83
individualism 15, 29; highly regarded 30
industrialism 164, 178
inferences 50
infinite regress 170, 176
information 19, 20, 31, 45, 70, 72, 82, 116; converting things into 124; Cooper's work on 1, 4; effects of 5; environment receptive to multiple sources 77; limitations in human capacity to process 17–18; local 56–7; new 217; organization and 67–9; organization of 78–81; reactive 208; sudden shift in levels 76; transmitting 27; two characteristics 207
information technology 68, 130
innovation 21, 35, 47, 58, 67; technological 125, 128, 219
inside–outside problems 112, 127, 132
instability 72, 82, 127
institutionalization 1, 5, 54, 58, 59, 60, 61; dramatization 136; goal-setting activity 169; habitualization the precursor to 47; rules for modern science 115; 'squeezing thinking' 137; theorizing and teaching tradition 138
instrumentality 165, 174, 180, 181, 182, 183; language and 175–8; planning, make-believe and 167–71; play far removed from ideal conditions of 173; resources 179
intellectualism 1–5, 89, 91, 115, 168, 188, 197, 232
interaction 27, 98, 126, 146, 147, 149, 150; delimited modes of 47; hierarchy and 143–5; human–computer 77; informal 154; institutionalized 47, 59; organized forms 24; social 57, 60, 122, 143, 144, 156; software–hardware 75, 81; subject–object 177, 182; symbolic 93
interchange 35
interconnections 68, 79, 80, 82, 93, 128
interdependence 5, 60, 98, 112, 174, 179, 217, 227; inescapable 221
interlocking 15, 111–41
internal goods 54
internal markets 153
Internet 80
intervention 29, 33, 81, 163; purposive 227; technological 219; totalizing 189
invariance 131–2

Jacky, J. 74
Jacobs, S. 118
Jacques, R. 30
Jameson, F. 15, 96–100
Japan 30, 128, 129, 210
Jaques, E. 168
Jeffcutt, P. 68
Jennings, M. 77
Jepperson, R. 173
jobs 17, 32, 144, 148, 201
Johannessen, K. 44, 51
Johnson, P. 44
Johnson and Johnson 148, 155
'joint-action' 23
Jones, J. 205
Joseph, T. T. 26, 32
'Joss' 29
judgement 225; deferral of 154; rational 30

Kahn, R. L. 118, 119
Kallinikos, Jannis 3, 166, 170, 171, 172, 175, 178, 181
Kant, Immanuel 16, 205
Kanter, R. 79
Katz, D. 118, 119
Keats, John 205, 207
Kets de Vries, F. R. M. 168
Kilduff, M. 29
'kinematic' conception 131, 134
kinship 151, 176
Knoespel, K. J. 71
Knorr-Cetina, Karin 90
knowledge 2, 26, 43, 62–6, 89–110, 129,

148, 181; acceptable and unacceptable 189; accumulated 166; bourgeois 199; claims 208, 225; codified 180; conventional 201; dangerous 188; deficit 167; disciplinary 88; foundational and experiential 180; generalizable 199; generating 15, 221; heterosexual 199; history of 23; local 28; male 199; narrative 44, 53–9, 60, 61, 177; new 217; objective 25, 217; power and 199, 230; production of 189, 199, 204, 213, 214, 215, 218; professional objects of 1; propositional 44–53, 59, 60, 61, 177; scientific 45, 217, 218, 221, 229; 'seduction' of 217; sociology of 23; structure of method in constituting 234; theory of 2; total 204; value-neutral 29; white 199

labour 5, 80, 148, 198, 210; demand for 190, 209; shedding 208; *see also* division of labour
laissez-faire 189
language 21, 27, 30, 31, 72, 90, 146, 157, 215; affirmative 197, 198; ancient 191; colonization of 197; computer programming 70, 71, 75; existence and 225; foreign 50–1; goodness, badness and 192; hegemonic use of 230; Heidegger on 3; instrumentality and 175–8; knowledge only possible through mediation of 199; loss and 4; negative 204; observational 134; operation of 228; playful nature of 167; post-structural theories of 71; pragmatics of 29, 32; qualitative and speculative 127; representation 20; sacred 34; scientific 25, 222; social action 24–5; sociopractical function of 26; technical 226; technique and 123; understanding of 67; viable 23; *see also* meaning(s); semantics; talking; words
'language games' 24, 130, 165
Lash, S. 68, 80
Latimer, J. 156
Latour, B. 45, 114, 126–7, 128–9, 149, 150
laughter 92
Law, J. 76, 81, 83, 111, 125, 144, 149, 158, 221, 231, 232, 233
Lawler, E. 17
Lawrence, P. R. 17
leadership 18, 22, 201, 211; effective 26; maintained as 'seductive game' 28; path-goal theory of 17
learning 77, 78, 126, 207; 'higher' 197; incremental process 129
Lecourt, D. 206
Lee, R. M. 47, 48, 50
legislation 101
Lerry, W. 15
Leveson, N. 69, 73, 74–5, 77, 81
Lévi-Strauss, C. 178, 179, 180, 181
Lewin, K. 121
liberation 198
Lilley, S. 143
Lincoln, J. R. 122, 123
Lindblom, C. E. 164, 165, 168, 180
literature: criticism 72; equivalence of science, philosophy and 3; popular 200; theory 15
Littlewood, B. 70, 77
Lobel, S. A. 18
location 4
Locke, E. A. 17
Locke, John 16, 20
Locke, R. 79
logic 18–19, 71, 112, 127, 128, 145–6, 173, 175; discursive 200; first-order 75; propositional 52, 53
logical positivism 16, 18
London Ambulance Service 74
Lorsch, J. 17
love 25
Lozada, H. 26
Luckmann, T. 46–7
Luhmann, N. 18
Lupton, T. 43
Lyon, D. 68, 69
Lyotard, J.-F. 32, 35, 68, 69, 89, 91, 101, 135, 165, 197–8, 199, 205, 206, 220, 234

McArthur, T. 5
McGibben, B. 15
McGowan, K. 188
McGregor, D. 202
McHugh, P. 224
McIntyre 52, 53–4, 55, 56, 60–1
McKelvey, B. 57
MacKenzie, D. 74, 76
McNeilly, F. S. 114
macro-organizational theories 18
make-believe 172, 174; instrumentality, planning and 167–71

INDEX

makeshifts 178–81
manageability 69, 79, 80, 81
management 76, 80, 153; 'appreciative' techniques 28; education and training programmes 18; human resource 210; participative 201; popular 200; rationing supply 190; relationships 33–4; risk 73; software, understanding 77; strategic 17, 137; stress 203; *see also* MBO techniques; 'new managerialism'
manipulation 50, 173, 178; detached 124
Mansfield, R. 43
March, J. G. 163, 164, 165, 166, 167, 168, 171, 175, 178
Marcus, G. E. 15
Marcuse, H. 175, 192, 197, 198, 204, 205
marketing 152, 153
marks 71–2
Marsden, P. V. 121
Martin, J. 26, 28, 30
Marx, Karl 89, 101, 168, 203, 232; Marxism 226
Marx, M. 43, 44
master-narratives 90
Masuch, M. 43, 44, 48, 51
materialities 91, 92, 94, 98, 100, 101; tensions that might be performed within and between 102
mathematics 72, 75, 78, 115, 117; Thales' 123; *see also* algebra; geometry
MBO (management-by-objective) techniques 17
meaning(s) 28, 58, 71, 73, 112–13, 181, 233; ability to prioritize 199; capacity to rationalize 227; concepts 218, 219, 226; cultural 29; double 53; first-order 226; forgotten 124; generating 223, 228; language and 24; literal 177; migration of 78; multiculturation of 25; multiplicity of 70, 72, 77; ontological 219; propositional knowledge 177; recontextualizing 31; scientific 226; stable 50, 73; subjective 118; taken-for-granted 230; transparency of 80; undecidability of 4
means–ends 167–71 *passim*, 173–7 *passim*, 179, 181
measurement 19, 127, 128, 182
Medawar, P. 45
media 200
medicine 51
Mehan, H. 224

Meindl, J. 26
memory 57, 222; collective 58, 60
Mercator, N. 98
Mészéros, I. 189
meta-languages 226
meta-narratives 89, 91, 92, 100–1, 102
metaphors 30, 33, 34, 52, 82, 170, 179; exploration 166; irreducibility 175; plans, play and 171–5; theatre 113
metaphysics 27, 123, 124, 135
method(ology) 23, 26, 27, 88, 101, 90, 112, 117, 158, 215; advancing 135; deductive/inductive 19; normalization of 80; performance of 94; positivist structure 214; rational-comprehensive 180; recasting social science as the study of 222–5; research 19; role of 217; scientific 217, 223; 'strong' 19; structure of 216, 223, 225, 228, 233, 234; successive-limited comparisons 180; textbooks 215; transformation-displacement networks 126–30; *see also* ethnomethodology
Meyer, J. W. 173, 178
microprocessors 75, 76
Miers, D. 47
Miles, R. E. 17
Miller, E. D. 30
Miller, E. J. 119
Miller, H. 15
Miller, S. 75, 166, 168
Mintz, S. I. 114
Mintzberg, H. 44, 137–8, 174
Mitroff, I. 174
Mizruchi, M. S. 122
mnemonics 57
mobility 45, 46
modernism/modernity 15, 31, 33, 34, 35, 91, 97, 176, 218; analysis 230; characterized 21; circumnavigation of 155; construction of a history of 101; defined 89; difference between postmodernism and 90, 95; formation of organizational science 16–21; fresh light on the nature of 2; implications 1; language and 22; model to which it aspires 98; ontologial and epistemological foundations 164; reflexivity 217; *see also* postmodernism/postmodernity
Moebius strip 127
molecular biology 90

250

moments 102
morality 53
Moreno, Jacob 120–1
Morgan, G. 25, 27, 31, 214, 215
motivation 202, 211
Mouritsen, J. 70
Mouzelis, N. 165
movement 4, 99–100, 101, 159; 'continuous double' 154
Mulgan, G. 69
Mulhall, S. 56
multicultural critiques 22
multinational organizations 33–5
Mumby, D. K. 28
Munro, R. 143, 149, 150, 152, 156
Murray, V. 26

narratives 30, 33, 34, 81; grand 25, 27, 32, 73, 78, 94; knowledge 44, 53–9, 60, 61, 177; of progress 21; unified 82; *see also* master-narratives; meta-narratives
Nath, R. 30
necessity 176, 177
negation 172; and impotence 188–212; simultaneous 173
Neil, M. 77
networks 91, 101; analysis 112, 120–3, 125, 127, 128; boundaries and margins 79; computer 45–6, 80; concepts and linguistic signs 181; consequential 174, 175; heterogeneous 81; hyperreal 98; interorganizational 122; narrow 92; sociotechnical 76, 111–12, 125, 126; *see also* TDNs
'new managerialism' 143, 145, 147, 149, 152, 154, 156
Newton, T. 230
Nielsen, E. H. 26
Nietzsche, Friedrich 24
Nkomo, S. 28
normativity 181
norms 119, 176
Norris, C. 73, 145

Oakeshott, M. 114, 126
Obel, B. 43, 44
objectivity 25, 91, 171, 218, 229
obligation 147
observation/observables 18, 19, 20, 23, 24, 132, 151; objective 134; separation between observer and observed 217; social processes in 26

obsolescence 128
Olsen, J. P. 163, 165, 168, 178
Olson, Charles 205
Ong, W. 170
ongoings 119, 126, 130, 131, 132, 214; cyclical character 133; networks of activities 136; number required 134; science and 135
ontology *see* reality (social)
optimality 181
optimization 175, 177, 189
order(ing) 4, 68, 72, 73, 76, 78, 82, 101, 120; appropriation, out of disorder 225; attainment of 113; built from other orders 131; desirable state of 117; emerging from chaos 114; general 116; hierarchy as a mode of 145; higher and lower 134; islands of 207; moral force that preserves 231; mutual constitution of disorder and 90; 'safe-enough' and 'managed-enough' 83; social 114, 134, 230; technology and 219; temporality and 124, 125; unruly 80
Orr, J. E. 51, 52, 55
Orwell, George 192
Ostrolenk, G. 77
other(ness) 5, 158, 179, 182, 198, 234; logic of 4; ontological 4; re-cognizing 213–41
Ott, S. 18
outcome 167, 174, 176, 178, 207; rationality as 182; unexpected 182
overwork 210
ownership 19

Paetzold, R. L. 218
paradox 52, 53, 80, 82, 117, 152, 158, 169, 175, 181; epitomized by polar distinctions 171; Escher's drawings 127; understanding 206
Parker, M. 15, 26, 230
Parsons, Talcott 19, 116, 118, 127
Pasmore, W. A. 26, 32
pasteurization 128–9
patterns 59, 82, 151; organized 131; recurring 47; shifting 80
Payne, R. 44
Peck, S. 30
Peitgen, H. 72
Pentium processor 'bug' 69
perception(s) 24, 77, 119, 222; topological theories of 132

251

performance 17, 18, 92, 93, 94; economic 130; limitations of 101; low 135; participatory 34, 55; security of 113
Perrow, C. 73, 77, 122
PERT (Program Evaluation and Review Technique) 121
Peters, T. 31, 32
Pettigrew, T. F. 30
Pfeffer, J. 165, 168, 218
Pfohl, S. 15
philosophy 15, 89, 115, 123, 206; Cooper's contribution 214; empiricist 18; equivalence of literature, science and 3; positivistic and positive trends 197
physics: atomic 217; high-energy 90; 'new' 217, 218; Newtonian 226
Piaget, J. 58
Pinder, C. C. 43
plans/planning 17; ameliorative 33; instrumentality, make-believe and 167–71; play, metaphor and 171–5; *see also* PPBS
play 166, 170, 171–5, 182; hermeneutical 226–8
pleasure 166, 171
pluralism/plurality 25, 26, 89, 168, 173; basic condition of 172; *de facto* 194; ideal form 196; intrinsic value 195; semantic 175, 177
pluralization 68, 69, 80, 82, 83
Polanyi, M. 58–9
Polaris 121
Pollner, Melvin 221–2, 224–5, 232
Pondy, L. R. 174
Poole, M. S. 47
Popper, Karl 150, 163
Portuguese oceanic navigation 125, 149
position 22, 153
Poster, M. 68, 70, 71
post-Fordism 32
postmodernism/postmodernity 3, 88, 97, 100, 230, 231; chosen authority on 89; construction of a history of 101; difference between modernism and 90, 95; implications 1; organizational science in context 15–42; political impotence of 90
post-structuralism 31, 67, 71, 77, 93, 158, 228; analyses of organization and technology 213; political impotence of 90; STS informed by 91; thinking 68, 214

potential: hidden 179; negative 206–8
Powell, W. W. 136
power 92, 93, 95, 124, 149, 152, 169, 180, 205; abdication of 151; absolute 194; access to 192; asymmetries of 199; attempts to exercise 117; challenge to 193; conditions of 192; equated with organizational rank 143; explanatory 196; knowledge and 199, 230; labour 198; negation and 189; persuasive 136; 'techno-mediatic' 200; 'terror' of 113
PPBS (Planning-Programming-Budgeting Systems) 17
practices 128, 129, 130; *see also* cultural practices; public/social practices
Prahalad, C. K. 32
Pratt, V. 69
predictability 60–1
predictions 5, 17, 19, 27, 169, 170; abbreviated 47; continuously threatened 29; increasingly precise 21
preferences 167
prescription 49, 165, 210
Pressman, R. S. 70
Preston, D. L. 233
Prigogine, I. 72, 77, 78, 82
privatization 189
probabilities 112, 121, 132, 163
problem solutions/solving 111, 113, 134, 200, 206; dysfunction and 202–3; perceived 208; possible, delineation of 190; technology/technical capacity 189, 209
problems 33–4, 68, 79, 95, 98; acceptable 200; cognitive and spatial 100; defining boundaries 120; endemic 209, 210; exclusionary ways of defining 208; inexhaustible source of 114; inside-outside 112, 127, 132; probabilistic 112; psychological 118; raised anew 116; redefinition of 211; scientific 129; 'scientifically relevant' 118; software 77, 80; structuring event 135; technical 121, 129, 175; uncertainty 127; *see also* problem solutions/solving
process(es) 47, 81, 98, 99, 112, 118, 123, 145, 170, 178; consequential 174; destructuring 133; differentiation 146; dynamic 226; ego-building 234; epistemology of 4; institutional 5; judgemental 225; learning 126, 129, 207; logic and primary of 3; negation

INDEX

200; ongoing 130, 131, 135, 214; prescriptive 210; progression of ideas 196; rational 18, 22; reality-building 233, 234; reflection 213; reproductive 207; social 26; software development 71; step-by-step 130, 134; structuring 138; substitution 129; transitional 67–8; trial-and-error 133
production 27, 153, 155, 172, 197; capitalist 175; developing new techniques 129; knowledge 189, 199, 204, 213, 214, 215, 218; science becomes a force of 35; simulated 171; useful outputs 208
professionals 137
profit 203, 210
profitability 201
Program Evaluation and Review Technique *see* PERT
progress 99; intrinsic requirement for 199; narrative of 21; only allowable meaning of 205; rubric for 200; systematic 21; unquestioning commitment to 189; vehicles of 79
proportion 115
propositional statements 44–5, 46, 57, 60; relationship between rules and 48
Prosch, H. 58–9
psychology: empirical 15; Gestalt 147; positivistic and positive trends 197; social 118; public/social practices 50, 51, 53, 54–5, 164
Pugh, D. S. 43
Putnam, L. 28
Putnam, R. 27

quantum theory 217

race 28
R & D (research and development) 129
randomness 72, 81, 133, 169
Rapoport, A. 115–16, 120
rational agents 16–18
rationality 118, 168, 171, 173, 175, 177, 196; culture-free 22; effects of 5; functional 18; individual 16–18, 20, 26; individual to communal 22–3; instrumental 183; rule of 163–7; scientific inquiry 217; transcendent 22; *see also* bounded rationality
realism 170, 176, 177; 'becoming-' 216; 'being-' 216

reality 18, 33, 165, 175, 231; building 233, 234; common sense ways of representing 223; creating 29, 31; empirical 219; 'lived' 98; methodical ways of accounting for 220; 'out there' 154; parochial forms 27; 'pictures' of 24; reason and 196; research 23; shared 182; simultaneous negation of 173; social 2, 60, 215, 228, 234; theory and 224; ultimate 116
Reason, P. 28
reason/reasoning 46, 70, 113, 128, 142–62; belief in 20; common sense 215; intuitive 43; logical 71; methodic 215; mundane 221, 222, 223; reality and 196
'reciprocal authentication' 189
reconstruction 34
Reed, M. 31
Reeves, S. 44, 46
referrals 123
reflection 35, 194, 213, 227; critical 28–30; theoretical 168
reflexivity 101, 217, 227, 234; radical 224, 225; self- 33
reflexivization 229, 230
regularities 46, 49, 59, 115, 128; patterned 7
relativism 35
relativities/relativizations 68, 69
reliability 78
religion 116
Renaissance man 115
reorganization 32
repetition 4, 46, 124, 125, 138
representation 3, 70, 80, 93, 112, 114, 116; abbreviated 45, 46; bounded entities 136; controllable 154; Cooper's work on 1, 124; departure from traditional way 134; detachable 154; effects of 5; Heidegger on 155; knowledge, unstable semantics of 50; laboratory 130; language as 20; manipulation of 50; metaphor as 113; objective 15; paper 142; philosophy of 123; produced and reproduced 130; project 121; real 123, 126; reality 223; 'spaces' of 149, 150, 154, 155, 156; spatial 115, 117; structure and organization of 5; TDN 127; technologies of 4; vital point of 154
repression 193, 195, 204, 232, 233; denial

191, 192; surplus 197; technological 198
reproduction 130, 176, 183, 203, 207, 230, 234
research 23, 57, 136; action 28; empirical 26, 224; inextricability of social action and 27–8; laboratory 171, 172; methodology 19; natural science 226; network-based 120, 121, 122; ongoing character 135; scientific 25, 27, 54, 217; technologies, place of 26–8; *see also* R & D
return on investment 210
Rice, A. K. 119
Richter, P. 72
Ricoeur, P. 173
risk 69, 79, 80, 164, 166; generation and identification of 217; high 75; increasing 74; managing 73; reducing 78
Robbins, S. 43
Roberts, J. 142
roles 47, 171, 210; decision-making 221; fabrication of 172; government 189; method 217; self-fulfilling 226; socialization 203; thought 196
Rorty, R. 15
Rosch, E. 44, 45, 50
Rosenau, P. M. 15
Rosenbrock, H. 51
Rosengren, W. 20
Rosile, G. A. 26
Rotman, B. 191, 194
Rowan, B. 178
Rowan, J. 28
Ruccio, D. 15
rules 47, 49, 51, 53, 79, 171, 173; bureaucratic 223; calculable 48; explicit 50, 61; generic 55, 57; 'if, then' structure 56; imperfect 48; institutionalization, for modern science 115; managing exclusively by 52; not conforming to 192; open-ended in application 58
ruling class 203
Rushing, W. 20

Saab Griffen aircraft crashes 74
safety 69; critical situations, software 73–8, 80, 82
Sartre, J.-P. 211
'satisficing' 18

scale 5, 77, 80
scale economies 129
Schank, R. 51
Schauer, F. 44, 47, 49, 51, 52
Schön, D. A. 27, 47, 55
Schultz, M. 26
Schutz, A. 222
science 45, 72, 126, 217; ambivalence about 89; analysing, as an ongoing activity 135; becomes a force of production 35; enduring presence 136; equivalence of literature, philosophy and 3; function of language in 20; modern, institutionalization rules for 115; phenomeno-technique 219–21; philosophy of 115; post-structural perception of 77; *see also* STS
scope 52
Scott, J. 122
Scott, W. R. 111, 119, 122
'selfish genes' 25
self-fulfilling prophecy 149
self-sufficiency 116, 119
Selznick, Philip 117, 118, 142
semantics 46, 175, 181, 189; stable 177; unstable 50
semiotics 22, 68
Sen, A. 164
sensibility 213–41
sequences/sequencing 4, 45, 72, 126
Serres, Michel 3, 117, 123, 124
sexual divides 80
Shafritz, J. M. 18
shapes 115
shortages 190
Shotter, J. 15, 23
Shrader, C. B. 122, 123
Shrivastava, P. 73
signification 172, 173, 174, 178, 181; ambiguous character 177; context-embedded 180; imaginary 176; indexical 180; pejorative 194; potential 179; recalcitrant nature of 182
silence 91, 92, 93, 94, 101, 198
Silverman, D. 165, 214, 218
Simon, Herbert 17–18, 28, 43, 79, 164, 165, 168, 175
Simon, W. 15
Simonds, Rollin 21
simplification 95, 100, 101
'simulacra' 135
simultaneous equating 172, 173

INDEX

Skinner, Q. 114
'slippage' 145, 147, 148, 226
Smircich, L. 26, 28
Smith, D. 27
Snow, C. C. 17
social action 158, 182, 221, 226; highly institutionalized forms 44; inextricability of research and 27–8; language as 24–5
social construction 22, 90; empirical method 23–4
social institutions: control of 43; managed transformation 21
socialization 149, 203
social theory modernization 112–17
socioeconomics 2, 68, 201, 203
sociograms 120–1
sociology 15, 23, 76, 89, 91, 118, 125–6; Cooper's contribution 214; ethnomethodology and 224; organizational charts and 142–3, 149; positivistic and positive trends 197
Socrates 191
software 72, 82, 83; 'bugs' and 'crashes' 80; engineering 69, 70–1, 75–81 *passim*; system safety 73–8
solidarity 116
Sommerville, I. 70, 74
space 89–90, 121, 123, 134, 150, 156; compression 68; empty 221; intermediate 182; meaningful 100; ontological 224; outer 125; stability and consistency in 182
specialization 20, 121, 146, 178, 207; increased 208
Spender, J.-C. 51, 57
Srivas, M. 75
Srivastva, S. 26, 28, 30, 34
stability 50, 99, 117, 150, 155; network 122; semantic 177; structural 130; time and space 182
Stalker, G. M. 122
standardization 19
standards 78; industrial 129; normalization of 80
'standing-reserve' 155, 156, 159
Starbuck, W. 44, 57–8
statements 195; factual 192; normative 165; prescriptive 165; scientific 215; *see also* propositional statements
Stewart, E. C. 29
Stillings, N. 44

Stinchcombe, A. L. 133
Stokman, F. N. 122
Strathern, M. 146
Strati, A. 30
Strauss, L. 114
stress 202–3
Strickland, A. J. 17
Strothman, Charlie 57–8
structuralism 91, 180; *see also* post-structuralism
structuration 227, 229
structure 81, 130, 222, 224, 227; evolving 121; functional, simplistic 148; method 216, 223, 225, 228, 233, 234; modernist understanding of 20; organic 201; problems of 68; social 117, 121, 190; thought 221; *see also* event-structure
STS (science, technology and society) 88–92, 100
subjectivity 25, 68, 91, 100
subjects–objects 166, 177, 181–3, 215, 234
sublime 206
subsidiaries 59
substitution 129, 173, 176, 179
superabundance 190, 208
supplementation 4
surveillance 67, 69, 80
Sutherland, E. 79
Swift, A. 56
Swiss watchmakers 128
symbolism/symbols 2, 46, 50, 188, 193; encoding 72
synergy 67, 194, 207
syntax 46, 93
synthesis 195, 196
systase 32
systematizing 117–23
systems 112–13, 117, 127, 134; adaptive 119; autopoietic 208; boundary-maintaining 126; 'death' 128; failing 209; formal 153; integral 136; 'legacy' 78; social 114, 116; 'technological' 115–16; systems/complexity theory 68

Taket, A. 15
talking 88, 92, 96, 97; with a computer 126
Tandon, R. 27
'tangency' 133
targets: efficiency 58; high-profit 210
tautologies 131
'taxonomic urge' 5

INDEX

Taylor, C. 50, 55
Taylorism 17
TDNs (transformation-displacement networks) 112, 133; expansion to the approach 132; objection to 130–1; requirements 126–30; towards a definition 125–6
technology 19, 29, 31, 35, 153, 157, 170; benefits of 190; conditions for better applications 167; effects of 5; excluded 158; gendering of 80; Heidegger on 3, 155; imaginary significations that permeate 176; information 68, 130; interdependence between modern organization and 5; new forms 25; organization and 123–5; phenomeno-technique 219–21; post-structuralist analyses of 213; prediction 169; representation 4; sensitization 27; social 220; understanding of 79; *see also* research technologies; STS
telecommunication 5
teleology 118, 132
Tenkasi, R. 26
tension 88–110 *passim*
text: creation of 70; software as 71–3, 77, 81
'texture' 93, 94
Thales 123, 124
Thatchenkery, T. J. 15, 26, 31
Thébaud, J.-L. 32
Therac-25 accidents 69, 74, 75, 76, 78
'there is no alternative' *see* TINA
thermodynamics 118
thesis 195, 196, 197; 'positive' or 'affirmative' 203
'thing' concept 191–4, 209–11
Thomas, M. 70, 75
Thompson, A. A. 17
Thompson, C. J. 29
Thompson, E. 44, 45, 50
Thompson, G. 122
Thompson, J. D. 19, 43, 163, 174
Thompson, V. A. 20
thought/thinking 22, 98, 99, 100, 192, 222; alternative 205; Cooper's commitment to 4; Cooper's style 3; critical 219; distal 215, 216, 224, 231, 232, 233, 234; dominant performative mode 2; dualistic 143, 150; foundation for all else 16–17; 'is/is not' structure 221; negative 189, 196; new, developing 194; post-structuralist 68, 214; 'process' 3; proximal 215, 216, 225, 231–2, 233, 234; rational 18; 'squeezing' 137; wishful 226; wishing 143
time 77, 99, 134, 170; compression 68; management of objectification of 169; spatial 123; stability and consistency in 182
TINA ('there is no alternative') 204
topology 120, 121, 127, 132
Torbert, W. R. 28
totalitarianism 16, 22, 191, 194
totalization 73, 189, 197, 198, 203
TQM (Total Quality Management) 17
training 18, 27, 137, 206; simulated 171
transferability 45
transformation 4, 71, 77, 111, 112, 181; broadly diffused 28; endless 148; managed 21; personal 213; postmodern 30; scientifically-managed 21; self 60; social 213, 232; *see also* TDNs
transition 67, 69, 79, 80, 83, 120; dynamically hybrid 82; socioeconomic 68
transnational nonprofit organizations 32
Traweek, Sharon 90
Trist, E. L. 119
truth 25, 26, 90, 147, 155, 229; absolute 199; capitalist regime of 201–3, 209; claims for 192; gradual accumulation of 200; lies changed into 198; micro- 196; model of 165; objective 21; pessimism about the possibility of 89; power and 193; revealed 204; speaking against 191
Tsivacou, I. 164, 170
Tsoukas, H. 47, 50, 52, 56
Tuck, R. 114
Turner, B. 71, 73, 76, 77
Turner, C. 69, 74–5
Twinnings, W. 47

uncertainty 70, 76, 79, 83, 93, 100, 127, 164, 166, 198, 207; attempts to transform 170; inherent 77; learning to live at ease with 206; semantic connections with 189; world a dangerous place because of 204
unconscious notion 168, 178, 216, 227
undecidability 4, 94, 145–7 *passim*, 149, 150, 228; formal relations and 154; intrinsic 225
understanding 46, 58, 82, 120, 176, 206;

alternative modes 27; binary nature of 193; bringing to consciousness 231; common sense 230; conventional ways of 209; intellectual and managerial 209; labour 210; language 67; modernist 20; perfect 199; pluralism of 25; post-Cartesian 217; primary 193; problem with 234; scientific 23, 72; self- 220; software management 77; technology 79
unemployment 190, 203
United Kingdom 189, 195, 204; Ministry of Defence 76, 78; Wages Councils 209–10
United States 29, 30, 74, 123
unity 21, 79, 114, 121, 134, 224; conjectured sense of 230
un-modern notion 81–3
unpredictability 77, 80, 169, 172, 177; inherent in human action 182
un-ready notion 220–1
Urry, J. 68, 80
utopia 67, 189, 190, 198, 199

validity 50, 71, 179
values 27, 29, 30, 35, 118, 138, 182, 196, 197; core 143, 153; fundamental 194; learned 136; shared 77, 119, 157; social 170, 176
Van der Knoop, J. 122
Van de Ven, A. H. 47
Van Orden, P. W. 32
Van Reijen, W. 135
Varela, F. 44, 45, 50
Vattimo, Gianni 123, 135, 136
Veerman, D. 135
verification 71, 76
Vickers, G. 52
Villoria, R. L. 121
Vroom, V. H. 17

Waddington, C. H. 4
wages 209; downward pressure on 210
Wagner, R. 145
Warner, M. 43
Wasseur, F. W. 122
'waterfall model' 70

Watkins, J. W. N. 114
Watzlawick, P. 49
Weakland, J. 49
wealth 22, 209
Weber, Max 47–8, 56, 118, 143, 175, 228
Weber, Samuel 137, 138, 220
Webster, J. 44
Weick, K. E. 32, 57, 58, 153, 166
Weider, D. L. 223–4
whistle-blowers 192, 195
Whitehead, Alfred North 3, 4
Wiginton, J. 57
Willinger, M. 129–30
Willmott, H. C. 29, 143, 214, 216, 220, 222, 227, 228, 230, 232
Wilson, J. 17
Winnicott, D. W. 182
Winograd, T. 50
Wittgenstein, Ludwig 23, 24, 50, 51, 53
Wolf, William 19
women 28, 90; single mothers 49, 50, 52, 53
Wood, H. 224
Wooley, B. 45
words 101, 102, 113, 124, 226
work 123, 142, 201, 209–11; *bricoleur's* 79; engineering 125; 'knowledge' 80; motivation to 202; physically and psychologically unhealthy 190; psychoanalytical studies 168; shifting places of 80; *see also* jobs; unemployment
'world pictures' 154, 158
Worldbest company 152, 153
'wrappers' 97, 98
writing 4, 5, 88, 150, 170–1, 232; computer software as a form of 71; Derridean theory of 72

Zammuto, R. 33
zero-hours contracts 210
Ziegler, R. 122
Zimmermann, D. H. 223–4
Zuboff, S. 67
Zucker, L. G. 47
Zuscovitch, E. 129–30